Taking a Case to the European Court of Human Rights

For Becky

Taking a Case to the European Court of Human Rights

Philip Leach

BA (Hons) (Dunelm), Solicitor
Visiting Research Fellow, University of Nottingham
Human Rights Law Centre

Series Editor: John Wadham

With a foreword by Sir Nicolas Bratza

BLACKSTONE
PRESS LIMITED

Published by
Blackstone Press Limited
Aldine Place
London
W12 8AA
United Kingdom

Sales enquiries and orders
Telephone +44-(0)-20-8740-2277
Facsimile +44-(0)-20-8743-2292
e-mail: sales@blackstone.demon.co.uk
website: www.blackstonepress.com

ISBN 1 84174 137 X
© Philip Leach 2001
First published 2001

British Library Cataloguing in Publication Data
A catalogue record for this book is available from the British Library

Typeset in 10/12pt Times by Montage Studios Limited, Tonbridge, Kent
Printed and bound in Great Britain by Antony Rowe Limited,
Chippenham and Reading

Contents

Foreword

The year 2000 was a momentous year in the history of the protection of human rights in the United Kingdom. The coming into effect in October of the Human Rights Act 1998 has been accurately described as representing one of the most important constitutional changes since the Bill of Rights, some 300 years ago.

The 'bringing of rights home' understandably overshadowed another important human rights milestone, which was celebrated in the millennium year. November 2000 marked the fiftieth anniversary of the first signing in Rome of the European Convention on Human Rights. In a public lecture given in London five years ago, Judge Rolv Ryssdal, the great President of the old European Court of Human Rights, described the birth and growth of the Convention in these terms:

> The arrival on the scene of international law of what was a new species of international instrument aroused little more than polite curiosity at the time. Its infancy was difficult and for many years its role and future were uncertain. Almost exactly forty-five years later, it has developed into a regional system of unparalleled effectiveness. Its scope, its influence and the number of States that have agreed to abide by its standards have grown far beyond the most optimistic predictions of its founders. It is ... no exaggeration to say that, at least as far as the democratic protection of individuals and institutions is concerned, the Convention has become the single most important legal and political common denominator of the States of the continent of Europe in the widest geographical sense.

Since that speech was delivered, the influence of the Convention has continued to spread: the number of contracting states has grown from thirty-six to forty-one, covering an area stretching from the Atlantic to the Pacific and with a total population substantially in excess of 800 million. Moreover, the dramatic increase in the number of applications resulting from the rapid expansion of the Convention system has brought about the most important constitutional change in the system since its inception: in 1998, the new permanent and full-time European Court of Human Rights came into being, replacing the part-time Commission and Court.

These developments have underlined the need for an up-to-date work describing the practice and procedures of the new Court, as well as recording its growing output of judgments and decisions. It is for this reason that I especially welcome this book, which amply fills this need. With his extensive knowledge and experience of the Convention system as both practitioner and commentator, Philip Leach has produced an admirable guide to the system, combining as it does a clear, accurate and practical exposition of the procedures with a concise and systematic overview of the case law of the Convention organs, both new and old.

Whether or not the new Act will have the effect of making recourse to Strasbourg from the United Kingdom less frequent, it will certainly not diminish the importance of knowledge of the Convention system. I therefore warmly recommend this book which will prove an invaluable guide to that system for practitioners and students alike.

Sir Nicolas Bratza,
European Court of Human Rights,
Strasbourg

Preface

This book is intended to be a practical guide on taking cases to the European Court of Human Rights. Forty-one European states have ratified the European Convention on Human Rights, allowing victims of human rights violations to challenge them in the European Court in Strasbourg. In its first fifty years, the European Convention system has had a profound effect in upholding and developing human rights standards across Europe. Applicants have been vindicated, but perhaps more importantly, European Court judgments have forced significant changes in the law, and in policy and practice.

The Strasbourg system has changed almost beyond all recognition since its beginnings in the 1950s when there were just ten member states. The 1990s has seen the Council of Europe's membership increased significantly by states from central and eastern Europe. The European Commission of Human Rights, and the former Court, have now gone, having been replaced by a single permanent Court at the end of 1998. The Committee of Ministers of the Council of Europe no longer has a judicial role in the system, but retains its function of supervising the enforcement of Court judgments.

It has been possible to challenge the UK Government in Strasbourg since 1966, although it was not until the mid to late 1970s that the first UK cases reached the European Court. By the 1990s the UK had become one of the worst offenders in Strasbourg, reflecting the failure of successive Governments to incorporate the European Convention on Human Rights into the domestic law. The effect of the Human Rights Act 1998 has been and will continue to be profound. Even prior to its implementation the Act dramatically changed the awareness and knowledge of human rights in the UK due to the scale of training not only of legal practitioners and the judiciary, but also within public authorities: including Government, local authorities, the police, the courts and the prison and immigration services.

Since October 2000, the domestic courts have been obliged to adjudicate on human rights cases. This will mean that many victims of human rights violations will rightly be able to obtain redress without recourse to the European Court. However, some commentators have suggested that the number of applications to

Strasbourg from the UK will increase, rather than decrease. This is in part due to increased public awareness of human rights and a better educated body of practitioners willing and able to spot and pursue human rights issues, but it is also due to the scheme established by the Act itself. Where legislation cannot be interpreted in accordance with the European Convention, the domestic courts will only be able to issue a 'declaration of incompatibility' with the Convention. Whilst such a declaration may lead to legislative changes, for the particular litigant the only recourse then available will be an application to the European Court.

Contents

Chapter 1 provides an overview of the Convention system and the main institutions. The practice and procedure of the Court are explained in chapters 2 to 4, from lodging the initial letter to the Court to the enforcement of judgments. These chapters include explanations of the Strasbourg legal aid system and the system for obtaining emergency relief (interim measures). Included in the appendices are the Court Rules, the Court's application form and a completed precedent application. There is also a case study of a UK application in which judgment was published by the Court in 2000 (*Caballero* v *UK* — chapter 11).

Chapter 5 deals with the Court's admissibility rules which are a critical element in the Convention system. Chapter 6 discusses the most important underlying principles of the Convention and chapter 7 provides an overview of the Convention case law, including Articles 1 to 14 and Protocols 1 and 6 (the two substantive rights Protocols which have been ratified by the UK). Sources of Convention case law, including law reports, journals, websites and texts, are set out in chapter 12. Chapter 8 deals with derogation and reservation from the Convention: the text of the UK's derogations and reservation are included at appendix 17. Chapter 9 explains the principles applied by the Court in awarding 'just satisfaction' (compensation and costs) and includes a table of awards in selected UK cases from 1998 to 2000. Protocol 12 to the Convention will create a new, free standing prohibition of discrimination, and is described in chapter 10.

Acknowledgements

I would like to thank a number of people who have kindly given their expert comments on draft chapters: Professor Bill Bowring (University of North London), Tim Eicke (Essex Court Chambers), Professor David Harris (University of Nottingham), Tim Otty (2 Temple Gardens) and Stephen Phillips (European Court Registry). My thanks to Kate Akester for providing JUSTICE's intervention in *T and V* v *UK*, and to Stephen Grosz for allowing the inclusion of Bindman and Partners' conditional fee agreement.

I would also like to thank the practitioners with whom I have worked on human rights cases whose commitment and expertise has been inspiring. They include Keir Starmer (Doughty Street Chambers), Ben Emmerson QC, Murray Hunt, Helen Mountfield, Jessica Simor and Rabinder Singh (Matrix), Dinah Rose (Blackstone Chambers) and the late Peter Duffy QC.

My thanks also to past and present colleagues at the NGOs, Liberty and the Kurdish Human Rights Project, and to Alistair, David, Ruth and the team at Blackstone Press.

Finally, I would like to thank Becky for her unfailing support, and Anna, Katie and Mary for their patience when I should have been reading them stories.

Philip Leach
January 2001

Table of Cases

Table of International Instruments

Table of International Rules

Table of Primary Legislation

Table of Secondary Legislation

Chapter One

Introduction: The Council of Europe and the European Convention on Human Rights

1.1 THE COUNCIL OF EUROPE: ORIGINS AND PRINCIPAL BODIES

The European Convention on Human Rights is a creation of the Council of Europe, which was established immediately after the second world war by the Statute of the Council of Europe 1949 with the aim of enhancing the cultural, social and political life of Europe and promoting human rights, democracy and the rule of law. The creation and early work of the Council of Europe (based in Strasbourg) was in part a reaction to the serious human rights violations encountered in Europe during the second world war. There were originally ten member states of the Council of Europe (including the UK) and there are now forty-one members.

The Council of Europe's primary decision-making bodies are the Committee of Ministers and the Parliamentary Assembly.

The Committee of Ministers is made up of the Ministers for Foreign Affairs of each member state who meet twice a year, with permanent representatives acting on a day-to-day basis. It is the executive organ of the Council of Europe which issues its decisions in the form of treaties, declarations, resolutions and recommendations. The Committee of Ministers is assisted by a Steering Committee for Human Rights which receives reports from Committees of Experts.

The Parliamentary Assembly is composed of groups of representatives from the national Parliaments of member states (currently 582 members). The size of the national delegation varies according to the population of the member state.

Non-member states can be given special guest status (currently Armenia, Azerbaijan and Bosnia-Herzegovina) or observer status. A series of specialist committees are appointed by the Assembly to work on particular issues. The Parliamentary Assembly also elects the judges of the European Court from a list of three candidates presented by each member state.

A third body, the Congress of Local and Regional Authorities in Europe was created in 1994 and comprises representatives (currently 582) from the local or regional authorities of the member states. The Congress has produced, for example, the European Charter of Local Self Government (1985).

More than 170 conventions and agreements have been adopted under the auspices of the Council of Europe. Most significant in the human rights field have been the establishment of the European Convention on Human Rights (1950), the Social Charter (1961), the European Convention for the Prevention of Torture and Inhuman and Degrading Treatment or Punishment (1987), the European Commission against Racism and Intolerance (1993) and the Framework Convention for the Protection of National Minorities (1994).

The Social Charter came into force in 1965 and is in effect the counterpart to the European Convention on Human Rights in the field of social and economic rights. Compliance with the Charter is monitored by the European Committee of Social Rights (ECSR) made up of nine independent and impartial experts, together with the Governmental Committee (made up of representatives of the states) and the Committee of Ministers. The ECSR monitors national reports and receives collective complaints from trade unions, employers' organisations and international non-governmental organisations (NGOs) with consultative status with the Council of Europe. Protocols were added to the Charter in 1988, 1991 and 1995 and in 1996 the revised Social Charter was opened for signature and will progressively replace the first Charter.

The European Convention for the Prevention of Torture came into force in 1989. It established a pro-active non-judicial system for monitoring compliance: the European Committee for the Prevention of Inhuman and Degrading Treatment or Punishment (CPT). The CPT comprises independent experts from various backgrounds (e.g., lawyers, doctors, prison experts) and has both a fact-finding and a reporting function. It makes periodic and ad hoc visits to places of detention (including e.g., prisons, police stations, psychiatric hospitals, barracks). The CPT may interview detainees in private and has the power to communicate freely with anyone who has relevant information. Its reports are confidential and may only be published with the agreement of the contracting state, but where there is no agreement the CPT may issue its own public statement.

The European Commission against Racism and Intolerance (ECRI) monitors states' legislation and policies in relation to racism and intolerance. ECRI carries out an in-depth study into each state, before issuing specific proposals. Following a confidential dialogue with state liaison officers, ECRI's reports are published.

The Framework Convention for the Protection of National Minorities came into force in 1998. It includes a periodic reporting process (every five years) and is monitored by the Committee of Ministers assisted by an Advisory Committee of twelve to eighteen independent experts in the field of national minorities. The Advisory Committee examines state reports (the first of which were received in February 1999) and produces an opinion on the steps taken by the state. It may request additional information and may receive information from other sources, such as NGOs.

1.1.1 Commissioner for Human Rights

Created in 1999,[1] the role of the Commissioner for Human Rights is non-judicial and preventive. The Commissioner's functions include the promotion of the effective implementation of human rights standards by member states, the provision of advice and assistance to states, to national human rights institutions and to the Committee of Ministers and the Parliamentary Assembly. The first Commissioner, Alvaro Gil-Robles, was elected by the Parliamentary Assembly in September 1999.

1.1.2 Directorate of Human Rights

The Directorate of Human Rights of the Council of Europe promotes awareness of human rights amongst the general public, groups with specialist interest, such as the legal profession, and amongst vulnerable groups, such as refugees. The Directorate produces publications and organises seminars, conferences and training programmes.

1.2 THE EUROPEAN CONVENTION ON HUMAN RIGHTS

The European Convention on Human Rights was adopted in 1950 and came into force in 1953. It was primarily intended to protect civil and political rights, rather than economic, social or cultural rights. It represented a significant step in the enforcement of particular aspects of the 1948 United Nations Universal Declaration of Human Rights.

The Convention created a right of individual petition — the right of individuals and organisations to challenge their Government through the Strasbourg process, by taking their case to the European Commission of Human Rights (established in 1954), and then to the European Court (established in 1959). The Court's judgments are binding on the state parties to the Convention. The substantive rights in the Convention have been supplemented by additional protocols to the

---

[1] Committee of Ministers Resolution (99)50.

Convention: the first protocol,[2] the fourth protocol,[3] the sixth protocol[4] and the seventh protocol.[5] Protocol 12 to the Convention will create a freestanding prohibition of discrimination (see chapter 10).

This right of individual petition was in many ways revolutionary, given the strength of notions of independent sovereignty of the state at the time of the creation of the Convention system. In other ways, however, the politicisation of the process was fundamental: the system was to be supervised by a political body, the Committee of Ministers; the European Commission initially had a majority of serving or former ministers, civil servants or MPs, rather than legal professionals; and the procedure before the Commission was kept confidential. The system has subsequently developed into a predominantly legal process over the years, although even the most recent changes (see Protocol 11 below at 1.2.1) have been significantly influenced by political considerations.

The Convention represents the minimum human rights standards which could be agreed by European states more than fifty years ago. The concept of human rights has developed enormously in those fifty years, leaving the Convention in some respects inadequate to uphold human rights in the twenty–first century. Despite the additional protocols and the accepted notion of the Convention as a 'living instrument', there are significant omissions of rights in the Convention and many have argued that the restrictions on the Convention rights are too widely drawn. Nevertheless, the Convention has also been extraordinarily influential on the development of legislation and policy in the human rights field throughout Europe. The European Convention is considered to be one of the most successful human rights systems in the world, particularly because of its enforcement mechanisms and its membership: it has been described by Rolv Ryssdal, the former President of the European Court, as 'the Basic Law of Europe'.

However, the Convention has also been the victim of its own success. The current caseload of the Court is incomparable to the early years. In the 1960s the Court produced just ten judgments, twenty-six in the 1970s and 169 in the 1980s. This number had increased by the early 1990s to more than fifty judgments a year. There has been a rapid expansion of the Convention system in the 1990s when a number of central and eastern European states have joined the Council of Europe and ratified the Convention: Bulgaria, Czech Republic and Slovakia (1992),

---

[2] Adopted 1952 and came into force in 1954.

[3] Adopted 1963 and came into force in 1968. The fourth protocol provides for the following rights: (1) no deprivation of liberty merely on the ground of inability to fulfil a contractual obligation; (2) freedom of movement and residence; (3) no expulsion of nationals; (4) prohibition of collective expulsion of aliens.

[4] Adopted 1983 and came into force in 1985.

[5] Adopted 1984 and came into force in 1988. The seventh protocol provides for the following rights: (1) conditions of expulsion of lawfully resident aliens; (2) right of review of criminal conviction or sentence; (3) compensation for miscarriages of justice; (4) no second criminal trial or punishment; (5) equality of rights of spouses.

Poland (1993), Romania and Slovenia (1994), Lithuania (1995), Albania, Andorra and Estonia (1996), Ukraine, Croatia, Moldova, 'the former Yugoslav Republic of Macedonia' and Latvia (1997), Russia (1998) and Georgia (1999). There are now forty-one member states which are all signatories to the Convention. Armenia and Azerbaijan will shortly become the forty-second and forty-third states to ratify the Convention.

The European Convention on Human Rights was ratified by the UK in 1951 and the right of individual petition against the UK was first introduced in 1966.

1.2.1   Protocol 11

The increased membership has placed even greater strains on the system which has meant long delays in the processing of cases which have been taking at least four to five years (in addition to the time taken to pursue domestic proceedings). Cases were initially processed by the European Commission of Human Rights, through first an admissibility stage and secondly a merits stage. Only then would cases proceed to the European Court or to the Committee of Ministers for the final determination. In the 1980s various proposals were discussed[6] to simplify and speed up the system, culminating in Protocol 11.

As from 1 November 1998, Protocol 11[7] to the Convention was brought into effect, abolishing the two-tier system of Commission and Court, and creating a single full-time permanent Court. Protocol 11 did not change the substantive provisions of the Convention or the admissibility criteria, but in addition to the abolition of the Commission, there were a number of other significant procedural changes, such as the creation of a rehearing procedure before the Grand Chamber of the Court and the removal of the quasi-judicial role of the Committee of Ministers (which continues to supervise the enforcement of judgments). The rehearing procedure appears to be the dubious result of political compromise (acknowledging those states which had pushed to retain a two-tier system by the creation of a court of first instance), but the removal of the power to decide cases not referred to the Court, from a political body, the Committee of Ministers, was a welcome development.

Protocol 11 is unlikely, however, to be sufficient for the Court to manage the ever-increasing flow of cases. Since November 1998, the backlog of Convention cases has continued to increase. In 1999 8,396 applications were registered, compared with 5,981 in the previous year.[8] The Court delivered 177 judgments in 1999, declared 731 applications admissible and 3,519 cases were either declared

---

[6] See *Reform of the Control System of the European Convention on Human Rights* (1993) 15 EHRR 321.

[7] *Protocol No. 11 to the Convention for the Protection of Human Rights and Fundamental Freedoms, Restructuring the Control Machinery Thereby*, Council of Europe, Doc. H (94) 5; (1994) 17 EHRR 501.

[8] Press release of the Registry of the European Court of Human Rights, 24.1.00.

inadmissible or struck off the Court's list. At the end of 1999, the Court had pending more than 12,000 registered cases.[9] In June 2000 senior European legal figures met in Strasbourg to discuss further changes, including an increased budget, the streamlining of procedures and further legislative reform through a new protocol.

1.2.2   Territorial application

Member states may extend the application of the Convention and the right of individual petition to any of their territories for whose international relations they are responsible (Article 56). To do so, the Secretary-General of the Council of Europe must be notified, either on ratification of the Convention or at any later time. The Convention will be applied in such territories 'with due regard ... to local requirements' (Article 56(3)).

1.2.3   Exclusion of other means of dispute settlement

In ratifying the Convention, member states agree that they will not seek to use other methods of dispute resolution (treaties, conventions or declarations) in order to solve a dispute arising out of the interpretation or application of the Convention (Article 55).[10]

1.2.4   Denunciation of the Convention

A member state may withdraw from the Council of Europe and the Convention system by the process of denunciation (Article 58). This may only be done from five years after the state becomes a party to the Convention and six months' notice must be given to the Secretary-General of the Council of Europe. Denunciation will take effect at the end of the six-month period, but the state will remain responsible for any violation of the Convention prior to that date.

1.2.5   Inquiries by the Secretary-General

The Secretary-General of the Council of Europe may institute inquiries under Article 52[11] into the domestic implementation of the Convention standards. The member states are obliged to provide the Secretary-General with an explanation as to how the Convention is implemented in national law, when requested to do so.

The power has been invoked six times to date. For example, in 1988 the Secretary-General asked member states to provide information about the

---

[9] In addition, there are provisional files which are not yet registered. In June 1999, there were more than 47,000 such provisional files pending at the Court (see European Court of Human Rights Registry press release, 21.6.99).

[10] Article 55 would, however, allow a State to do so 'by special agreement'.

[11] Formerly Article 57.

implementation of the right to a fair trial under Article 6(1) (in relation to various disciplinary and regulatory matter) and Article 6(3) (in relation to criminal and regulatory offences). The governments' replies were published in 1993.[12] The results of these inquiries may provide useful comparative material about the implementation of Convention principles, but there have been criticisms that the ambiguity of the questions has produced responses which are not comparable with one another.[13] Moreover, the responses of the governments are not critically scrutinised by the Council of Europe. In December 1999 the Secretary-General invoked Article 52 in relation to Chechnya.

1.3 THE EUROPEAN COURT OF HUMAN RIGHTS

The Convention as amended by Protocol 11 created in 1998 a new Court functioning on a permanent basis. Individuals now have a mandatory right to complain directly to the Court.

One judge is elected to the Court by the Parliamentary Assembly for each state party, who holds office for six years and may be re-elected. Each judge must retire at 70. There is a power of dismissal where a two-thirds majority of the judges consider that the judge has ceased to fulfil the required conditions. The Court is divided into four sections. The composition of the sections is intended to be balanced in terms of geography and gender and takes account of the different domestic legal systems. The composition of the sections is fixed for three years. A list of judges (by section and by Grand Chamber) is at appendix 15.

The Plenary Court is concerned with electing the President, Vice-Presidents, Presidents of Chambers, the Registrar and Deputy Registrar, and adopting rules. It has no judicial role. Most cases are decided on admissibility by committees of three judges (set up within each section for twelve-month periods and which may unanimously declare cases inadmissible), with the remaining cases being decided by chambers of seven judges constituted from each section on the basis of rotation. The judge elected in respect of the state concerned will sit in each case brought against that state which is decided by a chamber (as an *ex officio* member of the chamber, if he or she is not a member of the relevant section), but the national judge will not necessarily sit in committee.

The most important cases may be relinquished by a chamber to a grand chamber of seventeen judges provided that both parties consent to relinquishment. The grand chamber is established for three years and is formed by rotation within two groups which alternate every nine months. The groups are intended to be geographically balanced and reflect the varying domestic legal systems of member states. Cases decided by a chamber may be referred to a grand chamber

---

[12] H/SG (93) 1.
[13] H/SG (93) 1, p. 208.

for rehearing, subject to screening by a panel of five judges. Where this happens, the chamber President and the national judge will sit again in the rehearing. The Court procedures are discussed further in chapters 2 to 4.

1.3.1   Advisory opinions

The Court may issue advisory opinions on legal questions concerning the interpretation of the Convention, at the request of the Committee of Ministers (Article 47). In doing so, the Court is obliged to give reasons and judges may deliver separate opinions where there is disagreement (Article 49). However, this provision is very limited, as the Court's advisory opinions may not deal with the content or scope of the substantive Convention rights (Article 47(2)).

Chapter Two

Practice and Procedure of the European Court: Pre-admissibility

2.1 LODGING THE APPLICATION WITH THE COURT

The European Court of Human Rights has its own application form for applicants to use in lodging their case with the Court. A copy of the form is at appendix 3. The Court will require an applicant to complete this application form, but cases before the European Court of Human Rights can, in fact, initially be lodged simply by letter.

The Court's contact details are as follows:

The Registrar
European Court of Human Rights
Council of Europe
F-67075 Strasbourg Cedex
France

Telephone: (00) 333 88 41 20 18
Fax: (00) 333 88 41 27 30/62

Website: www.echr.coe.int

Practitioners who introduce a complaint by letter should identify the applicant(s), summarise the facts relevant to the issue being raised with the Court, refer to any domestic proceedings which have been brought by the applicant (or which are otherwise relevant to the applicant's particular case) and should set out the Articles of the Convention which the applicant claims have been breached.

At the time that an introductory letter needs to be lodged with the Court, it may well be that only limited instructions have been provided. Many Convention complaints will have a number of separate aspects to them. For example, Articles 13 and 14 should be considered in relation to every complaint: Article 13 requires an effective remedy in relation to other Convention rights; Article 14 prohibits discrimination in relation to the other Convention rights. If there is any doubt as to the extent of an applicant's case, it is of course advisable to draft the letter in as broad terms as possible, otherwise failure to mention an element of the applicant's claim might mean that that aspect is subsequently declared inadmissible, for failure to comply with the six months' time limit. A suggested form of introductory letter is set out below.

By Fax and Post

The Registrar
European Court of Human Rights
Council of Europe
F-67075 Strasbourg Cedex
France

[date]

Dear Sir/Madam

Re: *X* **v** *United Kingdom*

I represent Ms X of [address] and I am writing to introduce an application with the Court on her behalf under Article 34 of the European Convention on Human Rights.

On [date], the applicant was engaged in a peaceful protest outside the premises of a trade fair relating to genetically-modified crop production in the city centre of Norwich, Norfolk. With others engaged in the peaceful protest, the applicant handed out leaflets to people entering the exhibition and displayed a banner which read 'Think of our children: say No! to GM crops'.

At about 11.00 am, after the exhibition organisers had complained about the protest to the police, the applicant and three other protestors were arrested by the police for breach of the peace and obstructing the highway. Their leaflets and banner were confiscated. They were taken to the local police station and not released until 5.30 pm when the exhibition had ended. No further proceedings were brought against the applicant or the other people arrested.

The applicant brought civil proceedings for damages for wrongful arrest against the police. By a judgment of [date] the County Court found that the police had had lawful grounds for arresting the applicant for breach of the peace. The applicant has been advised that she would have no prospects of success whatsoever in bringing an appeal against the decision of the County Court.

The applicant submits that in the circumstances of this case there has been a violation of Article 5(1) on the basis that the domestic law permitting her arrest was so vague that her detention was not 'prescribed by law', and a violation of Article 5(3), because there was never any intention by the police to take her 'promptly before a judge or other officer authorised by law to exercise judicial power'. She submits that there has been a violation of Article 5(5), as she had no enforceable right to compensation in respect of the arrest in breach of Articles 5(1) and 5(3). She also submits that her removal from the site of the peaceful demonstration and the confiscation of her leaflets and banners violated her rights to freedom of expression and freedom of peaceful assembly under Articles 10 and 11, respectively. Finally, the applicant complains of a lack of an effective remedy in respect of her other Convention rights as referred to above, in violation of Article 13 of the Convention.[1]

This letter has been introduced within six months of the exhaustion of domestic remedies, in accordance with Article 35(1) of the European Convention. A completed application form, together with a file of relevant copy documents and a form of authority will be submitted shortly.

Please would you acknowledge receipt.

Yours faithfully

---

[1] See, *Steel and others* v *UK* (1999) 28 EHRR 603 and *Hashman and Harrup* v *UK* (2000) 30 EHRR 241.

The reason why it is common practice to introduce a case by letter to the Court is related to the admissibility requirements contained in Article 35 of the Convention, in particular the six months' time limit within which a case must be lodged with the Court. The admissibility rules are a critical part of the Convention system. In general, the admissibility rules are strictly applied by the Court and a high proportion of cases do not pass the admissibility hurdle. Therefore, it is essential for practitioners who intend to take European Court cases to be fully familiar with the admissibility requirements. The admissibility criteria are explained in more detail in chapter 5. In practice, the two most important admissibility rules are closely linked. They are set out in Article 35(1) of the Convention and they stipulate that the Court may only deal with a case after all domestic remedies have been exhausted (according to the generally recognised rules of international law) and within a period of six months from the date on which the final decision was taken.

It is now well established within the European Court system that a letter in the form described above will have the effect of stopping the clock for the purposes of calculating the six months' time limit (see Rule 47(5)). If you are running up against the six months' time limit it is likely to be far easier to submit a letter to the Court than to draft and lodge the full application and put together the relevant supporting documents. Submitting an introductory application by letter to the Court will mean that the applicant will have several more weeks to lodge the application form.

For some prospective applicants to the European Court, it may not be at all clear whether a particular form of redress would amount to a 'domestic remedy' for the purposes of Article 35. This is discussed in more detail in chapter 5 on the admissibility rules. However, if there is any doubt about the effectiveness of a particular 'remedy', practitioners should consider lodging an introductory letter with the Court in order to protect their client's position. If such a letter is not lodged, there is a danger that the Government might argue that the applicant had pursued a remedy that was not 'effective' for the purposes of Article 35 and therefore that the application should be declared inadmissible as having been submitted after the expiry of the six-month period. For example, the UK Government successfully argued such a point in the case of *Raphaie* v *UK* No. 2000/92, 2.12.93 on the basis that the applicant had pursued an internal prison complaint which was not 'effective'. Accordingly, should practitioners ever be in doubt about the effectiveness of a remedy, they should simply lodge an introductory letter with the Court *at the same time* as pursuing the remedy in question. The Court will not usually insist on a full application being lodged at that stage, but it should be kept informed of any further developments in the domestic remedies being pursued. A full application should be lodged with the Court once the domestic process has been completed.

The introductory letter may be sent by post or by fax. In either case, the date of the introduction of the case is taken by the Court to be the date of the letter or fax itself, *not* the date of receipt by the Court. In most cases, of course, the date of receipt of letters by the Court will be several days or possibly a week after they were sent. Nevertheless, it is absolutely clear that it is the date of the letter itself which stops the six-month clock. Exceptionally, where a letter is received by the Court a long time after its purported date, the Court may look more carefully into the question of timing, in order to prevent backdating of letters.

An application to the European Court can also be introduced by e-mail. This method will be sufficient, provided that the e-mail is in fact received by the Court. It would therefore be advisable to back up e-mail letters by fax and/or post.

Whilst it may be common practice to lodge the application by letter, there will be situations where the applicant will want to submit the full application at the outset. This will be the case where an applicant seeks expedition of the Strasbourg proceedings, as a case can only be registered by the Court once it has received the formal application. The registration process is explained below at 2.4. It will also be the case where the applicant proposes to request the Court to apply interim measures (under Rule 39), as the Court's practice is only to consider interim measures when an application has been registered. The interim measures procedure is a form of emergency procedure by which the Court may request during the course of an application that a respondent Government should refrain from carrying out particular steps or that it should take certain steps in order to protect the applicant. This procedure is in practice limited to cases where there is an imminent and serious risk to life. It is explained more fully below at 2.4.10.

2.1.1   Court Rules

The Court's Rules, adopted on 4 November 1998, are at appendix 2. The relevant Rules are referred to throughout this chapter.

2.1.2   Languages

Although the official languages of the Court are English and French, the introductory letter can be submitted in any of the official languages of the state parties to the Convention. In fact, any communication with the Court (including any pleading) on behalf of an applicant prior to the admissibility decision, may be in any one of the official languages of one of the state parties (Rule 34(2)). After admissibility, the parties must obtain the permission of the President of the chamber to continue to use one of the official languages of one of the state parties, otherwise they will be required to use either English or French (Rule 34(3)).

The state parties are required to use either English or French unless the President of the chamber allows otherwise (Rule 34(4)). The Court may request the state party to provide a translation of its submissions to the Court in one of the official languages of that country, in order to assist the applicant. Witnesses, experts and others appearing before the Court may use their own language if they do not have sufficient knowledge of either English or French.

2.1.3   Representation

There is no requirement that an application to the European Court should be submitted by a lawyer. Indeed, many applications to the Strasbourg Court are submitted directly by applicants.

It is a requirement of the Court that if, however, an applicant is legally represented, the lawyer must be authorised to practise in one of the European Convention states and be resident in one of the Convention states, otherwise the representative will have to obtain the approval of the President of the relevant chamber (Rule 36(4)(a)). Accordingly, solicitors, barristers and legal executives authorised to practise in the UK would not need the Court's permission to represent an applicant before the Court, but, for example, an academic lawyer not authorised to practise would need the Court's permission. Representatives are required to supply to the Court a power of attorney or written authority to act from the applicant (Rule 45(3)). A copy of the form, which is supplied by the Court, is at appendix 4.

In exceptional circumstances, where the 'circumstances or the conduct' of the representative 'so warrant', the Court has the power to direct that the appointed lawyer may no longer represent or assist the applicant and that the applicant should seek alternative representation (Rule 36(4)(c)).

2.2   COSTS, LEGAL AID AND FEES

European Court cases usually take at least four to five years to progress through the system (if they pass through the admissibility stage) and some cases take longer. Whilst these delays can be extremely frustrating to applicants, in other respects the Convention system is more accessible and litigant-friendly than domestic court procedures.

2.2.1   The respondent Government's costs

Significantly, there is no provision in the Convention for the respondent Government's costs to be paid by the applicant in any circumstances. Therefore, even if an applicant withdraws or settles a complaint before judgment or if an applicant is ultimately unsuccessful following a contested hearing before the Court, he or she cannot be required to pay the Government's costs. This may be a hugely significant factor in deciding whether European Court proceedings should be taken in the first place. Whereas many litigants in domestic proceedings will face the daunting prospect of having to pay some or all of the opponent's costs if they are unsuccessful, according to the usual rule that costs follow the event, there is no such risk in Strasbourg. This, it is suggested, is a very important element in making the Convention system relatively accessible to even the poorest of applicants.

2.2.2 The applicant's costs

An applicant's reasonable costs incurred can be recovered from the respondent Government, either as an element of a settlement or if costs are awarded by the Court to a successful applicant. Under Article 41 of the Convention, if the Court finds that there has been a violation of the Convention, it may award 'just satisfaction' to the applicant. As well as pecuniary and non-pecuniary damages, the Court may award the applicant costs and expenses under Article 41. The Court will only award costs to the extent that it is satisfied that they were actually and necessarily incurred and that the amount was reasonable. Therefore it is absolutely essential that practitioners should accurately record all costs and expenses incurred from the start of the case and, when the question of costs is ready to be considered, they should be able to provide the Court with the same detail as would be provided in a bill of costs prepared for domestic litigation. Practitioners should therefore include in their client letter at the start of the case a reference to the client's liability to pay, which can later be produced to the Court, if necessary, to show that the applicant has actually incurred the costs in question. The recovery of the applicant's costs is dealt with in more detail below in chapters 4 and 9.

European Court proceedings can be taken on a conditional fee basis. There is a precedent conditional fee agreement at appendix 5.

2.2.3 Court fees

There is no court fee payable at any stage by an applicant to the European Court. Applicants to the European Court can therefore instruct solicitors on a conditional fee basis and combined with the lack of court fees and the absence of any requirement to pay the Government's costs, a Strasbourg case may not amount to the sort of stressful financial gamble that domestic litigation may represent.

2.2.4 Legal aid

A limited form of legal aid is available for Strasbourg proceedings. A small set fee is payable (by the European Court) in respect of each stage that a case reaches in the Court proceedings. A schedule of the legal aid fees (in Euros) is at appendix 10. The amounts are limited and are generally considered to represent a contribution to an applicant's costs. However, if legal aid is granted, it will also pay for reasonable travel expenses to Strasbourg for a hearing before the Court.

Legal aid cannot be applied for prior to starting European Court proceedings, or even on registration of a case. Legal aid can only be applied for if and when a case is communicated to the Government to reply. If legal aid is granted at that stage, the applicant will then receive the appropriate set fee for lodging the initial application. Legal aid is dealt with in more detail below at 2.5.5.

2.3   GETTING ASSISTANCE

There are a number of human rights non-governmental organisations in the UK with substantial experience and expertise in bringing or advising on European Court applications. Practitioners might consider contacting these NGOs for advice or assistance on both the European Convention law and the procedure. Two NGOs, Liberty and the AIRE Centre, have particular experience in representing applicants before the European Court. For example, Liberty's recent cases include the following:

- *Rowe & Davis* v *UK* (2000) 30 EHRR 1: public interest immunity and 'ex parte' hearings in criminal cases
- *Caballero* v *UK* (2000) 30 EHRR 643: automatic denial of bail for rape suspect with a previous serious conviction
- *Smith and Grady* v *UK* (2000) 29 EHRR 493: ban on homosexuals in the armed forces
- *Steel and others* v *UK* (1999) 28 EHRR 603: arrest of peaceful demonstrators
- *McLeod* v *UK* (1999) 27 EHRR 493: police entry of home to prevent breach of the peace.

The AIRE Centre advises applicants from across Europe. Its recent cases include the following:

- *TP & KM* v *UK*, No. 28945/95, 10.9.99: exclusion of negligence claims against social services on public policy grounds
- *Osman* v *UK* (2000) 29 EHRR 245: public policy immunity for the police in negligence proceedings relating to the prevention and investigation of crime.

JUSTICE is the British section of the International Commission of Jurists (ICJ) and has extensive human rights research and policy expertise. Whilst it does not represent or provide advice to applicants before the European Court, JUSTICE has intervened as a third party in European Court proceedings, including the following:

- *T & V* v *UK* (2000) 30 EHRR 121: fairness of criminal proceedings brought against children (see appendix 23)

- *Teixeira de Castro* v *Portugal* (1999) 28 EHRR 101: incitement of offences by police officers.

Both Liberty and JUSTICE frequently intervene as third parties in European Court cases. So do a number of other NGOs in the UK, including Article 19 (freedom of expression cases), Amnesty International, the Committee on the Administration of Justice (Northern Ireland cases) and Interights. The Northern Ireland Human Rights Commission has also submitted third party interventions to the European Court.[2] If a case has important policy considerations affecting more people than just the client, practitioners might consider contacting one of these NGOs to discuss whether they would be interested in submitting a third party intervention to the Court. The process for intervening is considered below at 2.6.

The contact details for these NGOs are as follows:

Liberty
21 Tabard Street
London SE1 4LA

Tel: 020 7403 3888
Fax: 020 7407 5354

E-mail: info@liberty-human-rights.org.uk
Web: www.liberty-human-rights.org.uk

The AIRE Centre
74 Eurolink Business Centre
49 Effra Road
London SW2 1BZ

Tel: 020 7924 9233
Fax: 020 7733 6786

E-mail: aire@btinternet.com

JUSTICE
59 Carter Lane
London EC4V 5AQ

DX 323 CHANCERY LANE

Tel: 020 7329 5100
Fax: 020 7329 5055

E-mail: admin@justice.org.uk

---

[2] See, *Shanaghan* v *UK*, No. 37715/97, 4.4.00; *Kelly* v *UK*, No. 30054/96, 4.4.00; *Jordan* v *UK*, No. 24746/94, 4.4.00; and *McKerr* v *UK*, No. 28883/95, 4.4.00.

Article 19
Lancaster House
33 Islington High Street
London N1 9LH

Tel: 020 7278 9292
Fax: 020 7713 1356

E-mail: info@article19.org
Web: www.article19.org

Amnesty International
1 Easton Street
London WC1X 8DJ

Tel: 020 7413 5733
Fax: 020 7956 1157

Web: www.amnesty.org.uk

Interights may be able to provide assistance in freedom of expression cases (across Europe) and any category of human rights cases relating to central and eastern Europe.

Interights
Lancaster House
33 Islington High Street
London N1 9LH

Tel: 020 7278 3230
Fax: 020 7278 4334

Web: www.interights.org

In relation to cases in Northern Ireland, applicants will be able to obtain advice from the Northern Ireland Human Rights Commission:[3]

Northern Ireland Human Rights Commission
Temple Court
39 North Street
Belfast BT1 1NA
Northern Ireland

---

[3] Under s. 69, Northern Ireland Act 1998 the Commission may give assistance to individuals who apply to it for help in relation to proceedings involving law or practice concerning the protection of human rights.

Tel: 028 9024 3987
Fax: 028 9024 7844

E-mail: nihrc@belfast.org.uk
Web: www.nihrc.org

The NGO, the Committee on the Administration of Justice (CAJ) may also be able to advise on European Convention cases.

Committee on the Administration of Justice
45/47 Donegal Street
Belfast BT1 2FG
Northern Ireland

Tel: 028 9096 1122

Web: www.caj.org.uk

In Scotland, the Scottish Human Rights Centre may be able to provide assistance.

The Scottish Human Rights Centre
146 Holland Street
Glasgow G2 4NG

Tel: 0141 332 5960
Fax: 0141 332 5309

E-mail: shrc@dial.pipex.com

The UK Government has not ruled out establishing a human rights commission. A Joint Committee on Human Rights is due to be established by both Houses of Parliament, the terms of reference of which include considering whether there is a need for a human rights commission. If a human rights commission is established in the UK, it is suggested that one of its important roles should be to provide advice to prospective applicants in taking cases to the European Court of Human Rights.

2.4 REGISTRATION OF THE CASE

On receipt of an introductory letter, the Court will open a provisional file and the application will be given a provisional file number.

A lawyer in the Court Registry will send the applicant's representative (or the applicant if unrepresented) an application form and a power of attorney form.

2.4.1 Time limits

The application form and power of attorney should be completed and returned to the Court within the time limit specified by the Court, which is usually six weeks. Unlike the six-month time limit for lodging an initial application, it is possible to obtain extensions of time of this and subsequent time limits set by the Court. Requests should be made in writing explaining the reasons for the further time needed. In relation to a first request for an extension of time, the Court will generally not require exceptional reasons. The Court will usually grant a first request for an extension for a number of reasons, which may include difficulties in obtaining instructions, the need to carry out further research or even the unavailability of counsel.

Any written observations filed after the expiry of a time limit may not be included in the case file, unless the President of the chamber decides otherwise (Rule 38). Therefore, time limits should be observed and requests for extensions of time limits should be made in good time. If a practitioner is running up against a time limit or if an extension is urgently required at the eleventh hour then it may be advisable to telephone the Court to speak to a Registry lawyer.

2.4.2 Power of attorney

The Court's power of attorney form is at appendix 4. The form should be signed (and dated) by the client to confirm that the named lawyer is authorised to act on the client's behalf (Rule 45(3)).

If there is a change of representation at any stage during the proceedings, the Court will require that a new power of attorney should be submitted by the new representative.

2.4.3 The Court Registry

The Court Registry is staffed by teams of lawyers who administer the cases, draft the case correspondence and draft Court decisions for consideration by the Judge Rapporteur. Many of the Court Registry lawyers have an in-depth knowledge of the case law of both the European Commission and Court. While much of the Court's correspondence with the applicants or their representatives is written in the name of the section Registrars, practitioners will be able to find out which lawyer is dealing with their case either from the initials on the reference on the Court's letter, or simply by telephoning the Court. The Registry lawyer will be able to advise on progress of the case and may also advise on both the law and procedure of the Court. They are very much more accessible than can often be the case with domestic court personnel. If practitioners have particular questions about their case or Court procedure more generally, the simplest and quickest solution is often to contact the relevant Court registry lawyer.

The cases brought against the UK are usually dealt with by one of the following Court Registry lawyers: Anna Austin, Lawrence Early, Claire Ovey, Stephen Phillips, Karen Reid or Stephanos Stavros.

2.4.4   Completing the application form

A copy of the Court's application form is at appendix 3. Applicants are required to use this form (Rule 47(1)), unless the President of the relevant section decides otherwise. Each application should set out the following (according to Rule 47(1)):

(a)   the name, date of birth, nationality, sex, occupation and address of the applicant;

(b)   the name, occupation and address of the representative, if any;

(c)   the name of the respondent Government against which the application is made;

(d)   a succinct statement of the facts;

(e)   a succinct statement of the alleged violations of the Convention and the relevant arguments;

(f)   a succinct statement on the applicant's compliance with the admissibility criteria (exhaustion of domestic remedies and the six-month rule) laid down in Article 35(1) of the Convention;

(g)   the object of the application, as well as a general indication of any claims for just satisfaction which the applicant may wish to make under Article 41 of the Convention.

Applicants should indicate in the application form whether they have submitted their complaints to any other procedure of international investigation or settlement (Rule 47(2)(b)). This might include complaints, for example, to the UN Human Rights Committee in relation to the obligations under the International Covenant on Civil and Political Rights. The UK has not, however, ratified the Optional Protocol to the Covenant and so this system cannot yet be used against the UK. For further discussion of this condition, see chapter 5.

Applicants should also provide the Court with copies of any relevant documents, particularly the decisions (judicial or otherwise) relating to the object of the application and those showing that the admissibility criteria have been satisfied (Rule 47(1)(h) and (2)(a)). Grounds of appeal may also be relevant, in order to show that the points raised before the Court have been canvassed, as far as possible, before the domestic courts.

The application form itself has sections corresponding to each of (a) to (g) above. Practitioners are very likely to require more space than the form allows, in which case the Court will accept an annex to the application. In practice, the details required in (a) to (c) above can be completed on the first page of the form and the remaining substantive sections can be included in an annex, with the form cross-referring to the annex. An example of a completed application (in the form of an annex) is at appendix 21.

It is not necessary to provide a detailed claim for compensation under Article 41 in the initial application. This will not be required until after admissibility. It will be usual to include in the initial application three aspects under Article 41:

(i)   a claim for a declaration that there has been a violation of the relevant Articles of the Convention;

(ii)   a claim for compensation;

(iii)   a claim for costs (including, where relevant, a claim for the costs of any domestic proceedings).

However, it is wise to obtain all the information and evidence necessary at the outset, as European Court cases take several years to progress through the system, by which time it may be much more difficult to obtain the evidence needed to sustain a claim under Article 41.

Applicants are required to keep the Court informed of any change of address and of all circumstances relevant to the application (Rule 47(6)).

2.4.5   Strategy

Practitioners are well advised to submit the strongest possible application at the outset of a Convention case, rather than rely on augmenting the applicant's case at each stage in reply to the Government's arguments. It is of course possible to develop an applicant's case in response to the Government's submissions as the case progresses, but it is extremely important to remember that a case may be declared inadmissible by the Court at the initial stages, without the case even being referred to the Government. Under the Court's admissibility conditions, cases can be declared inadmissible as being 'manifestly ill-founded'. This condition amounts, in effect, to a preliminary test of the case on its merits (see chapter 5 as to the admissibility rules). Convention applications are frequently declared inadmissible as being manifestly ill-founded, accordingly the more authoritative and convincing an initial application, the less likely it is to fall at this troublesome early hurdle.

Careful consideration should also be given to the scope of the applicant's case. There may be a number of Convention points which could be taken in any case. For example, in a criminal case, practitioners will want to consider each of the separate limbs of Article 5 (liberty and security of the person) and Article 6 (fair trial), but they may also want to give consideration to Article 7 (no punishment without law), to Article 13 (effective remedy), Article 14 (prohibition of discrimination) and even the extent of any interference caused by the criminal proceedings with the rights under Articles 8 to 11. If there are various different arguments which could be made, practitioners will want to consider to what extent to focus on the main arguments and how far to rely on the subsidiary points. Of course, if an alleged violation of an Article of the Convention is not included at all in the initial application, it may be declared inadmissible for failing to comply with the six months rule. Practitioners would therefore be well advised to include all arguable points in the initial application. It is quite possible that as the case develops, and in the light of the Government's observations in reply, the subsidiary arguments may get weaker or stronger. Once the Government's cards are also on the table, the applicant's representative may then decide that the weak points can be dropped, without the applicant being penalised in any way.

2.4.6 Supporting documents

Copies (not originals) of all relevant documents should be lodged at the Court with the application form, preferably in an indexed file. These may include domestic court claim forms, affidavits and judgments and relevant correspondence, reports and other non-judicial decisions. It may be necessary to include copies of domestic judgments on which the applicant relies, but it is not necessary to submit copies of European Convention case law.

It is not necessary for the supporting documents to be paginated. If relevant documents are omitted, the Court will ask for copies of specified documents to be submitted.

2.4.7 Confidentiality

The Court operates on the general principle that information about proceedings before the Court should be in the public domain. Not only are Court judgments and admissibility decisions publicly available documents, but the Court also publishes regular bulletins about its caseload which include brief details of cases which have only reached the stage of being communicated to the respondent Government. Therefore an applicant's identity could be publicly available as early as communication of the case (or perhaps earlier if the Court issues a press release).

However, the President of the relevant chamber of the Court may permit an applicant's anonymity in 'exceptional and duly justified cases' (Rule 47(3)). An applicant who does not wish her or his identity to be disclosed in the proceedings should therefore write to the Court giving their full reasons for requesting anonymity. If the application for confidentiality is successful, the applicant will be referred to by his or her initials or by an 'anonymous' initial, such as X or Y.

2.4.8   Legal aid

Legal aid is not available at this stage, but if legal aid is subsequently granted, a limited, set fee is recoverable for the preparation of the application (see the section on legal aid below at 2.5.5).

2.4.9   Registration

The application is registered on receipt of the completed application form. Registration may be delayed pending the submission of all relevant supporting documents. The Court will reply in writing to confirm the case number and the date of introduction of the complaint. This is the date at which the clock is deemed to have been stopped for the purposes of the six months rule. It is worth checking that the date is correct, as errors do sometimes occur within the Court Registry. It is open to the Court to reconsider the date of introduction if new circumstances come to light (see Rule 47(5)), but this rarely happens in practice. The case number should be cited in all subsequent correspondence with the Court.

The Court may also refer in the letter in reply to the applicant's representative to any apparent problems as to the admissibility of the application. It is an important function of the lawyers in the Court Registry to weed out the weakest cases, to enable the Court to concentrate its limited resources on the strongest cases. A practitioner who is sent such a letter should consider it carefully and should try to answer the points made. It may be that there is an issue of admissibility which was missed and which clearly will lead to the application being declared inadmissible. However, it may also be that the Court has not been provided with all the required information, for example, as to the extent to which the applicant has sought to exhaust effective domestic remedies. In either case, in fact, the letter from the Court is not a decision of the Court, it is merely an indication from the Registry as to how the case is likely to be dealt with. The applicant can nevertheless insist that the case should proceed to a formal admissibility decision.

2.4.10   Urgent cases: interim measures

There is no injunctive process as such within the European Convention system. However, in urgent cases where the applicant's life is at risk or where there is a substantial risk of serious ill-treatment, the Court may apply 'interim measures' (under Rule 39, formerly Rule 36). A chamber of the Court, or its President, may indicate to the parties any interim measures which it considers should be adopted in the interests of the parties or the proper conduct of the proceedings. The Court may also request information from the parties in connection with the implementation of any interim measure which it has indicated.

In considering requests for interim measures, the Court applies a threefold test:

- there must be a threat of irreparable harm of a very serious nature; and
- the harm threatened must be imminent and irremediable; and
- there must be an arguable (*prima facie*) case.

Interim measures may therefore be applied for where an applicant is threatened with expulsion to a country where there is a danger of torture or death. For example, interim measures were sought by the applicants in the cases of *Soering* v *UK* (1989) 11 EHRR 439 and *D* v *UK* (1997) 24 EHRR 423 (both of which are referred to below at 2.4.11). In both cases interim measures were granted in order to prevent the removal of the applicants in circumstances in which their lives were at risk in the receiving country. The applicant in *Soering* faced extradition to the United States and a death sentence for a murder charge and in *D*, the applicant, who was in the advanced stages of AIDS, was threatened with removal to his country of birth, St Kitts, where, he argued, medical treatment for his condition would be totally inadequate. During the course of the case of *Chahal* v *UK* (1997) 23 EHRR 413, which concerned the proposed deportation on national security grounds of an alleged Sikh militant, the Commission invoked the interim measures procedure in requesting the Government not to deport. When the case went before the Court, the Government undertook to provide the Court with at least two weeks' notice of any intended deportation.

However, requests for interim measures in respect of removal of applicants to other European Convention signatory states are not usually granted, on the basis that it is assumed that the state will comply with its Convention obligations, unless there is clear evidence to suggest otherwise.

In the case of *Öcalan* v *Turkey*, No. 46221/99, 14.12.00, concerning the prosecution of the leader of the Kurdish Workers' Party (PKK), the Court requested that the Turkish Government should take all necessary steps to ensure that the death penalty (which had been passed by the State Security Court in Turkey) was not carried out.[4] This followed an earlier request under Rule 39 in February 1999 which was refused by the Court, although the chamber did seek clarification from the Government about the circumstances of the applicant's arrest and detention, particularly his access to lawyers.[5]

Interim measures are relatively rarely sought and very rarely granted. By 1989 there had been 182 requests for interim measures in cases concerning expulsion, which had been granted in only thirty-one cases.[6] Between 1987 and 1996 there were a total of 1,017 requests for interim measures, of which only twenty-one were granted.[7]

---

[4] Press Release, European Court of Human Rights, 30.11.99.
[5] Press Release, European Court of Human Rights, 23.2.99.
[6] *Cruz Varas* v *Sweden* (1992) 14 EHRR 1, para. 55.
[7] N. Bratza and M. O'Boyle, *The Legacy of the Commission to the New Court under the Eleventh Protocol* [1997] EHRLR 211, 222.

An applicant seeking interim measures should fax a completed application form to the Court (including an explanation as to how domestic remedies have been exhausted). The applicant's representative should also lodge any supporting documents showing risk to life or of ill-treatment. These may include both general documents about the situation in the relevant country, such as reports of UN Rapporteurs, Amnesty International and other NGOs, and documents relating to the applicant's specific situation. It is advisable to contact the Registry by telephone as soon as practicable. If the request is granted, the Government is informed immediately by the Court. The case will often be communicated to the respondent Government at the same time as notification of the interim measures request.

When the Court indicates interim measures which it considers should be adopted by a Government, the request will almost always be complied with. In *Cruz Varas v Sweden* (1992) 14 EHRR 1, the Court commented that there had been almost total compliance with interim measures indications. However, the Convention system does not enable the Court to order a Government to carry out particular measures. It is merely a request.[8]

The enforceability of an interim measures request was considered by the Court in a case where the respondent Government did not comply with the request of the Commission not to expel the applicants to their native Chile: *Cruz Varas v Sweden*. The applicants, a married couple and their young son, had sought political asylum and refugee status in Sweden because of the first applicant's political activity against the Pinochet regime in Chile. He alleged that he had been tortured. Their requests were refused by the Swedish authorities. An application was lodged on their behalf with the European Commission on 5 October 1989. At 9.10 am the Swedish Government was informed by telephone that the Commission had indicated that the applicants should not be deported. Nevertheless, Mr Cruz Varas was deported at 4.40 pm later that day. The European Court subsequently had to decide whether the Government's failure to comply with the Commission's request had violated the duty not to hinder the effective exercise of the right of individual petition (then under Article 25, now Article 34 of the Convention). It found that the Rule could not create a binding obligation on Convention states.[9] By just ten votes to nine, the Court held that the failure to comply with the interim measures request did not violate the Swedish Government's obligation not to hinder European Convention applications. In view of the slender majority in the Court (which 'overturned' the decision of the Commission in that case), this is a matter which may be (and, it is suggested, should be) considered again by the new Court.

---

[8] Compare Rule 39 with, for example, Article 41 of the Statute of the International Court of Justice and Article 63(2) of the American Convention on Human Rights.
[9] *Cruz Varas v Sweden* (1992) 14 EHRR 1, paras 94–103

The Court may request information from the parties 'on any matter connected with the implementation of any interim measure it has indicated' (Rule 39(3)).

2.4.11 Expediting cases

The usual procedure of the Court is to deal with cases in the order in which they are lodged with the Court. Of course, once registered, the time which cases will take to progress through the Court system may vary enormously, depending upon the particular circumstances of the case and the 'route' it takes through the Court.

However, the Court can give notification of the introduction of urgent cases to the respondent Government, by any available means (Rule 40). The Court can and does also give priority to particular cases (under Rule 41). The reasons for expediting cases are not set out in the Rules and therefore will be at the discretion of the Court. If an applicant seeks expedition, full reasons should be given to the Court at the earliest possible stage in the proceedings.

One case which was given priority by the (former) Court was *Soering* v *UK* (1989) 11 EHRR 439 which was processed by the Court within twelve months from the application being lodged to the judgment of the Court. *Soering* concerned the applicant's threatened extradition from the UK to face a capital murder charge in the United States, which clearly required expedition by the European Court. The chronology of the case (under the pre-Protocol 11 system, involving both the European Commission and Court) was as follows:

Application lodged with European Commission	July 1988
Communication of case to the respondent Government and Government requested not to extradite applicant (under 'interim measures' procedure)	August 1988
Respondent Government's observations submitted	September 1988
Applicant's observations in reply	October 1988
Commission hearing on admissibility and merits	November 1988
Commission's admissibility decision	November 1988
Supplementary observations submitted by the applicant and respondent Government	December 1988
Commission's Article 31 report (merits)	January 1989
Case referred to the Court	January 1989
Court indicated that the applicant should not be extradited (under 'interim measures' procedure)	January 1989
Memorials of the applicant and respondent Government lodged	March 1989

Amnesty International sought leave to submit written comments	March 1989
Amnesty International granted leave to submit written comments	April 1989
Further evidence and observations submitted by the parties	April 1989
Court hearing	April 1989
Judgment of the Court	July 1989

A more recent example of a case given priority by the Convention system was the case of *D* v *UK* (1997) 24 EHRR 423 concerning the removal of the applicant, who was suffering from the advanced stages of AIDS, from the UK to St Kitts. It was dealt with by the Commission and Court within fifteen months:

Application lodged with European Commission and respondent Government gave assurances that applicant would not be expelled pending examination of the case	February 1996
Communication of case to the respondent Government	March 1996
Respondent Government's observations submitted	March 1996
Applicant's observations in reply	April 1996
Commission hearing on admissibility and merits	April 1996
Commission's admissibility decision	June 1996
Supplementary observations submitted by the applicant and respondent Government	August 1996
Commission's Article 31 report (merits)	October 1996
Case referred to the Court	October 1996
Court indicated that the applicant should not be deported (under 'interim measures' procedure)	October 1996
Memorials of the applicant and respondent Government lodged	January 1997
Court hearing	February 1997
Judgment of the Court	May 1997

2.4.12   Joinder of cases

The Court can order the joinder of cases (Rule 43), which it will do where cases raise identical or very similar points. Applicants should consider applying for joinder with other cases if they raise the same issues and if it is considered that to do so would strengthen the case. For example, the joinder of similar cases may underline to the Court that the issue raised is not just a one-off problem, but is likely to lead to repeated Convention violations. The Court can order joinder of its own motion.

The Court can also order cases to be conducted simultaneously, whether or not joinder is ordered (Rule 43(2)).

2.4.13   Public access to documents

Following registration, all documents lodged with the Court (except those related to friendly settlement negotiations) are accessible to the public, unless the President of the chamber decides otherwise. The President may decide to restrict public access either at his or her own motion, or at the request of one of the parties or 'any other person concerned' (Rule 33(3)). The President may exclude public access in the interest of morals, public order or national security in a democratic society, where the interests of juveniles or the protection of the private life of the parties so require, or to the extent strictly necessary in the opinion of the chamber in special circumstances where publicity would prejudice the interests of justice (Rule 33(2)).

The extent of public access is new to the Convention system since the changes brought about by Protocol 11 in November 1998. Under the old system, the European Commission applied strict rules of confidentiality of proceedings. The new public access rules would allow practitioners to apply for copies of all documents, including Government submissions, in any registered case. This may be extremely useful where there are cases similar to a practitioner's proposed application which are already registered with the Court. The Court publishes summaries of selected cases in its monthly *Information Notes*, which include cases which have been communicated to the respondent Government. It would be open to practitioners to apply for copies of the parties' submissions in those cases.

2.4.14   Immunity of applicants and their representatives

The 1996 *European Agreement relating to persons participating in proceedings of the European Court of Human Rights* (see appendix 18) sets out various immunities available to those involved in European Court proceedings. The Agreement applies to anyone taking part in Court proceedings, including the parties, their representatives and advisers and witnesses and experts (Article 1). The Agreement establishes immunity in respect of oral or written statements and documents made or submitted to the Court, but it would not apply to statements made outside the Court (Article 2).

Governments are obliged to respect the right of applicants and their representatives to correspond freely with the Court and there are particular provisions protecting the rights of people in detention (Article 3). These provisions to a great extent overlap with the obligations which the Court has read into both Article 8 of the Convention (the right to respect for correspondence) and Article 34 (the duty not to hinder the right of individual petition). Parties and their representatives are to be permitted free movement in order to attend Court proceedings (Article 4). However, the Court is obliged to waive immunity where it would otherwise impede the course of justice (Article 5). The Agreement came into force on 1 January 1999. It was signed by the UK in October 1999, but has not yet been ratified.

2.5 PROCEDURE LEADING TO ADMISSIBILITY

2.5.1 The Judge Rapporteur

Once registered, an application is assigned to one of the Court judges, known as a 'Judge Rapporteur', whose function is to examine the case and consider its admissibility. The identity of the Judge Rapporteur is never disclosed to the applicant.

The Judge Rapporteur may ask either of the parties to provide further information, documents or other relevant material, within a specified time. The Judge Rapporteur will decide whether the admissibility of an application should be considered by a committee of three judges or a chamber of seven judges.

2.5.2 Admissibility decided by a committee

Convention cases which appear on their face not to satisfy the admissibility requirements are referred by the Judge Rapporteur to a committee of three judges which may declare a case inadmissible provided that the committee is unanimous (Article 28; Rule 53). In reaching its decision, the committee is required to take into consideration a report prepared by the Judge Rapporteur which includes brief statements of the facts and of the reasons underlying the proposal to declare the application inadmissible, or to strike a case out of the Court's list of cases (as to striking out, see below at 3.3). The Judge Rapporteur may take part in the deliberations of the committee.

The decisions of the committees usually take up no more than a page and provide no reasons relating to the particular case other than a formulaic response referring to the admissibility criteria under Article 35. The committees fulfil the role within the Convention system of disposing of the weakest cases. For example, in 1996, the committees (then of the Commission, rather than the Court) dealt with 2,108 of the 2,776 cases declared inadmissible.[10] An example of a committee decision is at appendix 11. The decision of a committee is final. There is no right of appeal against an admissibility decision, whether of a committee or a chamber.

---

[10] N. Bratza and M. O'Boyle, *The Legacy of the Commission to the New Court under the Eleventh Protocol* [1997] EHRLR 211, 217.

Applicants may be very dissatisfied if their case is declared inadmissible by a committee, particularly because of the lack of specific reasons. The applicant will not be able to obtain further reasons for the committee's decision, but, where cases are likely to be declared manifestly ill-founded, it is the general practice for the Registry lawyer to write to applicants (or their advisers) *prior to* a referral to a committee to set out the reasons why it is likely that the case will be declared inadmissible.

If a committee cannot reach a unanimous decision as to the inadmissibility of an application then it passes to a chamber for consideration.

2.5.3   Admissibility decided by a chamber

Once it is decided that a case is to be considered by a chamber of seven judges, a chamber is constituted by the President of the Section (Article 29; Rule 54). The chamber will consider a report on the case prepared by the Judge Rapporteur which will include a statement of the relevant facts and a summary of the Convention issues arising. The report will also include the Judge Rapporteur's proposals on admissibility and on any other action to be taken.

The chamber is required to take into account the report of the Judge Rapporteur. It may decide to declare the case inadmissible or to strike it out of the list. In those circumstances, the chamber produces a reasoned decision explaining the grounds for declaring the case inadmissible (see below at 2.5.8). As with committee inadmissibility decisions, there is no right of appeal against an inadmissibility decision made by a chamber.

Alternatively, the chamber may seek further information or documents from either of the parties.

2.5.4   Communication of a case

If there are no clear reasons for declaring an application inadmissible then the chamber will communicate the case to the respondent Government and ask the Government to submit its written observations.

When a case is communicated to the respondent Government, the Government will be provided with the Court's statement of facts and will be asked to reply to specific questions within a stipulated time. The statement of facts includes a summary of the relevant facts, the steps which the applicant has taken to exhaust domestic remedies, a summary of the relevant domestic law and practice and a summary of the applicant's Convention complaints. The Government may obtain one, or possibly more, extensions of time in order to lodge its observations, in the same way that the applicant can. At the same time, copies of the statement of facts and the list of questions are sent to the applicant who is notified that the case has been communicated and is informed of the time limit given to the Government to reply.

The Court's factual summary and list of questions will be the first indication for the applicant of the Court's initial view of the case. If the Court's list of questions to the Government omits any aspects of the applicant's case then it is likely that those elements of the case are considered to be weak (and therefore not matters which the Court considers merit a response from the Government). On the other hand, the Court may ask the Government specific questions in relation to a particular Article of the Convention which may give a good indication of the Court's thinking as to the crux of the case.

Following communication of a case, the Court may require any unrepresented applicant to obtain representation from an advocate who is authorised to practise in any of the state parties to the Convention, or who is otherwise approved by the President (Rule 36(2)).

2.5.5   Legal aid

Domestic legal aid is *not* available to bring European Court applications, but the European Court itself operates a legal aid system.

When a case is communicated to the respondent Government, the applicant is at that stage invited by the Court to apply for legal aid. The applicant is sent on request three copies of the Court's Declaration of Applicant's Means form (see appendix 8).

The assessment of financial means is carried out by the appropriate *domestic* body (Rule 93). Applicants in England and Wales are asked by the Court to complete the Declaration of Applicant's Means form, together with the relevant domestic legal aid financial form (CLS MEANS 1-4, and Form L17 if the applicant is employed) and to send the completed forms to the Legal Services Commission for assessment and certification. In cases relating to England and Wales, the forms should be sent to:

Legal Services Commission
London Regional Office
29–37 Red Lion Street
London WC1R 4PP

DX: 170 LON/CH'RY LN WC2

Tel: 020 7759 1500
Fax: 020 7759 1520

Applicants in Scotland should send the forms for certification to:

The Scottish Legal Aid Board,
44 Drumsheugh Gardens,
Edinburgh EH3 7SW

Tel: 0131 226 7061
Fax: 0131 220 4879

Applicants in Northern Ireland should send forms for certification to:

Incorporated Law Society of Northern Ireland,
Legal Aid Department,
Bedford House,
16-22 Bedford Street,
Belfast BT2 7FL

Tel: 01232 246441
Fax 01232 332548

The Legal Services Commission assesses the applicant's financial means in the same way that it would do so for civil legal aid applications in domestic proceedings. If the applicant would be eligible for domestic legal aid, the Commission sends the applicant a 'Certificate of Indigence' to that effect (see appendix 9). If not, the certificate will either state that the applicant would be eligible subject to contributions or ineligible.

Both the completed Declaration of Applicant's Means form and the Legal Services Commission Certificate of Indigence should then be sent to the Court within the stipulated time, if possible. It is often the case that the time given by the Court is insufficient for the forms to be completed by the applicant and certified by the Legal Services Commission, in which case practitioners should inform the Court of the delay. The Court will send an application for legal aid to the Government to comment on.

The test which the Court applies (under Rule 92) in considering requests for legal aid is twofold:

(a)   that it is necessary for the proper conduct of the case; and
(b)   that the applicant has insufficient means to meet all or part of the costs entailed.

In practice, if the Legal Services Commission certifies a client's eligibility, legal aid will be granted by the Court, unless there are any other particular reasons for the Court not to do so. However, it is important to remember that even if a client would not be financially eligible for legal aid in domestic proceedings, he or she may nevertheless be granted legal aid by the European Court. So it is worth applying to the Court, if you consider that the applicant cannot realistically afford to pay all or part of the costs which will be incurred. The extent to which the income of other members of the applicant's family is taken into account is a matter of discretion for the Court. A grant of legal aid can be revoked or varied by the Court at any time if it is satisfied that the conditions of eligibility are no longer fulfilled (Rule 96).

The grant of legal aid is retrospective and there is a set scale of fees for each stage of the proceedings. Applicants are never required by the European Court to pay contributions, as may happen in domestic proceedings.

Offers of legal aid are sent to the lawyer at each stage of the proceedings and should be signed and returned by the lawyer. Monies are paid by bank transfer.

The scale of legal aid fees is low, even by domestic legal aid standards in the UK (see the scale of fees at appendix 10). Therefore, legal aid should be considered as a contribution to an applicant's costs and expenses, rather than representing payment for the work done, however reasonable. Nevertheless, legal aid should always be applied for where possible, in particular because it will pay for the reasonable expenses incurred at any Court hearings, which can be considerable. If the Court decides to hold a hearing on the admissibility and/or the merits of an application (as to Court hearings, see below at 3.5), Strasbourg legal aid will pay for the applicant's and the applicant's lawyer's reasonable travel and subsistence expenses (Rule 94(2)). This will cover, for example, the costs of flights to Strasbourg and hotel costs for one night in Strasbourg.

Legal aid may cover the costs of more than one lawyer (Rule 94(1)). Prior to the changes brought about by Protocol 11 in November 1998, the European Commission's practice in UK cases was to offer legal aid for two lawyers, recognising the common practice in the UK of both solicitor and counsel being instructed. However, whilst it is still possible for the fees of two lawyers to be covered by legal aid, the usual practice of the Court is to offer legal aid for only one lawyer, unless there are exceptional circumstances. If legal aid is only obtained for one lawyer, it may be possible to cover some of the travel and hotel costs of a second lawyer from the 'per diem' fee of the first lawyer, provided of course that he or she is willing to waive the fee.

For applicants who represent themselves and who are granted legal aid, the practice of the Court is to pay their reasonable expenses, but not to pay them the equivalent of 'fees' for work done.

2.5.6   Government's observations

A copy of the Government's written observations will be sent by the Court to the applicant. The applicant may submit further written observations in reply (within a stipulated time). There is no prescribed form or even a set format for the observations in reply. It is of course essential that in the observations in reply the applicant must counter any arguments put by the Government as to the inadmissibility of the application, particularly in relation to the exhaustion of domestic remedies and the six months rule.

2.5.7   Admissibility hearings

It is possible for a chamber to hold a hearing to decide on the admissibility of an application (Rule 54(4)). Admissibility hearings used to be common, but the new Court's practice is to hold admissibility hearings very rarely, in view of the huge backlog of cases pending before the Court. The decision to hold a hearing can be taken by the chamber of its own motion, or at the request of either party.

If an applicant has particular reason to believe that he or she has a greater chance of success at a hearing on admissibility, rather than admissibility being decided on the papers, written reasons should be submitted to the Court as to the need for a hearing. In advance of the admissibility hearing, the parties may be asked specific questions by the Court, in order to assist in focusing the argument. Hearings on admissibility will usually only take place if the case raises difficult or new issues. One example of such a case is *T & V* v *UK*, where the Commission decided to hold a hearing on admissibility.

T & V v *UK*

In 1998 the European Commission decided to hold a hearing on admissibility in the cases of *T & V* v *UK*, Nos 24724/94 and 24888/94, 6.3.98. Those cases concerned the criminal proceedings brought against the two boys who, at the age of 11, were convicted of murdering Jamie Bulger and sentenced to detention during Her Majesty's pleasure. The applicants complained of their inability to take part in the trial proceedings, the penalty imposed and the procedure by which the 'tariff' period was imposed by the Home Secretary, invoking Articles 3, 5, 6 and 14 of the Convention. The admissibility hearing was originally fixed for September 1996 but was subsequently adjourned pending the outcome of the applicants' judicial review application. Following the judgment of the House of Lords on 12 June 1997,[11] the admissibility hearing was re-fixed for March 1998.

One of the arguments made by the Government was that in so far as the applicants complained that their trial had been unfair since they could not properly participate in the proceedings, the applicants had failed to exhaust domestic remedies since they had failed to make such complaints by way of appeal. The Commission rejected this argument on the basis that it was not satisfied that an application to the trial judge or on appeal would have had any chance of success. A similar argument about the exhaustion of domestic remedies was also made to the Court, as the respondent Government is entitled to do, but was rejected by the Court in its judgment of 16 December 1999.

If a hearing on admissibility is held, then the parties will usually also be asked to address issues arising relating to the merits of the case. The procedure adopted by the Court for oral hearings is discussed below. The usual order of oral pleading in admissibility hearings is for the Government to open and the applicant to reply (in merits hearings, the applicant opens — see 3.5 below).

---

[11] *R* v *Secretary of State for the Home Department, ex parte V and T* [1998] AC 407.

2.5.8   Decisions on admissibility by a chamber

Following communication of an application to the respondent Government and consideration of the parties' written submissions (and oral submissions, where relevant), the chamber will publish its decision on admissibility.

Admissibility decisions will contain the following sections:

- The facts: the particular circumstances of the case and the relevant domestic law and practice;
- Complaints: a summary of the applicant's Convention complaints;
- Procedure: a summary of the various stages of the application; and
- The law: a summary of the parties' submissions and the Court's findings.

The admissibility decision also includes the names of the seven judges making up the chamber, together with the Section Registrar. Admissibility decisions may be made unanimously or by a majority. In majority decisions, there are no published dissenting decisions (unlike the position for Court judgments) and the names of the dissenting judges are not revealed. There is no right of appeal against a finding of inadmissibility.

An application may be declared admissible/inadmissible in part, in which case the application proceeds in respect of the admitted aspects only.

2.5.9   Relinquishment to a grand chamber

In cases which are considered to raise important issues, a chamber may relinquish its jurisdiction to a grand chamber of seventeen judges (under Article 30; Rule 72). A case can be relinquished to the grand chamber at any time before a chamber has given its judgment. This might happen in one of two situations:

(a)   where a case raises a serious question affecting the interpretation of the Convention (or the protocols); or

(b)   where a judgment might be inconsistent with earlier jurisprudence.

Such cases will therefore be considered by the broadest composition of judges. It is possible, however, for one party to the case to veto relinquishment. The parties will be given one month from notification of the chamber's intention to relinquish jurisdiction to lodge any reasoned objection.

2.6   THIRD PARTY INTERVENTION

The European Court operates a well-established and important system for intervention in cases by third parties. Under Article 36 of the Convention, the Court may permit not only Convention states to intervene, but also 'any person concerned' if it is considered to be 'in the interest of the proper administration of justice'. A third party may be given permission by the Court to submit written comments or, in exceptional cases, to take part in hearings (Article 36(2); Rule 61(3)).

Any third party seeking to intervene should write to the President of the Court for permission to do so. If the request is granted, the Court will almost invariably set out certain conditions for intervening. These conditions will include a maximum length for the written submissions (commonly ten to fifteen pages), a specified time limit for lodging the submissions (usually within four to six weeks) and, importantly, conditions as to the matters which can be covered by the intervention. It is usual for the Court to indicate that the intervention should not comment on the particular facts or circumstances of the case (as those are matters for the parties). A copy of the request by Liberty to intervene in the case of *Khan* v *UK* is at appendix 22, together with the Court's letter in reply setting out conditions.

It is therefore suggested that a letter seeking permission to intervene should set out details about the intervener (including any relevant expertise and experience) and outline the issues which the intervener proposes to address in its submissions. The letter of request should be submitted within a reasonable time after the fixing of the written procedure (Rule 61(3)), which will mean within good time after a case is declared admissible. The written submissions are sent to the parties to the case who will be entitled to submit observations in reply. Those observations in reply will be sent to the intervener, but there will usually be no opportunity for the intervener to submit any further comments.

For the Court, the third party intervention process may assist in providing the context in which a particular policy or practice has been adopted by a Convention state. Frequently, the Court is assisted through this process by having relevant comparative international law materials before it which have been submitted by human rights organisations with particular experience and expertise in that area. For applicants, it may be of considerable assistance to have a respected human rights organisation making submissions which in effect support their position (although of course this will not always be the case).

Requests for permission to lodge third party interventions will usually be made in relation to the merits stage of the proceedings. But it is also possible to be granted permission to lodge a third party intervention for the purposes of deciding admissibility. For example, *TI* v *UK*, No. 43844/98, 7.3.00, concerned the removal to Germany of an asylum-seeker, a Sri Lankan national who had applied for asylum in Germany and then in the UK, who had previously been tortured in Sri Lanka. The Court accepted written observations submitted by the German government and the United Nations High Commissioner for Refugees.

In relation to the UK, it has been a regular practice of human rights organisations to seek and obtain leave from the Court to submit written comments in cases concerning significant points of law, practice or policy. By way of example, a copy of JUSTICE's intervention in *T and V* v *UK* is at appendix 23. Interventions have often considered the comparative situation under other international human rights provisions (such as the International Covenant on Civil and Political Rights), in other European Convention states or according to the domestic constitutions from both Convention and non-Convention states. For example, there were third party interventions in the following cases:

McCann and Others v *UK* (1996) 21 EHRR 97   Interventions by Amnesty International, British Irish Rights Watch, the Committee on the Administration of Justice (CAJ), Inquest and Liberty dealt in particular with standards demanded of the state by the right to life under international law.

John Murray v *UK* (1996) 22 EHRR 29   Interventions by Amnesty International, JUSTICE, British Irish Rights Watch, the Committee on the Administration of Justice (CAJ) and Liberty focused on the importance of the right to silence and access to lawyers in the adversarial system, in the Diplock courts and in international law.

Saunders v *UK* (1997) 23 EHRR 313   An intervention by Liberty considered the right to a fair trial and the privilege against self-incrimination under international human rights standards, in other European Convention states and under other domestic constitutions, notably South Africa.

Chahal v *UK* (1997) 23 EHRR 413   Amnesty International's intervention concerned, inter alia, the evidence of the risk of ill-treatment at the hands of the Punjab police. Interventions by JUSTICE, the AIRE Centre, the Joint Council for the Welfare of Immigrants (JCWI) and Liberty focused on whether a threat to national security allegedly posed by a person is a relevant consideration where the person is at risk of being tortured, the effect of claims of national security by a state on proper access to an effective remedy, and the requirements of Article 13 in such cases.

Sheffield and Horsham v *UK* (1999) 27 EHRR 163   An intervention by Liberty provided the Court with a comparative survey of the legal position relating to transsexuals in the other Convention states.

Teixeira de Castro v *Portugal* (1999) 28 EHRR 101   An intervention by JUSTICE concerned the incitement of offences by undercover police officers.

T and V v *UK* (2000) 30 EHRR 121   Both JUSTICE (see appendix 23) and the parents of the murdered child, Jamie Bulger, were given leave by the Court to submit written comments, and in addition the parents were granted leave to attend the hearing and make oral submissions (through their respective legal representatives).

Khan v *UK* No. 35394/97, 12.5.00   JUSTICE and Liberty were granted leave to submit joint observations in relation to the admissibility of unlawfully obtained evidence.

Shanaghan v *UK*, No. 37715/97, 4.4.00   The Northern Ireland Human Rights Commission made submissions relating to international standards (e.g. Inter-American Court of Human Rights and Human Rights Committee) on the right to life.

Interights and/or Article 19 have frequently submitted third party interventions to the Court, in particular in cases concerning freedom of expression, such as *Lingens* v *Austria* (1986) 8 EHRR 407, *Open Door and Dublin Well Woman* v *Ireland* (1993) 15 EHRR 244, *Informationsverein Lentia and others* v *Austria* (1997) 17 EHRR 93, *Otto Preminger Institut* v *Austria* (1995) 19 EHRR 34, *Goodwin* v *UK* (1996) 22 EHRR 123 and *Incal* v *Turkey* (2000) 29 EHRR 449.

Chapter Three

Practice and Procedure of the European Court: Post-admissibility

3.1 ESTABLISHING THE FACTS

Once an application is declared admissible, the Court will pursue the examination of the case and if necessary undertake an investigation (Article 38). The President of the chamber will specify time limits for the lodging of further written submissions on the merits and/or for producing further evidence, as required. The Court *may* examine witnesses and carry out on-the-spot investigations,[1] although this is rare. In most cases, the Court is able to establish the facts from the documentary evidence before it. In view of the Convention requirement to exhaust domestic remedies prior to bringing an application to the European Court, in many cases the significant facts are no longer in dispute, following the decisions of the domestic courts.

Where, however, there are fundamental factual disputes between the parties which cannot be resolved by considering the documents before it, the Court is able to carry out hearings to establish the facts, by hearing evidence from witnesses. For example, in the case of *Ireland* v *UK* 2 EHRR 25, concerning the arrest and detention of IRA suspects, 119 witnesses were heard by the Commission. The Convention requires that the respondent state should provide 'all necessary facilities' for any investigation carried out by the Court in order to establish the facts (Article 38(1)(a)) and the state will be specifically criticised by the Court under this provision if it fails to do so.[2] A failure to provide documentary evidence or to ensure that witnesses attend the Court's hearings may lead the Court to draw

---

[1] See, for example, the *Greek Case* (1969) 12 YB 1; the *Cyprus* v *Turkey* cases, Nos 6780/74, 6950/75, (1975) 2 DR 125; *Ireland* v *UK* 2 EHRR 25; *France, Norway, Denmark, Sweden and the Netherlands* v *Turkey*, Nos 9540-9544/82, DR 31.

[2] See, e.g., *Tanrikulu* v *Turkey*, No. 26763/94, 8.7.99, paras 71 and 98.

inferences as to the well-foundedness of the allegations (particularly where it is only the state which has access to information which could corroborate or refute the applicant's allegations).[3]

In a series of cases brought by individuals against Turkey from the mid-1990s, the former Commission and the new Court have held fact-finding hearings in Strasbourg and in Turkey in order to adjudicate on fundamental factual differences between the parties. The cases against Turkey have concerned gross violations, including village destruction, extrajudicial killings and torture occurring in the south-east of Turkey, which has been declared a state of emergency region. In many of these cases there was a failure by the domestic authorities to carry out any form of effective investigation into the allegations and accordingly there was no finding of fact by any domestic courts.

The Strasbourg organs have acknowledged their own limitations in establishing the facts in this way.[4] Witnesses cannot be compelled to attend and respondent Governments cannot be ordered to produce particular documents. There may also be problems in assessing evidence obtained orally through interpreters and the Commission and Court will of course not have direct familiarity with the particular conditions in the region in question. One example of a case in which the Commission held fact-finding hearings was the case of *Akdeniz and others* v *Turkey*, No. 23954/94, Comm. Rep. 10.9.99.

Mehmet Emin Akdeniz and others v Turkey

This case concerned complaints that the applicants' relatives disappeared after they were detained by soldiers during a military operation in south-east Turkey in 1993. They complained of ill-treatment of their relatives in detention and of the lack of any effective remedy. They also alleged discrimination in relation to these rights on the basis of their relatives' Kurdish origin. The applicants complained of violations of Articles 2, 3, 5, 13 and 14 of the Convention.

During the course of the case, three Commission delegates heard evidence from twenty-three witnesses in September–October 1997 and in May 1998. In a 114-page opinion published in September 1999, the Commission found violations of Articles 2, 3, 5 and 13 and found that Turkey had failed to comply with its obligations not to hinder the effective exercise of the right of petition to Strasbourg (under former Article 25, now Article 34). The fact-finding hearings were clearly critical, as there had been no findings of facts by any domestic court in relation to the matters raised by the applicants. In assessing the evidence of the oral witnesses, the Commission stated that '[the delegates] found the applicants and their witnesses to be honest and convincing in the way they gave evidence'. Their evidence was considered to be 'strongly consistent', the reliability of which was found to increase as more witnesses were heard.[5] On the other hand, the

---

[3] See, e.g., *Timurtaş* v *Turkey* No. 23531/94, 13.6.00, paras 66–67.
[4] See, e.g., *Mehmet Emin Akdeniz and Others* v *Turkey*, No. 23594/94, Comm. Rep. 10.9.99, para. 384.
[5] Para. 429.

Commission was very critical of some of the Government's witnesses, one of whom was found to be 'totally lacking in credibility' and 'evasive, glib and frequently contradictory'. Another was criticised as having 'a selective ignorance about events'.[6]

It is understood that the new Court may be less inclined to hold fact-finding hearings due to considerations of cost and delay (although the new Court appears to be holding fact-finding hearings in cases where a sufficiently strong prima facie case has been made out by the applicant). In cases such as *Akdeniz* concerning alleged gross Convention violations and in which there have been no domestic findings of fact, it is suggested that the Court's fact-finding role is an absolutely essential element of the European Convention process, without which victims of serious violations of their rights will find it extremely difficult to obtain redress in Strasbourg.

In order to establish the facts, the Court may hear any person as a witness or expert or in any other capacity (Rule 42(1)). The Court can deputise any number of judges to conduct an inquiry, carry out an on-the-spot investigation or take evidence in any other way. It can also appoint external experts to assist the Court's delegation (Rule 42(2)). Both the respondent Government and the applicant must assist the Court in its measures for taking evidence (Rule 42(4)). If measures are taken, such as obtaining an expert's report, at the request of one of the parties, the Court Rules provide that the costs are borne by the party in question, unless the Court decides otherwise. In practice, however, the applicant is rarely required to pay the experts' or witnesses' costs. In other situations, the Court will decide whether the costs are to be paid by the Council of Europe, or by one of the parties. Costs are taxed by the President of the chamber (Rule 42(5)).

In cases where the applicant considers it necessary for the Court to hold a fact-finding hearing, the applicant's representative should write to the Court as soon as possible after admissibility to set out the reasons why the applicant believes the Court should hear witnesses. The Court will subsequently inform the parties of its decision to take evidence (and may provide provisional dates). The Court will provide a provisional list of witnesses after considering proposals from the parties as to the witnesses to be called. The Court will require a brief outline or statement of the evidence which it is anticipated they will give.

The Court will then provide a provisional timetable for the hearings and will provide witness summons to be served via the parties. The Court will require reasons to be given if any witness summonsed does not attend. The hearings are usually conducted by a delegation of three judges, with the Section Registrar and a Court Registry lawyer in attendance. Following the hearing, the Court may require further documentary evidence from the parties, arising from the oral evidence.

---

[6] Para. 430.

3.2 FRIENDLY SETTLEMENT

The friendly settlement procedure (Articles 37–39 and Rule 62) provides the respondent Government and the applicant with an opportunity to resolve a dispute. The Court will write to the parties asking for any proposals as to settlement. The case is struck off the Court's list of cases if settlement is agreed. This may happen at any stage of an application (Article 37(1)).

Following the decision on admissibility, the Court will write to the parties to inform them that the Court is at the parties' disposal for the purpose of securing a friendly settlement and inviting proposals from either party (Article 38(1)(b) and Rule 62). In practice, such an invitation will be included with the Court's letter enclosing the admissibility decision. The Court will usually set a time limit for any proposals, of about two months. However, the time limit may be extended (the Court is keen for cases to be resolved and so is likely to grant more time if a settlement is a real possibility).

Prior to the implementation of Protocol 11, the European Commission's practice was to try to encourage the friendly settlement process by giving an indication on a confidential basis of the Commission's provisional view as to whether or not there had been a Convention violation. However, the new Court has tended not to continue this practice.

The Court's role in the friendly settlement procedure is usually little more than a post box. If proposals are made by either party, they will be sent on to the other party for comment. However, if no such proposals are put forward, the Court will usually take no further action to encourage settlement. Only in very rare cases will the Court actively become involved in facilitating settlement in a more proactive way. For example, where financial negotiations run into difficulties, the Court may be prepared to suggest what would represent a reasonable sum for settlement of the case. Rule 62 permits the Court to take any steps that appear necessary to facilitate settlement, which may include arranging a meeting between the parties.

Friendly settlement negotiations are confidential and are without prejudice to the parties' arguments in the contentious proceedings (Rule 62(2)). The details of the negotiations cannot be referred to or relied on in the substantive proceedings.

From the respondent Government's perspective, the friendly settlement procedure may offer an opportunity to deal with cases which it considers are likely to be successful at the Court, if pursued. A Government may be willing to settle a case where the particular problem has been identified (either as a result of the case being brought or even before the application was made) and has been, or is being, dealt with. If a Government proposes to revise a particular procedure or introduce new legislation to deal with an issue raised by a Convention application, then it is possible that it will be prepared to settle the case and therefore avoid a Court judgment finding a Convention violation. It may well be prepared to offer a sum of money and costs to the applicant to settle the case, in addition to the substantive changes being made. More problematically, Governments could seek to avoid issues raising clear Convention violations by 'paying off' individual applicants. If, of course an applicant is prepared to settle a case on payment of a certain sum, it is possible for a case to be settled without any attempt by the Government to deal with the substantive issue in question.

For the applicant, the friendly settlement procedure *may* represent an opportunity to achieve more than would be obtained from a Court judgment itself (other than a finding of a violation). Whilst a Court judgment may provide the applicant with a declaration of a finding of a violation and payment of 'just satisfaction' (see chapter 9), it is important to remember that as a procedure of *settlement*, the applicant can of course attempt to negotiate for any form of redress, including compensation and costs, but also to obtain Government commitments to revise policy or practice or to introduce new legislation. Any settlement might also include a requirement that steps be taken by the Government within a specified time, in which case the applicant may be able to obtain a remedy well in advance of a Court judgment, were the case to proceed. The Government may be willing to pay higher rates of compensation (and costs) in settlement than would be likely to be granted by the Court. For some applicants, however, the achievement of obtaining a successful Court judgment may itself be very important and a strong disincentive to settle.

The Court will be willing to facilitate settlement of cases as this will mean a reduction in the Court's substantial backlog of cases. If terms are agreed, both parties should write to the Court to confirm the terms of the settlement agreement and requesting that the case be struck out of the Court's list of cases. The Court will publish a decision or judgment (if concluded post-admissibility) recording the facts of the case and the terms agreed between the parties and formally striking the case out of the list (Article 39). Settlements therefore have a higher 'visibility' than was previously the case prior to the implementation of Protocol 11. This in itself may be an important factor when advising on settlement negotiations.

However, the Court's role in agreed friendly settlements is not merely to 'rubber-stamp' the decision. In accordance with Article 37(1) of the Convention, in striking out applications, the Court will continue the examination of the case 'if respect for human rights as defined in the Convention and the protocols thereto so requires'. The factors affecting this decision will include the importance of the issue raised by the case, the terms of settlement proposed by the parties and whether the issue has previously been considered by the Court.

Two examples of settled Convention cases are summarised below. The first, *AV* v *UK*, No. 34546/97, 20.5.98, was concluded by the European Commission, prior to the Protocol 11 reforms. The second, *JT* v *UK*, No. 26494/95, 30.3.00, was struck out following a friendly settlement, by the new Court.

AV v *UK*

In 1987 a child, T, was born to V's wife, C, and was registered with V named as the child's father. At the time, the couple were in the process of divorcing, the decree absolute being granted later in 1987. V remarried in 1992 and had a child by his new wife in 1994.

Shortly after T's birth in 1987 V was told by C that he was not T's father. C subsequently brought affiliation proceedings against the real father and an order was made against him in respect of maintenance of T. Blood tests excluded V from paternity of the child. For the purpose of further Court proceedings, C provided a sworn affidavit stating that V was not T's father.

V began proceedings to amend T's birth certificate. He applied to the Registrar of Births, Deaths and Marriages, but he was informed that the error in the birth certificate could only be amended by production of two statutory declarations by two 'qualified informants' of the birth, or two 'credible persons having knowledge of the truth of the case'.[7]

Neither C nor T's real father would provide a statutory declaration and neither could be compelled to do so. The doctor who had carried out the blood test in the affiliation proceedings had since died and his records could not be obtained. Other medical experts who were approached were not able to comment on or interpret the doctor's report. V was therefore unable to find a second person to provide a statutory declaration.

The matter was then taken up by V's MP. The Parliamentary Under-Secretary of State replied to express great sympathy with V, but to say that the legislation did not permit the birth certificate to be amended without a second statutory declaration. In April 1996 V's MP initiated an adjournment debate in the House of Commons during which the Economic Secretary to the Treasury said that there was nothing further which could be done.

In July 1996 V introduced an application with the European Commission claiming violations of Article 8 (right to respect for private and family life), Article 13 (right to an effective remedy) and Article 14 (prohibition of discrimination) in conjunction with Articles 8 and 13. Under Article 8, he argued that the failure to provide a mechanism to allow him to correct T's birth certificate did not accord respect to his true family status or private life. This interference was not 'necessary in a democratic society' and could not be justified by any of the exceptions set out in Article 8(2). He also argued that Article 13 had been violated as there was no effective remedy available in relation to the breach of Article 8. Finally, he argued he had suffered discrimination on grounds of marital status in respect of the power to ensure that the birth register is correct as between putative fathers who are married to the mother of a child and putative fathers who are not.

In September 1997 the application was communicated to the UK Government which subsequently made settlement proposals on the basis that it was prepared to amend the relevant statute. In May 1998, the case was struck off the Commission's list of cases, on the following terms:

1.   The United Kingdom Government undertook to place a Deregulation Order before Parliament, pursuant to section 1 of that Act, to amend section 29(3) of the Births

---

[7] Section 29(3) of the Births and Deaths Registration Act 1953.

and Deaths Registration Act 1953. The Government proposed to permit correction of a birth record either upon presentation of two statutory declarations, or, alternatively on presentation of one statutory declaration from a qualified informant together with an unequivocal order of the court in place of the second statutory declaration confirming that the person in question is or is not the biological parent of the child.

2.   The Government would use its best endeavours to ensure that the order was brought into force as soon as possible, it being anticipated that the order might be made and brought into force by April 1999 at the earliest.

3.   The Government would pay the applicant compensation of £500.

4.   The Government would pay the applicant's reasonable costs incurred in bringing the application to the European Commission of Human Rights.

JT v UK

The applicant, an involuntary psychiatric detainee, complained under Article 8 about the absence of any means by which she could apply to change the identity of her 'nearest relative'.

The applicant was committed in 1984 as an involuntary patient under s. 3 of the Mental Health Act 1983. Psychiatric and social work reports detailed the applicant's difficult relationship with her mother and referred to her repeated allegations that she had been sexually abused by her stepfather. The reports recorded that the applicant did not wish her mother to know of her whereabouts and that she wished to remove her as her 'nearest relative' and replace her with a social worker.

The application was introduced to the European Commission in February 1995. In May 1998 the Commission unanimously found a violation of Article 8. The case was referred to the Court in November 1998. In January 1999 the Government proposed settlement terms. The relevant legislation was to be amended to provide detainees with the power to make an application to court to have their 'nearest relative' replaced where the patient reasonably objected to a certain person acting in that capacity. The applicant also received £500 in compensation, together with her reasonable legal costs.

3.3   STRIKING OUT

In addition to the resolution of cases through the friendly settlement procedure, the Court may strike out a case at any stage in the proceedings where it considers that any of the following three situations applies (Article 37; Rule 44):

(a)   the applicant does not intend to pursue his or her application; or

(b)   the matter has been resolved; or

(c)   for any other reason it is no longer justified to consider the examination of the application.

In any of these situations, the Court will not, however, strike the case out if 'respect for human rights' requires that the case should continue. In *Tyrer* v *UK* 2

EHRR 1, for example, a case concerning corporal punishment, the Court refused to strike out the case even though the applicant wished to withdraw, as the case was considered to raise questions of a general character affecting the observance of the Convention which required further examination.[8] Cases struck off the list may be restored if the Court considers that there are exceptional circumstances for doing so (Article 37(2) and Rule 44(4)). Where a case is struck out by the Court, the costs are at the discretion of the Court. In practice, the Court will not award costs against an applicant.

Any case to be struck out following the admissibility decision will be struck out by way of a judgment (Rule 44(2)) which is then sent on to the Committee of Ministers to supervise the execution of any relevant undertakings.

3.4　FINAL SUBMISSION POST-ADMISSIBILITY

If a case is not resolved through the friendly settlement procedure (and most are not), the parties are invited by the Court to lodge final written submissions (commonly referred to as the 'Memorial').

As the final submission to the Court prior to any oral hearing, the Memorial should encapsulate the totality of the applicant's case. There is no prescribed format as such, but the Memorial will commonly follow the order of the original application: the facts; followed by the relevant law; followed by the argument as to why the Convention has been violated. It may differ from the original application in a number of ways. Any issues already found to be inadmissible cannot be pursued in the Memorial. The applicant's Memorial will of course also take into account the responses made by the Government to the applicant's arguments. An applicant may have decided not to pursue particular arguments (even if they were declared admissible) in the light of the Government's observations in reply, or an applicant may seek to emphasise the principal arguments over and above any subsidiary points. It should always be borne in mind that the European Convention system is primarily a written rather than an oral procedure. Advocates in the UK may be used to supplementing written submissions and skeleton arguments with lengthy oral arguments in domestic proceedings, but the European Court permits no such luxury. Court hearings usually take less than half a day from start to finish and an applicant's advocate will be strictly required to complete their submissions in thirty minutes, supplemented by about fifteen minutes to reply to the Government and sum up. Accordingly, the Memorial should always be written with the limitations of the oral hearing in mind. Indeed, in the majority of cases now there is no oral hearing at all (see below at 3.5).

---

[8] See especially paras 24–27.

Details of any costs or compensation which are being claimed (under Article 41) should either be included with the Memorial or should be submitted to the Court within two months of the admissibility decision (or any other stipulated time) (Rule 60).

Compensation claims can include both pecuniary and non-pecuniary losses. In either case, the applicant should include sufficient documentary evidence of the losses incurred. In many cases, the Court has refused to award compensation simply because the applicant has failed to substantiate their claims adequately or even at all. Pecuniary claims may include, for example, documentary proof of loss of earnings or other income. Non-pecuniary items may include claims for suffering and distress caused by the Convention violation in question, which should, if relevant, be supported by medical reports. In relation to both pecuniary and non-pecuniary claims, it may be advisable to submit a sworn affidavit from the applicant setting out the extent of the loss incurred. The submissions on compensation, whether in the form of an affidavit or otherwise, should also aim to establish clearly the link between the violation and the resulting loss. For example, it may be necessary to establish that but for the Convention violation in question, the applicant would have been expected to earn a certain level of salary. In that situation, the applicant should provide the Court with information about the salaries payable in the sorts of positions which the applicant would have attained.

Costs schedules should be as detailed as possible, including supporting documentation, failing which the applicant risks not being awarded some, or even all, of the costs. The Court will only award costs on provision of proof that they have been actually and necessarily incurred and provided that the amount of costs is reasonable. Practitioners are therefore advised to submit to the Court bills of costs which are as detailed as bills submitted to the domestic courts, setting out each aspect of the work carried out, the time taken and the hourly rate being charged. Practitioners should be able to satisfy the Court that the applicant has actually incurred the costs in question, for example, by being able to produce a client letter referring to the client's liability to pay. In *Öztürk* v *Germany* (1985) 7 EHRR 251, the applicant's costs claim was rejected by the Court, inter alia, because there was nothing to show that he paid or was bound to pay the sums in question.[9] Any reasonably incurred expenses can also be claimed under Article 41. These may include necessary travel costs (including the costs of attending a hearing in Strasbourg), telephone, photocopying, postage and couriers, translation and other fees.

The claim for costs and expenses can also include sums incurred in attempting to secure redress for the violation of the Convention through the domestic legal system. As with costs incurred during the European Court procedure, any claim for domestic court costs should be fully itemised.

---

[9] Para. 9. See also *Dudgeon* v *UK* (1983) 5 EHRR 573, paras 21–22.

Any claim by an applicant under Article 41 will be sent by the Court to the respondent Government for its observations in reply. Awards of just satisfaction under Article 41 are considered in more detail in chapter 9.

3.4.1   Calling of witnesses

Witnesses will generally only be called in respect of fact-finding hearings (see above at 3.1). The Registrar will issue a summons to any witness, expert or other person to be heard by the Court (Rule 65). The summons will indicate the case in connection with which it has been issued, the object of the inquiry or opinion, and any provisions for the payment of expenses. The Court Rules allow for their costs to be borne by the party requesting the appearance of the witness, unless the Court decides otherwise. However, in practice the Court will very rarely require the applicant to pay such costs. In other cases, the Court will decide whether the costs are to be paid by one of the parties or the Council of Europe. All costs are taxed by the President of the chamber.

Witnesses and experts are required to take an oath or make a solemn declaration before giving evidence (Rule 66). If there are objections to witnesses or experts, the Court will decide on any dispute arising (Rule 67). The witness and experts may be questioned by any of the judges. The President of the chamber will adjudicate if there is any objection to the relevance of any question put to a witness or expert (Rule 68). If a witness refuses to attend or otherwise fails to do so, or violates the oath or declaration, there is no sanction, other than that the Court may notify the state party to whose jurisdiction the person is subject (Rule 69).

3.5   ORAL HEARING

The practice of the Court of holding a hearing on the merits of a case is now the exception rather than the rule (in spite of the wording of Rule 59). The vast majority of cases are decided without a hearing. The Court is more likely to hold a hearing if further clarification is needed on the facts of the case or the relevant domestic law or practice. It is suggested that the legal or political importance of a case may also be relevant factors in assessing the need for a hearing.

The hearing date will usually be set by the Court without notice to the applicant's representatives. The Court is reluctant to change hearing dates, but it may be possible to do so. If the applicant or his or her representatives would be unavailable for a particular date for good reason, then it is advisable initially to speak to the Registry lawyer and follow up with a letter setting out the reason for requesting a change of date. The Registrar will usually issue a press release about the case prior to the hearing and a second press release is usually issued on the day of the hearing. A schedule of forthcoming hearings is included on the Court's website.

Prior to the hearing, the applicant's representative will be asked to provide a copy of the oral submissions to the Court for translation purposes, at least one week before the hearing. It is not compulsory to do so, but it is advisable if possible, as it will facilitate the simultaneous translation of the oral submissions. If the text of the proposed submissions cannot be sent in advance, then at least a summary of the main points should be sent. Of course, advocates are not bound by any text sent in advance, but are free to alter their submissions as they consider fit.

The parties are also asked by the Court to provide, two weeks prior to the hearing, the names of all those who will attend the hearing including legal representatives, advisers and applicants. The Court Rules require that an applicant must be represented at hearings by an advocate who is authorised to practise in any of the state parties to the Convention (Rule 36(3)). In relation to UK cases, both practising barristers and solicitors may represent applicants as advocates before the Court, as may other lawyers, with the Court's permission. The President may allow applicants to present their own cases, but this is in practice extremely rare. The hearings are usually conducted in one of the Court's official languages (English or French), but the President may allow the use of an official language of one of the state parties.

The conduct of hearings will be directed by the President of the relevant chamber (Rule 63). However, hearings usually take no more than two hours in total, either from 9.00 to 11.00 am or from 2.30 to 4.30 pm. Only exceptionally will the parties be allowed further time. Applicants are usually given thirty minutes to put their primary oral arguments. The respondent Government is then given thirty minutes in which to respond (in admissibility hearings the Government will usually open and the applicant will reply). These times are strictly adhered to and it is essential that advocates keep to their allotted maximum of thirty minutes, otherwise they will be stopped by the President whether or not their submissions have been completed. The President will usually convene a short informal meeting prior to the hearing to remind the parties about the need to keep to the allotted times and to discuss any other particular arrangements for the hearing.

Clearly, the presentation of oral submissions in the context of a European Convention application is in a number of respects quite different from advocacy in the domestic courts. The procedure is primarily written, concluded in some cases by a very short hearing before the Court. In thirty minutes, the representatives will be required to complement the written submissions already lodged with the final oral submissions on behalf of the parties. The submissions will be simultaneously translated and a number of the judges will be listening to the translators, rather than the advocates. Advocates are therefore advised not to speak too quickly.

The parties can expect the Judge Rapporteur to have an in-depth knowledge of the case, however this cannot necessarily be assumed of the other judges. Given the very limited time, it is not necessary to dwell on the facts of the case (unless there are particular factual disputes). It is not of course necessary to argue every point in issue, provided that each point has been included in the written submissions already lodged with the Court. It is usual for oral submissions to concentrate on the primary matters of dispute between the parties. Given the strict time limits, it is quite common for advocates to prepare written speeches which they have timed, in order to ensure that the thirty minutes are not exceeded.

After the parties have each made their thirty-minute submissions, the Court may ask questions of the representatives. The questions are often directed specifically at one of the parties, although this will not always be the case. Any of the judges may ask questions and they may be fired at the parties in very quick succession. The parties are provided at the Court with a sheet indicating the names of the judges in the order that they are sitting in the Court, which will assist in identifying which judge has asked which question. If the Court does have questions, there will usually be a fifteen-minute adjournment for the parties to consider their responses. The parties are directed to meeting rooms below the Court during the adjournment. This can be a very stressful period, when the parties will have to decide both how to respond to the Court's questions and how to respond to the other side's submissions. It is obviously important that the legal representatives, advisers and the applicant work together in a very focused way during the fifteen-minute period.

Following the adjournment, each party will usually have about fifteen minutes to answer the Court's questions and to reply to the other side, with the applicant opening and the Government responding.

The Court's hearings take place in public (unless there are exceptional circumstances for the hearing to be held in private) (Article 40 and Rule 33). Any party or any other person concerned may request that a hearing take place in private. Reasons should be given for the request and it should be specified whether all or just part of the hearing should be held in private. The Court can exclude both the press and the public from all or part of a hearing for any of the following reasons (Rule 33(2)):

(a) in the interests of morals; or
(b) in the interests of public order; or
(c) in the interests of national security in a democratic society; or
(d) where the interests of juveniles so require; or
(e) where the protection of the private life of the parties so require; or
(f) to the extent strictly necessary in the opinion of the chamber in special circumstances where publicity would prejudice the interests of justice.

Under Rule 59 the Court may dispense with an oral hearing if it considers that a hearing is unnecessary. For example, it was not considered to be necessary to hold a hearing in the case of *Scarth* v *UK*, No. 33745/96, 22.7.99, as in that case the Government had conceded the point at issue, namely that Article 6(1) requires public hearings in small claims cases. It also appears that the new Court is cutting down on the number of oral hearings in order to reduce its backlog of cases. If no oral hearing is held, the applicant will usually be given the opportunity to submit further observations in response to the Government's Memorial.

If a party fails to appear for a hearing without showing sufficient cause, the Court may nevertheless proceed with the hearing in the absence of the party, provided that the Court is satisfied that to do so would be consistent with the proper administration of justice (Rule 64).

The Court may make a verbatim record of the hearing (Rule 70). The proceedings are recorded on tape, but a verbatim record is not prepared unless the Court decides to do so. The verbatim record will include:

(a)   the composition of the Court;
(b)   a list of those appearing before the Court (including agents, advocates, advisers and third parties);
(c)   details of any witnesses, experts or other persons heard by the Court;
(d)   the text of statements made, questions put and replies given;
(e)   the text of any decision delivered during the hearing by the Court.

The verbatim record will be sent to the parties for them to correct within a specified time limit (although they may not correct the sense of what was said).

The Court deliberates in private and its deliberations remain secret (Rule 22). Any decisions made by the Court are made by a majority of the judges. If there is a tie, a fresh vote is taken, and if there is still a tie, the President has the casting vote (Rule 23(1)). Votes are taken by a show of hands and the President may take a roll-call vote, in reverse order of precedence (Rule 23(3)).

Chapter Four

Practice and Procedure of the European Court: Judgment and Enforcement

4.1 DELIVERY OF JUDGMENT

The Court's reasoned judgment is usually published several months after the hearing. The parties will be given several weeks' notice of the date and time of the judgment, which will also be posted in advance on the Court's website. The Court's legal aid does not cover the attendance of the applicant or the applicant's representatives at the judgment, which is not required or expected by the Court. It is therefore usual for the applicant not to be represented at the judgment. However, in high profile cases, applicants and their representatives may consider attendance advisable in order to deal with any press enquiries.

Grand chamber judgments are read out (in summary) at a public hearing by the President of the grand chamber or a judge delegated by the President. There is a rarely a public hearing in respect of chamber judgments, which are sent directly to the parties. Once judgment is handed down, the Court will issue a press release summarising the judgment. The press release will be posted on the Court's website immediately (see below at 12.2. below). The judgment itself will also be posted on the website on the day judgment is given (but usually not until later in the day). The parties are sent certified copies of the judgment by post by the Registrar who also sends copies to the Committee of Ministers, the Secretary General of the Council of Europe, any third party and any person directly concerned (Rule 77).

Judgments are written in a standard format, in accordance with Rule 74(1). All judgments will contain the following:

(a) the names of the President and the other judges constituting the chamber concerned, and the name of the Registrar or Deputy Registrar;

(b) the dates on which it was adopted and delivered;

(c) a description of the parties;

(d) the names of the agents, advocates or advisers of the parties;

(e) an account of the procedure followed;

(f) the facts of the case;

(g) a summary of the submissions of the parties;

(h) the reasons in point of law;

(i) the operative provisions;

(j) the decision, if any, in respect of costs;

(k) the number of judges constituting the majority;

(l) where appropriate, a statement as to which text is authentic.

Judges may append their separate opinion, dissenting from or concurring with the majority judgment (Article 45(2) and Rule 74(2)), or they may include a bare statement of dissent. Judgments are given in either or both of the official languages, English or French.

The Court's primary remedy is a declaration that there has been a violation of one or more Convention rights. Where the Court finds that there has been a violation of the Convention, the judgment may include an award for 'just satisfaction' under Article 41 (previously Article 50, prior to November 1998), if the question of compensation is ready for decision. This may include compensation for both pecuniary and non-pecuniary losses and legal costs and expenses. The Court can, and usually does, direct that interest at a prescribed rate is to be payable on any sums not paid within a specified time (usually three months). There is *no provision* in the Convention for costs to be awarded against an applicant.

If the Article 41 claim is not ready for decision (as, for example, was the case in *Smith and Grady* v *UK* (2000) 29 EHRR 493),[1] awards for just satisfaction may be reserved in order for the Court to receive further submissions. In those circumstances, the Court will subsequently fix the procedure for adjudication of the just satisfaction claim. The Court will usually be composed of the same judges in order to consider the Article 41 claim, but this may not necessarily be the case (Rule 75(2)). If an Article 41 claim is subsequently agreed between the parties, the Court will strike the case out of the list, provided it is satisfied that the agreement is equitable (Rule 75(4)). Levels of Article 41 awards are discussed further in chapter 9.

As there is provision for referral of the judgment of a chamber to the grand chamber (see below at 4.2), the judgment of a chamber is not immediately final. The judgment of a chamber will only become final when one of three conditions is satisfied (Article 44):

---

[1] See especially paras 140–143.

(a)   when the parties declare that they will not request that the case be referred to the grand chamber; or

(b)   three months after the date of the judgment, if reference of the case to the grand chamber has not been requested; or

(c)   when the panel of the grand chamber rejects the request to refer the case.

The judgment of a grand chamber is final (Article 44(1)). Once final, judgments have binding force (Article 46(1)).

Any clerical errors made in the Court's judgments can be rectified, but the parties should notify the Court within one month of the delivery of the judgment (Rule 81).

4.2   REFERRAL TO THE GRAND CHAMBER

One of the new aspects of the Convention system introduced by the Protocol 11 changes was the capacity for rehearings before the grand chamber (under Article 43). Within three months of a chamber giving judgment, in exceptional cases, any party may ask for the case to be referred to the grand chamber for a final judgment. The party seeking referral should specify its reasons. The request is considered by a panel of five judges from the grand chamber. Their role is to decide whether the case involves any of the following:

(a)   a serious question affecting the interpretation of the Convention; or

(b)   a serious question affecting its application (for example, if it necessitates a substantial change to national law or practice); or

(c)   a serious issue of general importance (for example, a substantial political issue or an important issue of policy) (Article 43(2)).

If a request is refused, the panel need not give reasons, but if it is accepted, the grand chamber will decide any such referral by means of a judgment (Article 43(3)).

The introduction of a rehearing process through the Protocol 11 changes represented a political compromise by the Convention member states. It appears that in very 'controversial' cases the Convention will now allow for a respondent Government to have a second attempt at trying to persuade the Court of the merits of its position. Article 43 sets out only very general requirements for rehearings, which do not require, for example, that new evidence has become available since the judgment of the chamber. The grand chamber may accept a referral merely because the case raises 'a serious issue of general importance'. It is suggested that this is a highly questionable innovation. It is true, of course, that any party, including an applicant, may make such a request. It is also clear from the text of Article 43 itself that the procedure will only be relevant to 'exceptional cases'. It is therefore expected that the panel of five judges will only very rarely allow such referrals.

4.3   INTERPRETATION OF JUDGMENT

Within a year of the delivery of a judgment, either party may request the interpretation of the operative provisions of a judgment (Rule 79). The original chamber will usually decide such requests, but not if the original chamber cannot be constituted. The request can be refused by the chamber if there is no reason to warrant considering it. Otherwise, the other party will be asked to comment on the request within a specified time limit. If the request is granted, the question will be decided by way of a judgment. In exercising its inherent jurisdiction to consider interpretation, the Court will go no further than to clarify the meaning and scope which it intended to give to a previous decision.[2] Requests for interpretation concerning the attachment of sums awarded by way of just satisfaction by the Court have been rejected as being beyond the scope of 'interpretation'.[3]

4.4   REVISION OF JUDGMENT

Parties may seek a revision of a judgment if a decisive new fact is discovered (Rule 80). The revision of judgments is considered to be an 'exceptional procedure',[4] not least because it calls into question the finality of judgments. The conditions for seeking revision are as follows:

(a)   a fact has been discovered which might by its nature have a decisive influence; and

(b)   when the judgment was delivered the fact was unknown to the Court; and

(c)   when the judgment was delivered the fact could not reasonably have been known to the requesting party.

The request must be made not later than six months after the fact became known to the party. The request should identify the relevant judgment, show that the necessary conditions have been complied with and include all supporting documents (Rule 80(2)). The original chamber will usually decide such requests, but not if the original chamber cannot be constituted. The request can be refused by the chamber if there is no reason to warrant considering it. Otherwise, the other party will be asked to comment on the request within a specified time limit. If the request is granted, the question will be decided by way of a judgment.

---

[2] See, e.g., *Ringeisen* v *Austria (No. 3)* 1 EHRR 513, para. 13; *Allenet de Ribemont* v *France*, Judgment of 26.6.96, para. 17.

[3] See, e.g., *Allenet de Ribemont* v *France*, Judgment of 26.6.96.

[4] *Pardo* v *France*, No. 13416/87, 10.7.96.

An example of the revision process is the case of *Pardo* v *France*, No. 13416/87, 10.7.96,[5] which concerned the Court's original 1993 judgment. The applicant had complained of various violations including his right to a fair trial under Article 6(1), and in particular that he had not had the opportunity of an oral hearing despite the fact that the President of the Court of Appeal had announced that there would be such a hearing at a later date. The Court found no violation of Article 6(1) in its 1993 judgment because the applicant had failed to produce sufficient evidence of his version of events. When the applicant obtained copies of certain key documents, which had been retained in the domestic court case-file, he applied for revision of the original judgment in 1995. In reconsidering the position, the Court in 1996 found that the documents revealed that the applicant's version of events had been correct and it could not exclude the possibility that the documents might by their nature have had a decisive influence on the proceedings. Therefore, by five votes to four, the request for revision was found to be admissible and was referred to the chamber which gave the original judgment. However, in its subsequent judgment in *Pardo*, judgment of 29.4.97, the Court dismissed the request for revision on the basis that the new documents did not cast doubt on the original decision of the Court in 1993.

4.5   ENFORCEMENT OF JUDGMENT

Judgments are transmitted to the Committee of Ministers which supervises execution of judgments (Article 46(2)). In practice, the respondent Governments will report to the Committee on any measures taken in response to a judgment of the Court. The Committee of Ministers will be concerned both with the specific remedies awarded by the Court to the applicant, and the more general legislative, administrative or policy changes which may be required by a judgment. The case will remain on the agenda of the Committee of Ministers until the respondent Government has reported on the action taken and the Committee is satisfied with the sufficiency of those measures.

The Committee of Ministers publishes interim resolutions in relation to compliance which will record whether or not payment of just satisfaction has been carried out and whether other steps have been taken by the respondent government following the judgment. Selected resolutions are published in the Council of Europe's *Human Rights Information Bulletin*. For example, a resolution in relation to the case of *Saunders* v *UK* (1997) 23 EHRR 313[6] referred to guidance issued by the Attorney-General and changes to be implemented by the Youth Justice and Criminal Evidence Act 1999. The Committee of Ministers decided to review the case again once the Act had come into force.

---

[5] See also *McGinley and Egan* v *UK*, Nos 21825/93 & 25414/94, 28.1.00.
[6] Interim Resolution DH (00)27, 14.2.00 (*Human Rights Information Bulletin*, No. 48, p. 28).

It is extremely important that applicants are clearly advised at the outset of proceedings as to what the European Court can and cannot do. The effect of a judgment in which the Court has found a violation of the Convention is to impose a legal obligation on the respondent state to put an end to the breach and to make reparation for its consequences in such a way as to restore as far as possible the situation existing before the breach (*restitutio in integrum*). If *restitutio in integrum* is in practice impossible, the respondent state is free to choose the means for complying with a judgment.[7] The Court may issue declarations of Convention violations and award compensation and costs. It will not quash decisions of the domestic authorities or courts (including convictions),[8] strike down domestic legislation or otherwise require a respondent Government to take particular measures within the national legal system (such as ordering the transfer of prisoners to the jurisdiction of another Convention state[9] or order repayment of fines). This reflects the fact that the European Court is adjudicating on breaches of international law.

Nevertheless, Court judgments are binding in international law on respondent Governments which undertake to abide by the final judgment of the Court in any case to which they are parties (Article 46(1)). Accordingly, a Government may decide that as a result of a particular judgment it should adopt a new policy or practice, amend the relevant legislation, overturn a decision or take other steps as necessary. For example, in relation to the UK in recent years, changes to legislation or regulations have followed the Court's judgments in *Findlay* (1997) 24 EHRR 221 (changes to the court-martial system),[10] *Benham* (1996) 22 EHRR 293 (provision of legal aid in civil proceedings where there is a risk of imprisonment)[11] and *Hussain and Singh* (1996) 22 EHRR 1 (detention at Her Majesty's pleasure).[12] In other cases, legal changes have followed judgments during the course of which the Government has acknowledged Convention violations. In *A v UK* (1999) 27 EHRR 611, the Government accepted before the Court that there had been a violation of Article 3 where a stepfather had been acquitted in proceedings for assaulting a child on the basis of the 'reasonable chastisement' defence. In *Scarth v UK*, No. 33745/96, 22.7.99,[13] the Government

---

[7] See, e.g., *Selçuk and Asker v Turkey* (1998) 26 EHRR 477, para. 125.

[8] See, e.g., *Schmautzer v Austria* (1996) 21 EHRR 511, paras 42–44.

[9] *Selmouni v France* (2000) 29 EHRR 403, paras 124–126.

[10] The Armed Forces Act 1996 came into force on 1 April 1997 (see Resolution DH(98) 11 of 18.2.98).

[11] The Legal Advice and Assistance Regulations 1989 were amended in 1997 (see Resolution DH(97) 506 of 29.10.97).

[12] Under the Crime (Sentences) Act 1997, detainees at Her Majesty's pleasure are treated in the same way as discretionary lifers, once the tariff has expired (see Resolutions DH(98) 149 and 150 of 11.6.98).

[13] The relevant county court rule in force at the time was replaced by the Civil Procedure Rules (from April 1999) which provide the courts with a discretion to hold a hearing in private on various grounds, including confidentiality, national security and to protect the right of children and those suffering from mental incapacity.

conceded that Article 6(1) had been violated because of the failure to provide a public hearing in the course of county court proceedings for debt which were referred for arbitration.

In other cases, the Government has reversed decisions or changed policy or practice. For example, following the Court's judgment in *D* v *UK* (1997) 24 EHRR 423, the applicant was granted indefinite leave to remain.[14] Following the Court's judgments in *Smith and Grady* v *UK* (2000) 29 EHRR 493 and *Lustig-Prean and Beckett* v *UK* (2000) 29 EHRR 548, the Secretary of State for Defence announced in January 2000 the lifting of the ban on homosexuals in the armed forces and that there would be a new code of service conduct covering all personal relationships within the forces.

It is important to emphasise that it is the Government, not the Court, which decides what measures to take in response to a Court judgment. It is possible that a Convention violation was the result of a one-off action (for example, an arrest by a police officer in violation of Article 5) which does not require any amendment to policy or practice. For example, in the case of *Robins* v *UK* (1998) 26 EHRR 527 the Court found a violation of Article 6(1) arising from the length of costs proceedings. The proceedings had been delayed by ten months because of mistakes by the Legal Aid Board and by sixteen months because of inactivity by court staff. Following that judgment, the Government merely informed the Committee of Ministers that the judgment was circulated to the Legal Aid Board, the Department of Social Security and the Court of Appeal and that summaries of the judgment had been published in various legal reviews.[15] In cases which in effect do require the respondent Government to take action, and where the Government is reluctant to acknowledge this, change may be effected by the supervisory role of the Committee of Ministers or simply by further cases being brought by applicants raising the same issue. It is of course far preferable for Governments to take the necessary remedial action, without wasting time and expense (of both parties) in responding to further Convention applications.

The measures which are needed to remedy a Convention violation will of course depend upon the interpretation of the effects of the judgment. It is not uncommon for there to be clear differences of opinion as to the steps which should be taken to remedy a defect identified by the Court, and Governments are frequently criticised for failing to take sufficient steps.

If an applicant is dissatisfied with the failure of the Government to take adequate steps in response to a European Court judgment, the matter should be taken up with the Committee of Ministers as part of its role in supervising execution of the judgment. The Committee of Ministers is entitled to consider submissions from an individual who claims not to have received damages in

---

[14] See Resolution DH(98) 10, of 18.2.98.
[15] Resolution DH(98) 90 of 22.4.98.

accordance with a decision of the Court and any further information concerning the execution of a judgment. The Court itself will not, however, be able to take any further action. The Committee of Ministers has recognised that in certain cases the reexamination of a case by the domestic authorities or the re-opening of proceedings will be the most efficient means of achieving *restitutio in integrum* and has encouraged Convention states to ensure that it is possible to re-examine or reopen cases where the European Court has found a violation of the Convention.[16]

It may also be advisable for an applicant to take the matter up directly with the Government, and to seek the assistance of appropriate NGOs in drawing public attention to systemic problems. Whether or not applicants will succeed in pushing through changes of policy or practice will depend upon the extent to which they can establish that the Convention violation identified in their case revealed a general problem with the relevant system or practice, rather than a one-off incident.

---

[16] Recommendation No. R(2000)2 of 19.1.00.

Chapter Five

Admissibility Criteria

5.1 INTRODUCTION

The European Court's 'standing' and admissibility criteria are set out in Articles 34 and 35 of the Convention, which provide as follows:

Article 34

The Court may receive applications from any person, non-governmental organisation or group of individuals claiming to be the victim of a violation by one of the High Contracting Parties of the rights set forth in the Convention or the protocols thereto. The High Contracting Parties undertake not to hinder in any way the effective exercise of this right.

Article 35

1. The Court may only deal with the matter after all domestic remedies have been exhausted, according to the generally recognised rules of international law, and within a period of six months from the date on which the final decision was taken.
2. The Court shall not deal with any application submitted under Article 34 that
    (a) is anonymous; or
    (b) is substantially the same as a matter that has already been examined by the Court or has already been submitted to another procedure of international investigation or settlement and contains no relevant new information.
3. The Court shall declare inadmissible any individual application submitted under Article 34 which it considers incompatible with the provisions of the Convention or the protocols thereto, manifestly ill-founded, or an abuse of the right of application.
4. The Court shall reject any application which it considers inadmissible under this Article. It may do so at any stage of the proceedings.

The admissibility rules are a critical aspect of the European Convention system, not least because only about twenty per cent of cases are found admissible. For example, in 1999 the Court declared 731 applications admissible and 3,519 cases were found to be inadmissible (or struck off).[1] Article 34 (formerly Article 25) sets out the requirements relating to standing. Article 35 (formerly Article 26) sets out the admissibility criteria, the most important of which in practice are the requirement to exhaust effective domestic remedies and to submit an application to the Court within six months of the final decision in the domestic proceedings.

This chapter will discuss the following aspects of Articles 34 and 35:

5.2   Capacity and standing — who may petition the Court?
5.3   Who can claim to be a victim?
5.4   Exhaustion of domestic remedies
5.5   Six-month time limit
5.6   Anonymous applications
5.7   Applications substantially the same as a matter already examined by the Court
5.8   Applications already submitted to another procedure of international investigation or settlement
5.9   Incompatibility with the provisions of the Convention
5.10 Manifestly ill-founded
5.11 Abuse of the right of application.

The obligation on Governments not to hinder the right of application (in Article 34) is considered below at 6.20.

5.2 CAPACITY AND STANDING — WHO MAY PETITION THE COURT?

The European Court rules relating to capacity and standing are not restrictive, although they are inextricably linked to the requirement that an applicant must claim to be the victim of a violation of one or more Convention rights (which is dealt with below at 5.3).

Article 34 states that the Court may receive applications from 'any person, non-governmental organisation or group of individuals . . .'. Accordingly, individuals, groups of individuals, NGOs, companies (even if dissolved),[2] shareholders, trusts, professional associations, trade unions, political parties and religious organisations may all submit applications to the Court. Depending on the nature of the Convention violation alleged, a company itself may bring an application

---

[1] Press release of the European Court, 24.1.00.
[2] *Pine Valley Developments Ltd* v *Ireland* (1992) 14 EHRR 319, para. 42.

under the Convention, as may the chair and managing director of the company[3] and as may individual shareholders in exceptional circumstances.[4]

However, certain rights by definition can only be claimed by individuals and cannot extend to organisations, such as freedom of thought, conscience and religion,[5] the right to education[6] and the right not to be subjected to degrading treatment or punishment.[7]

Some examples of the different types of applicants are set out below.

5.2.1 Groups of individuals

Guerra and others v *Italy* (1998) 26 EHRR 357: forty inhabitants of an Italian town brought an application under Articles 2, 8 and 10 complaining of the risks of pollution or a major accident at a chemical factory a kilometre away.

Balmer-Schafroth v *Switzerland* (1998) 25 EHRR 598: ten applicants living in the vicinity of a nuclear power plant at Muhleberg challenged the granting of an operating licence, invoking Articles 2, 6(1), 8 and 13.

5.2.2 Companies and shareholders

Sunday Times v *UK* 2 EHRR 245: the publisher, editor and a group of journalists from the *Sunday Times* invoked Article 10 in challenging the obtaining of an injunction by the Attorney-General which prevented publication of articles concerning the thalidomide drug, which was the subject of legal proceedings.

Tinnelly & Son Ltd and others and McElduff and others v *UK* (1999) 27 EHRR 249: the applicants challenged the failure of the Government to grant them contracts, on the basis that the decision was discriminatory on religious grounds, and complained of the issue of Ministerial certificates which effectively barred them from bringing proceedings to challenge the decision, invoking Articles 6(1), 8, 13 and 14.

Pressos Compania Naviera SA and others v *Belgium* (1996) 21 EHRR 301: the applicant ship owners, mutual shipping insurance associations and an insolvency administrator complained of a retrospective amendment to the law affecting shipping negligence cases, invoking Article 1 of Protocol 1 and Article 6(1).

Autronic AG v *Switzerland* (1990) 12 EHRR 485: the applicant home electronics company challenged the refusal to grant a licence to receive television programmes from a Soviet telecommunications satellite, invoking Article 10.

---

[3] *Kaplan* v *UK* (1982) 4 EHRR 64.
[4] *Agrotexim and others* v *Greece* (1996) 21 EHRR 250.
[5] *X and Church of Scientology* v *Sweden* (1979) 16 DR 68.
[6] *Ingrid Jordebo Foundation & Christian Schools and Ingrid Jordebo* v *Sweden*, No. 11533/85, (1987) 51 DR 125.
[7] *Kontakt-Information-Therapie and Hengen* v *Austria*, No. 11921/86, (1988) 57 DR 81.

Kaplan v *UK* (1982) 4 EHRR 64: the applicant chairman and managing director of an insurance company could claim to be a victim of a violation of the company's rights which affected its business both because of his financial interest in the company and as an office holder, invoking Articles 6(1) and 13.

5.2.3   Building societies

National & Provincial Building Society and others v *UK* (1998) 25 EHRR 127: three building societies sought to claim restitution of monies paid out under invalidated tax regulations, invoking Article 1 of Protocol 1 and Articles 6 and 14.

5.2.4   Trade unions

Swedish Engine Drivers' Union v *Sweden* 1 EHRR 617: the applicant union challenged the system of collective bargaining which was carried out only with the State Employees' Union, invoking Articles 11, 13 and 14.

National Union of Belgian Police v *Belgium* 1 EHRR 578: the applicant union complained of the authorities' refusal to recognise it as a representative organisation which had the effect of debarring it from state consultation, invoking Articles 11 and 14.

Council of Civil Service Unions and others v *UK* (1987) 50 DR 228: the applicant union and civil servants employed at GCHQ challenged the removal of the right of GCHQ employees to belong to a trade union, and the deprivation of the union's role in industrial relations at GCHQ, invoking Article 11.

5.2.5   Religious bodies

Canea Catholic Church v *Greece* (1999) 27 EHRR 521: the church challenged its inability to take legal proceedings as a result of the civil court's refusal to acknowledge that it had legal personality, invoking Articles 6(1), 9, 14 and Article 1 of Protocol 1.

Holy Monasteries v *Greece* (1995) 20 EHRR 1: eight Greek Orthodox monasteries brought proceedings to challenge the deprivation of their property and their inability to bring proceedings in the domestic courts against the Greek state, invoking Article 1 of Protocol 1 and Article 6(1).

X and Church of Scientology v *Sweden* (1979) 16 DR 68: the applicants complained of the prohibition of particular wording in advertising for items sold by the Church of Scientology, invoking Article 9.

5.2.6   Non-governmental organisations (NGOs)

Christians Against Racism and Fascism v *UK* (1980) 21 DR 138: the applicant organisation challenged a ban imposed by the police on all public demonstrations in London, invoking Articles 5, 10, 11 and 14.

Plattform 'Ärzte für das Leben' v *Austria* (1991) 13 EHRR 204: the applicant organisation, an association of doctors complaining about abortion, sought to challenge the failure of the police to provide protection for their demonstrations against disruption by pro-abortion groups, invoking Articles 9, 10, 11 and 13.

Rai, Allmond and 'Negotiate Now' v *UK* (1995) 19 EHRR CD 93: the applicant organisation, which sought to promote peace in Northern Ireland, challenged the refusal to permit a rally in Trafalgar Square, invoking Articles 9, 10, 11, 13 and 18.

5.2.7 Political parties

Freedom and Democracy Party (Özdep) v *Turkey*, No. 23885/94, 8.12.99: the applicant political party complained about its dissolution by the Constitutional Court and the banning of its leaders from holding similar office in any other political party, invoking Articles 9, 10, 11 and 14.

The Liberal Party and others v *UK* (1982) 4 EHRR 106: the applicants complained about the simple majority electoral system in Britain, invoking Article 3 of Protocol 1 and Articles 10, 13 and 14.

5.2.8 Nationality and residence

Nationality and place of residence are irrelevant to the right to complain to the Court of violations of the Convention, reflecting the obligation in Article 1 for the parties to secure Convention rights to everyone within their jurisdiction (see also below at 7.1). The test applied is whether or not the applicant can claim to be a victim of a violation of his or her Convention rights.

5.2.9 Legal capacity

Lack of legal capacity will not generally affect the right of petition, but applicants may be represented by a relative or other suitable person. For example, in the case of *Winterwerp* v *Netherlands* 2 EHRR 387 an application was brought by a man who had suffered severe brain damage in an accident and who had been compulsorily detained under the Dutch mental health legislation. Similarly, the applicant in *Van der Leer* v *Netherlands* (1990) 12 EHRR 567 sought to challenge her compulsory detention in a psychiatric hospital. Where, however, applicants are represented before the Court by a relative or other person, the Court will require evidence of their authority to represent the applicant.

5.2.10 Children

Children may be applicants in cases before the European Court, both in conjunction with adult 'victims' arising from the same complaint and in their own right. For example, in *Marckx* v *Belgium* 2 EHRR 330, an unmarried mother and her young daughter complained of the illegitimacy laws in Belgium, including in relation to the bequeathing and inheritance of property. The case of *A* v *UK* (1999) 27 EHRR 611 concerned the severe ill-treatment of the applicant child by his stepfather and the failure of the state to provide the child with protection from ill-treatment. The cases of *T and V* v *UK* (2000) 30 EHRR 121 concerned the criminal proceedings brought against the applicants when they were aged eleven, in relation to the abduction and murder of a two-year-old boy committed when they were ten years old.

Children may also be represented by a parent (as in *Campbell and Cosans* v *UK* (1981) 3 EHRR 531 where the applicants complained on their children's behalf of the risk of corporal punishment in school), unless there is a conflict of interest or for any reason the parent does not have legal standing in domestic law to do so. In *Hokkanen* v *Finland* (1995) 19 EHRR 139 an application was brought by a father in respect of a child custody dispute with the child's maternal grandparents. The applicant father also lodged an application on behalf of his daughter, but that aspect of the case was declared inadmissible as it was found that he was no longer the child's custodian at the relevant time.

Children may be represented at the Court by others, such as solicitors, provided that the representative produces proof of authority to act. For example, in *SD, DP and T* v *UK* (1996) 22 EHRR CD 148, which concerned delay in care proceedings, the application was brought by a solicitor on behalf of the three children, supported by a letter of authority from the guardian ad litem appointed by the court to safeguard the interests of the children in the domestic proceedings. This was challenged by the Government which argued that neither the solicitor nor the guardian ad litem had authority to act on the children's behalf in the proceedings under the European Convention. However, the Commission rejected the Government's objections, emphasising that it would not take a restrictive or technical approach to such questions, as children generally relied on others to represent their interests, and required specific protection of their interests which had to be both practical and effective. No conflict of interests were found to arise and on the facts there was no alternative means of representation.

5.2.11   Death of an applicant

The Court will not accept applications in the name of a deceased person. However, it is well established that an application can be brought on behalf of the deceased by a close relative or heir. For example, the case of *McCann and others* v *UK* (1996) 21 EHRR 97, concerning the fatal shooting of three members of the IRA in Gibraltar by British soldiers, was brought by members of the victims' families who were representatives of the estates of the deceased. In *Keenan* v *UK*, No. 27229/95, 6.9.99, following her son's suicide in prison, the applicant complained of the prison authorities' failure to take adequate steps to safeguard her son's life. It is *not* necessary for an applicant in such cases to have to establish financial dependency or pecuniary loss. In *Keenan*, the applicant's son had been over eighteen when he died and he had no dependants, which effectively ruled out proceedings under the Fatal Accidents Act 1976 or for bereavement damages. The absence of any pecuniary loss did not prevent Mrs Keenan from making an application to the European Commission and indeed the very fact that she could not bring domestic proceedings in respect of her son's death led to a finding by the Commission of a violation of the right to an effective remedy under Article 13.

Where the standing of an applicant to bring Convention proceedings in respect of a deceased relative has been challenged, the Strasbourg institutions have underlined the objective and purpose of the Convention as being to provide practical and effective safeguards. Accordingly, in *Yaşa v Turkey* (1999) 28 EHRR 408 the Court held that the applicant, as the deceased's nephew, could legitimately claim to be a victim of an act as tragic as the murder of his uncle. It did not matter that there might have been closer relatives who could have brought proceedings on behalf of the deceased. It may be the case that the Convention rights of the deceased's relative have also been violated and therefore an application should be brought in the applicant's own right, as well as on behalf of the deceased. For example, in *Kurt v Turkey* (1999) 27 EHRR 373 the applicant complained of her son's disappearance in south-east Turkey, invoking Articles 2, 3, 5, 13, 14 and 18 in respect of her son, and Article 3 in respect of herself, because of the anguish and distress caused by her son's continued disappearance which she argued amounted to inhuman treatment. On the facts of the case, the Court found violations of Articles 5 and 13 in respect of the applicant's son, and a violation of Article 3 in relation to the applicant.

If an applicant dies whilst a case is pending before the Court, the case can usually be continued by the applicant's close relatives or heirs, if that person has a legitimate interest, or if the Court is satisfied that the complaint is of general importance. For example, the parents of a haemophiliac who had contracted HIV could continue an application brought in respect of the length of domestic proceedings for compensation following the applicant's death.[8] In *Laskey, Jaggard and Brown v UK* (1997) 24 EHRR 39, a case concerning criminal proceedings for assault brought in relation to sado-masochistic activities, there was no objection to the father of the first applicant continuing with the proceedings following the first applicant's death.

In *Lukanov v Bulgaria* (1997) 24 EHRR 121, a case concerning the arrest and prosecution of a former Prime Minister of Bulgaria, it was not disputed that the applicant's widow and two children could continue with the application after Mr Lukanov was shot dead outside his home. However, the right of the widow and children of the applicant to continue proceedings was disputed in *Ahmet Sadik v Greece* (1997) 24 EHRR 323. The applicant was a newspaper publisher and

---

[8] *X v France* (1992) 14 EHRR 483.

parliamentary election candidate who was prosecuted for publishing false and defamatory information about other election candidates and for inciting the Muslim population to disturb the peace. He died after the Commission had published its report on the merits and his widow and two children sought to continue the case. The Government argued that an application concerning an Article 10 violation could not be transferred to the applicant's heirs, but the Court held that his heirs had a legitimate moral interest in obtaining a ruling that the applicant's conviction infringed Article 10, as well as having a pecuniary interest in the case.

However, an executor may not have standing to bring an application. For example, in *Scherer* v *Switzerland* (1994) 18 EHRR 276, the application was struck out where, rather than any close relative, an executor proposed to continue the proceedings (for pecuniary reasons only) and the Court considered there to be no public policy reasons to pursue the case. It was a relevant consideration in striking the case out that the domestic law in question had been substantially changed since the events in question.

5.2.12   Public corporations

Public bodies, such as councils, cannot make applications to the European Court, as Article 34 only permits a 'person, non-governmental organisation or group of individuals' to petition the Court. A Spanish city council and a Swiss local government commune have both been thwarted from petitioning Strasbourg for this reason.[9]

In an application brought by the BBC against the UK, concerning a witness summons served on the BBC to produce relevant film material in the course of criminal proceedings, the Commission left open the question as to whether the BBC, an organisation set up by Royal Charter, could bring an application under the Convention.[10]

5.3   WHO CAN CLAIM TO BE A VICTIM?

In accordance with Article 34, an applicant must claim to be the *victim* of a violation of one or more Convention rights. The Court will only consider the particular circumstances of each case and will not permit abstract challenges (*actio popularis*),[11] nor will the Court admit hypothetical breaches. This may lead to all or part of Convention applications being rejected. For example, in *Buckley*

---

[9] See *Ayuntamiento de M* v *Spain*, No. 15090/89, 68 DR 209 and *Rothenthurm Commune* v *Switzerland*, No. 13252/87, 59 DR 251

[10] *BBC* v *UK*, No. 25978/94, 84-A DR 129; [1996] EHRLR 322.

[11] See, e.g., *Lindsay and others* v *UK*, No. 31699/96, 17.1.97: application claiming to represent more than 1 million people in Northern Ireland declared inadmissible *ratione personae* with the provisions of the Convention.

v *UK* (1997) 23 EHRR 101 the applicant, who was a gypsy, complained that she was prevented from living in caravans on her own land with her family and from following a life as a traveller. The applicant also complained to the Court of the provisions of the Caravan Sites Act 1968 and the Criminal Justice and Public Order Act 1994 which criminalised the use of gypsy caravans in certain circumstances. However, the Court found that as measures had been taken against the applicant under neither statute, those particular complaints could not be considered.

The test applied by the Court is that the applicant must show that he or she has been personally or directly affected by the alleged Convention violation.

There are numerous examples of Convention applications in which the applicants have been found to have failed this test, in which case the application will be declared inadmissible *ratione personae*. For example, in *Magee* v *UK*, No. 24892/95, 6.4.95, the applicant barrister complained of the requirement to take an oath of allegiance for applicants to become Queen's Counsel, which he argued amounted to a violation of Articles 9, 10, 13 and 14 of the Convention. However, the case was declared inadmissible on the basis that as his application to become a Queen's Counsel had been turned down, he could not claim to be a victim of a violation under Article 34. In a case relating to common law developments restricting the use of 'discovered' documents which had been read out in court,[12] the applicants were journalists and a newspaper company who argued that their sources of information had been adversely affected because recipients of such information would be unwilling to allow journalists to see the information, and that the risk of contempt proceedings had a 'chilling effect' on their right to freedom of expression. However, the applicants were not considered to be victims because they had not themselves been restrained or fettered. In order to satisfy the 'victim' test, the detriment complained of had to be of a less indirect and remote nature.

Agrotexim and others v *Greece* (1996) 21 EHRR 250 concerned the alleged unlawful interference by the municipal authorities with various rights of a brewery company, the shareholders of which were the applicants. The Court held the application to be incompatible *ratione personae* with the Convention as the applicant shareholder companies were not 'victims'. The brewery company itself could have brought the application (despite being in liquidation): piercing the 'corporate veil' would only be exceptionally justified where it was established that it was impossible for the company itself to apply under the Convention.

The victim test may rule out some applicants in a case, but not others.[13] In *Ahmed and others* v *UK*, No. 22954/93, 12.9.95,[14] a complaint made by the union

---

[12] *Leigh, Guardian Newspapers Ltd and Observer Ltd* v *UK*, No. 10039/82, (1985) 7 EHRR 409, 451.
[13] See, e.g., *Bowman and the Society for the Protection of the Unborn Child* v *UK*, No. 24839/94, 4.12.95.
[14] See also, e.g., *Purcell and others* v *Ireland*, No. 15404/89, 16.4.91.

UNISON concerning the restrictions on the political activities of local government officers was declared inadmissible. The Commission found that the
regulations in question[15] did not affect the rights of the union as such (under
Articles 10 or 11) and therefore UNISON could not claim to be a victim of a
violation of the Convention. However, applications brought by individual local
government officers who were affected by the regulations were declared
admissible. Therefore, if there are doubts about an applicant organisation's victim
status, it is advisable to include at least one individual victim as an applicant.

The Strasbourg institutions have allowed a degree of flexibility in certain
circumstances in defining what is meant by a 'victim'. Where there is any doubt
about an individual's 'victim' status, practitioners should consider carefully
whether their clients fall into any of the categories set out below at 5.3.1 (potential
victims) or 5.3.2 (indirect victims).

5.3.1 Potential victims

Article 34 may permit an applicant to complain that the law itself violates their
Convention rights, even if there has been no specific measure implemented
against them. However, potential victims of Convention violations must satisfy
the Court that there is a real personal risk of being directly affected by the
violation.[16]

Those considered to be at risk have fallen into various categories, including
those at risk of criminal prosecution. The cases of *Dudgeon* v *UK* (1982) 4 EHRR
149, *Norris* v *Ireland* (1991) 13 EHRR 186, *Modinos* v *Cyprus* (1993) 16 EHRR
485 all concerned domestic legislation criminalising homosexual acts. In
Dudgeon, the applicant complained that he was liable to prosecution because of
his homosexual conduct and complained of the fear, suffering and psychological
distress caused by the very existence of the laws in question. He had been
questioned by the police about his homosexual activities and his house had been
searched, but criminal proceedings had not been brought against him. Nevertheless, the Court accepted that the very existence of the legislation continuously and
directly affected his private life. It was also relevant that the law in question was
not a 'dead letter'. A similar decision was reached by the Commission on the
applicant's status as a 'victim' in *Sutherland* v *UK*, No. 25186/94, 1.7.97, [1998]
EHRLR 117, which concerned the fixing of the minimum age for lawful
homosexual activities at eighteen rather than sixteen. Before he reached the age
of eighteen, the existence of the legislation directly affected the applicant's
private life, even though he had not even been threatened with prosecution. In
ADT v *UK*, No. 35765/97, 31.7.00, the applicant was prosecuted and convicted for

---

[15] The Local Government Officers (Political Restrictions) Regulations 1990, SI 1990 No. 851.
[16] See, e.g., *Open Door and Dublin Well Woman* v *Ireland* (1993) 15 EHRR 244, para. 44 and *Johnston
and others* v *Ireland* (1987) 9 EHRR 203, para. 42.

gross indecency. This was held to violate Article 8, but so too was the maintenance in force of legislation criminalising homosexual acts between men in private.

Those who fall into a particular group within society who might be affected by a particular measure or omission may also be considered as potential victims. In *Balmer-Schafroth* v *Switzerland* (1998) 25 EHRR 598[17] the Government argued that the applicants, who were residents living close to a nuclear power station, could not claim to be victims of a decision to extend the power station's operating licence because the consequences of the violations of which they complained were too remote to affect them directly and personally. However, the Court rejected those arguments, as the applicants' objections had been found admissible by the Swiss Federal Council and because there could be a Convention violation even in the absence of prejudice (which is relevant only in the context of Article 50 awards).

The case of *Open Door and Dublin Well Woman* v *Ireland* (1993) 15 EHRR 244 concerned an injunction imposed by the Irish courts preventing the dissemination of information to pregnant women on abortion facilities outside Ireland. The Government raised objections about the victim status of two of the applicants who joined the application as women of child-bearing age, but who were not pregnant. The Court held that the two applicants belonged to a class of women of child-bearing age which might be adversely affected by the restrictions imposed by the injunction. Therefore, they ran the risk of being directly prejudiced by the measure complained of.

In *Campbell and Cosans* v *UK* (1981) 3 EHRR 531 the Government argued that a complaint brought by parents on behalf of children who might be subjected to corporal punishment if they did not behave properly, could not satisfy the victim test. However, the Commission found that the threat of a potential use of corporal punishment as a means of discipline meant that the children had the requisite direct and immediate personal interest.

Potential violations of the Convention will also arise in cases concerning specific measures which, if implemented, would breach the Convention. This often arises in the context of immigration or extradition cases. The case of *Soering* v *UK* (1989) 11 EHRR 439 concerned the decision of the Home Secretary to extradite the applicant to the USA where he faced capital murder charges in Virginia and a possible death sentence. Therefore, if he were sentenced to death, he would be exposed to the 'death row phenomenon' which he claimed would violate Article 3. In those circumstances, the Court found that the responsibility of the state would be engaged where there were substantial grounds for believing that, if extradited, the applicant faced a real risk of being subjected to torture or inhuman or degrading treatment or punishment. That had to be the case, in order

---

[17] See especially paras 24–26. See also, e.g., *Amuur* v *France* (1996) 22 EHRR 533, para. 36.

to ensure the effectiveness of the Article 3 safeguards, given the serious and irreparable nature of the suffering which the applicant faced. There have been many examples of applicants complaining of prospective violations in deportation cases. In *Chahal* v *UK* (1997) 23 EHRR 413 the applicant complained that his deportation to India would violate his rights under Article 3 because as a Sikh political activist he risked being subjected to torture. The state's responsibility will be engaged where there are substantial grounds for believing that the applicant, if expelled, would face a real risk of inhuman or degrading treatment contrary to Article 3. In *D* v *UK* (1997) 24 EHRR 423 the applicant, who was suffering from the advanced stages of the AIDS virus, complained of a violation of Article 3 were he to be removed to St Kitts, where he was born, because the lack of adequate medical treatment would expose him to inhuman and degrading treatment.

Nevertheless, applicants will be required to wait for the final decision in any domestic proceedings and to exhaust available and effective avenues of appeal before their complaints will be admitted by the Court. The applicants in *Vijayanathan and Pusparajah* v *France* (1993) 15 EHRR 62 were found not to be 'victims' of a violation of the Convention where they had been ordered to leave French territory. As Sri Lankan citizens of Tamil origin, they claimed they would be at risk of torture were they to be returned to Sri Lanka. It was decisive that the direction to leave was not in itself enforceable, that no expulsion order had been made and were such an order to be made the applicants would have had a right of appeal.

The extent of the secrecy of legislation or measures taken by public authorities may have a bearing on the question of victim status. In *Klass and others* v *Germany* 2 EHRR 214, the applicant lawyers complained about the domestic law in Germany relating to secret surveillance, even though they had no evidence that they had been under surveillance themselves. The Court found that the applicants should not be prevented from claiming to be victims of the alleged violation where, because of the secrecy of the measures in question, it was not possible to prove any specific implementation against the applicants. Accordingly, applicants may in certain circumstances legitimately complain to the Court of being a victim of a violation because of the mere existence of secret measures.[18] The relevant factors that the Court will consider include the Convention rights in issue, the secret character of the measures objected to, and the connection between the applicant and those measures. This is an important aspect of the victim test given that the UK government's usual practice in cases concerning allegations of telephone or post interception is not to disclose to the Court to what extent, if at all, an applicant has been the subject of interception. For example, in *Malone* v

---

[18] See also, e.g., *Virginia Matthews* v *UK*, No. 28576/95, 16.10.96: allegation that applicant peace campaigner's telephone calls had been intercepted.

UK (1985) 7 EHRR 14, the Government merely conceded that as a receiver of stolen goods, the applicant was a member of a class of persons who were liable to have their communications intercepted.

5.3.2   Indirect victims

An individual who is not directly affected by a particular measure or omission may nevertheless have been 'indirectly' affected by the violation of the Convention rights of another person. This may often be the case in respect of close family connections, but it could also include other third parties. For example, family members of a person who is subject to a deportation decision might claim to be victims of a Convention violation. The case of *Chahal* v *UK* (1997) 23 EHRR 413 concerned the proposed deportation of Mr Chahal, a Sikh separatist leader, on grounds that he posed a threat to national security. Not only did Mr Chahal himself bring proceedings under the Convention, but so too did his wife and children, arguing that his deportation would violate their right to respect for family life under Article 8. In *Kurt* v *Turkey* (1999) 27 EHRR 373 the applicant complained of the disappearance of her son who had last been seen in the custody of the security forces. She successfully invoked Articles 5 and 13 in respect of her son, but she also obtained a finding of a violation of Article 3 in respect of her own anguish and distress which she had suffered over a prolonged period.

The case of *Abdulaziz, Cabales and Balkandali* v *UK* (1985) 7 EHRR 471 concerned the 1971 Immigration Act and Rules which prevented the applicants' husbands from remaining with them or joining them in the UK. The case was brought by the wives who were lawfully and permanently settled in the UK and the Court found a violation of Article 8 taken together with Article 14 (as victims of sex discrimination) and of Article 13.

5.3.3   Absence of requirement of 'prejudice'

There is no need for a 'victim' to have suffered 'prejudice' or 'detriment', which is relevant only in relation to awards of 'just satisfaction' under Article 41 of the Convention (formerly Article 50).[19] Article 41 awards are discussed in chapter 9.

For example, in *De Jong, Baljet and Van Den Brink* v *Netherlands* (1986) 8 EHRR 20 the Government objected to Mr Van den Brink's victim status because of the alleged lack of detriment to him. He was a military conscript who had refused to obey orders on grounds of conscientious objection and was therefore arrested and held in custody. The Government argued that he could not claim to be a 'victim' as his time spent in custody on remand was deducted from the sentence imposed upon him. However, the Court held that he had been directly

---

[19] See, e.g., *Balmer-Schafroth* v *Switzerland* (1998) 25 EHRR 598, para. 26 and *Amuur* v *France* (1996) 22 EHRR 533, para. 36.

affected by the decision in issue and that the deduction from sentence could not deprive the applicant of his victim status. A similar decision was made in *CC* v *UK*, No. 32819/96, 1.2.97 where the applicant complained of automatic pre-trial detention. The Commission found that the deduction of the period of pre-trial detention from his sentence did not remove his victim status as it did not constitute an acknowledgement that the Convention had been violated.

In *Eckle* v *Germany* (1983) 5 EHRR 1, which concerned the length of criminal proceedings for fraud brought against the applicant, the Court held that the mitigation of sentence and the discontinuance of the proceedings granted because of their excessive length, did not in principle deprive the applicant of his victim status. They were matters to be taken into consideration in assessing the extent of the damage he had suffered.

The position may be different, however, where the national authorities have acknowledged, either expressly or in substance, that there has been a violation of the Convention and where redress has then been provided to the victim.[20] This is discussed further below at 5.3.4.

5.3.4　Losing victim status

Applicants may lose their status as 'victims' for the purposes of Article 34. For example, an applicant's status may be affected by settlement of the domestic proceedings, or acquittal in criminal proceedings,[21] a successful appeal or discontinuation of the domestic proceedings. In *Caraher* v *UK*, No. 24520/94, 11.1.00 the applicant alleged violations of Articles 2 and 13 arising from the fatal shooting of her husband by British soldiers in Northern Ireland. Two soldiers were prosecuted for the shooting, but were acquitted. The application was introduced in Strasbourg in 1994. In 1998 the applicant settled a High Court action against the Ministry of Defence for aggravated damages in respect of the death of her husband on receipt of £50,000 in full and final settlement of all claims. The application to the European Court was subsequently declared inadmissible as the Court found that the applicant could no longer claim to be a victim of a violation of the Convention, having settled the civil proceedings.

In *Eckle* v *Germany* (1983) 5 EHRR 1,[22] the Court laid down a threefold test as to when an applicant would be considered to have lost their victim status:

(a)　where the national authorities had acknowledged that there had been a breach of the Convention, either expressly, or in substance; and

(b)　where the applicant had been provided with redress; and

---

[20] *Eckle* v *Germany* (1983) 5 EHRR 1, para. 66.

[21] However, a defendant's acquittal may not always exclude that person from claiming to be a victim of a violation of the procedural guarantees of Article 6. See, e.g., *Heaney and McGuinness* v *Ireland*, No. 34720/97, 21.12.00, paras 43–46; *Quinn* v *Ireland*, No. 36887/97, 21.12.00, paras 43–46.

[22] See para. 66.

(c) the applicant had been treated in such a way that there were sufficient indications to allow an assessment of the extent to which the violation was taken into account.

Applying this test in the case of *Lüdi* v *Switzerland* (1993) 15 EHRR 173, the Court rejected the Government's arguments that the applicant was no longer a victim of a Convention violation because his sentence had been reduced by the Court of Appeal. The Court found that rather than acknowledging that the use of an undercover agent in the criminal proceedings against the applicant had violated the Convention, the authorities had expressly decided that it had been compatible with the Convention's obligations.

In the case of *Moustaquim* v *Belgium* (1991) 13 EHRR 802, the applicant's deportation order had been suspended for a trial period of two years and he was allowed to remain in Belgium. However, the authorities had not made reparation for the consequences of living under threat of deportation for more than five years. Therefore, the Court rejected the Government's submissions that the case had become 'devoid of purpose'.

5.3.5 When inadmissibility arguments can be raised and decided

The Court may declare an application inadmissible at any stage of the proceedings (Article 35(4)). It may uphold a respondent Government's arguments that the applicants had failed to exhaust appropriate domestic remedies at the merits stage of the case, even though the case was previously declared admissible.[23] This was the case in *McGinley and Egan* (1998) 27 EHRR 1, concerning access to records relating to the applicants' participation in nuclear tests on Christmas Island in 1958. In its judgment in that case, the Court accepted the Government's arguments that the failure to utilise a procedure available before the Pensions Appeal Tribunal to obtain disclosure of relevant documents meant that it could not be said that the state had prevented the applicants from gaining access to the documents, or that the state had falsely denied the existence of relevant documents. The Commission, however, had found that the applicants would not have had a feasible means of obtaining the records, because of the Minister's power to refuse access to documents under the Pensions Appeal Tribunal procedure, on national security grounds.

However, the respondent Government will be estopped from raising new admissibility arguments at the merits stage, if those arguments were not previously raised at the admissibility stage,[24] unless there are developments after the admissibility decision which are relevant to the question of admissibility, such

---

[23] See, e.g., *Aytekin* v *Turkey*, No. 22880/93, 23.9.98.

[24] *Artico* v *Italy* (1981) 3 EHRR 1, paras 27–28; *Pine Valley Developments Ltd* v *Ireland* (1992) 14 EHRR. 319, para. 45.

as a reversal of domestic case law or the introduction by the applicant of a new complaint. In *McGonnell* v *UK* (2000) 30 EHRR 289, the Government argued before the Court that the applicant had failed to exhaust domestic remedies in relation to his complaint that the domestic proceedings had not been independent or impartial, as he had failed to appeal to the Court of Appeal. The Court found that the Government was estopped from relying on such arguments which had not been raised before the Commission.

5.4 EXHAUSTION OF DOMESTIC REMEDIES

5.4.1 Introduction

By far the most important admissibility rules, in practice, are the requirement to exhaust domestic remedies and to lodge an application with the European Court within six months from the date when the final decision was taken. The rules are closely linked, as the time limit for lodging an application will depend upon the extent of the domestic remedies available. Respondent Governments will frequently raise wherever possible any objection that domestic remedies have not been exhausted; therefore this is an area where practitioners need to be very clear about their client's position.

The rationale for the domestic remedies rule is the principle that the domestic authorities should always be given the opportunity to put right a Convention violation before the matter is to be considered by the European Court. The rule is based on the assumption, reflected in Article 13, that there is in the domestic system an effective remedy available in respect of the alleged breach, whether or not the Convention is incorporated into national law.[25]

5.4.2 Burden of proof

Applicants are required to set out in their application the steps taken to exhaust domestic remedies. The burden of proof is then on the respondent Government to raise non-exhaustion,[26] by pointing to a domestic remedy which in the circumstances of the particular case should have, but which had not, been invoked. The Government must satisfy the Court that the remedy was an effective one available both in theory and in practice at the relevant time. This will mean a remedy that was accessible, that was capable of providing redress in respect of the applicant's complaint and offered reasonable prospects of success. If the Government raises an available remedy which in its view should have been utilised, the applicant

---

[25] See, e.g., *Akdivar* v *Turkey* (1997) 23 EHRR 143, para. 65.
[26] *De Wilde, Ooms and Versyp* v *Belgium* 1 EHRR 373, para. 60; *Deweer* v *Belgium* 2 EHRR 439, para. 26.

must either show why the remedy was in fact exhausted, or why the purported remedy is not adequate or effective or that there were special reasons absolving the applicant from invoking the remedy (see below at 5.4.6).

A respondent Government whose submissions in relation to domestic remedies are inconsistent with its arguments in the domestic proceedings will be given short shrift by the Court. For example, in *Kolompar v Belgium* (1993) 16 EHRR 197,[27] the Government was prevented from arguing that the applicant had failed to exhaust domestic remedies where in the domestic proceedings, as the defendant, the state had contested the domestic court's jurisdiction in those proceedings.

An applicant should raise in domestic proceedings the substance of the complaint to be made to the Court[28] on the basis that the domestic courts should have the opportunity to decide on a claim before it is considered by the European Court. In *Guzzardi v Italy* (1981) 3 EHRR 333, the applicant, a suspected mafioso, complained about his three-year confinement on the island of Asinara. He argued that there had been violations of various Articles, but he did not refer to Article 5(1) which the Commission itself raised and considered and which was the only Article found by the Commission and Court to have been violated. It is therefore not strictly necessary to specify which Article, or even which right, is being invoked, provided that the applicant has in substance raised the issue in question. It is preferable specifically to invoke the Convention in domestic proceedings, but it is not absolutely necessary to do so. In *Ahmet Sadik v Greece* (1997) 24 EHRR 323, the applicant was found by the Court not to have exhausted domestic remedies as he had at no stage relied on Article 10, or on equivalent arguments, in the domestic courts, even though Article 10 was directly applicable in Greek law.

5.4.3 Compliance with domestic procedural rules

In raising the issue expressly or in substance in domestic proceedings, an applicant will be required to have complied with the formal and procedural rules, including time limits, in the domestic law and to have invoked any procedural means which might have prevented a breach of the Convention.[29] Domestic remedies will accordingly not be considered exhausted if an applicant has not pursued a remedy because the time limits or other procedural rules have not been complied with. In *Barbera, Messegue and Jabardo v Spain* (1989) 11 EHRR 360, the failure to raise during the trial allegations of a judge's hostility towards some defendants and witnesses, meant that the applicants were found not to have exhausted domestic remedies.

---

[27] See para. 31. See also *Pine Valley Developments Ltd v Ireland* (1992) 14 EHRR 319, para. 47.

[28] See, e.g., *Glasenapp v Germany* (1987) 9 EHRR 25, paras 42–46.

[29] *Cardot v France* (1991) 13 EHRR 853, para. 34.

5.4.4   Flexibility of the rule

The Court has said that the rule in Article 35 should be applied with 'some degree of flexibility and without excessive formalism'.[30] This flexibility reflects the fact that the rule is being applied in the context of a system intended to protect human rights.[31] Therefore the exhaustion of domestic remedies rule is not absolute, nor is it applied automatically. The circumstances of each case are always considered, including the general context in which the formal remedies operate and the personal circumstances of the applicant. The Court will then examine, in all the circumstances of the case, whether applicants have done everything that could reasonably be expected of them to exhaust domestic remedies.[32]

5.4.5   Availability, effectiveness and sufficiency of remedies

Whilst Article 35(1) states that the Court may only deal with a matter after all domestic remedies have been exhausted, an applicant is only required to pursue remedies which are available, effective and sufficient.

For a domestic remedy to be available, the applicant must be able to initiate the proceedings directly (without being reliant upon a public official). The unavailability of legal aid may affect the accessibility of a remedy, depending upon the applicant's financial resources, the complexity of the remedy and whether or not legal representation is compulsory in domestic proceedings.[33]

The European Court will not be satisfied with respondent Governments raising the existence of remedies which are only theoretically available. In this respect, the Court may require the Government to produce examples of the claimed remedy having been successfully utilised. For example, in *De Jong, Baljet and van den Brink v Netherlands* (1986) 8 EHRR 20, the applicant servicemen who were conscientious objectors complained about their detention for refusing to obey military orders. The respondent Government argued that the applicants had not exhausted domestic remedies because they could have brought a claim in the civil courts. However, that argument was rejected by the Court as there was not a single example of a detained serviceman having sued for damages and it was therefore not certain whether such a remedy was in fact available. Similarly, in *Van Oosterwijck v Belgium* (1981) 3 EHRR 557, it was held in relation to one form of redress raised by the Government, that in the absence of any decided domestic cases, the applicant could not be blamed for failing to bring such an action.

---

[30] See, e.g., *Guzzardi v Italy* (1981) 3 EHRR 333, para. 72; *Cardot v France* (1991) 13 EHRR 853, para. 34.

[31] *Akdivar v Turkey* (1997) 23 EHRR 143, para 69.

[32] See, e.g., *Yaşa v Turkey*, No. 22495/93, 2.9.98, para. 77.

[33] See *Airey v Ireland* 2 EHRR 305; *Faulkner v UK*, No. 30308/96, Comm. Rep. 1.12.98.

A remedy will be considered effective if it may provide redress for the applicant in respect of the alleged Convention violation. This includes not only judicial remedies, but also any administrative domestic remedy which may provide redress in the circumstances of the particular case.

The opportunity to request an authority (such as the legal aid board) to reconsider a decision it has already taken does not generally constitute a sufficient remedy.[34] Applicants will also not be required to have pursued remedies which are purely discretionary. In *Buckley* v *UK*, No. 20348/92, 3.3.94, the Commission rejected the Government's arguments that the applicant had not exhausted domestic remedies because she had not applied to the Secretary of State to exercise power under the Caravan Sites Act 1968 to direct a local authority to provide caravan sites. The Commission found that the Secretary of State had a very wide discretion and had only acted under the relevant provision of the 1968 Act in five cases. Similarly in *Temple* v *UK* (1986) 8 EHRR 252, the applicant was not required to apply to the Secretary of State under the Employment Act 1982 for compensation in respect of his dismissal as a railway shunter, as such a procedure was essentially discretionary and amounted to an application for an *ex gratia* payment. There was no legal entitlement to compensation even if the statutory eligibility criteria were satisfied.

In cases of doubt about the effectiveness of a domestic remedy, including an appeal process (see below), for the purposes of the European Court's exhaustion of domestic remedies test, the remedy should be pursued. This has been found to be particularly the case in a common law system, where the courts extend and develop principles through case law: 'it is generally incumbent on an aggrieved individual to allow the domestic courts the opportunity to develop existing rights by way of interpretation'.[35] The failure to bring proceedings in breach of confidence led to a finding of a failure to exhaust domestic remedies in *Earl and Countess Spencer* v *UK*, Nos 28851–2/95, 16.1.98 which concerned the publication in the tabloids of information about the Princess of Wales which was said to have been obtained from her close friends.

In general, applicants will be required to pursue processes of appeal available in the course of domestic remedies, if such an appeal process would or might provide a remedy for the alleged Convention violation.[36] However, it is not necessary for applicants to pursue a potential form of redress or an appeal process which would not in fact provide a remedy,[37] for example, where it is clear on settled legal opinion that it has no prospects of success.[38] In that situation, the applicant will have to satisfy the court that there were no such prospects of success

---

[34] *R* v *UK* (1993) 15 EHRR CD 100.

[35] *Earl and Countess Spencer* v *UK*, Nos 28851-2/95, 16.1.98.

[36] See, e.g., *Civet* v *France*, No. 29340/95, 28.9.99.

[37] See, e.g., *Hilton* v *UK*, No. 5613/72, 5.3.76; (1976) 4 DR 177.

[38] See, e.g., *De Wilde, Ooms and Versyp* v *Belgium* 1 EHRR 373, para. 62.

and practitioners should consider filing with the Court counsel's opinion to that effect. In *McFeeley* v *UK* (1981) 3 EHRR 161, a case concerning the conditions for prisoners in the Maze Prison in Northern Ireland, the Commission found that an order of certiorari could not have provided an effective remedy because of serious doubts as to whether the remedy would have been open to the applicants according to 'settled legal opinion' and whilst it could have been sufficient to redress the applicants' Article 6 complaints, it would not have provided redress for their complaints under Article 3.

The length of domestic proceedings will be a factor in the consideration of their effectiveness. For example, the case of *Tanli* v *Turkey*, No. 26129/94, 5.3.96 concerned the killing of the applicant's son in police custody. Criminal proceedings had been instituted but were still pending one year and eight months after the death of the applicant's son. In view of the serious nature of the crime involved, the Commission found that the criminal proceedings were an ineffective remedy.

A civil action for damages in respect of the death of the applicant's relative at the hands of an unidentified person was not considered to be an effective remedy where the claimant in such an action was required to identify the person believed to have committed the tort.[39] In the same circumstances, an administrative law action was found not be a sufficient remedy, where damages could be awarded against the state on a strict liability basis. The Court has held that in cases of fatal assault, damages will not satisfy the obligations under Articles 2 and 13 of the Convention, which also require an investigation which is capable of leading to the identification and punishment of those responsible.[40]

If there are a number of possible domestic remedies, an applicant will not be required to have exhausted them all, or even to have utilised more than one if they would not achieve anything more. The Court has held that an applicant cannot be criticised for not having had recourse to legal remedies which would have been directed essentially to the same end and would in any case not have offered better chances of success.[41]

Exhaustion of domestic remedies may take place after an application has been introduced with the Court, but such remedies must have been exhausted before the admissibility decision is made.[42]

5.4.6   Special circumstances

There may, exceptionally, be special circumstances absolving the applicant from exhausting domestic remedies. But 'special circumstances' will *not* include lack

[39] *Yaşa* v *Turkey*, No. 22495/93, 2.9.98, para. 73.
[40] *Yaşa* v *Turkey*, No. 22495/93, 2.9.98, para. 74.
[41] *A* v *France* (1994) 17 EHRR 462, para. 32.
[42] *Luberti* v *Italy*, No. 9019/80, 7.7.81, 27 DR 181.

of legal knowledge of the Convention, negligent advice by lawyers, or the applicant's depressive state.

Delay in the availability of a remedy may mean that it need not be utilised by the applicant. In *Reed* v *UK* (1981) 3 EHRR 136, the applicant complained of being assaulted in prison, invoking Article 3. The Government argued that he had failed to exhaust domestic remedies because he had not brought a civil action for damages. However, the applicant had been first required to allow the prison authorities to investigate his complaints and he was denied access to a solicitor for more than two years. In those circumstances, the applicant was not barred for non-exhaustion of domestic remedies, even where the remedy subsequently became available after the two-year period, as in principle, a remedy should have been immediately available to every aggrieved person, particularly in cases of alleged maltreatment.

In the case of *Akdivar* v *Turkey* (1997) 23 EHRR 143, concerning the burning of houses by security forces in south-east Turkey, the Court held that the failure of the national authorities to investigate or offer assistance in circumstances where serious allegations of misconduct or the infliction of harm by state agents were made, might constitute 'special circumstances'. The burden then shifts back to the Government to show what has been done in response to the scale and seriousness of the matters in issue.

5.5 SIX-MONTH TIME LIMIT

5.5.1 General principles

According to Article 35(1), the Court may only deal with a matter which has been submitted within six months of the final decision taken in the domestic proceedings.

The time limit is intended to promote legal certainty, to provide the authorities with a degree of protection from uncertainty, and to ensure that past decisions are not continually open to challenge. It is also intended to ensure that cases are dealt with within a reasonable time, and it increases the likelihood of evidence being available which might otherwise disappear. However, as Convention cases take on average four to five years to progress through the various stages (in addition to the time taken for the matter to be dealt with in the domestic courts), it is common for applicants and witnesses to be asked to produce evidence (usually documentary, and occasionally oral) many years after the original events which are the subject matter of the case.

The Court considers that the six months rule allows a prospective applicant time to consider whether to lodge an application and, if so, to decide on the specific complaints and arguments to be raised.

Time runs from the day after the date of the final decision in the domestic proceedings which the applicant is required to invoke under the exhaustion of domestic remedies rule. This will usually mean the date when judgment is given. But if judgment is not given publicly, time will run from the date when the applicant or their representative is informed of the decision.[43] This will mean that time will start to run when the applicant's solicitor receives notification of a decision, even if the applicant is not informed until later.

If reasons for a decision follow after the date when the decision itself was made public or notified to the applicant, the time will only start to run from the later date if the reasons given for the decision are relevant to the Convention application.[44] In *Worm* v *Austria* (1998) 25 EHRR 454, the applicant journalist had been prosecuted for publishing an article which was considered capable of influencing the outcome of criminal proceedings relating to a former Minister. The Government challenged the admissibility of the application as it had not been lodged within six months of the date when the operative provisions and the relevant reasons were read out by the Court of Appeal. The applicant was not, however, provided with a written copy of the judgment until more than five months later. The Court held that time only started to run after receipt of the written judgment, which contained more than nine pages of detailed legal reasoning.

If there are no domestic remedies, practitioners should lodge an application at the Court within six months of the incident or decision complained of, or within six months of the applicant's date of knowledge of the incident or decision.[45] This will be the Court's approach where it is clear that from the outset that no effective remedy was available to the applicant.

Where there has been a series of events which the applicant proposes to raise with the European Court, the safest course is to lodge an application within six months of the first incident. However, if the events are linked, it may be possible to lodge within six months of the final event in the series.

The six-month time limit can be satisfied by the lodging of a letter with the European Court which sets out the circumstances of the applicant's complaint. The requirements of the introductory letter and the application process are set out in chapter 2. An application may not, other than in very exceptional circumstances, be introduced by telephone. This would only be permitted where there was an overriding reason why it was not possible to submit a written application and where the fact that an application was being formally introduced by telephone was made express and unequivocal.[46]

---

[43] See, e.g., *KCM* v *The Netherlands*, No. 21034/92, 9.1.95, 80 DR 87.
[44] *Worm* v *Austria*, No 22714/93, 27.11.95 83-A DR 17.
[45] See, e.g., *X* v *UK*, No. 7379/76, 10.12.76, 8 DR 211; *Scotts of Greenock Ltd* v *UK*, No. 9599/81, 11.3.85, 42 DR 33.
[46] *West* v *UK*, No. 34728/97, 20.10.97.

However, if there is a significant delay between the initial letter and the submission of the completed application form, an applicant may fall foul of the six months rule.[47] It is only in exceptional cases that the six-month time limit might be suspended. For example, an applicant who introduced an application concerning the killing of her daughter and her husband lodged medical evidence setting out her medical and psychiatric treatment. The Commission accepted that for a certain time following her daughter's death, the applicant was unable to lodge an application because of the state of her health. Nevertheless the application was still declared inadmissible as being two years too late.[48]

The six months rule has a value in itself of promoting legal certainty and therefore cannot be waived by respondent Governments.[49]

5.5.2 Doubtful remedies

If an applicant pursues a remedy which proves to be ineffective, the six months may run from the final decision in the effective remedy pursued (or from the date of the incident itself, if there were no effective remedies). For some prospective applicants to the European Court, it may not be at all clear whether a particular form of redress would amount to a 'domestic remedy' for the purposes of Article 35. However, if there is any doubt about the effectiveness of a particular 'remedy', practitioners should consider lodging an introductory letter with the Court in order to protect their client's position. This can simply be done by a letter to the Court. The procedure is set out in chapter 2. The Court will not usually require a full application to be lodged in those circumstances, although applicants will be required to keep the Court informed of any developments in the domestic proceedings. A full application should then be lodged once the domestic remedy has been exhausted. If such a letter is not lodged, there is a danger that the Government might argue that the applicant had pursued a remedy that was not 'effective' for the purposes of Article 35 and therefore that the application should be declared inadmissible as having been submitted after the expiry of the six months period. For example, the UK Government successfully argued such a point in the case of *Raphaie* v *UK*, No. 20035/92, 2.12.93 on the basis that the applicant had pursued an internal prison complaint which was not 'effective'.

Where there is real doubt as to the availability or effectiveness of domestic remedies, the Court may be more flexible in applying the six months rule. The Court will, in general, not require an applicant to lodge a complaint before the position in relation to the matter in question has been settled at the domestic level.[50] If an applicant pursues an apparently existing remedy and only

---

[47] See, e.g., *J-PP* v *France*, No. 22123/93, 31.8.94, 79 DR 72.
[48] *H* v *UK and Ireland*, No. 9833/82, 7.3.85, 42 DR 53.
[49] See, e.g., *Walker* v *UK*, No. 24979/97, 25.1.00.
[50] See, e.g., *Scotts of Greenock Ltd* v *UK*, No. 9599/81, 11.3.85, 42 DR 33.

subsequently becomes aware of circumstances which render the remedy ineffective, the six months may only start to run from the date when the applicant first became aware, or ought to have become aware of the circumstances which made the remedy ineffective.[51]

The case of *Keenan* v *UK*, No. 27229/95, 22.5.98,[52] concerned the applicant's son's suicide in prison and the failure of the prison authorities to safeguard his life, given his history of threatening to kill himself in custody. The Government argued that the applicant had failed to comply with the six months rule as there had been no effective domestic remedies and the complaint should therefore have been lodged within six months of the applicant's son's death. The applicant had had a potential remedy under the Law Reform (Miscellaneous Provisions) Act 1934. She applied for and was granted legal aid. She obtained the opinion of a consultant psychiatrist and then obtained counsel's opinion. Counsel advised that there were no effective domestic remedies available to her. An application to the European Commission was lodged within six months of that advice. The Commission found that it was not until she had received counsel's advice that she could reasonably have known that there were no domestic remedies and accordingly the six months only ran from the date of that advice. The position might be different, however, if there were any evidence of abuse or delay by an applicant or an applicant's lawyer. It may be that in reaching this decision the Commission was influenced by the gravity of the case.

Care should be taken to ensure that if an applicant pursues domestic remedies or appeals, those remedies would be capable of providing redress for every complaint to be made to the European Court.[53] This frequently arises in criminal cases where the applicant wishes to complain about aspects of their detention, as well as the fairness of the proceedings. However, if the applicant's appeal against conviction would have no bearing on the question of the lawfulness of the pre-trial detention, then the question of the detention must be considered carefully and a Convention application lodged within six months of the end of the period of the detention at the latest (or within six months of the final decision in any domestic remedy relating to the detention). For example, in *Surriye Ali* v *UK*, No. 25605/94, 28.2.96,[54] the applicant complained under Article 6 about the fairness of the criminal proceedings against her and also under Article 5 about the lawfulness of her initial detention. The application concerning both aspects of the case was not lodged until after judgment was handed down by the Court of Appeal, but the applicant's Article 5 complaint was found to be out of time as the appeal proceedings were not capable of affecting the position in relation to the detention.

---

[51] See, e.g., *Laçin* v *Turkey*, No. 23654/94, 15.5.95, 81 DR 76.
[52] And see also [1998] EHRLR 648.
[53] See, e.g., *Lines* v *UK* (1997) 23 EHRR CD 58.
[54] And see also [1996] EHRLR 428.

5.5.3 Continuing breaches of the Convention

Where the matter which the applicant complains about is continuing, the time limit will not start to run until the breach ceases to have a continuing effect. Great care should of course be taken to ascertain that the violation is a continuing one, rather than a one-off decision. There will be a continuing breach, for example, where the applicant complains of the continued existence of particular laws, as in *Dudgeon* v *UK* (1982) 4 EHRR 149, which concerned the existence in Northern Ireland of laws which made homosexual acts between consenting adult males criminal offences.

There was a violation of the applicant's rights under Article 8 because of the non-enforcement of his right of access to his daughter in the case of *Hokkanen* v *Finland* (1995) 19 EHRR 139. The case was introduced in 1992 and the Court found that the violation arising from the non-enforcement of access had continued until September 1993 when the Court of Appeal decided that the applicant's access to his daughter could not be enforced against her wishes.

Where there is a continuing violation, an application could be lodged with the European Court several years after the violation first started.[55]

5.6 ANONYMOUS APPLICATIONS

Every application to the European Court must identify the applicant (Article 35(2)(a)). Any application which does not do so may be declared inadmissible on this ground alone.

In some cases applicants may have very good reasons for not wishing to have their identities disclosed. In such cases, the applicant's details (including name, address, date of birth, nationality and occupation) will have to be set out in the application form, but the applicant can request confidentiality. There is a section on confidentiality in chapter 2. If the applicant's request for confidentiality is accepted by the Court, the applicant will be identified in the case reports by their initials or simply by a letter.

5.7 APPLICATIONS SUBSTANTIALLY THE SAME AS A MATTER WHICH HAS ALREADY BEEN EXAMINED BY THE COURT

An application which is substantially the same as a matter that has already been examined by the Court and which contains no relevant new information will be declared inadmissible by the Court (Article 35(2)(b)). For example, repeated

---

[55] See, e.g., *De Becker* v *Belgium* (1962) Series B, No. 4 (concerning a statutory provision which created a continuing restriction on the applicant journalist's freedom of expression by preventing him publishing).

applications from the same applicant concerning the same matter will be declared inadmissible on this ground, unless relevant new information has come to light.

However, the exception concerning 'relevant new information' is important. For example, an applicant whose petition has previously been declared inadmissible for non-exhaustion of domestic remedies may resubmit the case to the European Court after having exhausted effective domestic remedies. There may also be new factual information, or new developments in domestic proceedings, which may justify a further application, such as the increased length of domestic proceedings.[56] However, additional legal arguments will not amount to 'relevant new information'.[57]

5.8   APPLICATIONS ALREADY SUBMITTED TO ANOTHER PROCEDURE OF INTERNATIONAL INVESTIGATION OR SETTLEMENT

The Court may not consider any application which has already been submitted to another procedure of international investigation or settlement, and which contains no relevant new information (Article 35(2)(b)). This has very rarely raised any difficulties in practice.

For example, a previous petition to the Human Rights Committee under the International Covenant on Civil and Political Rights would prevent an applicant also complaining to the European Court (even where an application was made to the Human Rights Committee to defer its decision until the European Commission had decided on admissibility).[58] But to be inadmissible on this ground, the contents of the applications would have to be essentially the same and submitted by the same applicant.[59] In *Pauger* v *Austria* (1998) 25 EHRR 105 the applicant complained of a violation of Article 6 because of the lack of a public hearing in proceedings concerning the discriminatory provision of a survivor's pension. A previous decision of the UN Human Rights Committee brought by the same applicant on the same facts did not, however, preclude an application to Strasbourg, because the petition to the Human Rights Committee concerned discrimination, whereas the European Convention application concerned the fairness of the proceedings. In relation to the UK, this particular avenue of redress is still not available as the UK has not ratified the Optional Protocol to the Covenant, which would allow the right of individual petition to the Human Rights Committee.

---

[56] See, e.g., *X* v *UK*, No. 8233/78, 3.10.79, 17 DR 122; *Vallan* v *Italy*, No. 9621/81, 13.10.83, 33 DR 217.

[57] *X* v *UK*, No. 8206/78, 10.7.81, 25 DR 147.

[58] *Cacerrada Fornieles & Cabeza Mato* v *Spain*, No. 17512/90, 6.7.92, 73 DR 214.

[59] See, e.g., No. 11603/85, (1987) 50 DR 228, where the Commission decided that an application brought by individuals was not the same as a complaint lodged with the International Labour Organisation (ILO) by the Trades Union Congress.

The fact that a case has been examined by the European Committee for the Prevention of Torture (CPT) would also not prevent an application to the European Court.[60]

5.9   INCOMPATIBILITY WITH THE PROVISIONS OF THE CONVENTION

Article 35(3) requires the Court to declare inadmissible any application which it considers 'incompatible with the provisions of the Convention or the protocols ...'. The concept of incompatibility with the Convention has four aspects to it:

- incompatibility of an application because of the limits of the state's jurisdiction (known as '*ratione loci*');
- incompatibility of an application because of the limits as to what the Convention rights cover (known as '*ratione materiae*');
- incompatibility of an application because of the limits in time as to the state's obligations under the Convention (known as '*ratione temporis*');
- incompatibility of an application because of the limits as to who may bring Convention applications and as to who may be respondents (known as '*ratione personae*').

These four categories are explained in more detail below.

5.9.1   Jursidiction: *ratione loci*

The alleged violation of the Convention must have occurred within the respondent state's *jurisdiction*. This includes a 'dependent territory' if the state has made a declaration under Article 56 that the Convention applies to the territory (see appendix 16 in relation to the UK).

For example, in the *Cyprus* v *Turkey* cases, Turkey has been found to be responsible for its armed forces in Cyprus. The Turkish armed forces in Cyprus were considered to have brought any persons or property there within the jurisdiction of Turkey, 'to the extent that they exercise control over such persons or property'.[61]

It is generally not possible to complain about the decision of an international organisation. But the transfer of state power to an international organisation does not necessarily exclude the state's responsibility, as otherwise the Convention guarantees could easily be excluded or limited. In cases concerning the applicants' secondment to the European Space Agency,[62] the Court has under-

---

[60] Explanatory Report to the Convention for the Prevention of Torture and Inhuman or Degrading Treatment or Punishment, CPT/Inf/C(89)1[EN], para. 92.

[61] See, e.g., *Cyprus* v *Turkey* (1976) 4 EHRR 482, para. 83.

[62] *Beer and Regan* v *Germany*, No. 28934/95; *Waite and Kennedy* v *Germany*, No. 26083/94, 18.2.99.

lined the principle that where states establish international organisations and give them powers and immunities, there may be implications for human rights, and it would be incompatible with the purpose and objectives of the Convention if contracting states were thereby absolved from their responsibility under the Convention.

5.9.2   *Ratione materiae*

Complaints about rights which are not protected by the Convention will be declared inadmissible on this ground, including rights clearly not covered by the Convention at all, and rights which are found not to fall within the scope of Convention Articles, for example, if an activity is not considered to be part of your 'private life' under Article 8. In *Botta* v *Italy* (1998) 26 EHRR 241 the applicant complained of the Government's failure to take measures to remedy the omissions of private bathing organisations which had the effect of preventing disabled people from getting access to the beach and the sea. The Court held that this did not fall within the scope of Article 8, particularly because the case concerned access to the beach away from the applicant's normal place of residence during holidays.

   However, it is very important to keep in mind the principle that the Convention is to be interpreted as a 'living instrument'.[63] Accordingly, the Court is obliged to interpret the Convention in the light of present day conditions, and not by assessing what the drafters of the Convention had intended by a particular provision. Practitioners should be aware of the possibilities of particular provisions being 'developed' to fall into line with present day situations. For example, it is arguably questionable whether those who drafted the Convention had envisaged that Article 8 would protect an applicant's home from the effects of a nearby privately-owned waste treatment plant. However, in *Lopez Ostra* v *Spain* (1995) 20 EHRR 277, the Court held that Article 8 was violated in such circumstances. Similarly, in *Guerra and others* v *Italy* (1998) 26 EHRR 357 Article 8 was found to have been breached because of the failure to provide the local population with information relating to the safety risks of a nearby chemical factory.

5.9.3   *Ratione temporis*

Complaints against a state which had not ratified the Convention or accepted the right of individual petition at the relevant date will be declared inadmissible on this ground. A table showing the ratification dates of each contracting state is at appendix 14. The UK Government accepted the right of individual petition in 1966.

---

[63] See, e.g., *Selmouni* v *France* (2000) 29 EHRR 403, para. 101.

Where the events complained of started before the entry into force of the Convention and continued afterwards, only the latter part can be the subject of a complaint, although the Court may take facts into account which have occurred before the entry into force of the Convention.[64] *Zana* v *Turkey*, No. 18954/91, 25.11.97 concerned the length of criminal proceedings which had started before Turkey had accepted the right of individual petition. In assessing the reasonableness of the length of the proceedings, the Court took into account that at that date the proceedings had already lasted two years and five months. In *Hokkanen* v *Finland* (1997) 19 EHRR 139,[65] concerning rights of custody and access over the applicant's daughter, domestic proceedings had begun in 1986. However, the Convention did not enter into force in relation to Finland until 1990. Therefore, the Court could only consider whether there had been a violation of the Convention arising out of the facts occurring after 1990, when the Convention entered into force. However, the Court took into account the background of events prior to 1990, particularly the large number of court actions brought by the applicant, the fact that all decisions in his favour had been effectively resisted by the grandparents and that the embittered relationship between the applicant and the child's grandparents did not favour a co-operative approach to resolving the dispute.

5.9.4 *Ratione personae*

This condition will in general exclude complaints which are not directed against the state (or any emanation of the state, such as a public authority, court or tribunal), but against a private individual or organisation.

However, the Court has emphasised that the state cannot absolve itself from responsibility by delegating its obligations to private bodies or individuals. In *Costello-Roberts* v *UK* (1995) 19 EHRR 112 the Court applied this principle in a case relating to corporal punishment in a private school. The Court found that the state has an obligation to provide children with their right to education, including responsibility for a school's disciplinary system; the right to education applies equally to pupils in independent schools as well as those in state schools.

There may also be exceptions to this condition where the state is found to be responsible for the alleged breach, by, for example, failing to take appropriate measures to protect an individual against the actions of others. For example, the case of *Young, James and Webster* v *UK* (1982) 4 EHRR 38 concerned former British Rail employees who had been dismissed for failing to comply with the closed shop agreement. The Court found the state to be responsible for the domestic law which made the treatment of the applicants lawful.

---

[64] See, e.g., *Kerojärvi* v *Finland*, No. 17506/90, 19.7.95, Series A, No. 328.
[65] See especially para. 53. See also, e.g., *Lukanov* v *Bulgaria* (1997) 24 EHRR 121, para. 40.

The responsibility of the state in cases concerning ill-treatment by private individuals will also be incurred under the Convention by virtue of the combined obligations under Articles 1 and 3. Article 1 requires the state to secure to everyone within its jurisdiction the rights and freedoms set out in the Convention. The state must therefore take the necessary steps to prevent individuals being subjected to inhuman and degrading treatment or punishment, even by private individuals. This will require that there is effective deterrence to prevent ill-treatment, in particular, of children and other vulnerable people, such as those with mental health problems.

A v *UK* (1999) 27 EHRR 611 concerned the applicant nine-year-old child's ill-treatment by his stepfather. The stepfather was prosecuted for assault occasioning actual bodily harm for beating the child with a garden cane, but was acquitted. The applicant complained, inter alia, of a violation of Article 3. The Court found that as it was a defence to a charge of assault that the treatment in question amounted to 'reasonable chastisement', the law did not provide adequate protection against the ill-treatment of the applicant, in violation of Article 3. This was accepted before the Court by the UK Government.

In *X and Y* v *Netherlands* (1986) 8 EHRR 235, the applicant complained that it was impossible to bring criminal proceedings against the perpetrator of a sexual assault on his daughter, because her mental illness meant that it was not possible to determine her wishes, as was required by the domestic law at the time. The Court found a violation of Article 8 as the criminal code failed to protect the victim.

In *Gustafsson* v *Sweden* (1996) 22 EHRR 409, the applicant restaurant owner complained of action taken by various unions representing employees, after he refused to allow collective bargaining, invoking, inter alia, Article 11 and Article 1 of Protocol 1, on the basis that the state had failed to protect the applicant against industrial action. The Court held that Article 11 was applicable, although it had not been violated, and that Article 1 of Protocol 1 did not apply as the case concerned contractual relationships between the applicant and his suppliers or deliverers.

Complaints against a state which has not signed the Convention or the relevant Protocol will also be excluded by this condition. For example, complaints against the UK in respect of Protocols 4 or 7 would be declared inadmissible on this ground, as the UK has ratified neither protocol.

Finally, an application from a person (or organisation) who could not properly claim to be a 'victim' of a Convention violation would be declared inadmissible *ratione personae*.[66] The definition of a 'victim' is discussed at section 5.3 above.

---

[66] See, e.g., *A and B* v *UK*, No. 25599/94, 9.9.96: father of child beaten by stepfather could not claim to be a direct or indirect victim, unlike the child himself who clearly was a victim.

5.10 MANIFESTLY ILL-FOUNDED

An application may be declared inadmissible as being 'manifestly ill-founded' (Article 35(3)), if on a preliminary investigation, the application does not disclose prima facie grounds that there has been a breach of the Convention. For example, where the applicant fails to adduce any evidence in support of the application, or if the facts complained of clearly fall within the limitations or restrictions on the Convention rights. For example, an applicant would need to produce sufficient evidence of telephone tapping or of torture, failing which the application would be declared admissible as being manifestly ill-founded.

In practice, this requirement amounts to a preliminary merits test and a large number of cases are declared inadmissible on this ground. It is in effect a filtering mechanism, intended to root out the weakest cases. This is perhaps an inevitable part of the Strasbourg system, given the very large number of cases which the Court has to deal with. However, it is something of a misnomer, as applications can still be declared 'manifestly ill-founded' even after the Court has decided that the case was worthy of being communicated to the respondent Government, and only in the light of the Government's submissions. Furthermore, such decisions do not require unanimity, but can be made by a majority of the chamber of the Court.

5.11 ABUSE OF THE RIGHT OF APPLICATION

Under Article 35(3), the Court will declare inadmissible any application which it considers an abuse of the right of application. Vexatious petitions[67] or petitions written in offensive language will be declared inadmissible on this ground. Deliberately concealing relevant information from the Court might lead to a declaration of inadmissibility on this ground.[68]

The application in *Foxley* v *UK*, No. 33274/96, 12.10.99 was declared partly inadmissible for failure to comply with the six months rule, but the Commission found that as there was evidence of the applicant's original representative having forged a letter purportedly from the Commission, it could equally have been rejected as an abuse of the right of application. In *Drozd* v *Poland*, No. 25403/94, 5.3.96[69] the application was struck off the Commission's list of cases following publication in a newspaper (of which the applicant was on the editorial board) of correspondence from the Commission, in breach of the Commission's confidentiality rules.

---

[67] See, e.g., *M* v *UK*, No. 13284/87, 15.10.87, 54 DR 214: a series of 'ill-founded and querulous complaints'.

[68] See, e.g., *F* v *Spain*, No. 13524/88, 12.4.91, 69 DR 185, where the applicant was found not to have deliberately concealed certain domestic proceedings in progress.

[69] And see [1996] EHRLR 430. The case was struck off under the then Article 30(1)(c).

In *Akdivar* v *Turkey* (1997) 23 EHRR 143, which concerned the destruction of homes by the security forces in south-east Turkey, the respondent Government sought to argue that the case amounted to an abuse of the right of petition. It was argued that the failure of the applicants to pursue domestic remedies was part of the general policy of the Workers' Party of Kurdistan (PKK) to denigrate Turkey and its judicial institutions. This argument was rejected by the Court on the basis that the Commission had in fact substantially upheld the applicants' complaints.

But this condition will *not* exclude 'political' applications or those made for purposes of gaining publicity. In *McFeeley* v *UK* (1981) 3 EHRR 161, the applicants complained about the conditions in the Maze prison in Northern Ireland. The Government argued that the application was an abuse of the right of petition as it was inspired by motives of publicity and propaganda and was intended to pressurise the Government into reintroducing the special category status. The Commission rejected these arguments, finding that a complaint of abuse might be upheld if an application were clearly unsupported by the evidence or outside the scope of the Convention.

Chapter Six

Underlying Convention Principles

6.1 INTRODUCTION

This chapter highlights key principles which run throughout the Convention and its case law. Some of the principles such as legality and proportionality are fundamental to the substantive Convention law, whereas others are issues of interpretation. The principles outlined below have application in a variety of substantive Convention Articles and in a variety of contexts. They are illustrated further in chapter 7 on the substantive Convention rights.

6.2 SUBSIDIARITY

The European Convention system for the protection of human rights is intended to be subsidiary to national systems safeguarding human rights. This is reflected in the requirement to exhaust effective domestic remedies before applying to the Court: 'States are dispensed from answering before an international body for their acts before they have had an opportunity to put matters right through their own legal system'.[1] The principle is also linked to the right in Article 13 to an 'effective remedy' in the domestic system, whether or not the Convention has been incorporated into national law.

The concept of the margin of appreciation (see below) is a further aspect of this principle of subsidiarity.

6.3 A DEMOCRATIC SOCIETY

The concept of a democratic society is said to prevail throughout the Convention[2] and is acknowledged as a fundamental feature of the European public order:

---

[1] See, e.g., *Akdivar* v *Turkey* (1997) 23 EHRR 143, para. 65.
[2] *Oberschlick* v *Austria* (1995) 19 EHRR 389, para. 58.

'democracy ... appears to be the only political model contemplated by the Convention and, accordingly, the only one compatible with it'.[3] It is referred to in the preamble to the Convention and it is a requirement that any restriction on the rights conferred by Articles 8–11 must be 'necessary in a democratic society'.

The Court will therefore be particularly concerned to uphold rights which touch on this concept. For example, freedom of political debate has been held to be at the very core of the concept of a democratic society, but it is also relevant to press freedom generally and may be a relevant consideration in cases concerning the rights to freedom of peaceful assembly, to freedom of thought, conscience and religion, and to the right to vote.

6.4 LEGAL CERTAINTY

The principle of the rule of law is referred to in the preamble to the Convention and in the Statute of the Council of Europe and was an important impetus in setting up the Convention system.[4]

The principle of legal certainty is accordingly inherent throughout the law of the Convention.[5] For example, Articles 8–11 require any interference with rights to be 'in accordance with the law' or 'prescribed by law' (see below at 7.8). Under Article 5, any detention must be lawful and 'in accordance with a procedure prescribed by law', referring to both procedural and substantive legality. Article 7 requires certainty of the criminal law.

This means that the legal basis (including statute, secondary legislation, common law and European Community law) for any interference with Convention rights must be adequately accessible and formulated with sufficient precision to enable a person to regulate their conduct: a person 'must be able — if need be with appropriate advice — to foresee, to a degree that is reasonable in the circumstances, the consequences which a given action may entail'.[6] The requirement for legality therefore not only requires a specific legal rule or regime authorising the interference, but also relates to the *quality* of the particular domestic legal provision. Where the domestic law confers a discretion, it should also indicate the scope of that discretion.[7] The Convention recognises that of course absolute certainty in the law is not, however, attainable. So, for example, incremental common law developments are acceptable under the Convention.[8] The degree of 'certainty' required in the law will differ depending upon the nature of the right being exercised and the nature of the interference.

---

[3] *United Communist Party of Turkey and others* v *Turkey* (1998) 26 EHRR 121, para. 45.
[4] See, e.g., *Golder* v *UK* 1 EHRR 524, para. 34.
[5] See, e.g., *Marckx* v *Belgium* 2 EHRR 330, para. 58.
[6] *Sunday Times* v *UK (No. 1)* 2 EHRR 245, para. 49.
[7] *Silver* v *UK* (1983) 5 EHRR 347, paras 88–89.
[8] See, e.g., *SW and CR* v *UK* (1996) 21 EHRR 363.

6.5 PROPORTIONALITY

Articles 8–11 only permit interferences with the substantive rights to the extent that they are 'necessary in a democratic society' in pursuit of particular legitimate aims. This means that there must be a 'pressing social need' for the measure and also that it is *proportionate* to the aim being pursued. In assessing the proportionality of a particular measure, the Court will consider whether there is an alternative means of protecting the relevant public interest without an interference at all, or by means which are less intrusive. The Court will assess whether the reasons for the interference are 'relevant' and 'sufficient' to justify it. The interference will be disproportionate if it does not in fact achieve the aim pursued. It is a further requirement that the decision-making process leading to the measure of interference should be fair. The existence of effective controls on measures taken by the authorities is also a relevant factor in assessing proportionality.

In assessing proportionality, the state is allowed a certain discretion or 'margin of appreciation' (see below at 6.6).

6.6 MARGIN OF APPRECIATION

In considering the proportionality of a particular interference with a Convention right, the Court will apply the margin of appreciation concept: that state authorities are in principle in a better position to give an opinion on the necessity of a restriction. It is a controversial notion which has been criticised as being wrong in principle and vague in application. It has been described by Rosalyn Higgins as 'objectionable as a viable legal concept', by Anthony Lester as being 'as slippery and elusive as an eel' and by Van Dijk as 'a spreading disease'.

In addition to its application within the concept of proportionality in Articles 8–11 (see below at 7.8), the margin of appreciation is also relevant in other contexts, for example, to Article 5 (e.g., in deciding whether an individual should be detained as being of 'unsound mind'),[9] Article 6 (e.g., in considering limitations on the right of access to court),[10] Article 14 (in assessing to what extent differences in otherwise similar situations justify a different treatment in law),[11] Article 15 (in assessing the existence of a public emergency), Article 1 of Protocol 1 (e.g., in considering the extent of the right of the authorities to enforce laws so as to control the use of property)[12] and Article 3 of Protocol 1 (e.g., in assessing limitations on the right to vote and stand for elections).[13]

---

[9] See, e.g., *Luberti v Italy* (1984) 6 EHRR 440, para. 27.
[10] See, e.g., *Osman v UK* (2000) 29 EHRR 245, para. 147.
[11] See, e.g., *Petrovic v Austria*, (1998) 5 BHRC 232, para. 38.
[12] See, eg. *Chassagnou and others v France* (2000) 29 EHRR 615, para. 75.
[13] See, e.g., *Gitonas v Greece* (1998) 26 EHRR 691, para. 39.

Depending upon the context, the breadth of the state's margin of appreciation will vary. For example, the state has a wide margin of appreciation in relation to the justification for interferences with property (under Article 1 of Protocol 1) and in assessing the existence of a public emergency (under Article 15), but it is narrow in respect of steps taken to maintain the authority and impartiality of the judiciary (under Article 10).

6.7   THE CONVENTION AS A 'LIVING INSTRUMENT'

The Convention is seen as a 'living instrument' and therefore the role of the Court is to interpret the Convention in the light of present day conditions and situations, rather than to try to assess what was intended by the original drafters of the Convention in the late 1940s. It applies a dynamic, rather than historical approach. This principle was applied, for example, in *Matthews* v *UK* (1999) 28 EHRR 361 in assessing whether Article 3 of Protocol 1 was applicable to the European Parliament even though that body was not envisaged by the drafters of the Convention. In *Selmouni* v *France* (2000) 29 EHRR 403,[14] the Court took the 'living instrument' principle into account in assessing the severity of the ill-treatment suffered by the applicant in police custody and found that acts which in the past had been classified as 'inhuman and degrading treatment', rather than torture could be classified differently in the future. The Court was influenced by the increasingly high standard being required in protecting human rights.

There is therefore no formal doctrine of precedent as such within the Convention system.

6.8   PRACTICAL AND EFFECTIVE RIGHTS

The provisions of the Convention are to be interpreted and applied so as to make the safeguards in the Convention 'practical and effective', not 'theoretical or illusory'. For example, the applicant in *Matthews* v *UK* (1999) 28 EHRR 361 complained that as a resident of Gibraltar she had no right to vote in the elections for the European Parliament. Applying this principle of practical and effective rights, the Court found that European legislation affected the population of Gibraltar in the same way as domestic legislation. Therefore, there was no reason why the UK should not be required to secure the right to vote under Article 3 of Protocol 1 in relation to European legislation.

There is a link here with the Court's acknowledgement that the application of the rule requiring the exhaustion of domestic remedies should make due allowance for its application in the context of machinery for the protection

---

[14] See especially para. 101.

of human rights.[15] Therefore, the rule should be applied flexibly. Applicants are not required to exhaust theoretical remedies: only domestic remedies which are sufficiently certain in practice need be utilised. This is discussed further in chapter 5.

6.9 AUTONOMOUS CONCEPTS

A number of terms used in the Convention, such as the meaning of a 'civil right' or 'criminal charge' under Article 6, the meaning of 'association' under Article 11 and the notion of a 'possession' under Article 1 of Protocol 1, are autonomous concepts. This means that the classification under national law will be a factor in the Court's determination as to whether the Convention is applicable, but it will not be decisive.

6.10 POSITIVE OBLIGATIONS

The Convention is to a great extent concerned with limits on interferences with rights by public authorities. However, there are a number of areas where it is established that there are positive obligations on the state to take action to prevent Convention violations. The cases concerning the recognition of transsexuals, such as *Sheffield and Horsham* v *UK* (1999) 27 EHRR 163 are about the extent to which the state has failed to comply with a positive obligation to ensure that their right to respect for their private lives is upheld, by allowing alteration of their birth certificates. In that sort of context, in order to decide whether there is a positive obligation, the Court will try to take account of the fair balance to be struck between the general interest of the community and the interests of the individual.

Another example is Article 2. The obligation on states in Article 2(1) to protect everyone's right to life has been interpreted as creating a positive duty to safeguard lives. In *Osman* v *UK* (2000) 29 EHRR 245,[16] for example, the Court found a positive obligation to take preventive operational measures to protect those whose lives were at risk from criminal attack.

The positive obligation may apply even as between private individuals or entities. For example, the right to peaceful assembly under Article 11 imposes on the authorities a general duty not to interfere with peaceful assemblies, but it may also require positive measures to protect demonstrators from counter-demonstrators.[17] Therefore, the State may be liable in certain circumstances for Convention violations by non-State bodies.

---

[15] See, e.g., *Akdivar* v *Turkey* (1997) 23 EHRR 143, para. 69.
[16] See especially para. 115.
[17] See, e.g., *Ezelin* v *France* (1991) 14 EHRR 362.

6.11   RESTRICTIONS ON RIGHTS

The Court has emphasised that inherent in the whole of the Convention is the fair balance to be struck between the general interest of the community and the interests of the individual.[18]

The aim to achieve such a balance is clearly evident in Articles 8–11 which include second paragraphs setting out the circumstances in which the right to respect for the private life or the right to freedom of expression etc. can be restricted (see chapter 7). However, the balance of rights is reflected throughout the Convention, for example, in the circumstances set out in Article 2 as to when deprivation of life may be permitted and the right of the authorities to enforce laws to control the use of property 'in accordance with the general interest' or to deprive a person of their possessions where it is in 'the public interest', under Article 1 of Protocol 1.

There are specific Convention provisions concerning restrictions in Article 16 (restrictions on the political activity of aliens) and in Article 18 (limitation on the use of restrictions in rights) which are considered below.

6.11.1   Restrictions on the political activity of aliens

Article 16 states that:

> Nothing in Articles 10, 11 and 14 shall be regarded as preventing the High Contracting Parties from imposing restrictions on the political activity of aliens.

In spite of the obligation on states enshrined in Article 1 to ensure that 'everyone within their jurisdiction' receives the protection of the Convention, Article 16 provides that in relation to the rights of freedom of expression, freedom of assembly and association and the prohibition of discrimination, states cannot be prevented from imposing restrictions on the political activity of aliens. There is no equivalent provision in the International Covenant on Civil and Political Rights.   .

Article 16 has, however, been interpreted so as to diminish its importance. *Piermont* v *France* (1995) 20 EHRR 301 concerned a German MEP who was invited to French Polynesia by the French Polynesian Liberation Front prior to parliamentary elections. Whilst in French Polynesia, the applicant denounced nuclear testing in the Pacific and as a result she was subsequently expelled and/or excluded from that territory and from New Caledonia. She argued that there had been violations of Article 2 of Protocol 4 (freedom of movement), Article 10 and Article 14 (taken together with Article 10). She claimed she had been discriminated against on grounds of national origin. In relation to her claim under

---

[18] See, e.g., *James* v *UK* (1986) 8 EHRR 123, para. 50.

Article 10, the French Government invoked Article 16, arguing that she could not rely on her status either as an MEP or as a European citizen. However, the Court decided that Article 16 could not be raised against her because she was a national of a member state of the European Union and an MEP, and found a violation of Article 10, by five votes to four. The four dissenting judges argued the reference to 'aliens' was unambiguous and had no express exceptions. Nevertheless, they also argued that Article 16 could not permit any restriction at all on the political activity of aliens, but that such restrictions would have to be limited.

6.11.2 Limitations on the use of restrictions on rights

Article 18 states that:

> The restrictions permitted under this Convention to the said rights and freedoms shall not be applied for any purpose other than those for which they have been prescribed.

Under Article 18, the Court may examine the reasons for a restrictive measure and if in fact the measure complained of was taken for reasons other than those invoked, then there may be a Convention violation. Article 18 is therefore linked to the underlying Convention concept of 'lawfulness' and, in particular, the prevention of arbitrary measures. Article 18 must be invoked with another Convention right, but there can be a violation of Article 18 (taken together with another Convention right), even if there is no violation of the other right taken alone. The Court will examine compliance of restrictions with Article 18 even if the point is not raised by an applicant.[19]

In practice, it may be very difficult to provide sufficient evidence to satisfy the Court of a violation of Article 18. Article 18 has been raised in the context of gross human rights violations perpetrated by the security forces in south-east Turkey, but the Court has repeatedly found no violation in such cases. For example, in *Kurt* v *Turkey* (1999) 27 EHRR 373,[20] a 'disappearance' case, the applicant argued that the authorities had acted outside the framework of domestic legislation in relation to detention, but the Court found the complaint under Article 18 unsubstantiated. An Article 18 claim also did not succeed in *Rai, Allmond and 'Negotiate Now'* v *UK* (1995) 19 EHRR CD 93 in which the applicants complained about the refusal to allow them to hold a rally in Trafalgar Square in order to promote peace negotiations in Northern Ireland. Article 18 was invoked in relation to a policy to ban demonstrations in Trafalgar Square which were not 'uncontroversial'. However, in declaring the case inadmissible, the Commission found that there was no indication that the restriction was applied for a purpose not prescribed by the provisions of the Convention.

---

[19] See, e.g., *McFeeley* v *UK* (1978) 20 DR 44.
[20] See especially paras 148–152.

6.12   PROHIBITION OF ABUSE OF RIGHTS

Article 17 states that:

> Nothing in this Convention may be interpreted as implying for any state, group or person any right to engage in any activity or perform any act aimed at the destruction of any of the rights and freedoms set forth herein or at their limitation to a greater extent than is provided for in the Convention.

Article 17 is intended to make it impossible for groups or individuals to derive from the Convention a right to do anything aimed at destroying any of the Convention rights and freedoms.[21] Article 17 applies only to an extent strictly proportionate to the seriousness and duration of the threat.[22]

Individuals or groups should not therefore use their Convention rights to undermine democracy or democratic institutions. For example, in *Retimag AG* v *Germany*, No. 712/60, (1962) 4 YB 384, Article 17 was invoked by the Commission in dismissing an application by the communist party in Germany (concerning its dissolution), as its objective of establishing a communist society through the dictatorship of the proletariat was considered to be incompatible with the Convention.

In *Glimmerveen and Hagenbeek* v *Netherlands* (1979) 18 DR 187 the applicants complained of being convicted of possessing leaflets inciting racial discrimination and of being prevented from taking part in municipal elections. They claimed violations of Article 10 and Article 3 of Protocol 1. However, the Commission found that such conduct amounted to an 'activity' within the meaning of Article 17 which was contrary to the text and spirit of the Convention. Similarly, *Kuhnen* v *Germany* (1988) 56 DR 205 concerned the conviction of a journalist for publishing pamphlets advocating the reinstitution of national socialism and racial discrimination. The Commission found that Article 10 may not be invoked in a sense contrary to Article 17.

In *Lawless* v *Ireland* 1 EHRR 15, the applicant member of the IRA complained of his arbitrary detention. The Irish Government tried to invoke Article 17 in arguing that as an active member of the IRA his activities fell within the scope of the Article and therefore he could not rely on Articles 5, 6 or 7, or any other Convention right. However, the Court found that Article 17 did not deprive the applicant of the protection of Articles 5 or 6, as he had not relied on the Convention in order to justify or perform acts contrary to the Convention, but had complained of being deprived of the Article 5 and 6 guarantees.

The Court has rejected attempts by the Turkish Government to invoke Article 17 in a series of cases brought following the dissolution of political parties in

---

[21] *Lawless* v *Ireland* 1 EHRR 15, para. 7.
[22] *De Becker* v *Belgium* (1962) Series, B No. 4, Comm. Rep., para. 279.

Turkey. For example, the United Communist Party of Turkey was dissolved in 1991 by the Constitutional Court for allegedly acting to the detriment of the unity of the Turkish nation. The Court held that Article 17 was not brought into play because there was no evidence that the party relied on the Convention to engage in activity or perform acts aimed at the destruction of any of the rights and freedoms in the Convention.[23]

6.13   INTERPRETATION OF THE SCOPE OF SUBSTANTIVE RIGHTS

In general, the scope of the substantive Convention rights should not be restrictively interpreted. It is a well-established principle that in assessing the scope of a Convention right 'it is necessary to seek the interpretation that is most appropriate in order to realise the aim and achieve the object of the treaty, and not that which would restrict to the greatest possible degree the obligations undertaken by the parties'.[24]

6.14   INTERPRETATION IN ACCORDANCE WITH THE VIENNA CONVENTION

In interpreting the Convention, the Court may take into account the Vienna Convention on the Law of Treaties (23 May 1969) (Articles 31–33 — see appendix 19). This means that the Court will assess the 'ordinary meaning' of the particular term in question and that it will also seek to take into account the object and purpose of the Convention'.[25]

6.15   INTERPRETATION IN THE LIGHT OF THE *'TRAVAUX PRÉPARATOIRES'*

In interpreting the Convention, the Court has on occasion[26] considered the *'travaux préparatoires'* or the preparatory documents related to the drafting of the Convention.[27] However, such a means of interpretation conflicts with the principle of the Convention as a 'living instrument' (see above at 6.7) which is more likely to prevail. The Court may also consider the meaning of the text of the Convention in French, which may have different nuances.[28]

---

[23] *United Communist Party of Turkey and others* v *Turkey* (1998) 26 EHRR 121, para 60. See also, *Socialist Party and others* v *Turkey*, No. 21237/93, 25.5.98, para. 53; *Freedom and Democracy Party (Özdep)* v *Turkey*, No. 23885/94, 8.12.99, para. 47.

[24] See, e.g., *Wemhoff* v *Germany* 1 EHRR 55, para. 8.

[25] See, e.g., *East African Asians* v *UK* (1981) 3 EHRR 76, para. 188.

[26] See, e.g., *Young, James and Webster* v *UK* (1982) 4 EHRR 38, paras 51–53 (whether Article 11 guarantees a right not to be compelled to join a union). For a recent example, see, *Witold Litwa* v *Poland*, No. 26629/95, 4.4.00, para. 63.

[27] *The Collected Edition of the Travaux Préparatoires of the European Convention on Human Rights*, Council of Europe.

[28] See, e.g., *Marckx* v *Belgium* 2 EHRR 330, para. 63.

6.16   ISSUES CONSIDERED BY THE COURT OF ITS OWN MOTION

The Court is not bound by the Convention violations pleaded by the parties. As the Court is master of the characterisation to be given in law to the facts of a case, it may consider and apply Articles of the Convention not raised by the applicant (applying the principle of *jura novit curia*).[29] The Court has full jurisdiction within the scope of a case as determined by the admissibility decision and may deal with any issue of fact or law arising. The Court is also not restricted to considering cases on the basis of material submitted to it, but may, if necessary, assess a case in the light of material obtained *proprio motu*.[30]

6.17   INABILITY TO CONSIDER CASES IN THE ABSTRACT

The Court will not admit applications which are theoretical or in the abstract (this is discussed further in chapter 5). The Court's role is not to assess whether legislation or policies in general violate the Convention,[31] but to assess in concrete cases whether the application of such laws or policies has breached the Convention. In doing so, it will however take account of the 'general context' in which the application arises.[32]

6.18   RULES OF EVIDENCE

The Court is not bound by strict rules of evidence, and may rely on all forms of evidence.[33]

6.19   USE OF OTHER SOURCES OF HUMAN RIGHTS LAW AND PRACTICE

The Court will frequently invoke human rights-related treaties, declarations, recommendations and case law from varied sources, including the Council of Europe, UN Conventions[34] and UN Human Rights Committee case law, other regional human rights mechanisms (such as the American Convention on Human Rights)[35] and relevant case law both from within Council of Europe states and from other jurisdictions.

---

[29] See, e.g., *Guerra and others* v *Italy* (1998) 26 EHRR 357, para. 44.
[30] See, e.g., *Cruz Varas* v *Sweden* (1992) 14 EHRR 1, para. 25.
[31] See, e.g., *McCann* v *UK* (1996) 21 EHRR 97, para. 153.
[32] See, e.g., *Young, James and Webster* v *UK* (1982) 4 EHRR 38, para. 53.
[33] *Ireland* v *UK* 2 EHRR 25, para. 209.
[34] See, e.g., *A* v *UK* (1999) 27 EHRR 611, para. 22 (Articles 19 and 37, UN Convention on the Rights of the Child).
[35] See, e.g., *Timurtaş* v *Turkey*, No. 33274/96, 13.6.00, paras 79–80.

Reports of non-governmental organisations, such as Amnesty International, may also be highly relevant. Intervention in European Court cases by third parties, including NGOs, is discussed above at 2.6.

6.20   THE EFFECTIVE EXERCISE OF THE RIGHT OF APPLICATION

As well as setting out the rules of 'standing' (see chapter 5), Article 34 (formerly Article 25) establishes a duty on Convention states not to hinder the effective exercise of the right to apply to the European Court. The Court has frequently emphasised that it is of the utmost importance for the effective operation of the system of individual petition that applicants or potential applicants should be able to communicate freely with the Court. Article 34 states that:

> The Court may receive applications from any person, non-governmental organisation or group of individuals claiming to be the victim of a violation by one of the High Contracting Parties of the rights set forth in the Convention or the protocols thereto. The High Contracting Parties undertake not to hinder in any way the effective exercise of this right.

Where a state prevents the effective right of application, the Court may find a violation of Article 34. Accordingly, if there is any evidence at any stage of a Convention application that the applicant's effective right of application is being restricted, then the matter should immediately be drawn to the Court's attention by lodging relevant evidence, including statements. The applicant's representative may plead a violation of Article 34 (albeit as a procedural, not a substantive right) and may request that the Court takes the matter up with the respondent Government. The right of application may be affected in a number of ways, including interception of the applicant's and/or the applicant's representative's communications[36] (post, telephone, e-mail etc.), or intimidation of the applicant, the applicant's family or potential witnesses.

Under Article 34, applicants must not be subjected to any form of pressure from the authorities to modify or withdraw their complaints. 'Pressure' includes direct coercion and flagrant acts of intimidation (of applicants, potential applicants, their families and legal representatives), but also any improper indirect acts or contacts designed to dissuade or discourage applicants from pursuing a Convention remedy. The questioning of applicants about their applications to the Court is considered to be a form of illicit and unacceptable pressure.[37] In assessing the

---

[36] See, e.g., *Foxley* v *UK*, Judgment of 20.6.00 (interception of applicant's mail by Receiver and Trustee in Bankruptcy led to finding of a violation of Article 8, and that it was not necessary to consider Article 34).

[37] *Assenov and others* v *Bulgaria* (1999) 28 EHRR 652.

degree of interference, the Court will take account of the vulnerability of the complainant and his or her susceptibility to influence exerted by the authorities.

Complaints of intimidation have frequently been made in cases against Turkey in the 1990s, and a number have been upheld. There was a violation of Article 25 (now Article 34) in *Akdivar v Turkey* (1997) 23 EHRR 143 where the applicants were directly asked about their petitions to Strasbourg and were presented with statements to sign declaring that no such applications had been brought (two applicants' interviews were filmed). The applicant in *Kurt v Turkey* (1999) 27 EHRR 373 alleged that she had been pressurised by the authorities to withdraw her application to the Commission. She also complained that steps had been taken to bring criminal proceedings against her lawyer in relation to the allegations in the application to the European Commission. The Court found that statements she had made repudiating all petitions in her name were not drafted on the initiative of the applicant (e.g. she was taken to the notary's office by a soldier and was not required to pay the notary's fee for drawing up a statement). The Court found there had therefore been improper pressure in violation of Article 25. In other cases where complaints of intimidation have been made, the Court has not been satisfied that there was sufficient evidence.[38]

The Court has held that Article 34 does not create a binding duty on states to comply with the Court's interim measures proposals[39] under Rule 39 (see above at 2.4.10).

There is a further obligation on states under Article 38(1)(a) to 'furnish all necessary facilities' in relation to the Court's examination of a case and its establishment of the facts (formerly Article 28(1)(a)) (see chapter 3). States which fail to do so may be criticised by the Court under this provision, but it will not in its own right give rise to a finding of a violation of the Convention. For example, in *Tanrikulu v Turkey*, No. 26763/94, 8.7.99, the Court found it to be 'a matter for grave concern' that the respondent state had failed to disclose certain documentary evidence or to ensure the attendance at oral fact-finding hearings of two public prosecutors. Such failings by the respondent Government may lead the Court to draw inferences as to the well-foundedness of the allegations (particularly where only the Government has access to information capable of corroborating or refuting the applicant's allegations).[40]

---

[38] See, e.g., *Aksoy v Turkey* (1997) 23 EHRR 553, para. 106 and *Aydin v Turkey* (1998) 25 EHRR 251, para. 117.

[39] *Cruz Varas v Sweden* (1991) 14 EHRR 1, para. 102.

[40] See, e.g., *Timurtaş v Turkey*, No. 23531/94, 13.6.00, paras 66–67.

Chapter Seven

The Substantive Rights of the European Convention

7.1 ARTICLE 1: OBLIGATION TO RESPECT HUMAN RIGHTS

The High Contracting Parties shall secure to everyone within their jurisdiction the rights and freedoms defined in section 1 of this Convention.

Article 1 of the Convention establishes the contracting parties' overriding obligation to ensure that everyone within their jurisdiction enjoys the rights and freedoms set out in section 1 of the Convention, namely the rights (and limitations on those rights) contained in Articles 2 to 18. Therefore, the contracting party is required to uphold those Articles, regardless of an individual's nationality, residence[1] or any other characteristic. The sole condition is jurisdiction.

Article 1 makes no distinction as to the type of rule or measure concerned, and does not exclude any part of a state's jurisdiction from scrutiny under the Convention.[2] The 'jurisdiction' of each contracting state includes, in addition to its geographical territory, all persons or property under the actual authority or responsibility of the state, such as the situation where the armed forces or other state agents act beyond the boundary of the territory of a state[3] or where a public official acts in an unauthorised way.[4] An applicant who complains to the European Court about a matter which is found not to be within the respondent state's

---

[1] See, e.g., *D v UK* (1997) 24 EHRR 423; *Amuur v France* (1996) 22 EHRR 533.
[2] *United Communist Party of Turkey and others v Turkey* (1998) 26 EHRR 121, para. 29.
[3] See, e.g., *Cyprus v Turkey* (1982) 4 EHRR 482, para. 83; *Reinette v France* (1989) 63 DR 189; *Loizidou v Turkey* (1997) 23 EHRR 513, para. 52; and *Issa and others v Turkey*, No. 31821/96, 30.5.00.
[4] *Wille v Liechtenstein* (1997) 24 EHRR CD 45.

jurisdiction will have their application declared inadmissible under Article 35(3). This is discussed further in chapter 5.

It is an important aspect of the Convention system that it does not specify how each contracting state is to ensure that the Convention is upheld. That is a matter for each state party. Article 1 does not, for example, necessarily require incorporation of the Convention into the domestic law of the state.

Because Article 1 itself defines the overriding obligation on state parties to ensure observance of the Convention's substantive rights, it cannot be the subject of a separate breach of the Convention. Accordingly, the European Commission rejected the Cypriot Government's arguments that Article 1 had been breached in *Cyprus* v *Turkey* (1982) 4 EHRR 482. Nevertheless, Article 1 may be invoked by the Court in conjunction with the other substantive rights and is linked to the fundamental principle that the Convention is to be interpreted in order to guarantee rights which are practical and effective, rather than theoretical or illusory[5] (see also above at 6.8). Article 1 is frequently referred to by the Court to strengthen the extent of the substantive rights. For example, Article 1 has been invoked in conjunction with the obligation to protect the right to life under Article 2, and to justify the finding that Article 2 requires some form of effective official investigation when individuals have been killed as a result of the use of force.[6]

It may also be invoked by the Court when the extent of the state's positive obligations are in question (see also above at 6.10). For example, in *A* v *UK* (1999) 27 EHRR 611, Article 1 was referred to by the Court in finding that the respondent Government could be liable under Article 3 of the Convention for its failure to ensure that the law adequately protected a young child from being beaten by his stepfather. The Court held that Article 1, taken together with Article 3, requires the state to take measures designed to ensure that individuals within its jurisdiction are not subjected to torture or inhuman or degrading treatment or punishment, including ill-treatment carried out by private individuals.[7] Consequently, the state must ensure that there is effective deterrence to prevent such treatment of children and other vulnerable people.

7.2   ARTICLE 2: THE RIGHT TO LIFE

1.   Everyone's right to life shall be protected by law. No one shall be deprived of his life intentionally save in the execution of a sentence of a court following his conviction of a crime for which this penalty is provided by law.

2.   Deprivation of life shall not be regarded as inflicted in contravention of this Article when it results from the use of force which is no more than absolutely necessary:

(a)   in defence of any person from unlawful violence;

---

[5] See, e.g., *Soering* v *UK* 11 EHRR 439, para. 87; *Cruz Varas* v *Sweden* (1992) 14 EHRR 1, para. 99.

[6] See, e.g., *McCann* v *UK* (1996) 21 EHRR 97, para. 161; *Tanrikulu* v *Turkey*, No. 26763/94, 8.7.99, para. 101.

[7] See also *Z* v *UK* (1999) 28 EHRR CD 65, para. 93.

(b) in order to effect a lawful arrest or to prevent the escape of a person lawfully detained;

(c) in action lawfully taken for the purpose of quelling a riot or insurrection.

The protection of the right to life is regarded as one of the most fundamental of the Convention rights and which 'enshrines one of the basic values of the democratic societies making up the Council of Europe'.[8] Under Article 15 of the Convention, there can be no derogation from Article 2 (other than in respect of deaths resulting from lawful acts of war). Article 2 comprises both positive and negative aspects: a positive duty to protect life (and adequately to investigate fatal incidents) and a negative obligation to refrain from the unlawful taking of life. Article 2(1) would permit the death penalty,[9] but in January 1999 the UK ratified Protocol 6 to the Convention, which has the effect of abolishing the death penalty (see below at 7.19).

Article 2 relates both to intentional and unintentional killings. Article 2(2) sets out an exhaustive list of the circumstances in which it is permissible to use force (no more than is *absolutely necessary*) which may result, as the unintended outcome of the use of force, in the deprivation of life,[10] as well as regulating the intentional taking of life. The use of force has to be strictly proportionate to the relevant Article 2(2) aim. This will require consideration of the nature of the aim pursued, the nature of the risk to life inherent in the particular case and the extent of the risk that loss of life might be caused.

The scope of Article 2 is discussed further below in the following contexts: police operations (7.2.1); deaths in custody (7.2.2); disappearances (7.2.3); suicide (7.2.4); victims of crime (7.2.5); environmental cases (7.2.6) and health care, abortion and euthanasia (7.2.7)

7.2.1 Police operations

In *McCann and others* v *UK* (1996) 21 EHRR 97, concerning the fatal shooting by the SAS of three members of an IRA Active Service Unit in Gibraltar, the Court emphasised that in judging whether force used was 'absolutely necessary', it should apply a stricter and more compelling test than that applied in considering whether state action is 'necessary in a democratic society'.[11] The Court rejected arguments that the incompatibility with Article 2 of national law and practice (as to the training and instruction of state agents) in itself violated the Convention, and that the inquest proceedings were inadequate. It also found that the soldiers had honestly and reasonably (albeit mistakenly) believed that it was necessary to

---

[8] See, e.g., *McCann* v *UK* (1996) 21 EHRR 97, para. 147

[9] However, in *Öcalan* v *Turkey*, No. 46221/99, 14.12.00, currently pending before the Court, the applicant is arguing that his death sentence amounts to an infringement of the right to life under Article 2 (and a violation of Article 3) on the basis that the contracting states have, through their practice over fifty years, abolished the exception provided for in the second sentence of Article 2(1). Turkey has not yet ratified Protocol 6 to the Convention.

[10] *Stewart* v *UK*, No. 10044/82, 10.7.84, 39 DR 162, pp 169–171.

[11] (1996) 21 EHRR 97, para. 149.

shoot the suspects in order to prevent them from detonating a bomb and causing serious loss of life. However, by ten votes to nine the Court held that Article 2 had been violated as a result of the failures in the conduct and planning of the operation. The Court focused on the decision not to prevent the suspects from travelling into Gibraltar, the authorities' failure to make sufficient allowances for the possibility that their intelligence assessments might, at least in part, have been wrong, and the automatic recourse to lethal force when the soldiers opened fire.

The Court was again split by the narrowest of margins in *Andronicou and Constantinou* v *Cyprus* (1998) 25 EHRR 491, which perhaps reflects the difficulties inherent in assessing police operations. There, the Court found no violation of the right to life (by five votes to four) arising from the fatal shooting by the police of a man and his fiancée whom he had taken hostage in his flat. They were shot dead when the police stormed the flat following several hours of negotiation. The Court held that the use of lethal force had not exceeded what was 'absolutely necessary' and found that the rescue operation had been adequately planned and organised. The test applied in such situations is that the operations should minimise to the greatest extent possible any risk to the lives of those involved.

In *Stewart* v *UK*, No. 10044/82, 10.7.84, 39 DR 162, the accidental fatal shooting of a thirteen-year-old boy by a British soldier in Belfast was found by the Commission not to violate Article 2 on the basis that the use of plastic bullets had been justified in the circumstances to quell a riot (Article 2(2)(c)) and that the death had occurred because, as the soldier fired, aiming at the legs of a person leading the riot, he was hit by missiles and his aim was deflected. In *Kelly* v *UK*, No. 17579/90, 31.1.93, 74 DR 139 the applicant's son was shot dead by soldiers whilst he was joyriding and driving through a roadblock in Belfast. In rejecting the application as manifestly ill-founded, the Commission accepted that the soldiers' actions were intended to effect a lawful arrest (Article 2(2)(b)) of people who were reasonably believed to be terrorists and that their use of force was justified (when assessed 'against the background of the events in Northern Ireland').

From the mid-1990s the Commission and Court have considered a series of applications arising from the activities of the security forces which have led to fatalities in south-east Turkey. For example, in *Ogur* v *Turkey*, No. 21594/93, 20.5.99, the Court found a violation of Article 2 arising from the planning and execution of an operation of the Turkish security forces which led to Musa Ogur's shooting, and a separate violation of Article 2 resulting from the ineffective investigations following the incident carried out by the national authorities[12] (as to the requirement to investigate, see also below at 7.2.2 on deaths in custody). In *Ergi* v *Turkey*, No. 23818/94, 28.7.98, the Court again found violations of Article

---

[12] Paras. 71–84. See also *Demiray* v *Turkey*, No. 27308/95, 9.11.00.

2 on account of defects in the planning and conduct of a security forces operation and the lack of an adequate and effective investigation.[13] However, in a number of cases, including *Ergi*,[14] the Strasbourg institutions have concluded that there has been an insufficient factual and evidential basis on which to conclude beyond reasonable doubt that the victims had been intentionally killed by state agents. Accordingly, in *Ergi*, the Court found no further violation of Article 2 arising from the alleged unlawful killing itself of the applicant's sister.

7.2.2   Deaths in custody

Article 2 imposes a positive obligation upon the authorities to ensure that the law adequately protects the right to life, and an obligation to enforce the law. Article 2 should always be considered together with Article 13 which, because of the fundamental importance of the right to protection of life, imposes stricter requirements in relation to the investigation of fatal incidents.[15] This will require in the context of a death in police custody that there is a thorough and effective official investigation into the circumstances in which the death occurred, and that those responsible are held accountable (whether by prosecution or otherwise). It will also require that the complainant has effective access to the investigatory procedure and that the procedure is capable of leading to the identification and punishment of the offenders.[16]

Ordinarily, the burden is on the applicant to establish a violation of the Convention. However, the burden shifts to the state where death has occurred during custody. In those circumstances, the burden of proof is on the authorities to provide a 'satisfactory and convincing explanation' or a 'plausible explanation' for the events leading to a detainee's death'[17] and to keep appropriate records. In *Salman* v *Turkey*, No. 21986/93, 27.6.00 the Court described the obligation in this way:

> Persons in custody are in a vulnerable position and the authorities are under a duty to protect them. Consequently, where an individual is taken into police custody in good health and is found to be injured on release, it is incumbent on the State to provide a plausible explanation of how those injuries were caused. . . . The obligation on the authorities to account for the treatment of an individual in custody is particularly stringent where that individual dies.

---

[13] Paras. 68–86.

[14] Paras. 77 and 78.

[15] See, e.g., *Kaya* v *Turkey* (1999) 28 EHRR 1, para. 107; *Yaşa* v *Turkey* (1999) 28 EHRR 408, paras 114–115.

[16] See, e.g., *Aksoy* v *Turkey* (1997) 23 EHRR 553, para. 98; *Kaya* v *Turkey* (1999) 28 EHRR 1, para. 107; *Aydin* v *Turkey* (1997) 25 EHRR 251, para. 103; *Yaşa* v *Turkey* (1999) 28 EHRR 408; *Tanrikulu* v *Turkey*, No. 26763/94, 8.7.99, para. 117.

[17] See, e.g., *Velikova* v *Bulgaria*, No. 41488/98, 18.5.00, para. 70 and *Salman* v *Turkey*, No. 21986/93, 27.6.00.

Where the events in issue are wholly, or in large part, within the exclusive knowledge of the authorities, as in the case of persons within their control in custody, strong presumptions of fact will arise in respect of injuries and death occurring during that detention. Indeed, the burden of proof may be regarded as resting on the authorities to provide a satisfactory and convincing explanation.[18]

The standard which the Court requires in assessing evidence of a Convention violation is proof beyond reasonable doubt. This test may be satisfied by 'the co-existence of sufficiently strong, clear and concordant inferences or of similar unrebutted presumptions of fact'.[19] In the context of cases of ill-treatment in custody (see below at 7.3.2), the requirement for the applicant to prove a violation beyond reasonable doubt has been criticised by some members of the Court due to the difficulties of those held in custody obtaining the necessary evidence,[20] which may be entirely in the hands of the authorities, or which may depend upon efficient investigation by the authorities. Therefore, in such circumstances the standard of proof 'on the balance of probabilities' has been proposed. It is suggested that the difficulties of obtaining evidence may be even greater for the relatives of those who have died in police or prison custody.

7.2.3 Disappearances

The Court initially assessed cases of enforced 'disappearance', primarily under Article 5, rather than Articles 2 or 3. In *Kurt* v *Turkey* (1999) 27 EHRR 373, the applicant's son had been last seen surrounded by soldiers and had not been seen for four and a half years. In considering whether there arose a positive obligation under Article 2 to carry out an effective investigation into the circumstances of the alleged unlawful killing, the Court applied a test as to whether there was 'concrete evidence' which could establish beyond reasonable doubt that the applicant's son had been killed by the authorities. In *Kurt* there was no such evidence and accordingly the Court found that the case was to be assessed in relation to Article 5, rather than Article 2. However, more recently in *Timurtaş* v *Turkey*, No. 23531/94, 13.6.00, the Court found a violation of Article 2 in relation to the disappearance of the applicant's son who had been taken into detention by the security forces and nothing further had been heard of him for six and a half years. Finding that the period of time was a relevant factor, although not decisive, the Court was satisfied that the applicant's son could be presumed dead. *Timurtas* represents a welcome change in approach which arguably should have been applied in *Kurt*.

---

[18] See paras 99 and 100. See also *Velikova* v *Bulgaria*, No. 41488/98, 18.5.00

[19] See, e.g., *Salman* v *Turkey*, No. 21986/93, 27.6.00, para. 100.

[20] See, e.g., *Veznedaroğlu* v *Turkey*, No. 32357/96, 11.4.00.

7.2.4 Suicide

The authorities have an obligation under Article 2 to take appropriate steps to safeguard the lives of detainees under their control, even where death or injury occurs as a result of suicide or attempted suicide. In the case of *Keenan* v *UK*, No. 27229/95, Comm. Rep. 6.9.99, concerning the suicide of the applicant's son in prison, applying the *Osman* test (see below at 7.2.5) the Commission found no violation of Article 2 on the facts of the case, taking into account the extent of the knowledge of the prison authorities about the applicant's condition and the reasonableness of the steps the authorities had taken.

7.2.5 Victims of crime (state and non-state actors)

In a series of cases concerning south-east Turkey in the 1990s, the Strasbourg organs have found that the authorities have failed to investigate allegations of wrongdoing by the security forces, which have led to findings that the procedural obligation under Article 2 has been violated.[21] In *Tanrikulu* v *Turkey*, No. 26763/94, 8.7.99, for example, the Court found a violation of Article 2 arising from the failure of the Turkish authorities to carry out an effective investigation into the circumstances surrounding the shooting of the applicant's husband.

The duty to prevent and investigate fatalities applies not only to cases concerning deaths at the hands of state officials, but also to any case in which the authorities are informed of a fatal incident.[22] In *Osman* v *UK* (2000) 29 EHRR 245 the Court considered the extent of the positive obligation on the state in the circumstances of a fatal shooting by a teacher of the father of a former pupil, with whom he had developed an obsession. In the context of the duty on the authorities to prevent and suppress offences, the Court found that it must be established that the authorities knew or ought to have known at the time of the existence of a real and immediate risk to the life of an identified individual from the criminal acts of a third party, and that they failed to take measures within the scope of their powers which, judged reasonably, might have been expected to avoid that risk. However, on the facts of the *Osman* case, the Court found no violation of Article 2 on the basis that the applicants had failed to point to any decisive stage in the sequence of events leading up to the shooting when it could be said that the police knew or ought to have known of a real and immediate risk to the lives of the Osman family. Applying the *Osman* test in the context of south-east Turkey, the Court found a violation of Article 2 in *Kaya, Mahmut* v *Turkey*, No. 22535/93, 28.3.00 because of the ineffectiveness of the criminal law protection in the region in relation to the actions of the security forces which

---

[21] See, e.g., *Kaya* v *Turkey*, No. 22535/93, 28.3.00, para. 96.

[22] See, e.g., *Ergi* v *Turkey*, No. 23818/94, 28.7.98, para. 82 and *Yaşa* v *Turkey* (1999) 28 EHRR 408, para. 100; *Tanrikulu* v *Turkey*, No. 26763/94, 8.7.99, para. 103.

meant that there had been a failure to prevent a real and immediate risk to life of a doctor who was suspected of giving assistance to wounded members of the PKK.

7.2.6   Environmental cases

The obligation on the state to protect life under Article 2 may be invoked in cases concerning environmental hazards which risk endangering life. In considering what positive steps should be taken under Article 2, the Court will assess whether 'the state did all that could have been required of it to prevent ... life from being avoidably put at risk'.[23] This may include an obligation to provide advice and to monitor the health of individuals considered to be at risk.[24] Article 2 may therefore be in issue even where there has been no death. However, cases of severe environmental pollution are likely to raise issues under Article 8, rather than Article 2 (see below at 7.9.10, and, for example, *Guerra and others* v *Italy* (1998) 26 EHRR 357).

7.2.7   Health care, abortion and euthanasia

Article 2 may give rise to arguments about the extent of the obligation to take adequate measures to protect life in the context of medical care.[25] However, given the difficulties about the allocation of limited financial resources for health care, it is suggested that only in very exceptional cases would the Court find a violation of Article 2 arising from failures in medical care. In *Powell* v *UK*, No. 45305/99, 4.5.00, the Court stated that:

> It cannot be excluded that the acts and omissions of the authorities in the field of health care policy may in certain circumstances engage their responsibility under the positive limb of Article 2. However, where a contracting state has made adequate provision for securing high professional standards among health professionals and the protection of the lives of the patients, it cannot accept that matters such as errors of judgement on the part of a health professional or negligent co-ordination among health professionals, in the treatment of a particular patient are sufficient of themselves to call a contracting state to account from the standpoint of its positive obligations under Article 2 of the Convention to protect life.

However, the Court confirmed in that case that Article 2 requires an effective independent system for establishing the cause of death of an individual under the care and responsibility of health professionals and any liability on their part.

---

[23] *LCB* v *UK* (1999) 27 EHRR 212, para. 36.
[24] *LCB* v *UK* (1999) 27 EHRR 212, para. 38.
[25] See, e.g., *Association X* v *UK*, No. 7154/75, (1978) 14 DR 31

In *D* v *UK* (1997) 24 EHRR 423, it was undisputed that the applicant's removal to St Kitts would hasten his death, because he was terminally ill with AIDS and the medical treatment he needed was unavailable there. The Court found that the issues under Article 2 were indistinguishable from those raised under Article 3 which was held to have been violated. In *Barrett* v *UK* (1997) 23 EHRR CD 185 the European Commission recognised that the provision for alcohol consumption at a naval base, combined with the failure to take any steps to control drinking to excess and inadequate care and treatment, would raise issues under Article 2.

The Strasbourg institutions have not decided whether an unborn child is protected by Article 2,[26] reflecting the varying attitudes towards abortion amongst Council of Europe states. Similarly, there has been no substantive decision about euthanasia in the context of Article 2, or of competing interests under Articles 3 or 8.

7.3   ARTICLE 3: PROHIBITION OF TORTURE AND INHUMAN OR DEGRADING TREATMENT OR PUNISHMENT

No one shall be subjected to torture or to inhuman or degrading treatment or punishment.

The absolute prohibition on torture and inhuman or degrading treatment or punishment enshrined in Article 3 is so fundamental that it has no limitations or exceptions whatsoever and it may not be subject to derogation under Article 15 of the Convention.[27]

For any treatment to violate Article 3, it must be of a minimum level of severity, which depends upon all the circumstances of the case, such as the duration of the treatment, its physical or mental effects, and, in some cases, the sex, age and state of health of the victim.[28] In many Convention cases, concerning a wide variety of circumstances, no violation of this Article has been found simply because the treatment in question is not considered to be sufficiently severe.[29] In less severe cases, consideration should be given to the right to respect for physical and moral integrity under Article 8 (see below at 7.9.1).

Sufficient evidence of a detainee's ill-treatment must be produced. There was found to be insufficient evidence in *Assenov and others* v *Bulgaria* (1999) 28

---

[26] See, e.g., *Paton* v *UK* (1981) 3 EHRR 408 and *Open Door and Dublin Well Woman* v *Ireland* (1993) 15 EHRR 244.

[27] Under Article 15(2) no derogation is permitted from Articles 2 (except in respect of deaths resulting from lawful acts of war), 3, 4(1) or 7.

[28] *Ireland* v *UK* 2 EHRR 25, para. 162.

[29] For a comprehensive analysis of the generally higher standards imposed by the European Convention on the Prevention of Torture and Inhuman or Degrading Treatment, see R. Morgan and M. Evans (Eds), *Protecting Prisoners — The Standards of the European Committee for the Prevention of Torture in Context*, Oxford University Press, 1999.

EHRR 652 to confirm that the applicant had been beaten in police custody with truncheons. Similarly, the applicant in *Klaas* v *Germany* (1994) 18 EHRR 305 alleged that injuries sustained during the course of her arrest by the police violated Article 3 (the fact of the arrest had not been disputed in the course of domestic proceedings). The Court found no violation because there was no further evidence which could lead it to depart from the findings of the domestic court that the applicant could have injured herself while resisting arrest and that the arresting officers had not used excessive force.

The standard of proof required by the Court in assessing allegations of ill-treatment is 'beyond reasonable doubt', although this has rightly been the subject of criticism in cases of ill-treatment of detainees where the only available evidence may be in the hands of the authorities[30] (see also above at 7.2.2 re deaths in custody). In expulsion cases, however, the Court applies a test of whether there are substantial grounds of a real risk of treatment contrary to Article 3 (see below at 7.3.3).

A threat of treatment which violates Article 3 would also itself amount to a breach of that provision, provided the threat is sufficiently real and immediate.[31]

Article 3 also imposes on states a positive obligation to carry out an effective official investigation into an allegation of serious ill-treatment, which is capable of leading to the identification and punishment of those responsible.[32] This obligation will be supplemented by Article 13, which requires an effective remedy, entailing effective access for the complainant to the investigatory process and the payment of compensation where appropriate. In a series of cases brought against Turkey from the mid-1990s, the Court has found violations of Article 13 arising from the failure to investigate allegations of torture or ill-treatment in custody.[33]

7.3.1 Definitions

The Court has applied the following definitions:

Torture: deliberate inhuman treatment causing very serious and cruel suffering.[34]

Inhuman treatment or punishment: intense physical or mental suffering.[35]

Degrading treatment or punishment: treatment which arouses in the victim feelings of fear, anguish and inferiority capable of humiliation and debasement and possibly

---

[30] See, e.g., the dissenting judgment of Bonello J. in *Veznedaroğlu* v *Turkey*, No. 32357/96, 11.4.00.
[31] *Campbell and Cosans* v *UK* (1982) 4 EHRR 293, para. 26.
[32] *Assenov and others* v *Bulgaria,* (1999) 28 EHRR 652, para. 102.
[33] See, e.g., *Aksoy* v *Turkey* (1997) 23 EHRR 553; *Aydin* v *Turkey* (1998) 25 EHRR 251, *Kaya* v *Turkey*, No. 22535/93, 28.3.00, para. 96.
[34] *Ireland* v *UK* 2 EHRR 25, para. 167.
[35] *Ireland* v *UK* 2 EHRR 25, para. 167.

breaking physical or moral resistance.[36] It is sufficient if the victim is humiliated in his or her own eyes.[37]

However, in a significant decision in 1999 in the case of *Selmouni v France* (2000) 29 EHRR 403, the Court found that, because of the need to interpret the Convention as a 'living instrument', acts which had previously been classified as inhuman and degrading treatment rather than torture, could be classified differently in future:

> ... the increasingly high standard being required in the area of the protection of human rights and fundamental liberties correspondingly and inevitably requires greater firmness in assessing breaches of the fundamental values of democratic societies.

The requirements of Article 3 are discussed further below in the following contexts: arrest and detention (7.3.2); immigration, asylum and extradition (7.3.3); discrimination (7.3.4); child care (7.3.5); corporal punishment (7.3.6); and medical treatment (7.3.7).

7.3.2   Arrest and detention

Where an individual is taken into custody in good health, but is found to be injured at the time of release, the obligation lies on the state to explain how the injuries occurred.[38] In assessing allegations of ill-treatment, the Court will take into account the particular vulnerability of a person detained in custody. The Court has consistently emphasised that the use of physical force against detainees, which has not been made strictly necessary by the individual's own conduct, diminishes human dignity and in principle infringes Article 3.[39]

The protections provided by Article 3 as to the physical integrity of individuals cannot be limited, even in the context of the fight against terrorism or crime.[40]

In the case of *Ireland v UK* 2 EHRR 25 the Court assessed five interrogation techniques (wall-standing, hooding, subjection to noise, sleep deprivation and deprivation of food and drink) used during the detention of five IRA suspects as against the obligations imposed by Article 3. Used in combination and for hours at a time, such treatment, causing at least intense physical and mental suffering and leading to acute psychiatric disturbances, was held to be inhuman and degrading treatment in violation of Article 3, but was not considered to amount to

---

[36] *Ireland v UK* 2 EHRR 25, para. 167.
[37] *Tyrer v UK* 2 EHRR 1, para. 23; *Smith and Grady v UK* (1999) 29 EHRR 493, para. 120.
[38] *Tomasi v France* (1993) 15 EHRR 1, paras 108–111; *Ribitsch v Austria* (1996) 21 EHRR 573, para. 34; *Selmouni v France* (2000) 29 EHRR 403, para. 87. But contrast these cases with *Klaas v Germany* (1994) 18 EHRR 305, where the domestic courts found that the applicant could have injured herself while resisting arrest and that the arresting officers had not used excessive force.
[39] *Ribitsch v Austria* (1996) 21 EHRR 573, paras 36 and 38.
[40] *Tomasi v France* (1993) 15 EHRR 1; *Assenov and others v Bulgaria* (1999) 28 EHRR 652, para. 93.

torture. However, severe beatings of the body and feet, and other treatment including electric shocks and the use of a vice, inflicted by the Athens security police on political detainees in order to extract information, was found to amount to torture and inhuman treatment in breach of Article 3.[41]

In a series of cases brought against Turkey, arising from the actions of the security forces in south-east Turkey, the Court has found the treatment of detainees by the Turkish authorities to be in violation of the prohibition against torture in Article 3. For example, the applicant in *Aydin* v *Turkey* (1998) 25 EHRR 251 was found to have been raped, beaten, kept blindfolded, paraded naked and pummelled with high pressure water whilst being spun around in a tyre. In *Aksoy* v *Turkey* (1997) 23 EHRR 553[42] the applicant was found to have been subjected to 'Palestinian hanging', that is, he was stripped naked, with his arms tied together behind his back, and suspended by his arms, leading to paralysis. This treatment was found to have been administered with the aim of obtaining admissions or information. In *Selmouni* v *France* (2000) 29 EHRR 403, the applicant was subjected to prolonged assaults by police officers over several days, which included being beaten, dragged by his hair, being urinated over and threatened with a blowlamp and a syringe. This treatment, taken as a whole, was considered to amount to torture in violation of Article 3 (for which the applicant was awarded 500,000 French francs in just satisfaction under Article 41).

The mental anguish and distress caused by the 'disappearance' of a close relative may give rise to a violation of Article 3, as was the case in *Kurt* v *Turkey* (1999) 27 EHRR 373, where the applicant was found to have suffered anguish for a long period of time over the disappearance of her son and in view of the complacency of the authorities in response to her complaints. In *Selçuk and Asker* v *Turkey* (1998) 26 EHRR 477, the Court found a violation of Article 3 arising from the destruction of the applicants' homes by the security forces, which they had to stand by and watch. This was found to amount to inhuman treatment.

The use of handcuffs may in certain circumstances breach Article 3. In the case of *Kaj Raninen* v *Finland*, No. 20972/92, Comm. Rep., 24.1.96, the applicant, who objected to military service, was handcuffed by military police for two hours and appeared in public handcuffed in the presence of his support group. The Commission found that the use of force had not been strictly necessary as a result of the applicant's conduct, nor of any other legitimate consideration, diminishing his human dignity and amounting to degrading treatment in violation of Article 3. The Court, however, unanimously found no violation of Article 3 because it was not convinced that the incident had adversely affected the applicant's mental state

---

[41] *Greek Case*, Nos 3321–3/67, 3344/67, 5.11.69; (1969) 12 Yearbook 1.
[42] See also, *Tekin* v *Turkey*, No. 22496/93, 9.6.98, paras 48–54 (applicant held in a cold and dark cell, blindfolded and wounded and bruised during interrogation was found to have been subjected to inhuman and degrading treatment).

or that the handcuffing had been aimed at debasing or humiliating him.[43] An intimate body search may amount to degrading treatment, if the particular circumstances were such that the Article 3 threshold had been reached.[44]

Conditions in which detainees are held may also violate Article 3, depending upon the particular circumstances. Relevant factors might include the standards of the provision of heating, ventilation, lighting, food and water, medical treatment, toilets, facilities for sleeping and for recreation and the means of contact with others not in detention.[45]

7.3.3 Immigration, asylum and extradition

The state may be found to be liable under Article 3 where an individual is to be deported or extradited to a country where there are substantial grounds for believing that they face a real risk of treatment contrary to Article 3 (the relevant time being when the European Court considers the case).[46] Article 3 may apply not only where the risk in question is created by public authorities in the receiving country, but also by private organisations or individuals, in circumstances where the risk is real and the authorities in the receiving state are not able to provide appropriate protection.[47]

In *Soering* v *UK* (1989) 11 EHRR 439[48] the Court held that there would be a violation of Article 3 if the applicant were deported to the United states on capital murder charges, where he faced exposure to the 'death-row phenomenon'. The Court found that the responsibility of the state would be engaged where there were substantial grounds for believing that, if extradited, the applicant faced a real risk of being subjected to torture or inhuman or degrading treatment or punishment. The Court held that Article 3 did not generally prohibit the death penalty itself,[49] but the prospect of six to eight years on death row gave rise to a breach of Article 3.

In *Chahal* v *UK* (1997) 23 EHRR 413 the applicant complained that his deportation to India on national security grounds would violate his rights under Article 3 because, as a Sikh political activist, he risked being subjected to torture. In an important passage in that case, the Court affirmed that it was inappropriate to apply any balancing act in such circumstances: Article 3 provides absolute

---

[43] *Raninen* v *Finland* (1998) 26 EHRR 563.

[44] There was, however, no breach in *McFeeley* v *UK*, No. 8317/78, 15.5.80, (1980) 20 DR 44; (1981) 3 EHRR 161.

[45] See, e.g., the *Greek Case*, Nos 3321–3/67, 3344/67, 5.11.69; (1969) 12 Yearbook 1. There was, however, no violation on the facts in *Assenov and others* v *Bulgaria* (1999) 28 EHRR 652.

[46] See, e.g., *Chahal* v *UK* (1997) 23 EHRR 413, para. 86.

[47] *HLR* v *France* (1998) 26 EHRR 29, paras 40–41.

[48] But see *Çinar* v *Turkey*, No. 17864/91, 5.9.94: no risk of treatment contrary to Article 3 arising from the death row phenomenon where there was a clear and established policy of not authorising enforcement of the death penalty.

[49] But see *Öcalan* v *Turkey*, No. 46221/99, 14.12.00.

protection and the activities of the individual, 'however undesirable or danger-
ous', cannot be a material consideration. There was therefore no need for the
Court to assess the threat which Mr Chahal allegedly posed to national security.
Article 3 therefore provides wider protection than Articles 32 and 33 of the UN
Convention on the Status of Refugees.

Article 3 may be engaged even where the source of the risk of the proscribed
treatment in the receiving country arises from factors which cannot engage (either
directly or indirectly) the responsibility of the public authorities of that country,
or which in themselves do not infringe Article 3. In *D* v *UK* (1997) 24 EHRR 423
the applicant, who was suffering from the advanced stages of the AIDS virus,
successfully argued that there would be a violation of Article 3 were he to be
removed to St Kitts, where he was born, because the lack of adequate medical
treatment would expose him to inhuman and degrading treatment. The Court did
emphasise that the decision was made 'in the very exceptional circumstances' of
the case and 'given the compelling humanitarian considerations at stake'.[50]

See also below at 7.9.8 in relation to immigration and asylum issues under
Article 8, and at 7.3.4 in relation to discrimination.

7.3.4   Discrimination

Discriminatory treatment may in itself amount to degrading treatment, whether
the discrimination is based on race or on other grounds. Whether Article 3 is
engaged will depend upon the application of the Court's 'severity' test (see above
at 7.3). In the *East African Asians case* (1981) 3 EHRR 76[51], the Commission
reiterated that 'a special importance should be attached to discrimination based on
race; that publicly to single out a group of persons for differential treatment on the
basis of race might, in certain circumstances, constitute a special form of affront
to human dignity ...'. In that case the Commission found that there had been
degrading treatment in violation of Article 3 because of the application of
immigration legislation which prevented British passport holders in East Africa
from obtaining rights of residence in the UK.

In *Smith and Grady* v *UK* (2000) 29 EHRR 493,[52] which concerned the armed
forces ban on homosexuals, the Court held that it 'would not exclude that
treatment which is grounded upon a predisposed bias on the part of a heterosexual
majority against a homosexual minority ... could, in principle, fall within the
scope of Article 3'.

---

[50] See para. 54
[51] The case was never referred to the Court and the Committee of Ministers did not agree on its
resolution. See also *Abdulaziz, Cabales and Balkandali* v *UK* (1985) 7 EHRR 471; and *Hilton* v *UK*
(1976) 4 DR 177, re racial harassment.
[52] See especially paras 117–123.

7.3.5 Child care

The Commission has found that the protection of children (who, it is acknowledged are not capable of looking after themselves because of their age and vulnerability) requires not merely that the criminal law provides protection against treatment prohibited by Article 3, but also that in appropriate circumstances there will be implied a positive obligation on the authorities to take preventive measures to protect a child who is at risk from another individual.[53] There will be a positive obligation on, for example, a local authority to take such steps that could reasonably be expected of it to avoid a real and immediate risk of ill-treatment contrary to Article 3 of which the authority was aware or ought to have been aware. However, in assessing the extent of the obligation on local authorities, any competing interests of parents or other family members under Article 8 will be relevant.

In *Z* v *UK* (1999) 28 EHRR CD 65 the Commission unanimously found a violation of Article 3 arising from the failure of the local authority to take action in respect of the serious ill-treatment and neglect caused to four siblings by their parents over a period of more than four and a half years. This included under-nourishment, insanitary living conditions and physical abuse, causing behavioural disturbances and developmental delays, and such treatment was found to have reached the level of severity prohibited by Article 3.

7.3.6 Corporal punishment

Corporal punishment will violate Article 3 if the minimum threshold is reached, whether it is administered by the judicial system[54] or in state[55] or private[56] schools. In *Costello-Roberts* v *UK* (1995) 19 EHRR 112 there was no violation of Article 3 where a seven-year-old boy had been slippered three times on the buttocks. Relevant factors included the fact that the punishment had been administered in private and there was no evidence of any severe or long-lasting effects.

The state may also be found to be responsible for the failure of the law to protect children against the ill-treatment of others, even those acting in a 'private' capacity. *A* v *UK* (1999) 27 EHRR 611 concerned the applicant nine-year-old child's ill-treatment by his stepfather. The stepfather was prosecuted for assault occasioning actual bodily harm for beating the child with a garden cane, but was acquitted. The applicant complained of a violation of Article 3. The European Court noted that it was a defence to a charge of assault that the treatment in question amounted to 'reasonable chastisement' and despite the fact that the treatment was sufficiently severe to fall within the scope of Article 3, the jury

---

[53] *Z* v *UK* (1999) 28 EHRR CD 65, para. 93.
[54] *Tyrer* v *UK* 2 EHRR 1.
[55] *Campbell and Cosans* v *UK* (1982) 4 EHRR 293.
[56] *Costello-Roberts* v *UK* (1995) 19 EHRR 112.

acquitted the stepfather. Therefore, the Court found that the domestic law did not provide adequate protection against the ill-treatment of the applicant, in violation of Article 3.

7.3.7   Medical treatment

The failure to provide adequate medical treatment may violate Article 3 in certain circumstances, as in *Hurtado* v *Switzerland* (1994) Series A, No. 280-A. In *D* v *UK* (1999) 27 EHRR 611 the lack of adequate medical treatment in St Kitts for an applicant suffering from the AIDS virus, led to a finding of a violation of Article 3 were he to be removed to St Kitts.

7.4   ARTICLE 4: PROHIBITION OF SLAVERY AND FORCED LABOUR

1.   No one shall be held in slavery or servitude.
2.   No one shall be required to perform forced or compulsory labour.
3.   For the purposes of this Article the term 'forced or compulsory labour' shall not include:

(a)   any work required to be done in the ordinary course of detention imposed according to the provisions of Article 5 of this Convention or during conditional release from such detention;

(b)   any service of a military character or, in case of conscientious objectors in countries where they are recognised, service exacted instead of compulsory military service;

(c)   any service exacted in case of an emergency or calamity threatening the life or well-being of the community;

(d)   any work or service which forms part of normal civic obligations.

Article 4 prohibits slavery and servitude absolutely and prohibits forced or compulsory labour subject to the exceptions set out in Article 4(3). According to Article 15 there can never be any derogation from Article 4(1).

The term 'slavery' has not been defined by the Court or Commission. However, in *Ould Barar* v *Sweden* (1999) 28 EHRR CD 213, the Court found that the expulsion of a person to a country where there was an officially recognised regime of slavery might raise an issue under Article 3. The applicant, a Mauritanian national, applied for asylum in Sweden, claiming he had left his country to escape slavery. He stated that he had to report once a year to his father's master and carry out various minor tasks. The Government acknowledged that although slavery was prohibited in Mauritanian law, it appeared that slavery still existed. On the facts, the Court found there was, however, no indication of ill-treatment.

The term servitude implies being compelled to live on someone else's property, as well as being required to work.[57] In *Van Droogenbroeck* v *Belgium* (1982) 4 EHRR 443 the applicant, a persistent criminal offender who was put at the 'disposal of the state' for ten years after his prison sentence expired, was found not to have been held in servitude, as there had been no violation of Article 5(1) in his case and he was found not to have been subjected to a 'particularly serious' form of 'denial of freedom'.

Forced labour involves 'physical or mental constraint', while compulsory labour has been defined as 'work exacted under the menace of any penalty and also performed against the will of the person concerned, that is work for which he has not offered himself voluntarily'.[58] It can include paid work.[59] *Van der Mussele* v *Belgium* (1984) 6 EHRR 163 concerned the obligation on pupil advocates to act without payment when required. The consequence for failing to act pro bono was striking off the role of pupils which was considered to be sufficiently serious enough to amount to a penalty. However, the obligation was found not to amount to 'forced labour' as: the services carried out were not outside the usual ambit of an advocate; there were compensatory advantages arising from his membership of the profession; the services also contributed to his professional training; the obligation ensured that his client obtained legal representation and was therefore 'founded on a conception of social solidarity'; and Mr Van der Mussele was not considered to have suffered a disproportionate burden, having provided only seventeen to eighteen hours of work.

It has not as yet been decided whether employment below the minimum wage level would violate Article 4.

Article 4(3) has the effect of excluding various forms of labour from the prohibition on forced or compulsory labour: work during detention (or during conditional release); military service or work in lieu of military service; emergency work; and work carried out as part of civic obligations.

It does not violate Article 4 to require work in prison, even for insufficient pay. There will also be no breach of Article 4 where a prisoner is forced to work in detention and the conviction is subsequently quashed or where there was no opportunity to challenge the legality of detention, in violation of Article 5(4).[60] In *De Wilde, Ooms and Versyp* v *Belgium* 1 EHRR 373, the work imposed on the applicants, who had given themselves up voluntarily to the police and who were detained under vagrancy laws, was found not to exceed the ordinary limits under Article 4(3)(a) because it was aimed at their rehabilitation and because there were similar laws in other Council of Europe states.

---

[57] *Van Droogenbroeck* v *Belgium* Comm Rep 1980, paras 79–80.
[58] *Van der Mussele* v *Belgium* (1984) 6 EHRR 163, para. 34.
[59] *Van der Mussele* v *Belgium* (1984) 6 EHRR 163, para. 40.
[60] *De Wilde, Ooms and Versyp* v *Belgium* 1 EHRR 373, para. 89.

The term 'normal civic obligations' has been found to include compulsory work for the fire service, or a compulsory financial levy in lieu of such service. However, such obligations which applied to men but not women, were found in *Schmidt* v *Germany* (1994) 18 EHRR 513 to violate Article 14 in conjunction with Article 4(3)(d).

7.5   ARTICLE 5: RIGHT TO LIBERTY AND SECURITY OF THE PERSON

1.   Everyone has the right to liberty and security of person. No one shall be deprived of his liberty save in the following cases and in accordance with a procedure prescribed by law:

(a)   the lawful detention of a person after conviction by a competent court;

(b)   the lawful arrest or detention of a person for non-compliance with the lawful order of a court or in order to secure the fulfilment of any obligation prescribed by law;

(c)   the lawful arrest or detention of a person effected for the purpose of bringing him before the competent legal authority on reasonable suspicion of having committed an offence or when it is reasonably considered necessary to prevent his committing an offence or fleeing after having done so;

(d)   the detention of a minor by lawful order for the purpose of educational supervision or his lawful detention for the purpose of bringing him before the competent legal authority;

(e)   the lawful detention of persons for the prevention of the spreading of infectious diseases, of persons of unsound mind, alcoholics or drug addicts or vagrants;

(f)   the lawful arrest or detention of a person to prevent his effecting an unauthorised entry into the country or of a person against whom action is being taken with a view to deportation or extradition.

2.   Everyone who is arrested shall be informed promptly, in a language which he understands, of the reasons for his arrest and of any charge against him.

3.   Everyone arrested or detained in accordance with the provisions of paragraph 1(c) of this article shall be brought promptly before a judge or other officer authorised by law to exercise judicial power and shall be entitled to trial within a reasonable time or to release pending trial. Release may be conditioned by guarantees to appear for trial.

4.   Everyone who is deprived of his liberty by arrest or detention shall be entitled to take proceedings by which the lawfulness of his detention shall be decided speedily by a court and his release ordered if the detention is not lawful.

5.   Everyone who has been the victim of arrest or detention in contravention of the provisions of this article shall have an enforceable right to compensation.

Article 5 of the Convention is aimed at preventing arbitrary detention and has been one of the most frequently invoked Convention Articles. Article 5 requires that every arrest or detention is lawful (both procedurally and substantively) and that it has in fact been carried out for one of the six specified reasons in sub-paragraphs 5(1)(a) to (f), which amounts to an exhaustive list of circumstances.[61] There are also a number of procedural rights. Anyone arrested must be promptly given the reasons for their arrest, they must be taken promptly before the judicial authorities (if arrested on reasonable suspicion of an offence) and they must be entitled to challenge their detention in court. There must also be a right to compensation whenever any of these requirements has been breached.

One of the first issues to consider in an apparent case of arrest or detention is whether it in fact amounted to a 'deprivation of liberty'. Article 5 is *not* concerned with mere restrictions of freedom of movement,[62] as opposed to arrest or detention. Relevant factors which are taken into account in this respect include the nature, duration, effects and manner of execution of the measure in question. In *Amuur* v *France* (1996) 22 EHRR 533, the Court held that holding the applicant asylum seekers for twenty days in an airport transit zone amounted to a deprivation of liberty, even though they were technically free to return to their country of origin. An important factor in the Court's decision was the lack of legal or social assistance provided to the applicants. Article 5 can be relied on in relation to any 'deprivation of liberty', even if the detention lasts only for a short period.[63] Article 5 will be in issue even where a person gives himself or herself up to be taken into detention.[64]

The requirement that any deprivation of liberty must be in accordance with a procedure prescribed by law means not only that there must be compliance with domestic substantive and procedural rules, but also that prospective detainees are protected from arbitrary action.[65] This means that there must be conformity with the purposes of the restrictions permitted under the relevant sub-paragraph of the Article.[66] Therefore an arrest will violate Article 5 if it is not in fact made for its ostensible purpose. For example, in *Bozano* v *France* (1987) 9 EHRR 297, the applicant's detention breached Article 5(1) when, after the French courts had declined to order his extradition, he was served with a deportation order and forcibly taken by French police to the Swiss border and expelled. Such action was held to amount to a 'disguised form of extradition' designed to circumvent a domestic court ruling.[67] The obligation to comply with the law procedurally

---

[61] *Engel and others* v *Netherlands* 1 EHRR 647, para. 57.

[62] *Engel and others* v *Netherlands* 1 EHRR 647, para. 58. See also *Guzzardi* v *Italy* (1981) 3 EHRR 333, para. 93, where the Court held that the difference between deprivation of and restriction upon liberty was one of degree or intensity, and not one of nature or substance. See also *Riera Blume and others* v *Spain*, No. 37680/97, 14.10.99, paras 28–30, where the Court found the applicants (who were allegedly members of a sect) to have been deprived of their liberty after having been taken by Catalan police to a hotel and confined by their families for ten days and allegedly subjected to a 'deprogramming' process.

[63] See, e.g., *X* v *Austria*, No. 8278/78, 18 DR 154 (1979) and *X and Y* v *Sweden*, No. 7376/76, 7.10.76, (1977) 7 DR 123.

[64] *De Wilde, Ooms and Versyp* v *Belgium* 1 EHRR 373, para. 65.

[65] *Winterwerp* v *Netherlands* 2 EHRR 387, para 45; *Bozano* v *France* (1987) 9 EHRR 297, para. 54.

[66] *Winterwerp* v *Netherlands* 2 EHRR 387, para. 39.

[67] *Bozano* v *France* (1987) 9 EHRR 297, para. 60.

meant that the failure of the courts to hear a voluntary psychiatric patient before she was ordered to be confined compulsorily in hospital for six months (despite the domestic law requiring such a hearing) violated Article 5(1).[68]

Benham v *UK* (1996) 22 EHRR 293 concerned the applicant's imprisonment by the magistrates' court for failing to pay the community charge. The lawfulness of the detention under the domestic law depended on whether or not the magistrates had acted within their jurisdiction. However, the domestic courts had not subsequently had to decide this issue, because the relevant question on appeal was whether or not they had acted in bad faith, rather than whether they had acted within their jurisdiction. The European Court accordingly found that it had not been established that the order for detention was invalid and there was therefore no violation of Article 5(1).

7.5.1 Article 5(1)(a): detention following conviction

Article 5(1)(a) permits detention after conviction by a competent court. There must be a sufficient connection between the conviction and the detention, which must result from and depend upon, or occur by virtue of, a conviction.[69] This provision will be breached, for example, where a court lacks the power to order detention. A conviction has been defined as a finding of guilt and the imposition of a penalty.[70] To be a 'competent court', the body in question must be independent of the parties and of the executive, it must have the power to order release and it should provide appropriate guarantees in the circumstances of the detention in question.[71]

7.5.2 Article 5(1)(b): detention for non-compliance with a court order or to secure compliance with a legal obligation

The first limb of Article 5(1)(b) permits detention for failing to comply with the lawful order of a court, which would allow, for example, an arrest for being in contempt of court or for failing to comply with a court injunction.

The second limb, which provides for detention to secure the fulfilment of an obligation prescribed by law, only concerns cases where the law permits the detention of a person to compel him or her to fulfil a 'specific and concrete obligation'.[72] A detention therefore cannot be justified on the basis of a general duty of obedience to the law. The distinction between these two situations was considered by the Commission in the case of *McVeigh, O'Neill and Evans* v *UK* (1988) 5 EHRR 71 in the context of the United Kingdom's Prevention of

---

[68] *Van der Leer* v *Netherlands* (1990) 12 EHRR 567.
[69] *Weeks* v *UK* (1988) 10 EHRR 293; *B* v *Austria* (1990) Series A, No. 175.
[70] See, e.g., *X* v *UK* (1982) 4 EHRR 188, para. 39.
[71] *De Wilde, Ooms and Versyp* v *Belgium* 1 EHRR 373
[72] *Engel and others* v *Netherlands* 1 EHRR 647, para. 69.

Terrorism legislation. The applicants were arrested in Liverpool on arrival from Ireland, and were detained for about forty-five hours, searched, questioned, photographed and had their fingerprints taken. They were, however, not charged with any offences. Even though there had been no specific prior breach of a legal duty, the Commission found no violation of Article 5(1)(b). The domestic legislation imposed a requirement to 'submit to examination' which the Commission found to be a sufficiently specific and concrete obligation. The Commission did emphasise, however, that the decision was made in the context of measures taken to combat terrorism and specifically noted that the obligation to submit to examination only arose in limited circumstances and had a limited purpose.

7.5.3 Article 5(1)(c): arrest on reasonable suspicion of an offence

Article 5(1)(c) permits an arrest for the purpose of bringing a person before the competent legal authorities (1) on reasonable suspicion of having committed an offence; or (2) where it is reasonably considered necessary to prevent an offence; or (3) where it is reasonably considered necessary to prevent a person fleeing after having committed an offence.

7.5.3.1 The meaning of 'offence'
The approach of the Strasbourg institutions to this question has been to consider in the first place whether or not the provision defining the offence forms part of the domestic criminal law. However, the notion of an offence is an autonomous Convention concept and depends not only upon the domestic classification, but also upon the 'very nature of the offence' and the degree of severity of the penalty.[73] *Steel and others* v *UK* (1999) 28 EHRR 603 concerned the arrest of the applicants on reasonable suspicion of their having committed a breach of the peace. The applicants had been involved in various protests or demonstrations at a grouse shoot, at the site of motorway building works and outside a fighter helicopter sales conference. Although breach of the peace is not a criminal offence according to domestic law,[74] it was found by the Court to be an 'offence' in Convention terms, taking into account the public nature of the duty to keep the peace, the available power of arrest, and the power to imprison anyone who refuses to be bound over to keep the peace. The Court rejected arguments in that case that the concept of breach of the peace was too vague and ambiguous to comply with the requirement of lawfulness under Article 5.[75] However, in

---

[73] *Schmautzer* v *Austria* (1996) 21 EHRR 511, para. 27.
[74] *R* v *County of London Quarter Sessions Appeals Committee, ex parte Metropolitan Police Commissioner* [1948] 1 KB 670 per Lord Goddard CJ at 673.
[75] See also *Öztürk* v *Germany* (1984) 6 EHRR 409, para. 53. The Court in *Steel*, supra, was, however, critical of the vagueness of the binding over order, particularly the requirement to be 'of good behaviour'.

Hashman and Harrup v *UK* (2000) 30 EHRR 241, where the applicant hunt saboteurs had been bound over to keep the peace and not to behave *contra bonos mores*, the Court held that the term *contra bonos mores* was so generally defined that it failed the 'prescribed by law' test (see above at 7.5).

What amounts to an 'offence' has also been considered in relation to the definition of terrorism in United Kingdom legislation as 'the use of violence for political ends', which includes 'the use of violence for the purpose of putting the public or any section of the public in fear'. In *Ireland* v *UK* 2 EHRR 25 such a definition was said by the Court to be 'well in keeping with the idea of an offence'. This position was confirmed by the Court in *Brogan and others* v *UK* (1989) 11 EHRR 117.

The second limb of Article 5(1)(c) would only allow detention to prevent the commission of a concrete and specific offence. It does not provide a general preventive power of detention.[76]

7.5.3.2   *Reasonable suspicion*

An arrest on reasonable suspicion of having committed an offence will not necessarily violate Article 5 if the detainee is not subsequently charged or taken before the magistrates' court, provided that the arrest had been made for that *purpose.*[77] This requirement applies to each of the circumstances in which an arrest may be lawful under Article 5(1)(c).[78] There is no requirement that the police should have obtained sufficient evidence to bring charges, either at the point of arrest, or while a person is in custody. The legality of continued detention depends upon the reasonable suspicion of the detainee persisting.[79]

The concept of 'reasonable suspicion' was defined by the Court in *Fox, Campbell and Hartley* v *UK* (1991) 13 EHRR 157 as meaning 'the existence of facts or information which would satisfy an objective observer that the person concerned may have committed the offence'. What is regarded as 'reasonable' will depend upon all the relevant circumstances. The Court found in that case that in the context of dealing with 'terrorist-type' offences in Northern Ireland, the reasonableness of the suspicion justifying such arrests could not always be judged according to the same standards as are applied in dealing with 'conventional crime'. However, the Court stressed that the exigencies of dealing with terrorism could not justify stretching the notion of 'reasonableness' to the point where the essence of the safeguard was impaired. Where, as in that case, the domestic law did not require 'reasonable suspicion' as such (but only 'honest suspicion'), the Court would have to have at least some facts or information capable of satisfying it that the arrested person had been reasonably suspected of having committed an

---

[76] But see *Eriksen* v *Norway* (2000) 29 EHRR 328.
[77] See, e.g., *Brogan and others* v *UK* (1989) 11 EHRR 117, para. 53.
[78] *Lawless* v *Ireland (No. 3)* 1 EHRR 15, para. 14.
[79] *Stögmüller* v *Austria* 1 EHRR 155, para. 4.

offence. Such evidence was not available (previous convictions for terrorist offences not being sufficient) and the Court found a violation of Article 5(1).

In *Murray* v *UK* (1995) 19 EHRR 193 the Court found that a material factor as to the level of suspicion required was the length of the deprivation of liberty at risk (limited to a maximum of four hours in *Murray*). No breach of Article 5(1)(c) was found in that case as the Court was satisfied that there was sufficient evidence to provide a 'plausible and objective basis' for a suspicion that the applicant may have been involved in collecting funds for the IRA.[80]

The requirement in Article 5(1)(c) to make an arrest only for the purpose of bringing a person before the competent legal authority should also be read in conjunction with Article 5(3) (see below at 7.5.8).

The third limb of Article 5(1)(c) requires reasonable grounds for believing that an offence has been committed. Accordingly, there is a substantial degree of overlap with the first limb.

7.5.4   Article 5(1)(d): detention of minors

Article 5(1)(d) permits the detention of minors (persons under 18) either by lawful order for the purpose of educational supervision, or lawful detention for the purpose of bringing them before the competent legal authority. In *Bouamar* v *Belgium* (1989) 11 EHRR 1 the applicant minor, who was suspected of various offences, was repeatedly detained in a remand prison on nine occasions on the interim orders of a juvenile court. The Court found that Article 5(1)(d) did not prevent an interim custody measure as a preliminary to a regime of supervised education, but such a regime had to be applied speedily following imprisonment. There was a violation of Article 5(1) in *Bouamar* because of the failure to implement such a regime.

7.5.5   Article 5(1)(e): detention of persons of unsound mind, alcoholics and vagrants etc.

Article 5(1)(e) provides for the lawful detention, for the prevention of the spreading of infectious diseases, of persons of unsound mind, alcoholics or drug addicts or vagrants. The Court has emphasised that the justification for the detention of persons in such categories is not only their danger to public safety, but also that detention may be necessary for their own interests.[81]

The term 'unsound mind' has not been defined by the Strasbourg organs, as its meaning is considered to be continually evolving, but there must be objective medical evidence of unsound mind (other than in emergencies). The disorder must also be such that it requires compulsory confinement and the detention can

---

[80] See para. 63.
[81] See, e.g., *Witold Litwa* v *Poland*, No. 26629/95, 4.4.00, para. 60.

only continue to be justified by the persistence of the disorder.[82] The Court has held that the lawfulness of the detention under Article 5(1)(e) will also depend upon detention in a hospital, clinic or other appropriate authorised institution, but subject to that, it has no bearing on the appropriateness of the treatment or conditions.[83] In *Johnson* v *UK* (1999) 27 EHRR 196, the release of the applicant, who had been detained under the Mental Health Act 1983, was ordered by the Mental Health Review Tribunal, conditional upon his living in a supervised hostel. However, his release was delayed because of the unavailability of a suitable hostel, which the Court found amounted to a violation of Article 5(1)(e) as in the circumstances the onus was on the state to provide suitable accommodation.

In *Witold Litwa* v *Poland*, No. 26629/95, 4.4.00, the Court held that the term 'alcoholics' should be interpreted in the light of the object and purpose of Article 5 and therefore the Article permits the detention of persons in a clinical state of 'alcoholism' as well as persons who are not medically diagnosed as alcoholics but whose conduct and behaviour under the influence of alcohol poses a threat to public order or themselves.

'Vagrancy' has not been defined, but in *De Wilde, Ooms and Versyp* v *Belgium* 1 EHRR 373,[84] the Court accepted that the then Belgian definition ('persons who have no fixed abode, no means of subsistence and no regular trade or profession') fell within the ambit of Article 5(1)(e) of the Convention.

7.5.6   Article 5(1)(f): detention relating to immigration, deportation or extradition

Article 5(1)(f) permits the lawful arrest or detention of persons to prevent their effecting an unauthorised entry into the country, or of a person against whom action is being taken with a view to deportation or extradition. The arrest must therefore be lawful according to domestic law and not arbitrary. There was a violation of this Article in the case of *Bozano* v *France* (1987) 9 EHRR 297 following the applicant's forcible removal at night by French police officers to the Swiss border where he was taken into Swiss police custody.

Article 5(1)(f) does not require that the detention be reasonably considered necessary, for example, to prevent the commission of an offence or to prevent a person fleeing. In fact, all that is required is that 'action is being taken with a view to deportation' and it is irrelevant whether the underlying decision to expel can be justified under national or Convention law.[85] However, detention under Article 5(1)(f) does require deportation proceedings to be in progress and to be

---

[82] See *Winterwerp* v *Netherlands* 2 EHRR 387, para. 39.

[83] *Ashingdane* v *UK* (1985) 7 EHRR 528, para. 44.

[84] See especially para. 68; see also *Guzzardi* v *Italy* (1981) 3 EHRR 333, para. 98.

[85] See, e.g., *Chahal* v *UK* (1997) 23 EHRR 413, para. 112.

prosecuted with due diligence.[86] In *Chahal* v *UK* (1997) 23 EHRR 413 the continued detention of the applicant, pending deportation, for more than three and a half years was found 'to give rise to serious concern', but was not held to violate this Article, in view of the complexity and the exceptional circumstances of the proceedings.[87]

7.5.7 Reasons for arrest

Article 5(2) requires reasons to be given promptly following any arrest or detention (see also below at 7.6.12 re provision of information on charge), including detention of a mental patient.[88] This has been interpreted by the Court as meaning that any arrested person 'must be told, in simple, non-technical language that he can understand, the essential legal and factual grounds for his arrest, so as to be able, if he sees fit, to apply to a court to challenge its lawfulness' in accordance with Article 5(4).[89] Written reasons are not required.

All of the requisite information need not, however, be provided by the arresting officer at the moment of arrest.[90] The applicants in *Fox, Campbell and Hartley* v *UK* were told on being taken into custody that they had been arrested under section 11 of the Northern Ireland (Emergency Provisions) Act 1978 on suspicion of being terrorists. That was found to be insufficient to meet the requirements of Article 5(2), but their subsequent interrogation by the police as to their suspected involvement in specific criminal offences and as to their membership of proscribed organisations was found to satisfy the Article. The fact that the questioning took place several hours after the applicants' arrests was nevertheless found to comply with the obligation to act promptly (the applicant was found to have been notified within six hours and twenty minutes of arrest). In *O'Hara* v *UK*, No. 37555/97, 14.3.00, notification during interview within six to eight hours of arrest was found to comply with the requirement of promptness. Similarly, in *Murray* v *UK* (1995) 19 EHRR 193 the reasons for the applicant's arrest were sufficiently brought to her attention during her subsequent interview. It should be noted that each of these cases was decided in the context of investigations into terrorism and it is suggested that these periods may not be sufficiently prompt in 'non-terrorism' cases.

7.5.8 Article 5(3): right to release pending trial

The first limb of Article 5(3) requires that an accused be brought promptly before a judge or other officer authorised by law to exercise judicial power. This

---

[86] *Quinn* v *France* (1996) 21 EHRR 529, para. 48.
[87] The Commission, however, had unanimously found a violation of Article 5(1).
[88] *Van der Leer* v *Netherlands* (1990) 12 EHRR 567, paras 27–29.
[89] *Fox, Campbell and Hartley* v *UK* (1991) 13 EHRR 157, para. 40.
[90] Ibid.

obligation has led to findings of violations against the UK in relation to detention of suspects in Northern Ireland. The issue of promptness depends upon an assessment of the 'special features' of each case.[91] In *Brogan and others v UK* (1989) 11 EHRR 117, periods of detention of four days and six hours, up to six days and sixteen and a half hours were held to violate the requirements of Article 5(3). Following that case, the UK Government entered a derogation under Article 15 of the Convention (relating to terrorism connected with the affairs of Northern Ireland). In the subsequent case of *Brannigan and McBride v UK* (1994) 17 EHRR 539 detentions for longer periods were also found to breach the same Article, but the derogation was found to comply with Article 15 and the applicants were therefore prevented from validly claiming a violation of the Convention.

The second limb of Article 5(3) provides for an entitlement 'to trial within a reasonable time or to release pending trial'. However, the Court has found that these are not alternatives: there is a right to be released pending trial unless detention can be justified.[92] Control must be exercised by a judicial officer who is independent of both the executive and the parties to the proceedings. The judge should review the circumstances for and against detention and decide 'by reference to legal criteria, whether there are reasons to justify detention'.[93] If not, the accused should be released. If the judge lacks the power to order release then Article 5(3) will be violated. In *Caballero v UK* (2000) 30 EHRR 643,[94] Article 5(3) was violated because of the effect of section 25 of the Criminal Justice and Public Order Act 1994 which was automatically to deny bail to anyone charged with certain serious offences and who had a previous conviction for any of those offences. In those circumstances, the magistrates' court had no power to order Mr Caballero's release.

Whilst there must continue to be reasonable suspicion of the accused's involvement in an offence for the detention to continue, that will not be enough in itself to satisfy the Article 5(3) requirements: 'after a certain lapse of time, it no longer suffices; the court must then establish whether the other grounds cited by the judicial authorities continue to justify the deprivation of liberty'.[95] The grounds must be both 'relevant' and 'sufficient' and the Court must consider whether the national authorities showed 'special diligence' in conducting the proceedings. Relevant grounds have been held to be a danger of absconding,[96]

---

[91] *Wemhoff v Germany* 1 EHRR 55, para. 10; *De Jong, Baljet and Van Den Brink v Netherlands* (1986) 8 EHRR 20, para. 52.

[92] *Wemhoff v Germany* 1 EHRR 55, paras 4–5.

[93] *Schiesser v Switzerland* 2 EHRR 417, para. 31.

[94] For full reasoning in that case see the Commission Report of 30.6.98 and the case study in chapter 11.

[95] *Letellier v France* (1992) 14 EHRR 83, para. 35.

[96] See, e.g., *Letellier v France* (1992) 14 EHRR 83 and *Tomasi v France* (1993) 15 EHRR 1.

interference with the course of justice,[97] the prevention of crime[98] and the preservation of public order.[99]

Article 5(3) also provides that 'release may be conditioned by guarantees to appear for trial'. Conditions which have been found to be permissible include residence requirements, an obligation to surrender travel documents and the imposition of a surety.

The right to trial within a reasonable time under Article 5(3) overlaps with the similar requirement in Article 6(1). Under Article 5(3), time will run from the initial arrest until first instance conviction or acquittal and/or sentence, but not appeal proceedings (which are covered by Article 6(1)). Rather than lay down specific time limits or even rigid criteria, the Court has stated that continued pre-trial detention must be justified by relevant and sufficient reasons. See also below at 7.6.8 in relation to Article 6(1).

7.5.9   Article 5(4): right of access to court to challenge detention

According to Article 5(4), everyone who is deprived of their liberty by arrest or detention is entitled to take proceedings to challenge the 'lawfulness' of the detention (in terms both of domestic and Convention law). Such proceedings should be decided by a body with the powers of a 'court' (see the relevant requirements set out above at 7.5.1 in relation to Article 5(1)(a)), including the power to order release if the detention is found to be unlawful.

The extent of the remedy required will depend upon the type of detention. In *Brogan and others* v *UK* (1989) 11 EHRR 117, for example, the Court acknowledged that the habeas corpus procedure satisfied the requirements of Article 5(4). However, in *Chahal* v *UK* (1997) 23 EHRR 413, the Court found that neither habeas corpus, nor judicial review, nor the 'advisory panel procedure' were sufficient to challenge detention on the grounds of national security. Article 5(4) necessarily implies various procedural requirements which in general will be similar to the obligations imposed by Article 6, but they may not always be the same and they will vary according to the deprivation of liberty in question.[100] The remedy must of course be available in practice, not just in theory.[101]

The Article 5(4) guarantees also apply to situations where the relevant factors justifying detention may change over time. In those circumstances, there must be periodic reviews of the need for continued detention. Accordingly, the Court has held that there must be periodic reviews of the lawfulness of detention of mental

[97] See, e.g., *Clooth* v *Belgium* (1992) 14 EHRR 717.
[98] See, e.g., *Muller* v *France*, No. 21802/93, 17.3.97.
[99] See, e.g., *Letellier* v *France* (1992) 14 EHRR 83.
[100] See, e.g., *Winterwerp* v *Netherlands* 2 EHRR 387; *Wassink* v *Netherlands* (1990) Series A, No. 185–A.
[101] *RMD* v *Switzerland* (1999) 28 EHRR 224.

health patients,[102] those sentenced to a discretionary life sentence (after expiry of the tariff period)[103] and juveniles sentenced to detention during Her Majesty's Pleasure.[104]

Article 5(4) requires that the determination by the Court must be carried out 'speedily', which will depend upon the circumstances of each case, including any delays caused by both the detainee and the authorities.[105] The initial review should take place particularly quickly. This requirement under Article 5(4) is much stricter than the right under Article 6(1) to a fair hearing within a reasonable time (see below at 7.6.8).

7.5.10   Article 5(5): right to compensation for unlawful detention

Article 5(5) provides for the right of a person arrested or detained unlawfully to an enforceable right to compensation. Therefore, for the Court to find a violation of Article 5(5), there must be a finding of a violation of one or more elements of Article 5. A requirement that the detainee must have suffered damage in order to claim compensation does not contravene Article 5(5), but 'damage' includes both pecuniary and non-pecuniary loss.

In cases such as *Fox*, *Campbell* and *Hartley*, *Brogan*, *Brannigan* and *McBride* and *Caballero* there was no such enforceable claim to compensation available to the applicants, and so in each case the Court found the UK in violation of Article 5(5).

7.6   ARTICLE 6: THE RIGHT TO A FAIR HEARING

1.   In the determination of his civil rights and obligations or of any criminal charge against him, everyone is entitled to a fair and public hearing within a reasonable time by an independent and impartial tribunal established by law. Judgment shall be pronounced publicly but the press and public may be excluded from all or part of the trial in the interests of morals, public order or national security in a democratic society, where the interests of juveniles or the protection of the private life of the parties so require, or to the extent strictly necessary in the opinion of the court in special circumstances where publicity would prejudice the interests of justice.

2.   Everyone charged with a criminal offence shall be presumed innocent until proved guilty according to law.

3.   Everyone charged with a criminal offence has the following minimum rights:

     (a)   to be informed promptly, in a language which he understands and in detail, of the nature and cause of the accusation against him;

     (b)   to have adequate time and facilities for the preparation of his defence;

---

[102] See, e.g., *X* v *UK* (1982) 4 EHRR 188, paras 58–61.
[103] *Thynne, Wilson and Gunnell* v *UK* (1991) 13 EHRR 666, paras 68–80.
[104] *Hussain* v *UK* (1996) 22 EHRR 1, para. 54; and see *T and V* v *UK* (2000) 30 EHRR 121.
[105] See, e.g., *Sanchez-Reisse* v *Switzerland* (1987) 9 EHRR 71.

(c) to defend himself in person or through legal assistance of his own choosing or, if he has not sufficient means to pay for legal assistance, to be given it free when the interests of justice so require;

(d) to examine or have examined witnesses against him and to obtain the attendance and examination of witnesses on his behalf under the same conditions as witnesses against him;

(e) to have the free assistance of an interpreter if he cannot understand or speak the language used in court.

The general requirement set out in Article 6(1) for a fair hearing applies to both criminal and civil proceedings, but the additional rights set out in Articles 6(2) and 6(3) apply only in criminal cases. The rights set out in Article 6(3) are aspects of the general right to a fair trial and are not therefore exhaustive.

Despite its fundamental importance, Article 15 does not preclude derogation from Article 6.

7.6.1 The criminal/civil distinction

The distinction between the Convention classification of cases as being 'civil' or 'criminal' is important as Article 6(1) applies to both types of proceedings, but Articles 6(2) and 6(3) only apply to proceedings classified according to the Convention as criminal.

The terms 'civil rights' and 'criminal charge' are autonomous Convention concepts. Therefore, the domestic classification of proceedings may be relevant, but will not necessarily be decisive.

In assessing whether proceedings are criminal in nature, the Court will consider the nature of the proceedings in question and the nature and degree of severity of the penalty. For example, proceedings for the non-payment of the community charge in the UK were classified in domestic law as being civil. However, in *Benham* v *UK* (1996) 22 EHRR 293 the Court found such proceedings to be criminal in nature, on the basis that they were brought by a public authority under statutory powers of enforcement and that the applicant faced a maximum penalty of three months' imprisonment and had in fact been ordered to be imprisoned for thirty days.

In criminal cases, Article 6 will usually apply as from the time when a suspect is charged, but it may apply earlier (such as from the point of arrest) where a suspect's situation has been 'substantially affected' by any other measure.[106]

7.6.2 The application of Article 6 to civil proceedings

For Article 6 to apply in civil cases, there are three requirements:

(a) that there is a *civil right or obligation* in issue; and

---

[106] See, e.g., *Eckle* v *Germany* (1983) 5 EHRR 1, para. 73. See also *Heaney and McGuinness* v *Ireland*, No. 34720/97, 21.12.00, para. 42; *Quinn* v *Ireland*, No. 36887/97, 21.12.00, para. 42.

   (b)   that there is a *dispute* in relation to a civil right; and

   (c)   that there is a *determination* of such a dispute.

In general, a 'civil right' will amount to a private law right, rather than a public law right. The term has an autonomous meaning and so the domestic law classification may be relevant, but will not be decisive. Therefore, 'civil rights' clearly arise, for example, in the context of tort and family law. Public law proceedings may also fall within the ambit of Article 6(1) if they are decisive of a private law right (such as pecuniary rights). The distinction may not always be obvious and has understandably been criticised as being vague and unclear.[107] For example, the Court has found the following to amount to 'civil rights': the right to property in the context of planning proceedings;[108] the right to statutory sickness allowance[109] and disability allowance;[110] the right to practise a profession (in relation to the individual's pecuniary interests);[111] the right to operate a commercial venture, for example, in the context of the removal of a licence;[112] and a civil claim for compensation against the state.[113]

The following have been found *not* to amount to 'civil rights': the right to stand for election,[114] the discretionary award of compensation following acquittal in criminal proceedings[115] and the right to freedom of movement within the EU.[116]

Article 6(1) will apply to private law disputes as between private employers and their employees, but public officials whose posts involve the exercise of powers conferred by public law generally fall outside its scope.[117]

The second condition is the existence of an actionable claim in domestic law in relation to the civil right in question. This requirement has created most contention in cases where there has been a procedural limitation to a substantive right. For example, in *Osman* v *UK* (2000) 29 EHRR 245[118], the Government argued that there was no substantive right in domestic law to sue the police in negligence for failing to prevent the shooting of the second applicant and his son and therefore Article 6(1) had no application. The European Court, however, found that Article 6(1) was applicable on the basis that the applicants did have a right to sue in negligence which had been subject to a rule, applied by the

---

[107] P. Van Dijk, 'The interpretation of "civil rights and obligations" by the European Court of Human Rights — one more step to take', in *Protecting Human Rights: the European Dimension* (1990).

[108] See, e.g., *Bryan* v *UK* (1996) 21 EHRR 342.

[109] *Feldbrugge* v *Netherlands* (1986) 8 EHRR 425.

[110] *Salesi* v *Italy* No. 13023/87, 26.2.93.

[111] *De Moor* v *Belgium* (1994) 18 EHRR 372.

[112] See, e.g., *Bentham* v *Netherlands* (1986) 8 EHRR 1.

[113] See, e.g., *Aksoy* v *Turkey* (1997) 23 EHRR 553.

[114] *Pierre-Bloch* v *France* (1998) 26 EHRR 202.

[115] *Masson and van Zon* v *Netherlands* (1996) 22 EHRR 491.

[116] *Adams and Benn* v *UK* (1997) 23 EHRR CD160.

[117] *Pellegrin* v *France*, No. 28541/95, 18.12.99.

[118] Discussed further below at 7.6.3. But see also *Powell and Rayner* v *UK* (1990) 12 EHRR 355.

domestic courts on public policy grounds, excluding the police from liability in negligence in the context of the investigation and suppression of crime. In *TP and KM v UK*, No. 28945/95, 10.9.99 the Commission was split ten to nine in finding that the striking out on public policy grounds of a negligence claim against a local authority for failing to prevent a child's ill-treatment amounted to a restriction on an existing civil right which violated Article 6. On the other hand, the child's mother had had no arguable claim in domestic law, because she was owed no duty of care, and therefore Article 6 did not apply.

The third condition is that the procedure must lead to a *determination* of a 'civil right'. The result of the proceedings in question must be 'directly decisive' of a 'civil right'; mere tenuous connections or remote consequences will not bring Article 6 into play. In *Fayed v UK* (1994) 18 EHRR 393, the applicants complained about the publication of a report by Government inspectors about the House of Fraser company. They argued that the inspectors' findings of dishonesty meant that the inquiry was decisive for their civil right to a good reputation. However, the Court held that the inspectors' functions were essentially investigative and were not determinative of any of the applicants' civil rights. Proceedings determining liability for costs and in relation to enforcement will also be subject to Article 6(1).

Where a determination is made by an administrative body which does not comply with Article 6(1), there may nevertheless be no breach of the Convention if that body is subject to a court or tribunal which does provide the Article 6(1) protections (see 7.6.9 below).[119] The availability of judicial review proceedings before the High Court may satisfy the Article 6 standards (but see *Kingsley v UK*, No. 35605/97, 7.11.00).

Specific aspects of the right to a fair trial in civil, as well as criminal, proceedings are discussed below at 7.6.3 to 7.6.9.

7.6.3 Access to court

Although not expressly referred to in Article 6, the European Court has found the right of access to court to be an inherent element of Article 6.[120] The effective exercise of this right may create other obligations on the state, such as the provision of legal aid in civil proceedings[121] where legal representation is made compulsory for certain types of litigation or simply because of the complexity of the procedure or the particular case. In *Faulkner v UK*,[122] the unavailability of civil legal aid in Guernsey was found to violate the applicant's right of access to court.

---

[119] See, e.g., *Bryan v UK* (1996) 21 EHRR 342.

[120] *Golder v UK* 1 EHRR 524.

[121] *Airey v Ireland* 2 EHRR 305.

[122] The case was settled before the Court, inter alia, on the Government's undertaking to establish a civil legal aid system in Guernsey (Judgment of 30.11.99).

The state is left a free choice of the means to secure the right of access to court which may be subject to limitations, provided that they do not impair the very essence of the right,[123] and provided that they are in pursuance of a legitimate aim and are proportionate. Limitations considered by the Court have included, for example, the imposition of security for costs,[124] restrictions on the right to bring proceedings by particular categories of litigants[125] and limitation periods.[126]

Another limitation is immunity from suit, which was considered by the Court in *Osman* v *UK* (2000) 29 EHRR 245, which concerned the 'civil right' to bring proceedings in negligence. There, the Court found a violation of Article 6 arising from the domestic courts' application of the immunity that the police enjoyed from liability in negligence in relation to the investigation and suppression of crime. Ahmet Osman had been injured (and his father shot dead) by a former teacher who had developed an obsession with him. The shooting followed a series of incidents involving the teacher which had been reported to the police. The applicants (Ahmet Osman and his mother) brought negligence proceedings against the police for failing to take adequate measures to apprehend the teacher. The action was struck out by the Court of Appeal on the basis that public policy required immunity from suit for the police in such situations. It was considered that the imposition of liability in negligence might lead to 'detrimentally defensive' policing and that a great deal of police time, trouble and expense might be diverted away from the suppression of crime and into defending litigation and that the threat of litigation itself would be a distraction.[127] The European Court, however, unanimously found that the application of the exclusion of liability, without consideration of competing public interest factors, operated in a disproportionate manner to restrict the applicants' right of access to court, in violation of Article 6(1). In coming to this conclusion, the Court noted that the applicants had satisfied the proximity test applied in negligence proceedings and that this test would serve as a threshold to limit the number of negligence cases against the police that would be likely to proceed to trial.

7.6.4   Fair hearing

The right to a fair hearing in Article 6(1) applies both to criminal and civil proceedings. The Court has constantly emphasised that its role is to consider

---

[123] *Winterwerp* v *Netherlands* 2 EHRR 387.
[124] See, e.g., *Tolstoy Miloslavsky* v *UK* (1995) 20 EHRR 442, para. 59 and *Ait-Mouhoub* v *France* [1999] EHRLR 215.
[125] *Winterwerp* v *Netherlands* 2 EHRR 387.
[126] *Stubbings* v *UK* (1997) 23 EHRR 213.
[127] *Osman and another* v *Ferguson and another* [1993] 4 All ER 344. See also, *Hill* v *Chief Constable of West Yorkshire* [1989] AC 53 and *Swinney and another* v *Chief Constable of Northumbria* [1996] 3 All ER 449.

whether the proceedings as a whole were fair.[128] The Court may overlook minor infringements provided that overall the proceedings were fair and, conversely, unfairness may still arise even though the relevant formal requirements may have been complied with. The Court has reiterated that it will not be concerned with applicants' complaints about errors of fact or law committed by domestic courts, unless rights protected by the Convention have as a result been infringed. It is not a 'court of appeal' from the domestic courts.

For example, the Court has held that it is a requirement of fairness that the prosecuting authorities disclose to the defence all material evidence for or against the accused. The failure to do so gave rise to a defect in the trial proceedings in *Edwards* v *UK* (1993) 15 EHRR 417, but there was no violation of Article 6 as the defects in the original trial were found to have been remedied by the subsequent procedure before the Court of Appeal which had examined the transcript of the trial and considered the impact of the new information on the conviction.

The application of this general principle is discussed further below in relation to the following aspects: admissibility of evidence (7.6.5); privilege against self-incrimination and the right to silence (7.6.6); and equality of arms (7.6.7).

7.6.5 Admissibility of evidence

Article 6 does not lay down any rules as to the admissibility of evidence as such, which is considered to be primarily a matter for domestic regulation.[129] The Court has declined to decide whether, as a matter of principle, unlawfully obtained evidence should be inadmissible, but will consider whether the proceedings as a whole, including the way in which evidence was obtained, were fair. This will entail an examination of the 'unlawfulness' in question and the nature of any violation of another Convention right. The applicant in *Khan* v *UK*, No. 35394/97, 12.5.00 complained about the admission in evidence of material obtained from a police bugging device, the use of which was found by the Court to violate Article 8 because of the lack of any domestic legal regulation. Applying the overall fairness test, the Court found no violation of Article 6. It was noted that the use of the listening device had not been contrary to domestic criminal law and whilst the material was the only evidence against the applicant, it was considered to be very strong evidence. Finally, the Court noted that the applicant had had ample opportunity to challenge the authenticity and use of the recording and that the domestic courts had assessed the effect of the admission of the evidence on the fairness of the trial.

---

[128] See, e.g. *Khan* v *UK*, No. 35394/97, 12.5.00, paras 34 and 38.

[129] See, e.g., *Schenk* v *Switzerland* (1991) 13 EHRR 242 and *Teixeira de Castro* v *Portugal* (1999) 28 EHRR 101.

See also below at 7.6.14 as to the attendance and examination of witnesses.

7.6.6   Privilege against self-incrimination and the right to silence

The Court has found that the privilege against self-incrimination and the right to silence are at the heart of the notion of a fair procedure under Article 6. These rights have usually been considered by the Court in relation to Article 6(1), rather than Article 6(2).[130] The privilege against self-incrimination may be invoked in order to prevent the use of certain evidence in criminal proceedings, although it may not prevent the authorities from obtaining the information, as in *Saunders* v *UK* (1997) 23 EHRR 313[131]. There, the admission in evidence in criminal proceedings of statements taken by DTI inspectors under statutory powers of compulsion, was found to violate the privilege against self-incrimination.

The privilege against self-incrimination is primarily concerned with respecting the right of the accused to remain silent. It does not prevent the admission in evidence of material which has an existence independent of the will of the suspect, such as breath, blood or urine samples, bodily tissue for the purpose of DNA testing, or documents obtained under a warrant.[132]

The right to silence is not an absolute right, but the drawing of adverse inferences from silence may violate Article 6, depending on all the circumstances of the case, including the situations where inferences may be drawn, the weight attached to them by the national courts in their assessment of the evidence and the degree of compulsion involved. It will be incompatible with the right to silence to found a conviction solely or mainly on the accused's silence or on a refusal to answer questions or give evidence. However, the accused's silence may be taken into account in situations which clearly call for an explanation.[133]

In *Condron* v *UK*, No. 35718/97, 2.5.00, the applicants remained silent when interviewed by the police on advice from their solicitor that they were unfit to answer questions, because of the effect of drugs. The Court found that Article 6 had been violated because of the insufficient direction to the jury: 'as a matter of fairness, the jury should have been directed that if it was satisfied that the applicants' silence at the police interview could not sensibly be attributed to their having no answer or none that would stand up to cross-examination it should not draw an adverse inference'. This was particularly important given that it was impossible to know what weight was given to the applicants' silence by the jury. The European Court also noted that the Court of Appeal had no means of making that assessment and was concerned with the 'safety' of the conviction, rather than whether there had been a fair trial.

---

[130] But see, e.g., *Heaney and McGuinness* v *Ireland*, No. 34720/97, 21.12.00 and *Quinn* v *Ireland*, No. 36887/97, 21.12.00 – violations of both Article 6(1) and 6(2).

[131] See also *IJL, GMR and AKP* v *UK*, Nos 29522/95, 30056/96 and 30574/96, Judgment of 19.9.00. But see *Staines* v *UK*, No. 41552/98, 16.5.00.

[132] *Saunders* v *UK* (1997) 23 EHRR 313, para. 69.

[133] *John Murray* v *UK* (1996) 22 EHRR 29, paras 44–47.

7.6.7 Equality of arms

The principle of 'equality of arms' is a fundamental aspect of the broader right to a fair hearing and applies in both criminal and civil cases. It has been defined by the Court as requiring 'that each party must be afforded a reasonable opportunity to present his case under conditions that do not place him at a substantial disadvantage *vis-à-vis* his opponent'.[134] The principle has application, for example, in relation to the duty of disclosure,[135] and to the failure to admit evidence or to hear or allow the cross-examination of witnesses. In relation to criminal proceedings, it is therefore likely to overlap with other constituent rights in Article 6(3) (see below at 7.6.11).

7.6.8 Rights relating to hearings and judgments

The right to a public hearing[136] is expressly included in Article 6(1), as is the public pronouncement of judgments. The press and public may only be excluded for the reasons set out in the Article. In criminal cases there is a general right for the accused to be present at the hearing, although this right may be waived and trial in absentia may be permissible. The right to a public hearing can also be waived, provided that waiver is unequivocal and that there are no public interest reasons for the public's presence. It is not always necessary for administrative or other tribunals determining 'civil rights' to hold public hearings, provided that a public appeal court hearing is available.

The prosecution of children will raise particular issues as to their ability to participate effectively in criminal proceedings. Full account must be taken of their age, level of maturity and intellectual and emotional capacities and steps must be taken to promote their ability to understand and participate in the proceedings. There was a violation of Article 6(1) in *T and V v UK* (2000) 30 EHRR 121, arising from the Crown Court trial of eleven-year-old defendants for murder, because of the incomprehensible and intimidating formality and ritual of the court, which was accompanied by a blaze of publicity, and the defendants' inability to follow the proceedings and take decisions in their own best interests.

Although Article 6 does not provide on its face for limiting the public pronouncement of a judgment, the right has in fact been found to be satisfied by its publication in writing.[137] There is a duty under Article 6 to give reasons in both civil and criminal cases, although the extent of the reasoning required will vary depending on the nature of the decision.

---

[134] See, e.g., *De Haes and Gijsels v Belgium* (1998) 25 EHRR 1.
[135] See, e.g., *McMichael v UK* (1995) 20 EHRR 205 and *Feldbrugge v the Netherlands* (1986) 8 EHRR 425.
[136] See, e.g., *Scarth v UK*, No. 33745/96, 22.7.99.
[137] *Pretto and others v Italy* (1984) 6 EHRR 182.

The right to a hearing within a reasonable time applies to both civil and criminal proceedings. In civil cases time will generally start to run from the outset of the proceedings and in criminal cases from charge, and will continue until the proceedings are determined, including appeals processes. The Court will not lay down particular time limits: what is 'reasonable' will depend upon the particular circumstances of each case, taking into account its complexity, the extent to which the authorities, other parties or the applicant are responsible for any delays, and what is at stake for the applicant.[138] For example, in *Robins* v *UK* (1998) 26 EHRR 527 the Court found that a period of more than four years to resolve straightforward costs proceedings, in part due to unjustifiable delays caused by the court and the Department of Social Security, violated the reasonable time requirement in Article 6(1). In *Cherakrak* v *France*, No. 34075/96, 2.8.00 criminal proceedings which had lasted for four years and nine months were found to violate Article 6(1).

7.6.9 Independent and impartial tribunal established by law

Article 6(1) expressly includes the right to a hearing by an independent and impartial tribunal established by law. This must be a body capable of reaching binding decisions. The test of independence applied by the Court (in both civil and criminal proceedings) includes consideration of the following: the manner of appointment of the tribunal's members, their term of office, the existence of guarantees against outside pressure and whether the tribunal presents an appearance of independence. In *Bryan* v *UK* (1996) 21 EHRR 342, the Court found that a planning inspector did not have the requisite appearance of independence, given that the Home Secretary could at any time revoke the inspector's power to decide an appeal and in circumstances where the policies of the executive could be in issue (even where the power had not in fact been exercised). However, even where an adjudicatory body determining disputes over civil rights does not comply with Article 6(1), there will be no violation where that body is itself subject to the control of an Article 6-compliant judicial body with full jurisdiction. In *Bryan*, the scope of the review of the inspector's decision provided by the High Court was found to be sufficient. This can be contrasted with, for example, *Kingsley* v *UK*, No. 35605/97, 7.11.00 where judicial review was found to be insufficient as, where the applicant complained of lack of impartiality by the Gaming Board, the High Court had no power to refer the case back for a new decision by an independent body.

Article 6(1) requires independence not only from the parties but also from the executive, in both civil and criminal proceedings. For example, the involvement of Ministers in any aspect of the criminal justice process is likely to cause problems under Article 6. In *T and V* v *UK* (2000) 30 EHRR 121, the Court found

---

[138] See, e.g., *Matter* v *Slovakia*, No. 31534/96, 5.7.99.

that in setting the applicants' tariff following their convictions for murder and sentences of detention during Her Majesty's pleasure, the Home Secretary was exercising sentencing powers but was clearly not independent of the executive.

There are two aspects to the requirement of impartiality: the tribunal must be subjectively free of personal prejudice or bias, and it must be impartial from an objective viewpoint. The Court has stressed that it is of fundamental importance in a democratic society that the courts inspire confidence in the public, and above all in the accused. The concepts of independence and objective impartiality are therefore closely linked. In *McGonnell* v *UK* (2000) 30 EHRR 289, which concerned the objective impartiality of the Bailiff of Guernsey in relation to planning proceedings, the Court found that the mere fact that the Bailiff presided over the legislature when the relevant regulation was adopted, was capable of casting doubt on his impartiality when he subsequently determined, as the sole judge of the law in the case, the applicant's planning appeal. Even in the absence of any actual bias or prejudice, the applicant was considered to have had legitimate grounds for fearing that the Bailiff may have been influenced by his prior participation in the adoption of the regulation in question.

The personal impartiality of both judges and jurors will be presumed, unless there is contrary proof. In *Sander* v *UK*, No. 34129/96, 9.5.00,[139] the applicant complained that he had not been heard by an impartial tribunal because the jury had been racially prejudiced. During his trial the judge had been passed a note from a juror stating that other jurors had been making racist remarks and jokes, which was admitted by one juror. The European Court found that that did not in itself amount to evidence that the juror was actually biased against the applicant. However, the judge's redirection to the jury was held to be insufficient to dispel the reasonable impression and fear of a lack of impartiality: 'given the importance attached by all Contracting States to the need to combat racism ... the judge should have reacted in a more robust manner than merely seeking vague assurances that the jurors could set aside their prejudices and try the case solely on the evidence'. There was therefore a violation of Article 6(1) (by four votes to three).

7.6.10 Presumption of innocence

Article 6(2) guarantees the presumption of innocence in criminal proceedings which may be in issue, for example, where the burden of proof is transferred to the accused to establish a defence or where a presumption of law or fact is applied against the accused. Such presumptions must be confined within reasonable limits which take into account the importance of what is at stake and maintain the rights of the defence.[140] Article 6(2) will be violated if, without any finding of guilt,

---

[139] But see *Gregory* v *UK* (1997) 35 EHRR 577.
[140] *Salabiaku* v *France* (1991) 13 EHRR 379 para. 28.

there is a judicial decision reflecting that an accused is guilty, such as the refusal to pay costs to an acquitted defendant.[141] Restrictions on the right to silence in the UK have been considered by the Court in relation to Article 6(1), rather than Article 6(2)[142] (see above at 7.6.6).

The presumption of innocence may also prevent prejudicial public comment concerning suspects. It may apply to a person who has been arrested by the police, even before being charged. In *Allenet de Ribemont* v *France* (1995) 20 EHRR 557 senior police officers, together with a Minister, gave a press conference about the applicant, who had just been arrested, and named him as having been involved in the murder of an MP. The applicant was subsequently charged with aiding and abetting murder, but was later released and discharged. The Court held that Article 6(2) applied because at the time of the press conference a judicial investigation into the case had begun, and accordingly the applicant was considered to have been 'charged with a criminal offence'. Article 6(2) was violated because there had been a clear statement of the applicant's guilt which would have led the public to consider him guilty and which prejudged the findings of the judicial authorities. The Court acknowledged that in view of the right in Article 10 of the authorities to receive and impart information, Article 6(2) could not prevent the police from informing the public about on-going criminal investigations, but they should do so with all the discretion and circumspection necessary if the presumption of innocence was to be respected.[143]

7.6.11   Article 6(3): further rights in criminal cases

The following further rights under Article 6(3) are discussed below: prompt information on charge (7.6.12); adequate time, facilities and legal representation (7.6.13); attendance and examination of witnesses (7.6.14); and interpreters (7.6.15).

7.6.12   Prompt information on charge

Whereas Article 5(2) requires prompt reasons for an arrest (see above at 7.5.7), Article 6(3)(a) requires prompt information to be given when a suspect is charged or otherwise at the start of criminal proceedings. In *Brozicek* v *Italy* (1990) 12 EHRR 371 this obligation was satisfied by the provision of information to the applicant which was intended to inform him of the institution of proceedings against him (for resisting the police, assault and wounding), which listed the offences of which he was accused, with places and dates, and which named the victim and referred to the relevant criminal code provisions. However, Article 6(3)(a) was violated because it was not communicated in a language which the

---

[141] *Minelli* v *Switzerland* (1983) 5 EHRR 554, paras 37–41.
[142] See, e.g., *Condron* v *UK*, No. 35718/97, 2.5.00, para. 72.
[143] (1995) 20 EHRR 557, para. 38.

applicant could understand, even after he notified the authorities that he could not understand Italian.

7.6.13 Adequate time, facilities and legal representation

Articles 6(3)(b) and (c) provide that everyone charged with a criminal offence has the right to have adequate time and facilities for the preparation of his defence, and to defend himself in person or through the provision of legal assistance of his own choosing.[144] The adequacy of the time given will depend upon the complexity of the particular case.

The right to be represented by a lawyer of the defendant's choice is subject to limitations: the wishes of the defendant may be overriden where there are relevant and sufficient grounds in the interests of justice.[145] Accordingly, it may be justified for the state to appoint representation.

In the context of Article 8, the importance of the right of communication with a lawyer has been emphasised in a series of cases concerning prisoners, such as *Campbell* v *UK* (1993) 15 EHRR 137 in which the Court stressed that procedures concerning communication with lawyers should 'favour full and uninhibited discussion'. In *S* v *Switzerland* (1992) 14 EHRR 670 the applicant was arrested, with twenty-seven others, and detained on suspicion of his involvement in cases of arson and attacks using explosives. Correspondence with his lawyer was intercepted and visits from his lawyer were supervised by police officials. In finding a violation of Article 6(3)(c), the Court rejected the Government's arguments that the possibility of collusion between defence counsel could justify such interferences. The Court emphasised that 'an accused's right to communicate with his advocate out of the hearing of a third person is one of the basic requirements of a fair trial in a democratic society'.[146]

It has been acknowledged that the right of access to legal advice is of particular importance in the context of restrictions on a suspect's right to silence. In *John Murray* v *UK* (1996) 22 EHRR 29[147] the Court found a violation of Article 6(1) in conjunction with Article 6(3)(c) where the applicant had been denied access to a lawyer for the first forty-eight hours of his detention. Under the Criminal Evidence (Northern Ireland) Order 1988, the drawing of adverse inferences was permitted from the refusal to answer questions in interview and in such circumstances the Court held that the denial of access to a lawyer violated Article 6.

Free legal assistance will only be required where the defendant has insufficient means to pay and where it is required in the interests of justice, which will depend

---

[144] See, e.g., *Bonzi* v *Switzerland*, No. 7854/77, 12.7.78, 12 DR 185.
[145] *Croissant* v *Germany* (1993) 16 EHRR 135, para. 29.
[146] (1992) 14 EHRR 670, para. 48.
[147] See also, *Magee* v *UK*, No. 28135/95, 6.6.00, and *Averill* v *UK*, No. 36408/97, 6.6.00.

upon both the severity of the penalty and the complexity of the case in question (can the defendant present a case adequately without a lawyer?). Where deprivation of liberty is at stake, the interests of justice in principle require legal representation. Applying these criteria, the Court found a violation of Articles 6(1) and 6(3)(c) in *Benham* v *UK* (1996) 22 EHRR 293 where legal aid was not available for magistrates' court proceedings for non-payment of the community charge.

7.6.14   Attendance and examination of witnesses

Article 6(3)(d) provides defendants with the right both to examine prosecution witnesses and to call witnesses and have them examined under similar conditions: 'all the evidence must normally be produced in the presence of the accused at a public hearing with a view to adversarial argument'.[148] The admission of hearsay evidence may therefore violate Article 6, depending upon the overall fairness of the proceedings. The use of anonymous witnesses (for example, where there is a threat of witness intimidation) may violate the Convention because the defence is unable to test the witness's reliability or question their credibility.[149] The Convention system recognises that there may be competing interests of the defendant and prosecution witnesses. Only such measures restricting the rights of the defence which are strictly necessary are permissible under Article 6(1).[150] The use of evidence obtained as a result of police incitement (for example, by undercover agents) will not, however, be justified by the public interest.[151]

Where evidence is withheld on public interest grounds, it should be the trial judge, rather than the prosecution, who attempts to assess the importance of concealed information to the defence and weigh this against the public interest in keeping the information secret. For this reason there was a violation of Article 6(1) in *Rowe and Davis* v *UK* (2000) 30 EHRR 1.[152] There, the Court held that the defect in the trial proceedings was not remedied by the Court of Appeal which was dependent for its understanding of the possible relevance of the undisclosed material on transcripts of the Crown Court hearings and on the account of the issues given by prosecuting counsel. The Court also noted that the first instance judge would have been in a position to monitor the need for disclosure throughout the trial, whereas the Court of Appeal was obliged to carry out its appraisal *ex post facto*.

---

[148] See, e.g., *Lüdi* v *Switzerland* (1993) 15 EHRR 173, para. 47.

[149] See, e.g., *Kostovski* v *Netherlands* (1990) 12 EHRR 434 and *Doorson* v *Netherlands* (1996) 22 EHRR 330 (where, exceptionally, the maintenance of witnesses' anonymity did not violate Article 6).

[150] See, e.g., *Van Mechelen and others* v *Netherlands* (1998) 25 EHRR 647.

[151] *Teixeira de Castro* v *Portugal* (1999) 28 EHRR 101, para. 36.

[152] But see also *Jasper* v *UK* (2000) 30 EHRR 441 and *Fitt* v *UK* (2000) 30 EHRR 480.

7.6.15   Interpreters

Article 6(3)(e) provides an unqualified right to free interpretation for those who cannot understand or speak the language used in court. This right extends prior to trial to the translation or interpretation of all documents and statements in the proceedings which it is necessary for a defendant to understand in order to have a fair trial.[153]

7.7   ARTICLE 7: NO PUNISHMENT WITHOUT LAW

1.   No one shall be held guilty of any criminal offence on account of any act or omission which did not constitute a criminal offence under national or international law at the time when it was committed. Nor shall a heavier penalty be imposed than the one that was applicable at the time the criminal offence was committed.

2.   This article shall not prejudice the trial and punishment of any person for any act or omission which, at the time when it was committed, was criminal according to the general principles of law recognised by civilised nations.

Article 7 prevents the retrospective application of the criminal law. It also requires sufficient accessibility and precision of the criminal law: in *Kokkinakis* v *Greece* (1994) 17 EHRR 397 the Court stated that Article 7:

embodies, more generally, the principle that only the law can define a crime and prescribe a penalty . . . and the principle that the criminal law must not be extensively construed to an accused's detriment, for instance by analogy; it follows from this that an offence must be clearly defined in law. This condition is satisfied where the individual can know from the wording of the relevant provision and, if need be, with the assistance of the courts' interpretation of it, what acts and omissions will make him liable.

Article 7 must be construed in line with its object and purpose, so as 'to provide effective safeguards against arbitrary prosecution, conviction and punishment'.[154] No derogation from Article 7 is ever possible.

Article 7 applies only in circumstances where there is a finding of guilt in criminal proceedings and/or the imposition of a criminal penalty. However, the fact that proceedings may be defined by the domestic authorities as 'civil' rather than criminal will not be decisive: the Court has found 'criminal proceedings' to be an autonomous concept.

The prohibition of the retrospective application of the criminal law includes developments through the common law where the definition of a criminal offence is extended to include conduct that had not previously been considered to be a

---

[153] *Luedicke, Belkacem and Koç* v *Germany* 2 EHRR 149, para. 48 and *Kamasinski* v *Austria* (1991) 13 EHRR 36, para. 74.
[154] *SW and CR* v *UK* (1996) 21 EHRR 363.

crime. There will be no breach of Article 7, however, where common law developments are consistent with the essence of the offence in question and where they could have been reasonably foreseen. For example, the applicants in *SW and CR* v *UK* (1996) 21 EHRR 363 argued that the House of Lords' removal of the marital rape exemption violated Article 7. However, the Court held that the change in the law had been gradually evolved through judicial interpretation and was reasonably foreseeable and accordingly Article 7 had not been violated.

The second limb of Article 7(1) prevents the imposition of a heavier penalty than that which could have been imposed when the offence was committed. Like 'criminal offence', the term 'penalty' has an autonomous meaning:[155] so the classification of a particular provision under domestic law will not be decisive. In *Welch* v *UK* (1995) 20 EHRR 247 the Court applied the following factors in determining whether a confiscation order imposed under the Drug Trafficking Offences Act 1986 amounted to a penalty: whether the measure was imposed following conviction for a criminal offence; the nature and purpose of the measure in question; its characterisation under national law; the procedures involved in the making and implementation of the measure; and its severity. In *Welch*, the Court found the following to be indicative of a regime of punishment under the 1986 Act: the statutory assumptions that all property passing through the offender's hands over a six-year period was the fruit of drug trafficking unless he could prove otherwise; the fact that the confiscation order was directed to the proceeds involved in drug dealing and was not limited to actual enrichment or profit; the discretion of the judge in fixing the amount of the order to take into consideration the degree of culpability of the accused; and the possibility of imprisonment in default of payment by the offender. The Court concluded that 'looking behind appearances at the realities of the situation, whatever the characterisation of the measure of confiscation, the fact remains that the applicant faced more far-reaching detriment as a result of the order than that to which he was exposed at the time of the commission of the offences for which he was convicted'.[156]

Cases challenging the requirement to register with the police under the Sex Offenders Act 1997 have been declared inadmissible by the Commission and Court.[157] The applicants claimed a violation of Article 7 on the basis that the requirement to register with the police amounted to a heavier penalty than that which could have been imposed at the time the offences were committed. However, the registration scheme was found not to amount to a 'penalty' within the meaning of Article 7.

According to Article 7(1), retrospectivity in the application of the criminal law will not, however, violate the Convention if the act in question had been a crime under international law at the time of its commission. Article 7(2) also permits

---

[155] *Welch* v *UK* (1995) 20 EHRR 247.
[156] (1995) 20 EHRR 247, para. 34.
[157] *Ibbotson* v *UK* (1999) 27 EHRR CD 332 and *Adamson* v *UK* (1999) 28 EHRR CD 209.

retrospectivity in relation to conduct which 'was criminal according to the general principles of law recognised by civilised nations'.

7.8 OVERVIEW OF ARTICLES 8 TO 11

Articles 8 to 11 set out the extent of the rights to respect for private and family life, home and correspondence, to freedom of thought, conscience and religion, to freedom of expression, and to freedom of assembly and association. In each case the right is not absolute; the Convention expressly permits interferences with the rights on certain conditions. The burden is primarily on the respondent to justify an interference with these rights.

Articles 8 to 11 were given a similar structure in that the first paragraph describes in general terms the extent of the right and the second paragraph describes the circumstances in which interferences with the rights are permissible. In each case, any interference must be 'in accordance with the law' or 'prescribed by law', and must be 'necessary in a democratic society' for one of the legitimate aims set out in the second paragraph. Because of their similar structures, each of these Articles can be considered by asking five questions in turn:

1. Can the applicant claim that the right under the first paragraph of the relevant Article is *engaged*?

The first question to consider is therefore whether the matter complained about falls within the scope of the relevant substantive right. For example, in *Halford* v *UK* (1997) 24 EHRR 523 the Government argued that telephone calls made by the applicant, the former Assistant Chief Constable of Merseyside, from her workplace, fell outside the scope of Article 8 because she could have had no reasonable expectation of privacy in relation to them. However, the Court rejected the Government's submissions, finding that telephone calls from business premises were covered by the notions of 'private life' and 'correspondence' under Article 8(1).

In *Botta* v *Italy* (1998) 26 EHRR 241, however, the applicant's complaints in relation to his right as a disabled person to gain access to the beach and the sea on his holidays were not found to fall within the scope of 'private life' under Article 8.

2. If so, has there been an *interference* with the applicant's right?

Whether there has been an 'interference' with a substantive right is rarely disputed. For example, in *Bowman* v *UK* (1998) 26 EHRR 1, the applicant (the director of the Society for the Protection of the Unborn Child) had been prosecuted and acquitted under the Representation of the People Act 1983 for spending more than £5 on publications prior to an election in order to publicise the candidates' views on abortion. The Government argued that there had been no restriction of the applicant's right to freedom of expression. The Court acknowledged that the Act did not directly restrain freedom of expression, but limited elections publication expenditure, and that it did not restrict expenditure on the transmission of information or opinions generally, but only expenditure incurred during an election period with a view to promoting the election of a candidate. Nevertheless, the Court found that the applicant's freedom of expression had been restricted.

3. Was the interference with the right '*in accordance with the law*' or '*prescribed by law*'?

The legal basis for any interference must be both adequately accessible and must be formulated with sufficient precision to enable a person to regulate their conduct: a person 'must be able — if need be with appropriate advice — to foresee, to a degree that is reasonable in the circumstances, the consequences which a given action may entail'.[158] It is therefore a very important principle that this condition not only requires a specific legal rule or regime authorising the interference, but also relates to the *quality* of the particular domestic legal provision. This means that, for example, where the domestic law confers a discretion, it should also indicate the scope of that discretion.[159] The degree of 'certainty' required in the law will differ depending upon the nature of the right being exercised and the nature of the interference. There are a number of examples below at 7.9 to 7.12 of interferences carried out both in the absence of any legal regulation and where the relevant law was insufficiently precise. Perhaps the strictest application of this test has been in relation to state surveillance (see below at 7.9.5).

4. Did the interference pursue one or more of the *legitimate aims* set out in the second paragraph?

The aims listed in the second paragraph are very broadly drawn. Respondent states will often raise more than one such aim. The state must produce some evidence that the particular aim was being pursued by the measure in question, but in many cases this is not disputed.

The second paragraphs of Articles 8 to 11 differ slightly. For example, Article 8(2) includes the 'economic well-being of the country' and Article 9 has no national security limitation.

---

[158] *Sunday Times* v *UK (No. 1)* 2 EHRR 245, para 49.
[159] *Silver* v *UK* (1983) 5 EHRR 347, paras 88–89 (restriction on prisoners' correspondence on the basis of unpublished prison orders).

5. Was the interference *'necessary in a democratic society'*?

The condition that any interference must be 'necessary in a democratic society', requires the existence of a 'pressing social need' and that the interference is proportionate to the legitimate aim pursued.[160] 'Necessity' is more than 'useful', 'reasonable', or 'desirable'.

In assessing the proportionality of a particular measure, the Court will consider whether there is an alternative means of protecting the relevant public interest without an interference or by means which are less intrusive. The Court will assess whether the reasons for the interference are 'relevant' and 'sufficient' to justify it. The interference will be disproportionate if it does not in fact achieve the aim pursued. It is a further requirement that the decision-making process leading to the measure of interference should be fair. The existence of effective controls on measures taken by the authorities is also a relevant factor in assessing proportionality.

In considering proportionality, the Strasbourg organs have developed the concept of the 'margin of appreciation' (see also above at 6.6): that national authorities are in principle in a better position to give an opinion on the necessity of a restriction, and that it is for the national authorities to make the initial assessment of the reality of the pressing social need. This doctrine reflects the European Court's status as a supervisory mechanism. The extent of the margin of appreciation will vary depending on the issue in question. For example, the state has a wider discretion in relation to the protection of morals, but it is narrower in relation to maintaining the authority and impartiality of the judiciary. The latter is considered to be a more objective notion in respect of which there is a lot of common ground amongst law and practice of the contracting states.

The scope of the margin of appreciation will vary from case to case. The extent of the discretion allowed to states will depend upon a number of factors:

- the importance of the protected right;
- whether there is a 'European standard' on the issue in question — if there is, it is more difficult for the state to justify an interference with a right, contrary to that standard;
- the weight of the (other, public) interest being protected;
- the extent or significance of the interference — what were the effects in the particular circumstances of the case?

These concepts will be examined and illustrated further below at 7.9 to 7.12 in connection with Articles 8 to 11.

---

[160] See, e.g., *Olsson v Sweden (No. 1)* (1989) 11 EHRR 259, para. 67.

7.9 ARTICLE 8: THE RIGHT TO RESPECT FOR PRIVATE AND FAMILY LIFE, HOME AND CORRESPONDENCE

1.　Everyone has the right to respect for his private and family life, his home and his correspondence.

2.　There shall be no interference by a public authority with the exercise of this right except such as is in accordance with the law and is necessary in a democratic society in the interests of national security, public safety or the economic well-being of the country, for the prevention of disorder or crime, for the protection of health or morals, or for the protection of the rights and freedoms of others.

Article 8(1) has four elements: private life; family life; home; and correspondence. The state's primary obligation under Article 8 is negative, that is, not to interfere with those rights. However, in certain circumstances the Article imposes positive obligations, that is, a duty to take appropriate steps to ensure protection of the rights in question (see, e.g., *Chapman* v *UK*, No. 27238/95, 18.1.01 and related cases on the positive obligation to 'facilitate the gypsy way of life'). It is well established that positive obligations are inherent in the concept of the right to 'respect' for private life under Article 8.[161] Such obligations may arise directly in relation to a public body, but the obligations under Article 8 may also arise where there is, or ought to be, a duty on a public authority to prevent an individual (or other private entity) from violating the rights of another individual. In any particular case, in order to determine whether or not a positive obligation exists, the Court will assess the fair balance between the general interests of the community and the interests of the individual.

7.9.1　Private life

The concept of private life has not been conclusively defined, but it has been invoked in a very wide range of contexts. The Court has held that the notion of privacy is not limited to the 'inner circle' of an individual's private life, but includes the right to establish and develop relationships with other human beings. Private life includes physical and moral integrity,[162] the right to determine personal identity (including sexual identity) and sexual orientation and relations.

7.9.2　Family Life

Whether an applicant can invoke the right to respect for family life will depend on the particular circumstances of each case. The Court in *Marckx* v *Belgium* 2 EHRR 330 has stated that this means that the domestic legal system must allow people 'to lead a normal family life' and for family ties to develop normally. Clearly, where there are biological ties, there is a strong presumption that family

---

[161] See, e.g., *Sheffield and Horsham* v *UK* (1999) 27 EHRR 163, para. 52.

[162] See *X and Y* v *Netherlands* (1986) 8 EHRR 235, para. 22 (sexual assault on 16-year-old girl with mental health problems).

life exists[163] and only in exceptional circumstances will such relationships not be protected by the concept of family life. Family life not only protects families based on marriage, but also other 'de facto' relationships, demonstrated by living together or other factors. Depending upon the circumstances, family life may include unmarried adults, relations with illegitimate children, and adoptive and foster families. Links between grandparents and grandchildren, aunts and uncles and other relatives may fall within the notion of family life, provided that there are found to be sufficiently close links.

It is an important principle that the Convention is to be interpreted as a 'living instrument', which in this context means that the notion of family life will continue to evolve. The Court has yet to accept a homosexual relationship as being within the concept of family life, but, for example, in *X, Y and Z v UK* (1997) 24 EHRR 143,[164] the Court held that family life included the relationship between a woman, her transsexual partner and a child born to the woman by artificial insemination from an anonymous donor.

7.9.3 Home

The notion of 'home' includes permanent and temporary places of residence (and offices). It also includes the right to enjoy the home. There will often be an element of overlap with other aspects of Article 8(1) and with property rights under Article 1 of Protocol No. 1 (see below at 7.16).

7.9.4 Correspondence

Article 8 will be engaged where there is interference with a wide range of communications, including by post, telephone, telex, fax, and e-mail. These forms of communication may be protected by the other elements of Article 8(1), such as private and family life, as well as the right to respect for correspondence.

The various constituent elements of Article 8(1) and the justification for interferences with the rights are examined and illustrated below under the following headings: communications, surveillance and policing (7.9.5); police information (7.9.6); family relations (7.9.7); immigration and asylum (7.9.8); sexual identity and relations (7.9.9); environmental issues (7.9.10); access to personal records (7.9.11) and confidentiality of personal data (7.9.12).

7.9.5 Communications, surveillance and policing

Cases of secret surveillance, notably by telephone tapping, have often focused on the adequacy of the legal regime regulating such surveillance. As a suspected receiver of stolen goods, the telephone conversations of the applicant in the case

---

[163] See, e.g., *Kroon v Netherlands* (1995) 19 EHRR 263, para. 30.
[164] But see *G v Netherlands* (1993) 16 EHRR CD 38 (sperm donor).

of *Malone* v *UK* (1985) 7 EHRR 14 were intercepted by the police under a warrant issued by the Home Secretary.[165] After his acquittal, he challenged the legality of such interceptions in the domestic courts and under the Convention. In its judgment in the *Malone* case, the Court acknowledged that where the state exercises its powers in secret, there are obvious risks of arbitrariness. However, the Court agreed with the UK Government that the requirements of the Convention (particularly in relation to foreseeability) cannot be the same in the context of police investigations as they are where the aim of the law is to restrict the conduct of individuals. Nevertheless, the Court emphasised that there has to be an adequate indication of the circumstances in which the police or other authorities can rely on 'this secret and potentially dangerous interference with the right to respect for private life and correspondence' in order to protect against arbitrary interference. The Court held that Article 8 had been violated in *Malone* because of the obscurity and uncertainty of the relevant domestic law which applied at that time.[166] As a result of this judgment, the UK Government introduced the Interception of Communications Act 1985 to regulate the interception of communications by mail and by telephone (including mobile phones). In a subsequent admissibility decision concerning allegations of the interception of telexes sent by trade unions in Eastern Europe to the General Secretary of the Scottish TUC, the European Commission found that this system provided the requisite degree of certainty (*Campbell Christie* v *UK*, No. 21482, 27.6.94, 78-A DR 119).[167]

In the case of *Halford* v *UK* (1997) 24 EHRR 523 the Court found a violation of Article 8 arising from the interception of Alison Halford's telephone calls by her employer, Merseyside Police, within the internal telephone system at the Merseyside Police Headquarters. In those circumstances, as the Interception of Communications Act 1985 only applied to a 'public telecommunications system', it did not regulate interception of internal systems, and on that basis the Court found that the interference was not 'in accordance with the law'.[168]

The absence of legal regulation has also been decisive in relation to the use of police bugging devices. In the case of *Michael Govell* v *UK*, No. 27237/95, 26.2.97 the Commission unanimously found a violation of both Articles 8 and 13 arising from the use of a listening device which had been placed in the partition wall between the applicant's house and the adjoining house by West Yorkshire Police. The use of listening devices had been subject only to non-statutory Home

---

[165] The UK Government's usual practice, as was the case in *Malone*, is not to disclose the extent to which an applicant has been the subject of surveillance, if at all. They did accept, however, that Malone was a member of a class of persons who were liable to be the subject of interception: para. 64.

[166] Post Office Act 1969, s. 80.

[167] The Commission's admissibility decisions in *Esbester* v *UK*, No. 18601/91, 2.4.93 and *Hewitt and Harman* v *UK*, No. 20317/92, 1.9.93; (1992) 14 EHRR 657, came to similar conclusions in relation to the analogous system for the Security Service established by the Security Service Act 1989.

[168] (1997) 24 EHRR 523, para. 51.

Office guidelines,[169] the disclosure of which to the applicant was refused on the basis of public interest immunity. There was no domestic law whatsoever regulating the use of covert listening devices at the relevant time and accordingly the Commission found that the interference was not 'in accordance with the law'. In *Khan* v *UK*, No. 35394/97, 12.5.00, which also concerned the planting of a listening device on private premises by the police, the Court found a violation of Article 8 on the same basis.

The *quality* of the law regulating telephone tapping in France (which was permitted under warrant issued by an investigating judge) also led to findings of violations of Article 8 by the Court in *Kruslin* v *France* (1990) 12 EHRR 547 and *Huvig* v *France* (1990) 12 EHRR 528. Whilst interception was regulated by the French Criminal Code, the Court found there were insufficient controls in a number of ways. For example, there was no definition of the categories of people liable to be subject to interception or the nature of offences which might give rise to an order for interception. There was also no obligation to limit the duration of the warrant, and there was no procedure for the destruction of the tapes, particularly following discharge or acquittal.[170] In *Rotaru* v *Romania*, No. 36437/97, 4.5.00 the Court found insufficient legal controls on the collection and storage of information by the Romanian secret services, in violation of Article 8.

In the context of secret surveillance, the Court has stressed that 'the values of a democratic society must be followed as faithfully as possible in the supervisory procedures if the bounds of necessity, within the meaning of Article 8(2), are not to be exceeded'.[171] In *Klass and others* v *Germany* 2 EHRR 214, concerning the system of secret surveillance in Germany, the Court stated that 'in a field where abuse is potentially so easy in individual cases and could have such harmful consequences for democratic society as a whole, it is in principle desirable to entrust supervisory control to a judge'. *Kopp* v *Switzerland* (1999) 27 EHRR 91 concerned the interception of a law firm's telephone calls, and therefore brought into play the question of legal professional privilege. There, the Court found it 'astonishing that this task should be assigned to an official of the Post Office's legal department, who is a member of the executive, without supervision by an

---

[169] *Guidelines on the Use of Equipment in Police Surveillance Operations*, Home Office, 1984. See also *PG and JH* v *UK*, No. 44787/98, 24.10.00 (surveillance devices used in police cells and carried by police officers in police stations) and *Taylor-Sabori* v *UK*, No. 47114/99, 27.6.00 (interception of pagers).

[170] *Kruslin* v *France* (1990) 12 EHRR 547, paras 34–35; *Huvig* v *France* (1990) 12 EHRR 528, paras 33–34. See also *Lambert* v *France* (2000) 30 EHRR 346 – unanimous violation of Article 8 where the domestic courts refused the applicant's complaint of the interception of his telephone calls on the ground that it was a third party's line which had been tapped. In *Nasir Choudhary* v *UK*, No. 40084/98, 4.5.99, the Court found that the Interception of Communications Act 1985, s. 1 was sufficiently clear for the purposes of Article 8(2) in permitting interception of telephone calls where there are reasonable grounds for believing that one of the parties to the call has consented to the interception.

[171] *Klass and others* v *Germany* 2 EHRR 214, para. 55.

independent judge, especially in this sensitive area of the confidential relations between a lawyer and his clients, which directly concern the rights of the defendant'.[172]

The searching of premises by the authorities has been examined both in respect of the legality of the measures used and their proportionality. In *Funke* v *France* (1993) 16 EHRR 297,[173] which concerned the search of the applicant's home by French customs authorities and the seizure of financial papers, the Court considered that three of the four component rights protected by Article 8(1) were in issue, namely the right to respect for private life, home and correspondence. The measures taken were found to be disproportionate to the legitimate aim being pursued by the authorities. The prime reason was the absence of the need for a judicial warrant. The other relevant restrictions and conditions under French law were considered to be 'too lax and full of loopholes', leaving the customs authorities very wide powers, including the exclusive competence to assess the expediency, number, length and scale of inspections.[174] Where the authorities may order and carry out searches without a judicial warrant, there must be 'very strict limits' on such powers in order to prevent violations of Article 8.[175]

In *Chappell* v *UK* (1990) 12 EHRR 1 the applicant was a videotape dealer who operated from premises which combined his office with his home. The case concerned the execution of a search warrant by the police looking for obscene videos at the same prearranged time as an Anton Piller order (a search order) was executed by the plaintiff in proceedings for breach of copyright. The Court noted the High Court judge's concerns that simultaneous searches (by sixteen or seventeen people) made the execution of the order 'more oppressive than it should have been'[176] but the interference with the applicant's Article 8 rights was found to be proportionate to the legitimate aim of protecting the plaintiff's copyright.

The case of *Niemetz* v *Germany* (1993) 16 EHRR 97 confirmed that the search of office premises would fall to be considered under Article 8. There, the applicant lawyer's office was searched by the police who examined four filing cabinets containing information relating to clients. The search would therefore have included 'correspondence' and the Court noted that Article 8(1) did not include any qualification of the word 'correspondence', as it did for the word 'life'.[177] It did not matter that the correspondence was of a professional nature. The search was found to impinge on professional secrecy to an extent that was disproportionate, primarily because the warrant had been drawn in very wide terms, permitting the search and seizure of 'documents', without limitation.[178]

---

[172] (1999) 27 EHRR 91, para. 74.
[173] See also *Cremieux* v *France* (1993) 16 EHRR 357 and *Miailhe* v *France* (1993) 16 EHRR 332.
[174] (1993) 16 EHRR 297, para. 57.
[175] See also, *Camenzind* v *Switzerland* (1999) 28 EHRR 458, para. 45.
[176] (1990) 12 EHRR 1, para. 65.
[177] (1993) 16 EHRR 97, para. 32.
[178] (1993) 16 EHRR 97, para. 37.

In *McLeod* v *UK* (1999) 27 EHRR 493, the Court found that the entry of the police into the applicant's house in order to prevent a breach of the peace amounted to an interference with her rights under Article 8(1). The police entered the house ostensibly to prevent any disputes which might have arisen when the applicant's former husband sought to remove various items of property from the house. The power to enter premises to prevent a breach of the peace was considered to be sufficiently accessible and foreseeable in domestic law. The interference was found to be aimed at preventing disorder or crime, but the means employed by the police were held to be disproportionate to that aim. The police had failed to verify whether the ex-husband was entitled to enter the applicant's home (he had not been so entitled) and once the police had been informed that the applicant was not present, they should not have entered the house, as it should have been clear that there was little or no risk of disorder or crime. There was accordingly a breach of Article 8.

The interception of prisoners' letters has been the subject of a number of Convention cases. Whilst some measure of control of prisoners' correspondence is accepted, the fact that the opportunity to write and receive letters may be the only contact with the outside world is an important factor to be taken into account. In *Silver* v *UK* (1983) 5 EHRR 347 the legal regime for the interception of prison mail (statute, rules and standing orders) to MPs, solicitors and others was in various respects found to be insufficiently foreseeable or to impose unjustifiable restrictions in violation of Article 8. In *Campbell* v *UK* (1993) 15 EHRR 137, the Court emphasised the particular importance of correspondence with a lawyer, which in principle is privileged. Therefore, such correspondence should only be opened where there are reasonable grounds to believe it contains an illicit enclosure. Privileged letters should, even then, not be read, other than in exceptional circumstances.

The importance of legally privileged correspondence was reiterated in *Foxley* v *UK*, No. 33274/96, 20.6.00, where the applicant's post, including correspondence with his legal advisers, was redirected under a court order to his trustee in bankruptcy (who was also the court-appointed receiver), who opened the letters, read them, photocopied them and placed them on file. Such interference was found to be disproportionate in violation of Article 8.

Article 8 will also protect the right of detainees to contact their family. In *McVeigh, O'Neill and Evans* v *UK* (1983) 5 EHRR 71 the applicants complained of violations of their rights under Article 8 to respect for their family life on the basis that they were prevented from communicating with their wives during their detention by the police under the Prevention of Terrorism (Supplemental Temporary Provisions) Order 1976. The Commission found a violation of Article 8 in that case as there had been no risk that accomplices might have been alerted, or might have escaped, destroyed or removed evidence, or committed offences.[179] The Commission acknowledged that 'at the time when a person is arrested his ability to communicate rapidly with his family may be of great importance. The unexplained disappearance of a family member even for a short period of time may provoke great anxiety'.[180]

7.9.6 Police information

The issues of access to personal records and the confidentiality of personal data are considered below at 7.9.11 and 7.9.12.

The collection and retention in police records of information about suspects gives rise to a number of questions, such as the necessity of retaining the information and the circumstances in which the information should be disclosed to the suspect or to third parties. The right to respect for private and family life in Article 8 will provide a degree of protection for those about whom information is held on police files. An interference with a suspect's Article 8(1) rights may be justified by the police on the basis, for example, that the retention of the information is necessary for the prevention of disorder or crime or is in the interests of public safety, provided also, that the measure in question is both in accordance with the law and proportionate to the aim being pursued. Whether Article 8(1) is engaged in such circumstances is not usually in issue. For example, it was undisputed in *Murray* v *UK* (1995) 19 EHRR 193 that various measures carried out by the army, including the recording of personal details about the first applicant and her family, and their taking her photograph without her knowledge or consent, interfered with the applicants' rights under Article 8(1).

In *Leander* v *Sweden* (1987) 9 EHRR 433 it was not disputed that information contained in a secret police register related to the applicant's private life. The Court found that both the storing and the release of such information, coupled with a refusal to allow the applicant the opportunity to refute it, amounted to an interference with his right to respect for private life under Article 8(1). *Leander* concerned the retention of information relating to employment in national security sensitive positions. Swedish law conferred a wide discretion as to the collection of information on a secret police register, but it was limited in that information could not be recorded merely because by belonging to an organisation, or by other means, a person had expressed a political opinion. The discretion was further limited by Governmental instructions (only one of which was public and therefore sufficiently accessible to be taken into account by the Court) and by the requirements that the information had to be necessary for the secret police service and intended to serve the purpose of preventing or detecting 'offences against national security, etc.'. There were also explicit and detailed provisions as to what information could be disclosed, the authorities to which, and circumstan-

---

[179] (1983) 5 EHRR 71, paras 237–240.
[180] (1983) 5 EHRR 71, para. 237.

ces in which, information could be communicated, as well as the procedure to be followed when taking decisions to release information. Such requirements were considered by the Court to provide an adequate indication as to the scope and manner of exercise of the discretion conferred on the police.[181]

The collection and retention of information by MI5 concerning the private lives of Patricia Hewitt and Harriet Harman (when they were respectively General Secretary and Legal Officer of Liberty) was found by the Commission to violate Article 8 because such interference was based on a non-binding and unpublished Government directive and was not therefore 'in accordance with the law'.[182] In *Amann* v *Switzerland* (2000) 30 EHRR 843, the retention of information on the applicant by the police in a national security card index, identifying him as a contact with the Russian embassy, was found to violate Article 8, as the relevant domestic law was insufficiently foreseeable.

In *Friedl* v *Austria* (1996) 21 EHRR 83 the applicant took part in a demonstration in Vienna about homelessness. He was photographed and filmed by the police who also checked his identity and took down personal details. The information was stored in administrative files which were to be destroyed in 2001, but it was not retained on computer files. The Commission found that the taking and retention of the photographs did not interfere with the applicant's rights under Article 8(1), as there had been no intrusion into the 'inner circle' of his private life; they concerned a public incident in which the applicant had voluntarily taken part and they were taken solely for the purpose of recording and investigating the incident in question. The retention of personal information was considered to be an interference with the Article 8(1) rights, but was found to be necessary in a democratic society for the prevention of disorder or crime.

7.9.7   Family relations

The right to respect for family life protects the contact between family members (see above at 7.9.2 as to the definition of family) and in certain circumstances includes positive obligations on the state.[183] There have been many cases relating to Article 8 concerning contact with children, for example custody and access cases and the placing of children into care. The Court has underlined that the taking into care of a child should normally be a temporary measure and that any measures taken should be consistent with the ultimate aim of reuniting the natural parent and child.[184] The Convention upholds the right of a parent without custody to have access or contact with the child, subject to the child's best interests. Many cases therefore depend upon the proportionality of the restriction on access or custody.

---

[181] (1987) 9 EHRR 433, paras 54–56.
[182] (1992) 14 EHRR 657.
[183] See e.g., *Airey* v *Ireland* 2 EHRR 305, para. 32.
[184] See, eg. *Olsson* v *Sweden (No. 1)* (1989) 11 EHRR 259, para. 81.

In *Johansen* v *Norway* (1997) 23 EHRR 33, the Court emphasised that consideration of what was in the best interests of the child was of 'crucial importance', and that the national authorities have a wide margin of appreciation in assessing the necessity of taking a child into care. However, the Court will exercise a stricter scrutiny in relation to restrictions on parental rights and access on the basis that such restrictions could effectively curtail family relations between parent and child. The Court found the taking of the child into care to be proportionate in *Johansen*, but the deprivation of the mother's access and parental rights in respect of her daughter was held to be unjustified and beyond the state's margin of appreciation. In *K and T* v *Finland*, No. 25702/94, 27.4.00, the applicants' children had been taken into care following the mother's long history of mental illness. Her younger child was taken away directly from the hospital delivery room, without her even being able to feed the child. The Court found that the reasons given and the methods used for taking the applicants' children into care were arbitrary and unjustified and was critical of the failure of the social authorities to inform the applicants about their decisions. Article 8 was also violated because of the failure adequately to consider the termination of public care, despite evidence of an improvement in the situation which had led to the care orders.

Article 8 guarantees certain procedural rights, which were found to have been violated in relation to the placing of the applicants' son into care in the case of *McMichael* v *UK* (1995) 20 EHRR 205 because of the failure to disclose certain documents during the domestic legal proceedings: 'what . . . has to be determined is whether, having regard to the particular circumstances of the case and notably the serious nature of the decisions to be taken, the parents have been involved in the decision-making process, seen as a whole, to a degree sufficient to provide them with the requisite protection of their interests'.

In relation to parental access rights, the Court has held that what is decisive is whether the national authorities have taken all necessary steps to facilitate reunion as can reasonably be demanded in the special circumstances of each case.[185] In *Hokkanen* v *Finland* (1995) 19 EHRR 139 the applicant's daughter was cared for by her maternal grandparents after his wife's death. The grandparents refused to comply with court orders granting the applicant custody and access which were not enforced by the authorities. The Court found a violation of the applicant's right to respect for his family life arising from the denial of access up to the point when the child had become sufficiently mature enough for her opinion, which was to oppose the applicant's access, to be taken into account. The separation of a mother and her baby in prison will also engage Article 8 rights.[186]

---

[185] *Olsson* v *Sweden (No. 2)* (1994) 17 EHRR 134, para. 90.
[186] *Togher* v *UK* (1998) 25 EHRR CD 99.

Issues relating to adoption may raise questions under Article 8. In *Keegan* v *Ireland* (1994) 18 EHRR 342 there was a violation of the right to family life where the domestic law permitted the mother of a child to place the child for adoption shortly after her birth without the knowledge or consent of the father: 'such a state of affairs not only jeopardised the proper development of the applicant's ties with the child but also set in motion a process which was likely to prove to be irreversible, thereby putting the applicant at a significant disadvantage in his contest with the prospective adopters for the custody of the child'.[187] However, in *Söderbäck* v *Sweden* (2000) 29 EHRR 95, there was no violation of Article 8 following the adoption of the applicant's child, even where its effect was totally to deprive the applicant of a family life with his daughter, because of the infrequency of the contact between him and his daughter and because she had been living with her adoptive father since she was eight months old.

In *Marckx* v *Belgium* 2 EHRR 330 the illegitimacy laws in Belgium, which included restrictions on giving or bequeathing property, were found to violate the right to respect for family life under Article 8. In *Kroon* v *Netherlands* (1995) 19 EHRR 263 the applicant father's paternity of his child could not be recognised unless the mother's husband denied paternity. This was found to violate Article 8: 'respect for family life requires that biological and social reality prevail over a legal presumption which, as in the present case, flies in the face of both established fact and the wishes of those concerned without actually benefiting anyone'.[188]

7.9.8 Immigration and asylum

Article 8 does not provide a right of entry or residence or a right to remain in a Convention state. The Court acknowledges that it is for states to maintain public order, 'in particular by exercising their right, as a matter of well-established international law and subject to their treaty obligations, to control the entry, residence and expulsion of aliens'.[189] Article 8 may, nevertheless, be engaged, depending upon the extent of the effects upon family life, by a decision to deport, exclude or expel.

Article 8 protects only established families, it does not guarantee a right of entry to create a new family.[190] There are a number of factors which the Court will weigh up in deciding whether a family is established in the Convention state. These factors include the length of time members of the family have lived in the country in question and the length of any periods of separation of family members. The Court will consider how easy it would be for the family to settle in

---

[187] *Keegan* v *Ireland* (1994) 18 EHRR 342, para. 55.

[188] *Kroon* v *Netherlands* (1995) 19 EHRR 263, para. 40.

[189] See, e.g., *Beldjoudi* v *France* (1992) 14 EHRR 801, para. 74.

[190] *Abdulaziz, Cabales and Balkandali* v *UK* (1985) 7 EHRR 471.

the country of origin of the non-national family member, which includes consideration of how 'adaptable' any children would be to living in the other country. The Court may also take into account difficulties connected with language, health, employment and other social, cultural and religious issues.

If the Court is satisfied that the right to family life is engaged, then it will apply the usual tests to any interference: is it 'in accordance with the law' and does it pass the test of proportionality?

In *Moustaquim* v *Belgium* (1991) 13 EHRR 802, the applicant's deportation following his conviction for various offences was found to be a disproportionate interference with his right to respect for family life under Article 8. It was important that the applicant, a Moroccan national, had been only two years old when he arrived in Belgium and he had lived there for about twenty years, and that at the time of the deportation order, all his close relatives had been living in Belgium for a long period. It was also relevant that the applicant had returned just twice to Morocco, for holidays, and that he had received all his schooling in French. Similarly, in *Beldjoudi* v *France* (1992) 14 EHRR 801, the proposed deportation of a convicted criminal, an Algerian citizen, was held to be a disproportionate interference with family life. Mr Beldjoudi was born in France of French parents, but had lost his French nationality because of his parents' failure to make a declaration on his behalf. He had spent his whole life (forty years) in France, had married a Frenchwoman, had been educated in French, appeared not to know Arabic and had no links with Algeria. However, in *Boughanemi* v *France* (1996) 22 EHRR 228 the Court found no violation of Article 8 in similar circumstances. The decisive difference with *Moustaquim* and *Beldjoudi* was the seriousness of the offences of which Mr Boughanemi had been convicted, and, apparently, that he kept his Tunisian nationality and 'never manifested a wish to become French'. The Court's approach to such cases has been rightly criticised as being arbitrary.[191] A deportation of an applicant where there is no criminality will be more difficult to justify under Article 8.[192]

In cases where an individual may be expelled to a country where he or she risks ill-treatment in any form, Articles 2 or 3 may be engaged (see above at 7.2 and 7.3).

7.9.9   Sexual identity and relations

The Court has acknowledged that sexual relations are 'a most intimate aspect' of a person's private life. Where there are restrictions on an intimate aspect of an individual's private life, there must be 'particularly serious reasons' to satisfy Article 8(2). In *Dudgeon* v *UK* (1982) 4 EHRR 149, the Court found that the criminalisation in Northern Ireland of consensual homosexual activity between

---

[191] See, e.g., the dissenting judgment of Martens J in *Boughanemi* v *France* (1996) 22 EHRR 228.
[192] See, e.g., *Berrehab* v *Netherlands* (1989) 11 EHRR 322.

men over the age of twenty-one violated the right to respect for private life under Article 8. Despite the lack of enforcement of the legislation, its very existence was considered to have affected the applicant's private life and there was held to be no pressing social need for the legislation. There have been equivalent decisions in the case of *Norris* v *Ireland* (1991) 13 EHRR 186, and in *Modinos* v *Cyprus* (1993) 16 EHRR 485.

Sutherland v *UK*, No. 25186/94, Comm. Rep. 1.7.97 concerned the discrimination in having a homosexual age of consent at eighteen rather than sixteen. By a majority of fourteen to four the Commission decided that the law violated Euan Sutherland's right to respect for his private life, and that the provision was discriminatory. The Commission rejected the arguments that men between sixteen and twenty were in special need of protection against being 'recruited' into homosexuality by predatory older men. The Commission also did not accept that 'society's claimed entitlement to indicate disapproval of homosexual conduct and its preference for a heterosexual lifestyle' could provide an objective or reasonable justification for the inequality of treatment under the criminal law. In overturning the Commission's previous case law on the age of consent issue going back more than twenty years,[193] the case represents a good example of the Convention being interpreted as a living instrument.

The applicant members of the armed forces in *Smith and Grady* v *UK* (2000) 29 EHRR 493 and *Lustig-Prean and Beckett* v *UK* (2000) 29 EHRR 548, complained about investigations into their homosexuality and about their automatic discharge from service solely on the ground of their sexual orientation. Neither was found by the Court to be justified under Article 8(2). The investigation process was found to be exceptionally intrusive and offensive, as it included detailed questions about particular sexual practices and preferences. The effect of discharge had a profound effect on the applicants' careers and prospects. The absolute and general character of the armed forces' policy was also decisive: immediate discharge followed, irrespective of an individual's conduct or service record. The Government was found to have failed to substantiate the allegation that the policy was required in order to maintain operational effectiveness. As to the reported negative attitudes amongst armed forces personnel towards homosexuals, the Court held that: 'to the extent that they represent a predisposed bias on the part of a heterosexual majority against a homosexual minority, these negative attitudes cannot, of themselves ... amount to sufficient justification for the interferences with the applicants' rights ... any more than similar negative attitudes towards those of a different race, origin or colour'.[194]

Like the issue of the age of consent, the Strasbourg cases concerning transsexual and transgendered people illustrate the notion that the European

---

[193] *X* v *UK*, No. 7215/75, DR 19 66; *WZ* v *Austria*, No. 17279/90, 13.5.92; *HF* v *Austria*, No. 22646/93, 26.6.95.
[194] (2000) 29 EHRR 493, para. 97.

Convention is a 'living instrument', in other words that the rights contained in the Convention are not static, but can evolve and develop with changes in society. There have been a number of cases aimed at achieving legal recognition of gender reassignment, by challenging the refusal to alter birth registers and arguing that this refusal fails to respect the right to a private life. In 1986 the case of *Rees* v *UK* (1987) 9 EHRR 56 was rejected by a twelve to three majority of the Court, although the Court specifically acknowledged the seriousness of the problems and the distress caused. But by 1990, in the case of *Cossey* v *UK* (1991) 13 EHRR 622, the majority against the applicant was down to ten to eight. Whereas in 1986 the Court found that only five European countries recognised gender reassigment through allowing changes to the birth register, by 1990 that number had risen to fourteen. In *Sheffield and Horsham* v *UK* (1999) 27 EHRR 163, the Court found against the applicants by an eleven to nine majority on the basis that the UK Government could rely on its margin of appreciation in refusing to recognise in law the sexual identity of a post-operative transsexual. It rapped the Government's knuckles for failing, since the earlier decisions in Rees and Cossey, to review the need for legal changes for the rights of transsexuals.

7.9.10   Environmental issues

The Court has held that an individual's well-being and the enjoyment of their home may be affected by severe environmental pollution, such that the right to private and family life may be adversely affected, even without there being any serious danger to health. In *Lopez Ostra* v *Spain* (1995) 20 EHRR 277, the Court found a violation of Article 8 arising from the failure of the municipal authorities to prevent pollution from a waste treatment plant: the authorities had failed to strike a fair balance between the interest of the town's economic well-being and the applicant's effective right to respect for her home and her private and family life.

The failure to provide environmental information may also violate Article 8. The forty applicants in *Guerra and others* v *Italy* (1998) 26 EHRR 357 lived within one kilometre of a chemical factory which had been classified as high risk. Article 8 was engaged by the direct effect of the factory's toxic emissions on the applicants' rights to respect for their private and family life, and the failure to provide them with information which would have enabled them to assess the risks which they faced from the factory was found to violate Article 8. The applicants in *McGinley and Egan* v *UK* (1998) 27 EHRR 1[195] had taken part, as servicemen, in the UK's nuclear testing programme in the 1950s and 1960s. The Court stated that 'where a government engages in hazardous activities ... which might have hidden adverse consequences on the health of those involved in such activities,

---

[195] In addition to Article 8, Article 6 was also in issue as a result of the effect of the non-disclosure of documents on the applicants' right of access to the Pensions Appeal Tribunal.

respect for private and family life under Article 8 requires that an effective and accessible procedure be established which enables persons to seek all relevant and appropriate information'.

7.9.11   Access to personal records

The question of access to personal records will engage Article 8. The applicant in *Gaskin* v *UK* (1990) 12 EHRR 36 sought documents from his local authority relating to the period of time when he was in care. Whilst acknowledging the applicant's interest in obtaining information about his childhood and early development, the Court also emphasised that the confidentiality of public records is of importance for receiving objective and reliable information, and that such confidentiality can also be necessary for the protection of third persons.[196] In such circumstances, in order to comply with the principle of proportionality, it should have been an independent authority which decided whether access should be granted. See also above at 7.9.10 (environmental issues).

7.9.12   Confidentiality of personal data

The Court has not to date found that Article 8 creates a general right of access to personal data, but it has acknowledged the fundamental importance of the protection of personal data under Article 8. There is also a recognition of the particular importance of health records:

> Respecting the confidentiality of health data is a vital principle in the legal systems of all the Contracting Parties to the Convention. It is crucial not only to respect the sense of privacy of a patient but also to preserve his or her confidence in the medical profession and in the health services in general.
>
>   Without such protection, those in need of medical assistance may be deterred from revealing such information of a personal and intimate nature as may be necessary in order to receive appropriate treatment and, even, from seeking such assistance, thereby endangering their own health and, in the case of transmissible diseases, that of the community.[197]

There must therefore be adequate safeguards in domestic law to prevent the communication or disclosure of personal health data in contravention of Article 8. Disclosure may be particularly damaging in certain circumstances, such as where it relates to HIV infection.

A case concerning the filming of a suicidal man in public by local authority closed-circuit television cameras (CCTV) and the subsequent disclosure of the

---

[196] (1990) 12 EHRR 36, para. 49.
[197] *Z* v *Finland* (1998) 25 EHRR 371, para. 95.

film to television companies and a newspaper, who published the pictures, is currently pending before the Court.[198]

In relation to police information, see above at 7.9.6.

7.10 ARTICLE 9: FREEDOM OF THOUGHT, CONSCIENCE AND RELIGION

1. Everyone has the right to freedom of thought, conscience and religion; this right includes freedom to change his religion or belief and freedom, either alone or in community with others and in public or private, to manifest his religion or belief, in worship, teaching, practice and observance.

2. Freedom to manifest one's religion or beliefs shall be subject only to such limitations as are prescribed by law and are necessary in a democratic society in the interests of public safety, for the protection of public order, health or morals, or for the protection of the rights and freedoms of others.

Freedom of thought, conscience and religion is said to be one of the foundations of a 'democratic society': 'It is, in its religious dimension, one of the most vital elements that go to make up the identity of believers and of their conception of life, but it is also a precious asset for atheists, agnostics, sceptics and the unconcerned'.[199] The right to freedom of thought, conscience and religion in Article 9 is closely connected to both the right to freedom of expression in Article 10 and the rights to peaceful assembly and of association in Article 11. In cases where the applicant's freedom of thought, conscience and religion is in issue, both Articles 10 and 11 should also be carefully considered.

Article 9(1) expressly clarifies the extent of the right to freedom of religion as including two aspects: the right to *change* one's religion or belief and to *manifest* one's religion or belief. To be able to rely on the right to manifest one's religion, an applicant must establish that he or she is in fact an adherent of the religion in question and that the manifestation in question is an essential part of that religion. Article 9(1) specifically refers to 'worship, teaching, practice and observance' as being forms of manifestation of one's religion or belief, which includes bearing witness in words and deeds and the right to try to convince others.

The scope of Article 9 has generally been interpreted widely in terms of the nature of the belief (which includes non-religious beliefs), but much more restrictively in relation to the manifestation or practices which are claimed to be motivated by one's religion or belief. The act in question must be 'intimately linked' to the religion or belief. Article 9 therefore does not protect every act

---

[198] *Peck v UK*, No. 44647/98.
[199] *Kokkinakis v Greece* (1994) 17 EHRR 397, para. 31.

which an individual considers to be required by their belief.[200] In general, Article 9 will not be violated by the application of general laws to individuals who object on the basis that the law offends against their religion or belief.

In *Buscarini and others* v *San Marino* (2000) 30 EHRR 208, the applicant MPs were required to swear an oath on the Gospels, or they would forfeit their parliamentary seats. This was found to violate Article 9 as the MPs were obliged to swear allegiance to a particular religion. In *Kokkinakis* v *Greece* (1994) 17 EHRR 397 the applicant, a Jehovah's witness, complained of his conviction for proselytism, which was found by the Court to be a disproportionate interference in violation of Article 9 given that the domestic courts had failed to set out in what way the applicant had used improper means. The Court made a distinction between bearing Christian witness through true evangelism and improper proselytism, through offering material or social advantages to gain new members, exerting improper pressure or even the use of violence or brainwashing. However, in *Otto-Preminger Institut* v *Austria* (1995) 19 EHRR 34, the Court stated that those who manifest their religion cannot reasonably expect to be exempt from all criticism: 'they must tolerate and accept the denial by others of their religious beliefs and even the propagation by others of doctrines hostile to their faith'. Measures taken by the authorities to restrict the publication or broadcast of provocative portrayals of objects of religious veneration may be justified to protect the respect for the religious feelings of believers.[201]

Article 9 cannot be relied on by corporate bodies, but churches can do so, on behalf of their members and as separate entities themselves.[202] Associations cannot invoke the right to freedom of conscience.[203]

In view of the express reference in Article 4 to compulsory military service, Article 9 has not as yet been interpreted so as to permit conscientious objectors to resist military service.[204]

It is important to note that the limitations set out in Article 9(2) only apply to the right to *manifest* one's religion or beliefs. Article 9(2) does not apply to the right to hold a particular belief or to the rights to freedom of thought or conscience, which are therefore unqualified.

Where it is accepted that Article 9(1) rights are engaged, the Court has frequently found the restrictions applied to be proportionate. For example, in *Pendragon* v *UK* (1999) 27 EHRR CD 179[205], a ban on assemblies at Stonehenge under the Public Order Act 1986 (which applied for four days over a four-mile radius) was found to have interfered with the rights of the applicant (who had

---

[200] See, e.g., *Arrowsmith* v *UK* (1978) 19 DR 5.

[201] See also *Wingrove* v *UK* (1997) 24 EHRR 1, paras 46–51.

[202] *Chappell* v *UK* (1987) 53 DR 214.

[203] *Vereniging Rechtswinkels Utrecht* v *Netherlands* (1986) 46 DR 200.

[204] But see the dissenting and concurring opinions in *Thlimmenos* v *Greece*, No. 34369/97, Comm. Rep. 4.12.98.

[205] See also *Christians Against Racism and Fascism* v *UK*, No. 8440/78, 16.7.80: police ban on processions in London not found to be disproportionate.

intended to hold a Druidic service at the summer solstice) under Article 11(1), and brought Article 9(1) into consideration. However, in view of the violence at Stonehenge in previous years, the restriction was not found to be disproportionate.

7.11   ARTICLE 10: FREEDOM OF EXPRESSION

1.   Everyone has the right to freedom of expression. This right shall include freedom to hold opinions and to receive and impart information and ideas without interference by public authority and regardless of frontiers. This article shall not prevent states from requiring the licensing of broadcasting, television or cinema enterprises.

2.   The exercise of these freedoms, since it carries with it duties and responsibilities, may be subject to such formalities, conditions, restrictions or penalties as are prescribed by law and are necessary in a democratic society, in the interests of national security, territorial integrity or public safety, for the prevention of disorder or crime, for the protection of health or morals, for the protection of the reputation or rights of others, for preventing the disclosure of information received in confidence, or for maintaining the authority and impartiality of the judiciary.

The Court has consistently underlined the importance of the right to freedom of speech as one of the essential foundations of a democratic society, acknowledging in particular the function which the press plays[206] (a vital role as 'public watchdog') and its duty to impart information and ideas of public interest, without overstepping certain bounds. This duty is said to be mirrored by the public's right to receive such information. Freedom of expression is also considered to be one of the basic conditions required for each individual's self-fulfilment.

Article 10 is related to, and frequently invoked with, Article 9 (freedom of thought, conscience and religion) and Article 11 (right to peaceful assembly and association). As with Articles 8, 9 and 11, the substantive right is set out in Article 10(1) and the permitted restrictions are set out in Article 10(2) (see also above at 7.8). These restrictions must be narrowly interpreted and the need for the restriction must be convincingly established.[207] The right to freedom of expression is therefore subject to duties and responsibilities, the extent of which will vary according to the context. For example, the Court has held that there is a duty not to be gratuitously offensive in relation to objects of religious veneration.[208] In assessing the proportionality of restrictions on the right to freedom of expression, the Court allows the authorities a discretion, or 'margin of appreciation' (see also above at 7.8) which varies according to the subject matter. For example, a wider margin of appreciation is allowed in respect of issues of morality and commercial speech, but a narrower margin of appreciation is applied in relation to political

---

[206] See, e.g., *Jersild* v *Denmark* (1995) 19 EHRR 1, para. 31.

[207] See, e.g., *Ahmed and others* v *UK* (2000) 29 EHRR 1, para. 55.

[208] See, e.g., *Wingrove* v *UK* (1997) 24 EHRR 1, para. 52.

speech. This variable application of the concept of the margin of appreciation in free speech cases has been criticised by some commentators.[209]

In principle, Article 10 will protect the right to express oneself in a way which may be seen as offensive, shocking or disturbing, reflecting the need in a democratic society for pluralism, tolerance and broadmindedness.[210] However, certain forms of expression, such as offensive racist statements may not be protected by Article 10 at all.[211] Where a form of expression is protected by Article 10(1), this will be subject to the permissible restrictions in Article 10(2). The majority of cases turn on whether or not an interference with the right was proportionate or not (which in some cases will be decided by the narrowest of margins). There may also be positive obligations under Article 10, for example, where the authorities fail to take steps to investigate and provide protection against unlawful acts of violence.[212]

As well as protecting the substance of the information or ideas expressed, Article 10 also protects the manner in which they are conveyed.

Whilst Article 10 expressly refers to the right to receive information, this has been narrowly interpreted as prohibiting the authorities from restricting a person from receiving information which others wish to impart. It has not been held to impose a positive obligation on the state to collect and disseminate information of its own motion. For example, in *Guerra and others* v *Italy* (1998) 26 EHRR 357[213] Article 10 was found not be applicable where the applicants complained that the authorities had failed to ensure that the public were informed about the risks created by the operation of a chemical factory.

The application of Article 10 is discussed further below under the following headings: political speech (7.11.1); public protest (7.11.2); print and broadcast media (7.11.3); artistic expression (7.11.4) and expression in the commercial context (7.11.5).

7.11.1 Political speech

Freedom of expression has particular importance for elected political representatives and so interferences with the freedom of speech of politicians will be closely scrutinised. In *Castells* v *Spain* (1992) 14 EHRR 445, for example, the conviction of a Basque opposition senator for writing an article critical of the Government was found to violate Article 10.

Freedom of political debate is considered by the Court to be at the very core of the concept of a democratic society and the freedom of the press provides the

---

[209] See, e.g., P. Mahoney, 'Universality versus Subsidiarity in the Strasbourg Case Law on Free Speech: Explaining some Recent Judgments' [1997] EHRLR 364 and A. Lester, 'Universality versus Subsidiarity: A Reply' [1998] EHRLR 73.

[210] See, e.g., *Handyside* v *UK* 1 EHRR 737, para. 49.

[211] See, e.g., *Jersild* v *Denmark* (1995) 19 EHRR 1, para. 35.

[212] See *Özgür Gündem* v *Turkey*, No. 23144/93, 16.3.00.

[213] See also, *Leander* v *Sweden* (1987) 9 EHRR 433, para. 74.

public with one of the best means of discovering and forming an opinion of the ideas and attitudes of political leaders.[214] For those reasons, whilst politicians are entitled to protect their reputations, the limits of acceptable criticism are wider in relation to a politician than a private individual. A politician 'inevitably and knowingly lays himself open to close scrutiny of his every word and deed by both journalists and the public at large, and he must display a greater degree of tolerance, especially when he himself makes public statements that are susceptible of criticism'.[215]

For example, the applicant journalist in *Oberschlick* v *Austria* (1995) 19 EHRR 389 was convicted of defamation for publishing a criminal information laid against the Secretary-General of the Austrian Liberal Party who had advocated discrimination against immigrant families in relation to family allowances. The Court found that the applicant had contributed to a public debate on an important political question and that a politician who expressed himself in such a way could expect a strong reaction from journalists and the public. The applicant was held not to have exceeded the limits of freedom of expression and there was therefore a violation of Article 10.

The limits of permissible criticism are wider still in relation to the Government which must be subject to the close scrutiny of the press and public. Whilst it may be appropriate for the authorities to invoke criminal sanctions in certain circumstances to achieve the Article 10(2) legitimate aims, the Court has stressed that the Government should exercise restraint in resorting to criminal proceedings, in view of its dominant position, and particularly where there are other means of replying to attacks from opponents or in the media.[216] A series of cases against Turkey, relating to criminal prosecutions for statements concerning the conflict in the south-east of the country has involved an assessment by the Court of the limits of permissible criticism. For example, in *Sürek* v *Turkey (No. 1)*, No. 26682/95, 8.7.99, the Court found no violation of Article 10 (by eleven votes to six) resulting from prosecutions relating to articles condemning military activity in south-east Turkey. One article was found to have named individuals and thereby exposed them to risk of physical violence and was considered to amount to hate speech and the glorification of violence.

Free political debate is closely related to, and one of the conditions needed to ensure, the right to free elections. Therefore the free circulation of opinions and information is particularly important prior to an election.[217] Article 10 was violated in *Bowman* v *UK* (1998) 26 EHRR 1 arising from the rules relating to election expenditure which prevented the applicant from informing the electorate about candidates' views on abortion.

---

[214] See, e.g., *Oberschlick* v *Austria* (1995) 19 EHRR 389, para. 58.
[215] Ibid.
[216] See, e.g., *Castells* v *Spain* (1992) 14 EHRR 445, para. 46.
[217] See, e.g., *Bowman* v *UK* (1998) 26 EHRR 1, para. 42.

Where the freedom of expression of public servants is in issue, the court will carefully consider the extent of their 'duties and responsibilities' which assume a 'special significance'.[218] The Court will attempt to strike a fair balance between the rights of the individual and the interests of the state in ensuring the functioning of the civil service.[219] Civil servants should enjoy public confidence and it may therefore be necessary to protect them from 'offensive and abusive verbal attacks'.[220]

7.11.2 Public protest

Linked to political speech is expression in the form of public protest or demonstration which will also engage Article 10. For example, *Steel and others* v *UK* (1999) 28 EHRR 603 concerned various forms of peaceful protest against a grouse shoot, a motorway extension and outside a fighter helicopter conference. Rejecting the Government's argument that Article 10 was not applicable because the protests were not peaceful, the Court found that although the applicants had physically impeded the activities of which they disapproved, they nonetheless constituted expressions of opinion within the meaning of Article 10. Three of the applicants had been protesting against the sale of fighter helicopters by handing out leaflets and holding up a banner which said: 'Work for peace and not war'. They were arrested on the basis that their conduct was likely to cause a breach of the peace and they were held for about seven hours. Subsequent proceedings against them were withdrawn by the magistrates when no evidence was produced. The Court found a violation of their right to freedom of expression as there were no reasonable grounds for the police to believe that the applicants' peaceful protest would cause a breach of the peace. Accordingly, their arrest and detention had not been 'necessary in a democratic society'.

7.11.3 Print and broadcast media

The importance of freedom of speech of the press is referred to in the introductory section above (7.11). Therefore, prior restraint of the media will require particular justification,[221] and orders requiring the disclosure of journalists' sources must be justified by an overriding requirement in the public interest.[222]

Article 10(1) expressly permits the licensing of broadcasting, television and cinema. The denial of licences or the extent of conditions placed on licences will be subject to the requirements of Article 10(2).[223]

---

[218] See, e.g., *Ahmed and others* v *UK* (2000) 29 EHRR 1, para. 61 (local government officers); *Glasenapp* v *Germany* (1987) 9 EHRR 25 and *Kosiek* v *Germany* (1987) 9 EHRR 328 (teachers).

[219] *Vogt* v *Germany* (1996) 21 EHRR 205, para. 53.

[220] *Janowski* v *Poland*, No. 25716/94, 21.1.99, para. 33.

[221] *Observer and Guardian* v *UK* (1992) 14 EHRR 153.

[222] *Goodwin* v *UK* (1996) 22 EHRR 123, para. 39.

[223] See, e.g., *Autronic AG* v *Switzerland* (1990) 12 EHRR 485.

In assessing the duties and responsibilities of journalists, the Court recognises that the audio-visual media often have a much more immediate and powerful effect than the print media.[224]

The Court has held that there will have to be particularly strong reasons for punishing journalists for assisting in disseminating the statements of others. In *Jersild* v *Denmark* (1995) 19 EHRR 1, the applicant was prosecuted and convicted after making a television documentary about self-proclaimed racist youths. The Court found that the applicant had not intended to propagate racist ideas, but to raise an issue of important public concern: news reporting based on interviews was said to be one of the most important means of fulfilling the public watchdog role of the press. Despite the low level of the fine, the fact that the applicant was convicted was disproportionate and was found to have violated Article 10 (by twelve votes to seven). See also the effect of Article 17 above at 6.12.

7.11.4   Artistic expression

The right to freedom of artistic expression is protected by Article 10. This was confirmed in *Müller and others* v *Switzerland* (1991) 13 EHRR 212, where the Court found Article 10 to be applicable to the confiscation of paintings under obscene publications laws and convictions for exhibiting the paintings. Artistic expression is seen as an aspect of the right to impart ideas. There was an interference with this right in *Wingrove* v *UK* (1997) 24 EHRR 1 arising from the refusal of the British Board of Film Classification to certify the applicant's video film *Visions of Ecstacy* (on the grounds it was blasphemous) and from the criminal sanctions applicable to the distribution of a video without a certificate.

7.11.5   Expression in the commercial context

Article 10 also protects commercial freedom of expression — the right is guaranteed to 'everyone', including profit-making corporate bodies. The state's margin of appreciation in regulating this area is likely to be wider: the Court has found the margin of appreciation to be essential in commercial matters, such as unfair competition and advertising.[225]

7.11.6   Maintaining the authority and impartiality of the judiciary

One of the legitimate aims in Article 10(2) (which is not to be found in Articles 8, 9 or 11) is the maintenance of the authority and impartiality of the judiciary.[226]

---

[224] See, e.g., *Jersild* v *Denmark* (1995) 19 EHRR 1, para. 31.

[225] *Casado Coca* v *Spain* (1994) 18 EHRR 1, para. 50 and *Jacubowski* v *Germany* (1995) 19 EHRR 64, para. 26.

[226] See, e.g., *Prager and Oberschlick* v *Austria* (1996) 21 EHRR 1 and *De Haes and Gijsels* v *Belgium* (1998) 25 EHRR 1.

This term has to be interpreted in a way which reflects the fundamental principle of the rule of law.[227] It encompasses both the machinery of justice or the judicial branch of government, as well as judges in their official capacity. The rationale for this restriction is that the public should have respect for and confidence in the courts' ability to fulfil their function of clarifying legal rights and deciding on legal disputes.

7.12 ARTICLE 11: FREEDOM OF PEACEFUL ASSEMBLY AND ASSOCIATION

1. Everyone has the right to freedom of peaceful assembly and to freedom of association with others, including the right to form and to join trade unions for the protection of his interests.
2. No restrictions shall be placed on the exercise of these rights other than such as are prescribed by law and are necessary in a democratic society in the interests of national security or public safety, for the prevention of disorder or crime, for the protection of health or morals or for the protection of the rights and freedoms of others. This article shall not prevent the imposition of lawful restrictions on the exercise of these rights by members of the armed forces, of the police or of the administration of the state.

The rights to freedom of peaceful assembly and association are linked to the right to freedom of expression in Article 10 and the right to freedom of thought, conscience and religion in Article 9. The Court has stressed that Articles 9 and 10 would be of very limited scope if there was not also a guarantee of being able to share beliefs and ideas in community with others, particularly through associations of individuals with the same beliefs, ideas or interests.[228] Equally, one of the objectives of the right to freedom of peaceful assembly and association is the freedom to hold opinions and to receive and impart information and ideas.[229] Where Articles 9, 10 and/or 11 are invoked together, the Court may decide to deal with one of those rights as the *lex specialis*, in which case in doing so it may take into account the other rights. The Court may also find violations of more than one of Articles 9 to 11, depending on the particular circumstances of the case.

7.12.1 Freedom of peaceful assembly

The right to freedom of peaceful assembly is considered to be one of the foundations of a democratic society and it is therefore not to be restrictively interpreted. The assembly must be peaceful: Article 11 does not protect those who

---

[227] See, e.g., *Sunday Times* v *UK (No. 1)* 2 EHRR 245, para. 55.

[228] See, e.g., *Chassagnou and others* v *France* (2000) 29 EHRR 615, para. 100.

[229] See, e.g., *Ahmed and others* v *UK* (2000) 29 EHRR 1, para. 70.

have violent intentions which result in public disorder.[230] Article 11 will, however, apply to an assembly where there is a real risk of a violent counter-demonstration, where the violence would be outside the control of the organisers.[231] The right has been applied to private meetings and meetings in the streets and other public places, marches, processions and 'sit-ins'. In *Anderson and others* v *UK* [1998] EHRLR 218 the applicants complained of their exclusion from a privately-owned pedestrianised shopping development which covered a large part of the centre of the town of Wellingborough. The Commission found that freedom of assembly does not guarantee a right to pass and repass in public places, or to assemble anywhere for purely social purposes. Meetings in public may legitimately require prior authorisation.[232]

Article 11 protects the communication of opinions by word, gesture and silent demonstrations.[233] Those who organise (both individuals and corporate bodies) and participate in a peaceful assembly can invoke Article 11.

General blanket bans on demonstrations will require far more justification than bans on particular assemblies. In *Rai, Allmond and 'Negotiate Now'* v *UK* (1995) 19 EHRR CD 93, the Commission found that banning the applicants from holding a rally in Trafalgar Square in London was not disproportionate as they were prevented from demonstrating in only one high profile location in central London. However, a general ban will only be justifiable if there is a real danger of disorder which cannot be prevented by other less stringent measures. An important factor to be taken into account is the effect on assemblies which do not pose a risk of disorder but which are nevertheless caught by the ban. In *Christians Against Racism and Facism* v *UK*, No. 8440/78, 16.7.80, the Commission found a blanket ban on demonstrations in London for two months, which was aimed at preventing a National Front march but which also prohibited the applicant's demonstration, to be 'necessary in a democratic society' because of the tense atmosphere at that time created by a series of National Front demonstrations. Where there is a foreseeable danger to public safety which the authorities must deal with at short notice, the state is likely to be given a wide margin of appreciation in placing restrictions on the right to assembly.[234]

In the context of the disruption of a demonstration by counter-demonstrators, the Court has confirmed that the right to freedom of assembly may entail positive obligations on the state to provide protection of peaceful protestors. In *Plattform 'Ärzte für das Leben'* v *Austria* (1991) 13 EHRR 204 the applicants complained about the lack of police protection to prevent the disruption of their anti-abortion demonstrations by pro-abortionist groups. The Court stated as follows:

---

[230] See, e.g., *G* v *Germany*, No. 13079/87, 6.3.89.
[231] *Christians Against Racism and Fascism* v *UK*, No. 8440/78, 16.7.80, para. 4.
[232] *Rassemblement Jurassien and Unité Jurassien* v *Switzerland*, No. 8191/78, 10.10.79.
[233] See, e.g., *Ezelin* v *France* (1992) 14 EHRR 362, para. 52.
[234] *Rassemblement Jurassien and Unité Jurassien* v *Switzerland*, No. 8191/78, 10.10.79, para. 9.

A demonstration may annoy or give offence to persons opposed to the ideas or claims that it is seeking to promote. The participants must, however, be able to hold the demonstration without having to fear that they will be subjected to physical violence by their opponents; such a fear would be liable to deter associations or other groups supporting common ideas or interests from openly expressing their opinions on highly controversial issues affecting the community. In a democracy the right to counter-demonstrate cannot extend to inhibiting the exercise of the right to demonstrate.

However, states have a wide discretion as to the reasonable and appropriate measures to be taken to enable lawful demonstrations to proceed peacefully.

7.12.2 Freedom of association

The right to freedom of association applies to private law bodies, but not public law bodies which are not considered to be 'associations' within the meaning of Article 11. In *Le Compte, Van Leuven and De Meyere* (1982) 4 EHRR 1 the applicant doctors complained about being required to join the *Ordre des Médecins* and being subjected to its disciplinary system. The Court held that the *Ordre* was not an 'association', taking into account its public law status and its functions of controlling the practice of medicine and maintaining the register of practitioners, as well as its administrative, rule-making and disciplinary powers. As there were also no restrictions on practitioners setting up or joining their own professional associations, there was no interference with the applicant's Article 11 rights.

The term 'association' is, however, an autonomous concept — the classification of an organisation in the national law will be a factor, but will not be decisive in establishing whether the right to freedom of association is applicable. For example, hunters' associations in France were found to be 'associations' within the meaning of Article 11, despite the Government's arguments that they were public law, para-administrative institutions outside its scope.[235]

Political parties are protected by the right to freedom of association under Article 11, not least because they are 'essential to the proper functioning of democracy'.[236] Because of this, the exceptions in Article 11(2) are to be strictly construed in relation to political parties: convincing and compelling reasons will be needed to justify restrictions and the state will be allowed only a limited margin of appreciation.

Article 11 includes a negative right of association and therefore prevents compulsory membership of associations, which may include professional associations and trade unions.[237]

---

[235] *Chassagnou and others* v *France* (2000) 29 EHRR 615, para. 100.

[236] *United Communist Party of Turkey and others* v *Turkey* (1998) 26 EHRR 121, para. 25. See also, *Socialist Party and others* v *Turkey* (1999) 27 EHRR 51 and *Freedom and Democracy Party (Özdep)* v *Turkey*, No. 23885/44, 8.12.99.

[237] See, e.g., *Sigurjonsson* v *Iceland* (1993) 16 EHRR 462.

7.12.3   Trade unions

Expressly included within the right to freedom of association under Article 11 is the right to form and to join trade unions. However, Article 11 has not been expansively interpreted in relation to trade unions. The Court has held that Article 11 does not guarantee any particular treatment of trade unions, such as the right to be consulted by the state or the right to strike.[238] However, Article 11 does require that trade unions should be heard[239] and that they should be able to take action to protect the occupational interests of their members,[240] an important aspect of which is the right to strike which may be limited by regulation in particular circumstances. The Commission has accepted that an obligation on a union to reveal its members' names to a third party could give rise to an unjustified interference with Article 11, but there was no violation in *NATFHE* v *UK* (1998) 26 EHRR CD 122 where the applicant union was required by statute to reveal the names of its members to an employer prior to balloting on industrial action, on the basis that such a duty did not adversely affect the union's capability to protect its members' interests.

Article 11 may protect the rights of those not wishing to join a union. *Young, James and Webster* v *UK* (1982) 4 EHRR 38 concerned the applicants' dismissal for failing to join one of three unions which had concluded a 'closed shop' agreement with their employer, British Rail, so that membership was a condition of employment. The Court found that the threat of dismissal and the exertion of pressure on the applicants to join an association contrary to their convictions went o the very heart of the protections provided by Article 11, which was found to be violated by such disproportionate measures. The Court has held that Article 11 binds the 'state as employer', whether relations with employees are governed by public or private law.[241]

7.12.4   Public officials

Article 11(2) expressly includes the right of the state to place 'lawful restrictions' on the exercise of the Article 11(1) rights by members of the armed forces, the police and members of the 'administration of the state'. This latter term is to be narrowly interpreted — in *Vogt* v *Germany* (1996) 21 EHRR 205 the Court left open the question as to whether the term included teachers. In *Vogt* the applicant teacher's dismissal for refusing to disassociate herself from the German Communist Party was an interference with her rights under Article 11 which was held to be disproportionate. The term 'lawful restrictions' has the same meaning as the terms 'in accordance with the law' and 'prescribed by law', in requiring not

---

[238] *Schmidt and Dahlstrom* v *Sweden* 1 EHRR 632, para. 36.
[239] *Swedish Engine Drivers' Union* v *Sweden* 1 EHRR 617, para. 40.
[240] *National Union of Belgian Police* v *Belgium* 1 EHRR 578, para. 39.
[241] See, e.g., *Schmidt and Dahlstrom* v *Sweden* 1 EHRR 632, para. 33.

only conformity with domestic law but also a certain quality of the law and sufficient foreseeability[242] (see also above at 7.8).

7.13   ARTICLE 12: RIGHT TO MARRY

Men and women of marriageable age have the right to marry and to found a family, according to the national laws governing the exercise of this right.

Article 12 has been narrowly interpreted. It should always be considered in conjunction with the right to respect for private and family life under Article 8.

The Court has interpreted Article 12 as upholding 'traditional marriage between persons of opposite biological sex' and has found that Article 12 is mainly concerned to protect marriage as the basis of the family.[243] Article 12 has not therefore been interpreted as permitting two persons of the same sex to marry, nor to allow a person who has undergone gender reassignment surgery to marry someone of the opposite sex to that as which the person now lives.[244] However, in *Cossey v UK* (1991) 13 EHRR 622[245], the Court recognised that this might change: 'although some contracting states would now regard as valid a marriage between a person in Miss Cossey's situation and a man, the developments which have occurred to date cannot be said to evidence any general abandonment of the traditional concept of marriage'.

Article 12 also stipulates that the exercise of the right is subject to the national laws of the state parties; however, any limitations on the right must not restrict or reduce the right to an extent which would impair the very essence of the right. Therefore restrictions on the right to marry, such as procedural requirements or limitations as to capacity or age, will be subject to a test of proportionality.

Article 12 upholds the right to remarry,[246] but does not establish a right of divorce.[247]

7.14   ARTICLE 13: RIGHT TO AN EFFECTIVE REMEDY

Everyone whose rights and freedoms as set forth in this Convention are violated shall have an effective remedy before a national authority notwithstanding that the violation has been committed by persons acting in an official capacity.

---

[242] *Rekvényi v Hungary* (2000) 30 EHRR 519, para. 59.
[243] *Rees v UK* (1987) 9 EHRR 56, and, e.g., *Sheffield and Horsham v UK* (1999) 27 EHRR 163, para. 66.
[244] *Sheffield and Horsham v UK* (1999) 27 EHRR 163.
[245] See especially paras 46 and 40.
[246] See, e.g., *F v Switzerland* (1988) 10 EHRR 411.
[247] *Johnston and others v Ireland* (1987) 9 EHRR 203, paras 51–54.

The Court has held that Article 13 must be interpreted as guaranteeing an effective remedy before a national authority for everyone who claims that his rights and freedoms under the Convention have been violated.[248] The effect of Article 13 is therefore to require the provision of a domestic remedy allowing the competent national authority both to deal with the substance of the relevant Convention complaint and to grant appropriate relief. The remedy required by Article 13 need not be provided by a court (see further below). It must be 'effective' in practice as well as in law, in particular in the sense that its exercise must not be unjustifiably hindered by the acts or omissions of the authorities of the respondent state.[249] The Article expressly states that such remedies must be available even as against those acting in their official capacity.

Whilst Article 13 does not require a domestic remedy in relation to *any* grievance under the Convention, it can be properly invoked in relation to any *arguable claim* of a violation of another Convention right.[250] However, it is important to note that in spite of the literal wording of the Article, no other Convention right need be violated in order to establish a breach of Article 13.[251] The Court has not defined the notion of arguability, which it has said must be determined in the light of the particular facts and the nature of the legal issues raised in each case.[252] While Article 13 guarantees the availability of a suitable forum to obtain a remedy, it cannot of course require that the applicant's claim is in fact successful.

Article 13 does not guarantee a remedy to challenge domestic legislation. For example, on that basis, the Commission rejected a claim of a violation of Article 13 in *CC* v *UK*, No. 32819/96, Comm. Rep. 30.6.98 which concerned the automatic denial of bail under the Criminal Justice and Public Order Act 1994.

The 'remedy' need not be provided by a court, but the body in question providing the remedy must be capable of affording effective redress and must be sufficiently independent of the body being challenged. Remedies which are discretionary, or unenforceable, will not generally comply with Article 13. For example, the Prison Board of Visitors and the Parliamentary Ombudsman were found to lack sufficient powers in relation to a complaint concerning the interception of prisoners' mail.[253] The Commission in *Govell* v *UK*, No. 27237/95, Comm. Rep. 14.1.98 found that the police complaints system does not provide an effective remedy, within the meaning of Article 13, because of the system's lack of independence. In reaching its decision, the Commission took into account the fact that it is standard practice for a Chief Constable to appoint a member of his or her own force to carry out the investigation, and noted the role of the Home

---

[248] *Klass and others* v *Germany* 2 EHRR 214, para 64.
[249] *Aksoy* v *Turkey* (1997) 23 EHRR 553, para. 95
[250] See, e.g., *Silver* v *UK* (1983) 5 EHRR 347.
[251] *Klass and others* v *Germany* 2 EHRR 214, para. 64.
[252] *Boyle and Rice* (1988) 10 EHRR 425, para. 55.
[253] *Silver* v *UK* (1983) 5 EHRR 347.

Secretary in appointing, remunerating and dismissing members of the Police Complaints Authority. This decision was confirmed by the Court in *Khan* v *UK*, No. 35394/97, 12.5.00.

In exceptional situations, the aggregate of remedies provided by domestic law may satisfy Article 13, as was found to be the case in *Leander* v *Sweden* (1987) 9 EHRR 433 in the context of secret security vetting.

The scope of Article 13 will vary depending upon the nature of the Convention complaint. For example, in the context of allegations of torture, the Court has held that the notion of an 'effective remedy' under Article 13 requires 'a thorough and effective investigation capable of leading to the identification and punishment of those responsible and including effective access for the complainant to the investigatory procedure'.[254]

In relation to systems of secret surveillance by the state, the Court has recognised that an 'effective remedy' under Article 13 must mean a remedy 'that is as effective as can be having regard to the restricted scope for recourse inherent in any system of secret surveillance'.[255] In *Chahal* v *UK* (1997) 23 EHRR 413, however, given the importance of Article 3 and the potential irreversible harm to the applicant (a Sikh nationalist under threat of deportation to India), the Court emphasised that the notion of an effective remedy under Article 13 required independent scrutiny of the claim that there existed substantial grounds for fearing a real risk of treatment contrary to Article 3. Article 13 was found to have been violated in *Chahal* as neither the 'advisory panel' nor the domestic courts could review the decision to deport him with reference solely to the question of risk, quite apart from any national security considerations. The advisory panel was also found not to provide sufficient procedural safeguards for Article 13 purposes, as the applicant had not been entitled to legal representation, he was given only an outline of the grounds for the decision and the panel could not make a binding decision and its advice to the Minister was not disclosed.

Prior to the implementation of the Human Rights Act 1998, the European Court has found that in certain circumstances judicial review will amount to an effective remedy, but in other situations it will not. The Court has contrasted the 'most anxious scrutiny' applied by the domestic courts to the individual facts in extradition or asylum cases such as *Soering* v *UK* (1989) 11 EHRR 439 or *Vilvarajah* v *UK* (1992) 14 EHRR 248 (where the test applied by the domestic courts was found to coincide with the Court's own approach under Article 3) with cases where the High Court's jurisdiction was limited and where therefore there could be no application of the test of proportionality. In *Smith and Grady* v *UK*

---

[254] See, e.g., *Aksoy* v *Turkey* (1997) 23 EHRR 553, para. 98. See also *Aydin* v *Turkey* (1998) 25 EHRR 251, para. 103; *Kaya* v *Turkey* (1999) 28 EHRR 1, para. 107; *Kurt* v *Turkey* (1999) 27 EHRR 373, para. 104; *Tekin* v *Turkey*, No. 22496/93, 9.6.98, para. 66; *Yaşa* v *Turkey* (1999) 28 EHRR 408, para. 114.

[255] See, e.g., *Klass and others* v *Germany* 2 EHRR 214, para. 69.

(2000) 29 EHRR 493, which concerned the ban on homosexuals in the armed forces, the Court found that despite the availability of judicial review proceedings, there had been a violation of Article 13 because the threshold at which the domestic courts could find the policy in question to be irrational 'was placed so high that it effectively excluded any consideration by the domestic courts of the question of whether the interference with the applicants' rights answered a pressing social need or was proportionate to the ... aims pursued, principles which lie at the heart of the Court's analysis of complaints under Article 8 of the Convention' (see para. 138). The likely effect of the Human Rights Act 1998 is that there will be fewer findings by the European Court of violations of Article 13 in UK cases.

7.15   ARTICLE 14: PROHIBITION OF DISCRIMINATION

The enjoyment of the rights and freedoms set forth in this Convention shall be secured without discrimination on any ground such as sex, race, colour, language, religion, political or other opinion, national or social origin, association with a national minority, property, birth or other status.

Article 14 prohibits discrimination in relation to the other Convention rights only. It is therefore not a free-standing right and must be invoked in conjunction with another substantive Convention right (including the rights contained in the Protocols). The 'parasitic' nature of the right is one of the reasons why the Article 14 case law has been limited. Its narrow remit has frequently been the subject of criticism. However, it is intended that Protocol 12 to the Convention will create a free-standing, non-discrimination provision. Protocol 12 is discussed in chapter 10.

The Strasbourg institutions can be criticised for failing to develop Article 14 notwithstanding its limited remit. For example, in the cases concerning the ban on homosexuals in the armed forces, *Smith and Grady* v *UK* (2000) 29 EHRR 493 and *Lustig-Prean and Beckett* v *UK* (2000) 29 EHRR 548 the Court found violations of the right to respect for private life (and of Article 13 in *Smith and Grady*), but it declined to consider Article 14, finding that it did not give rise to a separate issue. This case, concerning as it did an overtly discriminatory policy, illustrates the weakness of the application of Article 14. It has been the stated practice of the Court not to examine a complaint under Article 14 where a separate breach of the substantive Article has been found, unless a clear inequality of treatment is a fundamental aspect of the case.[256]

7.15.1   Applicability of Article 14

Article 14 can be relied upon provided that the complaint falls within the *ambit* of one or more of the other Convention rights, but it is not necessary to establish that

---

[256] See, e.g., *Dudgeon* v *UK* (1982) 4 EHRR 149, para. 67.

there has been a violation of another Convention right. In *Botta v Italy* (1998) 26 EHRR 241, for example, the applicant's complaint about discrimination in relation to access to bathing facilities on holiday for disabled people was not considered to fall within the ambit of Article 8 and therefore Article 14 had no application. However, in *Van der Mussele v Belgium* (1984) 6 EHRR 163, the complaint of a pupil advocate about having to perform *pro bono* work was found not to breach Article 4, but as the case fell within the ambit of Article 4, Article 14 was applicable.

Article 14 also applies not only to aspects of a Convention right which the state is obliged to protect, but also those aspects which a state chooses to guarantee, without being required to do so. In *Petrovic v Austria* (1998) 5 BHRC 232 the applicant father's complaint that the parental leave allowance was only available to mothers fell within the scope of Article 8 (despite the fact that there was no positive obligation to provide such financial assistance) because by granting such an allowance, the aim of the state was to promote family life.

7.15.2 Grounds of discrimination

Article 14 expressly prohibits discrimination on *any* ground: examples includes sex, race, colour, language, religion, political or other opinion, national or social origin, association with a national minority, property, or birth. However, it also prohibits discrimination on grounds of 'other status', indicating that the list is open-ended. For example, the other grounds prohibited have been found to include marital status, sexual orientation,[257] illegitimacy, disability[258] professional status[259] and military status.[260]

7.15.3 The test of discrimination

A person is considered to have suffered discrimination if:

(a) he or she has been treated differently from people in a similar situation (on a prohibited ground); and
(b) there is no reasonable and objective justification for the difference in treatment.[261]

The applicant must establish that there has been less favourable treatment and that its basis was a prohibited ground of discrimination. However, there will be no violation of Article 14 if the difference in treatment related to people who were

---

[257] See. e.g., *Sutherland v UK*, No. 25186/94, Comm. Rep. 1.7.97.
[258] *Malone v UK* [1996] EHRLR 440.
[259] *Van der Mussele v Belgium* (1984) 6 EHRR 163.
[260] *Engel and others v Netherlands* 1 EHRR 647.
[261] See, e.g., *Belgian Linguistic Case* 1 EHRR 252.

not in analogous situations. Each of these elements can of course be very difficult to establish. In *Van der Mussele* v *Belgium* (1984) 6 EHRR 163, the applicant lawyer complained about discrimination between advocates and other professions in relation to the obligation to work without payment. However, the Court held that, in view of the fundamental differences between the professions (as to legal status, conditions for entry into the profession, the nature of the functions involved and the manner of exercise of those functions) there was no similarity between the disparate situations in question.

If an applicant establishes that there has been differential treatment in an analogous situation, then the state must prove that the difference in treatment had a 'reasonable and objective justification'. The test which the Court applies is twofold: that the difference in treatment pursued a legitimate aim; and that it was proportionate to that aim.

The test of proportionality (which is discussed further above at 6.5) requires an assessment of whether there is a reasonable relationship of proportionality between the means employed and the aim sought to be achieved. Any difference in treatment must strike a fair balance between the protection of the interests of the community and respect for the rights and freedoms safeguarded by the Convention.

In assessing the proportionality of a measure, the state is generally allowed a certain margin of appreciation, or discretion. However, the Court has found that discrimination on particular grounds, such as sex[262] and nationality[263] will have to be justified by 'very weighty reasons'. The Commission has also affirmed that 'a special importance should be attached to discrimination based on race'.[264] One of the relevant factors in considering the reasons for the difference in treatment is whether or not there is a common standard amongst Council of Europe states. In *Petrovic* v *Austria* (1998) 5 BHRC 232 the Court noted that there was no such common standard in respect of parental leave allowances for fathers (at the end of the 1980s most Council of Europe states did not provide for such payments) and accordingly the decision to refuse the applicant a parental leave allowance fell within the state's margin of appreciation.

Hoffmann v *Austria* (1994) 17 EHRR 293 concerned the dispute over custody of the applicant's children. In awarding custody to the applicant's ex-husband, the domestic courts had assessed the effects that the applicant's membership of the Jehovah's Witness community would have on the children, which included the effects on their social life of being associated with a religious minority and the hazards attached to the rejection of blood transfusions. The European Court found that there had been a difference in treatment on religious grounds which had a legitimate aim (the protection of the health and rights of the children), but which

---

[262] See, e.g., *Abdulaziz, Cabales and Balkandali* v *UK* (1985) 7 EHRR 471, para. 78.
[263] *Gaygusuz* v *Austria* (1997) 23 EHRR 364, para. 42.
[264] *East African Asians* v *UK* (1981) 3 EHRR 76, para. 207.

was disproportionate: a distinction based essentially on a difference in religion alone was not acceptable. However, this decision was reached by a majority of just five to four, with the dissenting judges arguing that the domestic courts had reached their decision not on religious grounds, but because of the consequences for the children of the applicant's membership of the Jehovah's Witnesses, which they considered to be legitimate grounds.

There was no reasonable and objective basis for the difference in treatment between men and women in the payment of contributions to a child benefit scheme in *Van Raalte* v *Netherlands* (1997) 24 EHRR 503. The domestic law exempted unmarried childless women over forty-five, but not men. The Court noted that 'just as women over forty-five may give birth to children, there are on the other hand men of forty-five or younger who may be unable to procreate',[265] and that women over forty-five might also become eligible for child benefit by, for example, marrying a man who had children from a previous marriage. In *Chassagnou and others* v *France* (2000) 29 EHRR 615 the Court found no objective and reasonable justification in allowing large-scale landowners, but not small-scale landowners, the right to opt out of membership of hunting associations.

The Court has also recently held that the right not to be discriminated against is violated when, without an objective and reasonable justification, there is a failure to treat differently, persons whose situations are significantly different. There was a violation of Article 14, in conjunction with Article 9, in *Thlimmenos* v *Greece*, No. 34369/97, 6.4.00 on that basis. There, the applicant, a Jehovah's Witness, had been refused an appointment to a post of chartered accountant, as a result of a prior criminal conviction for disobeying an order to wear military uniform, because of his religious beliefs. He complained of the fact that no distinction was made between persons convicted of offences committed exclusively because of their religious beliefs and persons convicted of other offences. The applicant's exclusion from the profession was held to be disproportionate and did not pursue a legitimate aim.

Positive discrimination is not automatically prohibited by Article 14; it will depend upon the justification for the difference in treatment in each case.[266]

7.16 ARTICLE 1 OF PROTOCOL 1: RIGHT OF PROPERTY

Every natural or legal person is entitled to the peaceful enjoyment of his possessions. No one shall be deprived of his possessions except in the public interest and subject to the conditions provided for by law and by the general principles of international law.

The preceding provisions shall not, however, in any way impair the right of a state to enforce such laws as it deems necessary to control the use of property in accordance with the general interest or to secure the payment of taxes or other contributions or penalties.

---

[265] (1997) 24 EHRR 503, para. 43.
[266] See, e.g., *Lindsay* v *UK* (1986) 49 DR 181.

Article 1 of Protocol 1 provides qualified protections to the right of property. The Article expressly allows public authorities a wide discretion to interfere with the right: it permits the deprivation of a person's possessions where it is 'in the public interest', and the second paragraph allows the state to impose 'such laws as it deems necessary' in relation to taxation and other contributions or penalties.

7.16.1 Possessions

A 'possession' has been broadly interpreted to include land and moveable goods, as well as planning permission,[267] unenforced expropriation orders and the prohibition on construction,[268] the economic interests arising from a licence to sell alcohol,[269] a permit for gravel extraction,[270] hunting rights over land,[271] shares,[272] patents,[273] an enforceable debt,[274] and legal claims for compensation and for the restitution of assets.[275] A 'possession' is an autonomous Convention concept and therefore the domestic classification will not be decisive.

7.16.2 The three principles

The Article covers three principles:

(a) the entitlement to peaceful enjoyment of possessions;
(b) the prohibition of deprivation of possessions, subject to specified conditions; and
(c) the right of the state to control the use of property, subject to specified conditions.[276]

These principles are inter-related: the second and third rules are to be construed in the light of the general principle contained in the first.

The notion of 'deprivation' covers both *de facto* deprivation as well as formal deprivation. It is frequently in dispute as to whether there had been a 'deprivation of possessions' (second rule) or a 'control of use of property' (third rule), as the former will require greater justification than the latter. For example, in *Fredin* v *Sweden* (1991) 13 EHRR 784 the Court rejected the applicants' arguments that the revocation of their permit for gravel extraction was so serious as to amount to a

---

[267] *Pine Valley Developments Ltd* v *Ireland* (1992) 14 EHRR 319.
[268] *Sporrong and Lönnroth* v *Sweden* (1983) 5 EHRR 35.
[269] *Tre Traktörer Aktiebolag* v *Sweden* (1991) 13 EHRR 309.
[270] *Fredin* v *Sweden* (1991) 13 EHRR 784.
[271] *Chassagnou and others* v *France* (2000) 29 EHRR 615.
[272] *Bramelid and Malmstrom* v *Sweden* (1982) 29 DR 64.
[273] *Smith Kline and French Laboratories* v *Netherlands* (1990) 66 DR 70.
[274] *Stran Greek Refineries and others* v *Greece* (1995) 19 EHRR 293.
[275] *Pressos Compania Naviera SA and others* v *Belgium* (1996) 21 EHRR 301, para. 31 and *National and Provincial Building Society and others* v *UK* (1998) 25 EHRR 127, para. 74.
[276] *Sporrong and Lönnroth* v *Sweden* (1983) 5 EHRR 35, para. 61.

de facto deprivation of possessions, finding instead that it amounted to a 'control of use of property'. Similarly, in *Air Canada* v *UK* (1995) 20 EHRR 150 the seizure of an aircraft by customs officials following the discovery of cannibis resin, and the requirement to pay £50,000 in order to have it returned, was also found to be a 'control of use of property'. This was because the seizure was temporary and did not involve a transfer of ownership, and it had been carried out as part of a scheme intended to prevent carriers from bringing prohibited drugs into the country. In *AGOSI* v *UK* (1987) 9 EHRR 1 the applicant company complained about the forfeiture of krugerrands which had been seized by Customs and Excise officers from third parties whilst attempting to smuggle them into the UK. The Court found that whilst the forfeiture did involve a deprivation of property, it had been a measure taken as part of the prohibition of the importation of gold coins into the UK and therefore the second paragraph of Article 1 applied. In *Pine Valley Developments Ltd* v *Ireland* (1992) 14 EHRR 319 the annulment of outline planning permission for the applicant's land was found to be a measure of control of the use of property.

7.16.3   Public interest

In assessing interferences with property under Article 1 of Protocol 1, the Court will attempt to strike a fair balance between the right of the individual and the general interest of the community. There must be a reasonable relationship of proportionality between the means employed and the aim pursued. The authorities are allowed a wide margin of appreciation both in respect of the means of enforcement and the justification of the measure taken in the general interest. The second paragraph of Article 1 is to be construed in the light of the principles set out in the first sentence.

The Court has stated that the notion of what is in the public interest is:

> necessarily extensive. In particular, the decision to enact laws expropriating property will commonly involve consideration of political, economic and social issues on which opinion in a democratic society may reasonably differ widely. The Court, finding it natural that the margin of appreciation available to the legislature in implementing social and economic policies should be a wide one, will respect the legislature's judgment as to what is 'in the public interest' unless that judgment be manifestly without reasonable foundation'.[277]

In *Air Canada* the measures taken were found to conform to the general interest in combating international drug trafficking. In *Hentrich* v *France* (1994) 18 EHRR 440, the legitimate objective in the public interest for the exercise by the Commissioner of Revenue of a right of pre-emption over land, was the prevention

---

[277] *Pressos Compania Naviera SA and others* v *Belgium* (1996) 21 EHRR 301, para. 37.

of tax evasion. In *James* v *UK* (1986) 8 EHRR 123 the applicants were trustees of a substantial estate under the Duke of Westminster's will. They complained of the deprivation of part of their land following the exercise by tenants of rights of acquisition under the Leasehold Reform Act 1967. The Court rejected the applicants' arguments that the transfer of property from one individual to another could not be in the public interest, as 'the taking of property in pursuance of a policy calculated to enhance social justice within the community' would satisfy the public interest requirement. Moreover, the fairness of the system governing property rights as between individuals was also a matter of public concern.

7.16.4   Compensation

The level of compensation paid where there has been a deprivation of property will be a material factor in assessing proportionality. The taking of property will normally require compensation with an amount reasonably related to the value of the property, but public interest considerations (including measures designed to achieve greater social justice)[278] may permit reimbursement of less than the full market value.[279] In *Holy Monasteries* v *Greece* (1995) 20 EHRR 1 the transfer of land from the applicant monasteries to the Greek state without compensation was therefore found to be a deprivation of property in violation of Article 1. However, the failure to pay compensation following the annulment of outline planning permission for the applicant's land in *Pine Valley Developments Ltd* v *Ireland* (1992) 14 EHRR 319 was not found to be disproportionate, having regard to the commercial venture undertaken by the applicants and the consequential element of risk.

7.16.5   Legal regulation

An interference with property must also be sufficiently regulated by law, which requires sufficient precision and foreseeability in domestic law and practice. In *Hentrich* v *France* (1994) 18 EHRR 440, this requirement was violated by the Commissioner of Revenue exercising a right of pre-emption following the applicants' purchase of land in a manner which was arbitrary, selective and 'scarcely foreseeable'.

7.16.6   Procedural requirements

The second paragraph has been held implicitly to include procedural requirements. In the *AGOSI* case, the Court considered two procedural issues: whether reasonable account had been taken of the relationship between the conduct of the company and the unlawful smuggling of gold coins, and whether the company

---

[278] *James* v *UK* (1986) 8 EHRR 123, para. 54.
[279] See, e.g., *Holy Monasteries* v *Greece* (1995) 20 EHRR 1, para. 71.

had an adequate opportunity to put its case to the authorities. In that case, the scope of judicial review (in challenging the discretion of the Commissioners of Customs and Excise) was held to satisfy the requirements of the second paragraph of Article 1.

7.17 ARTICLE 2 OF PROTOCOL 1: RIGHT TO EDUCATION

No person shall be denied the right to education. In the exercise of any functions which it assumes in relation to education and to teaching, the state shall respect the right of parents to ensure such education and teaching is in conformity with their own religious and philosophical convictions.

The prohibition of the denial of the right to education has not been generously interpreted. The overriding aim of the provision is to ensure a right of access, in principle, to 'the means of instruction existing at a given time'. It has been held to guarantee a right of access to existing educational institutions and the right to obtain official recognition of studies completed.

It does not require states to establish, either at their own expense, or to subsidise, education of a particular type or at a particular level. The Article also does not lay down requirements for the content and purpose of the education or teaching: the setting and planning of the curriculum falls in principle within the state's competence.

There is no requirement that education be available in any particular language, other than the national language (or one of the national languages).[280] However, in *Cyprus* v *Turkey*, No. 25781/94, Comm. Rep. 4.6.99 the failure to provide secondary education in Greek in northern Cyprus was found to violate Article 2. The Commission found that the pupils had a legitimate desire to preserve their own ethnic and cultural identity, and whilst Article 2 of Protocol 1 guaranteed access only to existing educational facilities, the Commission noted that such educational facilities had in fact existed in the past and had been abolished by the Turkish Cypriot authorities.

The right to education may be subject to regulation which will vary in time and place according to the needs and resources of the community and of individuals.

7.17.1 Education in conformity with parents' religious and philosophical convictions

The aim of the second sentence of Article 2 is to safeguard the possibility of pluralism in education.[281] At the time of signing the first Protocol, the UK Government entered into a reservation in respect of this provision, which is incorporated into the Human Rights Act 1998 (schedule 3):

---

[280] *Belgian Linguistic Case (No. 2)* 1 EHRR 252, paras 3 and 6.
[281] *Kjeldsen, Busk, Madsen and Pedersen* v *Denmark* 1 EHRR 711, para. 50.

... in view of certain provisions of the Education Acts in force in the United Kingdom, the principle affirmed in the second sentence of Article 2 is accepted by the United Kingdom only so far as it is compatible with the provision of efficient instruction and training, and the avoidance of unreasonable public expenditure.

The term 'philosophical convictions' has been defined as meaning 'such convictions as are worthy of respect in a "democratic society" and are not incompatible with human dignity'. In addition, such convictions must not conflict with the fundamental right of the child to education: the whole of Article 2 being dominated by its first sentence.[282] For example, opposition to corporal punishment satisfies these criteria.

The second sentence requires that information or knowledge included in the curriculum should be conveyed in an 'objective, critical and pluralistic manner', and without indoctrination.

In *Campbell and Cosans* v *UK* (1982) 4 EHRR 293 the applicants complained about the system of corporal punishment in state schools. The Court rejected the Government's arguments that the disciplinary system did not fall within the 'functions' relating to education or teaching, and confirmed that any function ancillary to education and teaching would be subject to Article 2 of Protocol 1. It was also held that the obligation to respect parents' philosophical and religious convictions not only applies to the content of education, but also to other functions including the organisation and financing of education and the disciplinary system. The existence of corporal punishment was found to violate the applicants' rights under the second sentence of the Article, and the suspension of Jeffrey Cosans from school for nearly a year was unreasonable and accordingly violated the first sentence.

The applicants in *Kjeldsen, Busk, Madsen and Pedersen* v *Denmark* 1 EHRR 711, as Christian parents, objected to compulsory sex education in schools. The Court found no violation of Article 2 on the basis that the relevant legislation did not advocate a specific kind of sexual behaviour or incite pupils to indulge in practices which might be dangerous for their stability, health or future. Therefore, it was not considered to offend the applicants' convictions to the extent forbidden by the second sentence of the Article.

The authorities are given a wide discretion in utilising resources to provide for the education of children with special educational needs.[283] For example, in *SP* v *UK*, No. 28915/95, 17.1.97, the applicant complained about the provision of education to her son who was dyslexic. The application was declared inadmissible as there had been no question of his being excluded from the educational facilities provided by the state.

---

[282] *Campbell and Cosans* v *UK* (1982) 4 EHRR 293, para. 36.
[283] See, e.g., *Molly McIntyre* v *UK*, No. 29046/95, 21.10.98.

Article 14 is frequently invoked in conjunction with Article 2. For example, a series of applications brought by gypsies complaining about discriminatory planning provisions were declared admissible in 1998.[284] The applicants argued that being denied permission to stay on their own land, threatening them with removal, undermined the stability of their children's education and would inevitably have a severely deleterious effect on their future education, in violation of Article 2 of Protocol 1.

7.18   ARTICLE 3 OF PROTOCOL 1: RIGHT TO FREE ELECTIONS

The High Contracting Parties undertake to hold free elections at reasonable intervals by secret ballot, under conditions which will ensure the free expression of the opinion of the people in the choice of the legislature.

The Court has described this Article as being 'of prime importance in the Convention system' as it enshrines a characteristic principle of democracy.[285] Unlike the majority of other Convention rights, it is primarily concerned with a positive obligation — to hold democratic elections. There is a strong link with Article 10: 'free elections and freedom of expression, particularly freedom of political debate, together form the bedrock of any democratic system'.[286]

Article 3 of Protocol 1 applies only to the election of a 'legislature'. In addition to national parliaments, the Court has held that, depending on the constitutional structure of the state in question, the Article may apply to other bodies. In *Mathieu-Mohin and Clerfayt* v *Belgium* (1988) 10 EHRR 1 the Court found that a regional council had sufficient competence and powers to make it a constituent part of the Belgian 'legislature'. However, metropolitan county councils were not considered to be 'legislatures' because their powers were delegated by Parliament.[287]

In *Matthews* v *UK* (1999) 28 EHRR 361 the applicant complained about the exclusion of Gibraltar from the franchise for the European Parliamentary elections. The Court rejected the Government's arguments that, as a supranational body, the European Parliament fell outside the ambit of Article 3 of Protocol 1. The Court in *Matthews* considered the actual powers of the European Parliament in the context of the EC legislative process, notably since the Maastricht Treaty, and concluded that it was sufficiently involved in the general democratic supervision of the EC to constitute part of the 'legislature' of Gibraltar. As the applicant had been

---

[284] See, e.g., *Coster* v *UK*, No. 24876/94, 4.3.98.
[285] *Mathieu-Mohin and Clerfayt* v *Belgium* (1988) 10 EHRR 1, para. 47.
[286] *Bowman* v *UK* (1998) 26 EHRR 1, para. 42.
[287] *Booth-Clibborn* v *UK* (1985) 43 DR 236.

completely denied the opportunity to express her opinion in choosing members of the European Parliament, Article 3 of Protocol 1 was violated.

Article 3 of Protocol 1 includes both the right to vote and the right to stand for election to the legislature (including the right to sit as an MP once elected).[288] The state has a wide margin of appreciation in setting conditions on those rights (such as minimum age requirements), but any conditions must pursue a legitimate aim and be proportionate and must not impair the very essence of the rights. Restrictions on the voting rights of prisoners have not as yet been found to violate the Convention. The Commission has found that the deprivation of the right to vote following a conviction by a court for uncitizenlike conduct does not affect the expression of the opinion of the people and is not arbitrary. This view is based on 'the notion of dishonour that certain convictions carry with them for a specific period, which may be taken into consideration by legislation in respect of the exercise of political rights'.[289] In *Moore* v *UK*, No. 37841/97, 30.5.00 the applicant invoked Article 3 of Protocol 1, together with Article 14, in challenging the rule preventing mental health patients from using the hospital as their residential address for the purposes of registering on the electoral roll. The case was struck off the Court's list of cases after the UK Government agreed to amend the Representation of the People Act 1983 to allow mental health patients to use the hospital as their address.

In *Matthews* v *UK* (1999) 28 EHRR 361, the Court distinguished the position of the applicant resident of Gibraltar, who had no voting rights in relation to the European Parliament, with that of people who live outside the jurisdiction on the basis that 'such individuals have weakened the link between themselves and the jurisdiction'. In *Labita* v *Italy*, No. 26772/95, 6.4.00, the applicant, who was suspected of belonging to the Mafia, was automatically struck off the electoral register even after his acquittal. This was found by the Court to be disproportionate and in violation of Article 3 of Protocol 1.

The Article does not require a particular electoral system, such as proportional representation, as states have a wide margin of appreciation in relation to appointments to the legislature. The Court has stated that : 'any electoral system must be assessed in the light of the political evolution of the country concerned; features that would be unacceptable in the context of one system may accordingly be justified in the context of another, at least so long as the chosen system provides for conditions which will ensure the free expression of the opinion of the people in the choice of the legislature'.[290]

---

[288] *Gaulieder* v *Slovak Republic*, No. 36909/97, Comm. Rep. 10.9.99.
[289] See, e.g., *Patrick Holland* v *Ireland*, No. 24827/94, 14.4.98.
[290] *Mathieu-Mohin and Clerfayt* v *Belgium* (1988) 10 EHRR 1, para. 54.

7.19 ARTICLES 1 AND 2 OF PROTOCOL 6: ABOLITION OF THE DEATH PENALTY

Article 1

The death penalty shall be abolished. No one shall be condemned to such penalty or executed.

Article 2

A state may make provision in its law for the death penalty in respect of acts committed in time of war or of imminent threat of war; such penalty shall be applied only in the instances laid down in the law and in accordance with its provisions. The state shall communicate to the Secretary-General of the Council of Europe the relevant provisions of that law.

Protocol 6 provides for the abolition of the death penalty in peacetime, but allows a state to maintain the death penalty in respect of acts of war or during imminent threat of war. Article 1 prevents states from either passing the death sentence or carrying out executions.

Articles 3 and 4 of Protocol 6 provide that there may be no derogation from the Protocol (under Article 15) and no reservation (under Article 57). Under Article 5, a state may specify, on ratification or signature of the Protocol, to which territories the Protocol will apply. The Protocol may subsequently be extended to other territories, or its application in relation to particular territories may be withdrawn, by notification to the Secretary-General of the Council of Europe.

The death penalty has been abolished in the UK and Protocol 6 was ratified by the UK in January 1999. Applicants who are under threat of deportation or expulsion from the UK to a country where they may face the death penalty will be able to argue before the Court that their expulsion would be in violation of Article 1 of Protocol 6 (as to the application of Article 3 in such cases, see above at 7.3.3).

Chapter Eight

Derogation and Reservation

8.1 DEROGATION

8.1.1 Introduction

The right of a state to derogate is set out in Article 15, which provides as follows:

> 1. In time of war or other public emergency threatening the life of the nation any High Contracting Party may take measures derogating from its obligations under this Convention to the extent strictly required by the exigencies of the situation, provided that such measures are not inconsistent with its other obligations under international law.
>
> 2. No derogation from Article 2, except in respect of deaths resulting from lawful acts of war, or from Articles 3, 4 (paragraph 1) and 7 shall be made under this provision.
>
> 3. Any High Contracting Party availing itself of this right of derogation shall keep the Secretary-General of the Council of Europe fully informed of the measures which it has taken and the reasons therefor. It shall also inform the Secretary-General of the Council of Europe when such measures have ceased to operate and the provisions of the Convention are again being fully executed.

Article 15(2) permits no derogation in relation to Article 3 (prohibition of torture and inhuman and degrading treatment or punishment), Article 4(1) (prohibition of slavery and servitude), Article 7 (prohibition of retrospective criminal penalties) and in relation to Article 2 (the right to life) other than in respect of acts of war. Therefore, derogation from Article 6 (the right to a fair hearing) is in theory possible, which it is suggested must be extremely difficult to justify.

Article 15 lays down a threefold test for a valid derogation. First, the state must satisfy the Court of the existence of war or a public emergency threatening the life of the nation. If that condition is satisfied, the state must then establish, secondly, that the measures it has taken were 'strictly required by the exigencies of the situation'. Finally, such measures must also comply with the state's international law obligations. In addition, there must be compliance with the procedural requirements. Each of these conditions is considered below.

The Court acknowledges that the state is in a better position to make judgements about the extent of an emergency and the measures necessary to deal with it. Accordingly, the respondent state is allowed a wide margin of appreciation in relation to Article 15,[1] although the discretion is not unlimited. The Court will take into account factors such as the nature of the rights affected by the derogation, the circumstances leading to the emergency situation, and how long it lasts.

8.1.2 Procedural requirements

For a derogation to be effective, there must be some formal, public act of derogation, such as a declaration of martial law or state of emergency. Article 15 will not apply if no such declaration is made, unless it is prevented by special circumstances. A Governmental proclamation[2] will suffice, as will a Ministerial statement in Parliament.[3]

States invoking the derogation provision are also required (by Article 15(3)) to keep the Secretary-General of the Council of Europe fully informed of the measures which it has taken and the reasons for doing so.[4] Undue delay in doing so might be prejudicial.[5]

8.1.3 Public emergency threatening the life of the nation

During peacetime, a derogation can only apply in circumstances where there is a public emergency threatening the life of the nation. This has been interpreted as meaning 'an exceptional situation of crisis or emergency which affects the whole population and constitutes a threat to the organised life of the community of which the state is composed'.[6]

In *Lawless* v *Ireland*, which concerned the applicant's detention without trial for five months, the Court found it was reasonable to have claimed the existence of a public emergency in the late 1950s because of the increasing threat of the IRA

---

[1] *Ireland* v *UK* 2 EHRR 25, para. 207.
[2] *Lawless* v *Ireland (No. 3)* 1 EHRR 15.
[3] *Brannigan and McBride* v *UK* (1994) 17 EHRR 539.
[4] This provision was found to be violated in the *Greek Case* (1969) 12 YB 1.
[5] *Lawless* v *Ireland (No. 3)* 1 EHRR 15, para. 47.
[6] *Lawless* v *Ireland (No. 3)* 1 EHRR 15, para. 28.

both within and outside Ireland. In *Ireland* v *UK* 2 EHRR 25, in the context of the early 1970s when there had been numerous attacks by the IRA including bombings and shootings, it was undisputed that a public emergency existed. Even where it is undisputed, the Court will nevertheless have to make its own assessment, but the state will be allowed a wide margin of appreciation. An 'emergency' in only part of a state may affect the whole population and therefore may threaten 'the life of the nation'.

In *Aksoy* v *Turkey* (1997) 23 EHRR 553[7] the Court found that a public emergency existed in south-east Turkey as a result of the particular extent and impact of PKK terrorist activity in the region in the mid-1990s.

The European Commission rejected the Greek Goverment's claim of a public emergency in the *Greek case* (1969) 12 Yearbook 1. The Government relied on the breakdown of public order, the constitutional crisis and the alleged threat of a communist takeover, but the Commission found no evidence for this, and so found Article 15 inapplicable.

8.1.4   Measures strictly required by the exigencies of the situation

Where the Court is satisfied that there exists 'a public emergency threatening the life of the nation', the respondent state may only take such measures as are 'strictly required by the exigencies of the situation'. For example, detention without trial of terrorist suspects in the context of the activities of the IRA in Ireland in the late 1950s was found to meet such criteria in *Lawless*. There, the Court took into account the dangerousness of the situation, which the ordinary criminal law had been unable to check, and the available safeguards, including Parliamentary supervision of the detention regime and a 'Detention Commission' with binding powers to order release.

The respondent Government will be allowed a wide margin of appreciation in assessing a situation and deciding what measures are necessary, on the basis that it is in a better position to do so than the European Court. The Court will consider various factors, including to what extent is the ordinary law inadequate; whether the continuance of the measures can be justified; and the proportionality of the measures introduced (is there another alternative?). Because of the difficulties faced by a state during an emergency, it will be allowed some leeway in introducing sufficient safeguards over time, rather than all at once.[8] The fact that a particular measure may be compliant with domestic law will not in itself be sufficient to justify measures derogating from the Convention.[9]

---

[7] See also *Demir and others* v *Turkey*, Nos 21380/93, 21381/93, 21383/93, 23.9.98, para. 45.
[8] *Ireland* v *UK* 2 EHRR 25, para. 220.
[9] *Demir and others* v *Turkey*, Nos 21380/93, 21381/93, 21383/93, 23.9.98, para. 52.

Whilst in *Brannigan and McBride* v *UK* (1994) 17 EHRR 539 the detention of terrorist suspects for up to seven days was considered not to exceed the state's margin of appreciation, in *Aksoy* v *Turkey* (1997) 23 EHRR 553, a fourteen-day detention was considered too long. The Turkish Government failed to explain why the fight against terrorism made judicial intervention impracticable. The Court found that there were insufficient safeguards: 'in particular, the denial of access to a lawyer, doctor, relative or friend and the absence of any realistic possibility of being brought before the court to test the legality of the detention meant that he was left completely at the mercy of those holding him'.[10]

A derogation will only be valid in respect of those parts of a state's territory which are explicitly referred to in the notice of derogation.[11]

8.1.5 Other obligations under international law

Any derogation must also be consistent with a state's other obligations under international law, including treaty obligations (e.g., the Geneva Conventions in relation to armed conflict), or customary international law. There is a similar general obligation under Article 53 which provides that the Convention should not be construed as limiting or derogating from the human rights protected by a state's laws or by any agreement to which it is a party.

8.1.6 UK derogation

Following the judgment in *Brogan and others* v *UK* (1989) 11 EHRR 117 in 1988 in which detention for more than four days was found to violate Article 5(3), the UK Government entered into a derogation in relation to Northern Ireland (which is incorporated into Schedule 3 of the Human Rights Act 1998) to permit detention without charge for up to five days. The text of the UK derogation is at appendix 17. The lawfulness of the UK derogation was upheld in *Brannigan and McBride* v *UK* (1994) 17 EHRR 539.

8.2 RESERVATION

The Convention allows states, at the point of signature or ratification, to make express reservations from particular provisions. Article 57 (formerly Article 64) provides as follows:

> 1.   Any state may, when signing this Convention or when depositing its instrument of ratification, make a reservation in respect of any particular provision of the Convention to the extent that any law then in force in its territory is not in conformity with the provision. Reservations of a general character shall not be permitted under this Article.

---

[10] *Aksoy* v *Turkey* (1997) 23 EHRR 553, para. 83.
[11] *Sakik* v *Turkey* (1998) 26 EHRR 662.

2.   Any reservation made under this Article shall contain a brief statement of the law concerned.

A reservation applies to the law in force at the time the reservation is made.[12] However, a reservation may extend to include a new law replacing an old law, provided that it does not extend beyond the scope of the reservation. A reservation must be interpreted in the language in which it was made.

If a reservation is upheld in relation to a particular application, then the application will be declared inadmissible under Article 35 (see chapter 5).

Under Article 57(1), a state may not make a general reservation, which has been defined as 'a reservation couched in terms that are too vague or broad for it to be possible to determine their exact meaning and scope'.[13] In *Belilos* v *Switzerland* (1988) 10 EHRR 466 this requirement was found to be breached by a reservation lodged by the respondent Government in relation to Article 6.

The purpose of Article 57(2) is to ensure that the reservation does not go beyond the provisions expressly excluded by the state. The requirement to provide a brief statement of the law is considered to be both an evidential factor and contributes to legal certainty. A reservation may be invalidated on this ground alone. This requirement was found to have been breached in *Belilos* v *Switzerland* where the Government conceded that no statement of law had been included with the reservation.[14] In *Chorherr* v *Austria* (1994) 17 EHRR 358, a reservation relating to Article 5 was found to be sufficiently specific as it included a limited number of laws which, taken together, amounted to 'a well-defined and coherent body of substantive and procedural administrative provisions'. In *Helle* v *Finland* (1998) 26 EHRR 159, a reservation aimed at relieving certain specified courts from holding oral hearings was found to be sufficiently specific to be valid.

8.2.1   UK reservation

The UK Government has made a reservation in respect of the right to education in Article 2 of Protocol 1, to the effect that the principle that education and teaching should be in conformity with parents' religious and philosophical convictions is accepted only so far as it is compatible with the provision of efficient instruction and training and the avoidance of unreasonable expenditure. The UK reservation (see appendix 17) has been incorporated into schedule 3 to the Human Rights Act 1998.

The Commission has raised questions about the validity of the UK reservation in *SP* v *UK* (1997) 23 EHRR CD 139 concerning the failure to provide adequate schooling for a dyslexic boy, on the basis that the relevant provisions had come into force after the reservation had been made. The case was declared inadmissible for other reasons.

---

[12] See, e.g., *Fischer* v *Austria* (1995) 20 EHRR 349, para. 41.

[13] *Belilos* v *Switzerland* (1988) 10 EHRR 466, para. 55.

[14] *Belilos* v *Switzerland* (1988) 10 EHRR 466. See also *Weber* v *Switzerland* (1990) 12 EHRR 508.

Chapter Nine

Just Satisfaction (Article 41)

9.1 INTRODUCTION

The European Court's primary remedy is a declaration that there has been a violation of the Convention. Where the Court finds that there has been a violation of the Convention, the judgment may include an award for 'just satisfaction' under Article 41 (previously Article 50, prior to November 1998), if the question of compensation is ready for decision. Judgments and their enforcement are discussed further in chapter 4. Article 41 states:

> If the Court finds that there has been a violation of the Convention or the protocols thereto, and if the internal law of the High Contracting Party concerned allows only partial reparation to be made, the Court shall, if necessary, afford just satisfaction to the injured party.

Just satisfaction under Article 41 may include compensation for both pecuniary and non-pecuniary loss and legal costs and expenses. Awards for just satisfaction are an equitable remedy, at the discretion of the Court.

The importance of obtaining adequate information and evidence about potential compensation claims, and of adequately recording legal costs, from the outset of a case, are discussed above at 2.4.4 and 2.2.2 respectively.

9.2 PECUNIARY AND NON-PECUNIARY COMPENSATION

In general, awards of damages are relatively low compared with damages awarded by the domestic courts of many Council of Europe states[1] (there is a

---

[1] See also 'Damages under the Human Rights Act 1998', Law Commission and Scottish Law Commission, October 2000 (Cm 4853).

schedule of recent awards in UK cases below at 9.4). This is probably due to a prevailing view that the primary remedy in Strasbourg is the finding of a violation of the Convention itself. Indeed in many cases, the Court will decline to award any damages on the basis that the declaration is 'sufficient' just satisfaction. In considering awards for just satisfaction, the Court is unlikely to take account of principles or scales of assessment used by domestic courts.[2]

Rather than lay down specific means of calculating damages awards (such as an hourly rate for unlawful detention), the Court applies general principles in assessing just satisfaction. The legal effect of a judgment is to place a duty on the respondent state to make reparation for its consequences in such a way as to restore as far as possible the situation existing before the breach (*restitutio in integrum*). The Court will frequently comment that it is unable to speculate on the outcome of the applicant's domestic proceedings, had there not been a violation of the Convention. This is often the position, for example, in cases where there has been a violation of the right to a fair trial in criminal proceedings.[3] In *Findlay* v *UK* (1997) 24 EHRR 221, for example, the applicant's claim for loss of income of £440,200 following his conviction and sentence by a court-martial which violated Article 6(1) was rejected for this reason by the Court. On many occasions, the Court states that its award is made 'on an equitable basis'.

The respondent state is usually expressly required to pay compensation and costs within three months of the date of the judgment. The Court usually directs that interest at a prescribed rate (currently 8 per cent in UK cases) is to be payable on any sums not paid within that time.

It is vital that particularised claims for just satisfaction are made by the applicant. Where an applicant fails to make such a claim, the Court will not consider an award of its own motion.[4]

Claims for punitive or aggravated damages have been rejected by the Court, without ruling out the possibility of making such awards.[5]

One of the highest awards for damages, inter alia, for personal injury, in recent years was the award of 500,000 French francs in *Selmouni* v *France* (2000) 29 EHRR 403 following the torture of the applicant by French police. In *Tomasi* v *France* (1993) 15 EHRR 1 the applicant who was also ill-treated in police custody, was awarded 700,000 French francs for both pecuniary and non-pecuniary loss.

The conduct of the applicant may also be a factor in assessing awards. No award was made in *McCann and others* v *UK* (1996) 21 EHRR 97 'having regard to the fact that the three terrorist suspects who were killed had been intending to plant a bomb in Gibraltar'.

---

[2] *Osman* v *UK* (2000) 29 EHRR 245, para. 164.
[3] See, e.g., *Hood* v *UK* (2000) 29 EHRR 365, para 86.
[4] See, e.g., *Moore and Gordon* v *UK* (2000) 29 EHRR 728, para. 28.
[5] See, e.g., *Selçuk and Asker* v *Turkey* (1998) 26 EHRR 477, para. 119 and *Hood* v *UK* (2000) 29 EHRR 365, para. 89.

In order to succeed in claiming pecuniary losses, the applicant must establish a causal link between the violation and the losses claimed. Awards may include loss of earnings (past and future), loss of pension scheme benefits, fines and taxes imposed, costs incurred, loss of inheritance, medical expences and the loss of the value of land. Interest may also be claimed as a pecuniary loss.[6] Awards for non-pecuniary damage may include elements in respect of pain and suffering, anguish and distress, trauma, anxiety, frustration, feelings of isolation, helplessness and injustice and for loss of opportunity, loss of reputation or loss of relationship. The court has recognised that corporte bodies may suffer pecuniary loss.[7] A schedule of Article 41 awards in recent cases against the UK is below at 9.4.

9.3   COSTS AND EXPENSES

The Court may award an applicant their costs provided that each of the following conditions is satisfied:

(a)   that the costs are actually incurred; and
(b)   that they are necessarily incurred; and
(c)   that they are reasonable as to quantum.

In addition to the costs of the European Court proceedings, a successful applicant may seek to recover from the Court costs incurred in domestic proceedings which were aimed at obtaining redress in respect of the Convention violation.[8] Domestic fee scales may be relevant, but they are not binding on the Court.

In order to attempt to recoup as much as possible of the costs and expenses actually and necessarily incurred, it is essential to submit to the Court a detailed bill of costs setting out the tasks carried out, the hours worked, the hourly rates and details of all expenses (see also chapters 2 and 4). There is, however, no prescribed format for a 'bill of costs' as such. Where possible, copies of invoices relating to expenses incurred should be provided to the Court. It should be noted that the Court very rarely awards all of the costs and expenses claimed by the applicant's representatives, especially where the respondent Government disputes the amount claimed. In many cases, costs awarded by the Court are significantly lower than the amounts claimed (see the schedule of recent UK just satisfaction awards at below 9.4).

Costs will not be deemed to have been incurred where a legal representative has acted free of charge and therefore they cannot in those circumstances be claimed under Article 41.[9]

---

[6] See, e.g., *Pine Valley Developments Ltd* v *Ireland* (1992) 16 EHRR 379.
[7] *Comingersoll SA* v *Portugal*, No. 35382/97, 6.4.00.
[8] See, e.g., *Lustig-Prean and Beckett* v *UK*, Nos 31417/96 and 32377/96, 25.7.00, paras 30-33.
[9] See, e.g., *McCann and others* v *UK* (1996) 21 EHRR 97, para. 221.

If the applicant has not succeeded in establishing a violation of the Convention in respect of part of their case, this may be a factor in the Court reducing the costs sought.[10]

Costs awards may be expressed to be inclusive or exclusive of VAT and any sums previously paid by the Court as legal aid will be deductible. There is no provision in the Convention for costs to be awarded against an unsuccessful applicant.

9.4   SCHEDULE OF ARTICLE 41 AWARDS IN SELECTED UK CASES (1998–2000)

Article 3

1.   *A* v *UK*, No. 25599/94, 23.9.98; (1999) 27 EHRR 611

Violation: Article 3

Pecuniary damages.	Claimed: None

Non-pecuniary damages.	Claimed: £15,000 Awarded: £10,000

Costs and expenses.	Claimed: £48,450 Awarded: £20,000 (amount claimed considered to be excessive in view of limited number of issues raised by case and absence of any detailed breakdown of costs)

Article 5(1)

2.   *Steel and others* v *UK*, No. 24838/94, 23.9.98; (1999) 28 EHRR 603

Violation: Article s 5(1) and 10

Pecuniary damages.	Claimed: None

Non-pecuniary damages.	Claimed: Amount not specified Awarded: £500 to each of three applicants imprisoned for seven hours

Costs and expenses.	Claimed: £53,889.62 Awarded: £20,000, less amounts paid by way of legal aid (violations found in respect of only part of three of the applicants' claims; decided on an equitable basis)

---

[10] See, e.g., *IJL, GMR and AKP* v *UK*, Nos 29522/95, 30056/96 and 30574/96, 19.9.00, para. 151

Article 5(3)

3. *Caballero* v *UK*, No. 32819/96, 8.2.00; (2000) 30 EHRR 643

Violation: Article 5(3) and 5(5)

Pecuniary damages.	Claimed: None
Non-pecuniary damages.	Claimed: Amount not specified Awarded: £1,000 (applicant submitted affidavit evidence, not disputed by Government, to the effect that had it not been for s. 25, Criminal Justice and Public Order Act 1994, he would have had good chance of being released on bail prior to trial — applicant also argued that any such release prior to trial could have been his last days of liberty given advanced age, ill-health and long sentence — decided on an equitable basis)
Costs and expenses.	Claimed: £32,225.09 Awarded: £15,250 less sums awarded for legal aid (considerable duplication between applicant's two representatives and counsel's number of hours excessively high — decided on an equitable basis)

4. *Hood* v *UK*, No. 27267/95, 18.2.99; (2000) 29 EHRR 365

Violation: Articles 5(3), 5(5) and 6(1)

Pecuniary damages.	Claimed: None
Non-pecuniary damages.	Claimed: £10,000 (Article 5) and £15,000 (Article 6) Awarded: None — judgment constituted sufficient just satisfaction (evidence did not support the view that applicant would not have been detained prior to court-martial had there been no breach of Article 5; impossible to speculate as to outcome of court-martial proceedings had violation of Article 6 not occurred)
Costs and expenses.	Claimed: £14,137.75 (for domestic and Strasbourg proceedings) Awarded: £10,500 (on an equitable basis)

5. *Jordan* v *UK*, No. 30280/96, 14.3.00

Violation: Article 5(3) and 5(5)

Pecuniary damages.	Claimed: None
Non-pecuniary damages.	Claimed: £5,000 Awarded: None (judgment constituted sufficient just satisfaction — the evidence, particularly applicant's previous

absence without leave, did not support the view that he would not have been detained prior to his court-martial or that he would have been released earlier had there been no breach of Article 5(3))

Costs and expenses.

Claimed: £4,441.50 (31 hours at £120 per hour, including 25 hours on drafting initial application)
Awarded: £3,500 (decided on an equitable basis)

Article 5(4)

6. *Curley* v *UK*, No. 32340/96, 28.3.00

Violation: Article 5(4) and 5(5)

Pecuniary damages.

Claimed: None

Non-pecuniary damages.

Claimed: £50,000 or £25,000
Awarded: £1,500 (Applicant must have suffered feelings of frustration, uncertainty and anxiety as for ten years he did not receive a review of his detention by a body compliant with Article 5(4) — domestic scales of compensation for unlawful detention not applicable where there was no equivalent finding of unlawfulness — decided on an equitable basis)

Costs and expenses.

Claimed: £4,882.40
Awarded: £3,664.40 less sums awarded for legal aid (amount of costs claimed after admissibility was disproportionate — decided on an equitable basis)

See: 16. *T* v *UK*; 17. *V* v *UK*

Article 5(5)

See 3. *Caballero* v *UK*; 6. *Curley* v *UK*; 4. *Hood* v *UK*; 5. *Jordan* v *UK*

Article 6(1) (criminal)

7. *Averill* v *UK*, No. 36408/97, 6.6.00

Violation: Article 6(1) and 6(3)(c)

Pecuniary/non-pecuniary damages.

Claimed: Amount not specified
Awarded: None (finding of a violation constituted just satisfaction — Court could not speculate on whether outcome of applicant's trial would have been different had he obtained access to a solicitor at the beginning of interrogation)

Costs and expenses.	Claimed: £8,812.50 for counsel's fees; £3,525 for solicitor's costs Awarded: £5,000 (decided on an equitable basis — violation found only in respect of complaint concerning access to solicitor)

8.   *Cable and others* v *UK*, No. 24436/94 etc., 18.2.99; (2000) 30 EHRR 1032

Violation: Article 6(1)

Pecuniary damages.	Claimed: Amount not specified (for reduction in income and in earning capacity) Awarded: None (no causal link between the alleged losses and the violation of the Convention)
Non-pecuniary damages.	Claimed: £10,000 plus punitive damages for failure to change court-martial system following the Commission Article 31 report Awarded: None (finding of a violation constituted just satisfaction — no basis for claim of punitive damages)
Costs and expenses.	Claimed: £228,891.46 (35 applicants) Awarded: £40,000 less sums awarded for legal aid (considerable overlap in 35 cases, which raised only limited questions in the wake of the judgments in *Findlay* v *UK* and *Coyne* v *UK* — decided on an equitable basis)

9.   *Condron* v *UK*, No. 35718/97, 2.5.00

Violation: Article 6(1)

Pecuniary damages.	Claimed: None
Non-pecuniary damages.	Claimed: None
Costs and expenses.	Claimed: £23,774.16 Awarded: £15,000 (on an equitable basis)

10.   *Magee* v *UK*, No. 28135/95, 6.6.00

Violation: Article 6(1) and 6(3)(c)

Pecuniary/non-pecuniary damages.	Claimed: Amount not specified Awarded: None (finding of a violation constituted just satisfaction — Court could not speculate on whether outcome of applicant's trial would have been different had he obtained access to a solicitor at the beginning of interrogation)

Costs and expenses.

Claimed: £52,426
Awarded: £10,000 less sums awarded for legal aid (Convention violation confined to complaint relating to denial of access to solicitor — decided on an equitable basis)

11. *Moore and Gordon* v *UK*, Nos 36529/97 and 37393/97, 29.9.99; (2000) 29 EHRR 728

Violation: Article 6(1)

No Article 41 claim made — Court not required to consider Article 41 of its own motion

12. *Perks and others* v *UK*, No. 25277/94 etc., (2000) 30 EHRR 33

Violation: Article 6(1) and 6(3)(c)

Pecuniary damages.

Claimed: None

Non-pecuniary damages.

Claimed: Amount not specified
Awarded: £5,500 for Perks; none for other seven applicants (no basis to speculate as to outcome of magistrates' court proceedings — finding of violation was sufficient just satisfaction)

Costs and expenses.

Claimed: £5,464.54 for Beattie; £13,860 for other seven applicants, plus £10,100 for counsel.
Awarded: £28,000 (less 23,958 French francs received by way of legal aid) (only minimal reduction due to partial finding of a violation; decided on an equitable basis)

13. *Sander* v *UK*, No. 34129/96, 9.5.00

Violation: Article 6(1)

Pecuniary/non-pecuniary damages.

Claimed: £458,000 in respect of lost earnings and property applicant had to sell during imprisonment; also claimed for future loss of earnings and compensation for three years in prison
Awarded: None (no causal link established between violation of Convention and claimed damage)

Costs and expenses.

Claimed: None

14. *Rowe and Davis* v *UK*, No. 28901/95, (2000) 30 EHRR 1

Violation: Article 6(1)

Pecuniary damages.

Claimed: None

Non-pecuniary damages.

Claimed: Amount not specified

<table>
<tr><td></td><td>Awarded: None (finding of a violation constituted just satisfaction)</td></tr>
<tr><td>Costs and expenses.</td><td>Claimed: £28,065.15 for Liberty's costs; £25,380 for counsel's fees (for Rowe and Davis, Jasper and Fitt)
Awarded: £25,000 less sums awarded for legal aid (decided on an equitable basis)</td></tr>
</table>

15. *Smith and Ford* v *UK*, No. 37475/97 and 39036/97, 29.9.99

Violation: Article 6(1)

No Article 41 claims made — Court not required to examine Article 41 of its own motion

16. *T* v *UK*, No. 24724/94, 16.12.99; (2000) 30 EHRR 121

Violation: Articles 6(1) and 5(4)

Pecuniary damages.	Claimed: None
Non-pecuniary damages.	Claimed: None
Costs and expenses.	Claimed: £12,740.08 solicitors' costs and £17,750 barristers' fees Awarded: £18,000 less sums paid by way of legal aid (reduced since violations of Articles 3 or 5(1) not established)

17. *V* v *UK*, No. 24888/94, 16.12.99; (2000) 30 EHRR 121

Violation: Articles 6(1) and 5(4)

Pecuniary damages.	Claimed: None
Non-pecuniary damages.	Claimed: None
Costs and expenses.	Claimed: £7,796.34 solicitors' costs, £30,000 barristers' fees and £4,580 costs and expenses in relation to hearing Awarded: £32,000, less sums paid by way of legal aid (reduced since violations of Articles 3 or 5(1) not established)

Article 6(1) (civil)

18. *McGonnell* v *UK*, No. 28488/95, 8.2.00; (2000) 30 EHRR 289

Violation: Article 6(1)

Pecuniary damages.	Claimed: None
Non-pecuniary damages.	Claimed: £50,000 Awarded: None (finding of a violation constituted just satisfaction)

Costs and expenses.   Claimed: £20,913.90
                                 Awarded: £20,913.90

19.   *Osman* v *UK*, No. 23452/94, 28.10.98; (2000) 29 EHRR 245

Violation: Article 6(1)

Pecuniary/non-pecuniary   Claimed: Amount not specified
damages.   Awarded: £10,000 for each applicant (assessment not by
                                 reference to principles or scales of assessment used by
                                 domestic courts)

Costs and expenses.   Claimed: £46,976.78
                                 Awarded: £30,000 (less 28,514 French francs in legal aid
                                 payments) (complaints under Articles 2 and 8 unsubstan-
                                 tiated; decided on equitable considerations)

20.   *Scarth* v *UK*, No. 33745/96, 22.7.99

Violation: Article 6(1)

Pecuniary damages.   Claimed: £21,590.17
                                 Awarded: None (no causal link between alleged losses and
                                 Convention violation)

Non-pecuniary damages.   Claimed: Amount not specified
                                 Awarded: None (finding of a violation constituted just
                                 satisfaction)

Costs and expenses.   Claimed: £705.82
                                 Awarded: £705.82 (decided on an equitable basis)

21.   *Tinnelly & Son Ltd and others and McElduff and others* v *UK*, No. 20390/92 and
23414/94, 10.7.98; (1999) 27 EHRR 249

Violation: Article 6(1)

Pecuniary/non-pecuniary   Claimed: £777,086 (T); £119,584 (M; including £30,000
damages.   non-pecuniary damages) (for loss of opportunity to secure
                                 a determination of their claims and for being victims of
                                 unlawful discrimination and to clear their business names
                                 and reputations — profits lost through being refused
                                 contracts and business opportunities lost as being tarnished
                                 as security risks)
                                 Awarded: £15,000 (T) and £10,000 (M) (decided on an
                                 equitable basis — Court could not speculate as to what
                                 outcome of proceedings would have been had the PII

certificates not been issued — but applicant's were denied opportunity to obtain ruling on merits of claims that they were victims of unlawful discrimination)

Costs and expenses.	Claimed: £1,200.14 (for two applicants to attend hearing) Awarded: £1,200.14

Article 6(3)(c)

See: 7. *Averill* v *UK*; 10. *Magee* v *UK*; 12. *Perks and others* v *UK*

Article 8

22. *ADT* v *UK*, No. 35765/97, 31.7.00

Violation: Article 8

Pecuniary damages.	Claimed: £10,929.05
Non-pecuniary damages.	Claimed: £10,000
	Awarded: £29,929.05 (total)

23. *Foxley* v *UK*, No. 33274/96, 20.6.00

Violation: Article 8

Pecuniary damages.	Claimed: None
Non-pecuniary damages.	Claimed: £3,500 for moral damage, including sense of humiliation applicant had suffered Awarded: None (alleged non-pecuniary damage adequately compensated by finding of violations of Article 8)
Costs and expenses.	Claimed: £8,482.33 Awarded: £6,000 minus amount received by way of legal aid (on an equitable basis)

24. *Khan* v *UK*, No. 35394/97, 12.5.00

Violation: Articles 8 and 13

Pecuniary damages.	Claimed: None
Non-pecuniary damages.	Claimed: None
Costs and expenses.	Claimed: £14,694.95 Awarded: £11,500 less sums paid by way of legal aid (on an equitable basis)

25. *Lustig-Prean and Beckett* v *UK*, No. 31417/96 and 32377/96, 25.7.00

Violation: Article 8

Pecuniary damages.

Claimed: £61,518.86 plus £4,875 (L: past loss of earnings); £69,610.18 plus £6,000 (B: past loss of earnings); £204,650 (L: future loss of earnings); £17,024 (B: future loss of earnings); £494,119.98 (L: loss of non-contributory service pension scheme); and unquantified sum for B's loss of non-contributory service pension scheme.

Awarded: L: £39,875 (past loss of earnings); £25,000 (future loss of earnings); and £30,000 (pensions scheme), a total of £94,875. B: £34,000 (past loss of earnings); £7,000 (future loss of earnings); and £14,000 (pensions scheme), a total of £55,000.

Non-pecuniary damages.

Claimed: £22,500 (L); £25,000, plus £20,000 for aggravated damages (B).

Awarded: £19,000 each (the investigation and discharges ... were profoundly destabilising events in the applicants' lives which had and, it cannot be excluded, continue to have a significant emotional and psychological impact on each of them; on an equitable basis).

Costs and expenses.

Claimed: L: £30,970.48 (domestic proceedings) and £42,954 plus £8,584.16 for Article 41 submissions (Convention proceedings); B: £45,567.09 plus unspecified sum for Article 41 submissions

Awarded: L: £18,000 (domestic proceedings) and £16,000 (Convention proceedings); B: £15,000 (Convention proceedings).

26. *McLeod* v *UK*, No. 24755/94, 23.9.98; (1999) 27 EHRR 493

Violation: Article 8

Pecuniary damages.

Claimed: None

Non-pecuniary damages.

Claimed: None

Costs and expenses.

Claimed: £5,523.39 for applicant's own costs of representing herself in domestic proceedings and before European Commission; £1,577.64 for applicant's travel and other expenses; £3,829.21 solicitors' costs; and £15,275 counsel's fees.

Awarded: £15,000 (applicant could not be compensated for her time spent on case; decided on an equitable basis)

27. *Smith and Grady* v *UK*, No. 33985/96 and 33986/96, 25.7.00

Violation: Articles 8 and 13

Pecuniary damages.	Claimed: S: £64,186.20 (past loss of earnings); £167,737 (future income); £358,299.20 (service pension). G: £185,497.09 (loss of earnings) and £599,217 (pension scheme). Awarded: S: £30,000 (past loss of earnings), £15,000 (future loss of earnings) and £14,000 (pension scheme), a total of £59,000. G: £25,000 (Future loss of earnings) and £15,000 (pension scheme), a total of £40,000.
Non-pecuniary damages.	Claimed: £30,000 (S) and £20,000 (G). Awarded: £19,000 each (the investigation and discharges ... were profoundly destabilising events in the applicants' lives which had and, it cannot be excluded, continue to have a significant emotional and psychological impact on each of them; on an equitable basis).
Costs and expenses.	Claimed: £50,731.57 Awarded: £32,000 (Convention proceedings) plus £200 (filing costs in domestic proceedings).

Article 10

28. *Bowman* v *UK*, No. 24839/94, 19.2.98; (1998) 26 EHRR 1

Violation: Article 10

Pecuniary damages.	Claimed: None
Non-pecuniary damages.	Claimed: £15,000 Awarded: None (finding of violation sufficient just satisfaction)
Costs and expenses.	Claimed: £1,633.64 for domestic proceedings; £35,490 for Strasbourg proceedings Awarded: Domestic costs awarded in full; £25,000 for Strasbourg proceedings (on an equitable basis)

29. *Hashman and Harrup* v *UK*, No. 25594/94, 25.11.99; (2000) 30 EHRR 241

Violation: Article 10

Pecuniary damages.	Claimed: None
Non-pecuniary damages.	Claimed: None
Costs and expenses.	Claimed: £6,000 Awarded: £6,000

See: 2. *Steel and others* v *UK*

Article 13

See: 24. *Khan* v *UK*; 27. *Smith and Grady* v *UK*

Article 3 of Protocol 1

30.   *Matthews* v *UK*, No. 24833/94, 18.2.99; (1999) 28 EHRR 361

Violation: Article 3 of Protocol 1

Pecuniary damages.	Claimed: None
Non-pecuniary damages.	Claimed: None
Costs and expenses.	Claimed: 760,000 French francs and £10,955 in costs; 6,976 French francs and £1,151.50 for travel expenses Awarded: £45,000 less sums awarded for legal aid (decided on an equitable basis)

Chapter Ten

Strengthening the Prohibition of Discrimination: Protocol 12

The widely acknowledged limitations of the existing prohibition of discrimination in Article 14 of the Convention have led to proposals within the Council of Europe to strengthen the provision. The main problem with Article 14 is that it does not provide a freestanding right to non-discrimination, but must be invoked in conjunction with another substantive Convention right (see above at 7.15 on Article 14).

The only other provision in the Protocols to the Convention bearing on discrimination is Article 5 of Protocol 7 concerning equality between spouses. Protocol 7 has not as yet been ratified by the UK.[1] It is also accepted that discriminatory treatment may amount to degrading treatment in violation of Article 3 (see above at 7.3.4).

The introduction of an additional protocol dealing with equality and non-discrimination has been debated within the Council of Europe since the 1960s, but received greater impetus in the 1990s in view of the recognition of the importance of countering discrimination on grounds of sex and race in particular. The Steering Committee for Equality between Women and Men (CDEG) considered the inclusion of a substantive right of women and men to equality. A new expert body, the European Commission Against Racism and Intolerance (ECRI) focused on concerns about racism, xenophobia, anti-Semitism and intolerance.

It is now proposed that an additional Protocol 12 to the Convention will create a freestanding anti-discrimination provision. The text of the protocol was adopted by the Committee of Ministers of the Council of Europe in June 2000 (see appendix 20). It has been open for signature as from November 2000 and it will enter into force when it has been ratified by ten Council of Europe states.

---

[1] It signalled its intention to do so in the White Paper *Rights Brought Home: the Human Rights Bill*, Cm 3782, 1997.

Article 1 of Protocol 12 provides as follows:

1.   The enjoyment of any right set forth by law shall be secured without discrimination on any ground such as sex, race, colour, language, religion, political or other opinion, national or social origin, association with a national minority, property, birth or other status.
2.   No one shall be discriminated against by any public authority on any ground such as those mentioned in paragraph 1.

The first paragraph prohibits discrimination in relation to 'any right set forth by law' rather than 'the rights and freedoms set forth in this Convention' as in Article 14. This may include international law.[2] It is important that the two paragraphs are read together, as they are intended to be complementary. The Explanatory Report to Protocol 12 (appendix 20) suggests that the combined effect of the two paragraphs will be to provide protection against discrimination in four situations:

(a)   in the enjoyment of any right specifically granted to an individual under national law;
(b)   in the enjoyment of a right which may be inferred from a clear obligation of a public authority under national law, i.e. where a public authority is under an obligation under national law to behave in a particular manner;
(c)   by a public authority in the exercise of discretionary power (e.g. granting certain subsidies);
(d)   by any other act or omission by a public authority (e.g. behaviour of law enforcement officers when controlling a riot).

The list of grounds in Protocol 12 is identical to the grounds listed in Article 14. It was decided not to include other grounds such as disability, sexual orientation and age expressly, on the basis that the list of grounds is in any event open-ended and that to include some additional grounds might be prejudicial to the consideration of other grounds which were not included. Be that as it may, the adoption by the Council of Europe of an additional anti-discrimination measure which expressly lists certain grounds, but omits disability, sexual orientation and age, is regrettable. The Parliamentary Assembly had recommended that non-discrimination based on sexual orientation and the principle of equality of rights between women and men should be explicitly included.[3]

The Explanatory Report acknowledges that the Protocol may create certain positive obligations, but suggests that as between private persons, this will be limited to relations in the public sphere normally regulated by law, for which the state has a certain responsibility (such as employment contracts).

---

[2] See the Explanatory Report of the Steering Committee for Human Rights, para. 29 (appendix 20).
[3] Opinion No. 216 (2000) of 26.1.00.

The preamble to the Protocol refers to the fundamental principle of equality before the law and equal protection of the law. It also reaffirms that the principle of non-discrimination does not prevent states from taking measures in order to promote full and effective equality, provided that there is an objective and reasonable justification. Accordingly, positive discrimination may be permissible.

Chapter Eleven

Case Study: *Caballero* v *UK*[1]

This case study describes the various stages of an application which was initially lodged with the European Commission in 1996, in which the European Court gave judgment in 2000 and which led to changes in the relevant domestic legislation. It is included with the permission of the applicant. A copy of the application in this case is at appendix 21.

In January 1996 C was arrested by the police on suspicion of attempted rape of a neighbour. He was taken before the magistrates' court where bail was refused because of the application of section 25 of the Criminal Justice and Public Order Act 1994. The effect of section 25 was automatically to exclude bail to defendants, such as C, who were charged with a serious offence (murder, attempted murder, manslaughter, rape or attempted rape) and who already had a previous conviction for a serious offence (in his case, manslaughter).

According to the admissibility requirements under the European Convention on Human Rights, any application has to be lodged within six months of the exhaustion of effective domestic remedies (Article 35(1)). When C's legal representatives met to consider his position under the European Convention in April 1996, C was still remanded in custody pre-trial. The primary Convention point in C's case was to argue that his rights under Article 5(3) had been violated because he had not been granted judicial determination of the question of pre-trial detention. Even though the criminal proceedings against C were still continuing, it was considered that the key decision was the magistrates' refusal to grant bail in January 1996. As the Magistrates had reached their decision by applying an unambiguous statutory provision, there was no domestic remedy in respect of the

---

[1] *Caballero* v *UK* (2000) 30 EHRR 643. The applicant was advised by John Skinner, Messrs Dundons, Keir Starmer, Doughty Street Chambers and the author. See also P. Leach, *Automatic Denial of Bail and the European Convention* [1999] Crim LR 300.

pre-trial detention. Therefore, an introductory letter was lodged with the (then) European Commission in June 1996, within six months of the Magistrates' initial decision to deny bail.

In order to establish that the applicant was not merely complaining about a theoretical violation of the Convention, the applicant's representatives submitted an affidavit from the applicant's solicitor in the domestic criminal proceedings which set out the reasons why the applicant would have had arguments to put forward in support of his being granted bail, had the court been able to consider such an application. Of course, the solicitor could not say that C would have been granted bail, but merely that there would have been reasonable arguments to submit on his behalf. The applicant's representatives were also able to refer to the debates in the House of Lords on the Criminal Justice and Public Order Bill when the then Government was challenged to give examples of judicial errors of judgment which the section was intended to prevent. The Government was not able to give any such examples.

In addition to the principal Article 5(3) argument, it was submitted that there had been a violation of Article 5(5) as C had no enforceable right to compensation for the violation of his rights under Article 5(3). It was also submitted that the effect of section 25 of the 1994 Act was to violate the applicant's right to be presumed innocent under Article 6(2) and that it imposed a heavier penalty for manslaughter than had been applicable at the time of (his first) conviction, contrary to Article 7. Finally, it was argued that the applicant had been discriminated against as a person previously convicted of manslaughter, in violation of Article 14 in conjunction with Article 5(3), as he automatically had had no right to bail, and that, in relation to Article 13, there was no effective remedy in respect of the violations of the other Convention rights.

In the domestic proceedings, in October 1996, C was found guilty of attempted rape and assault occasioning actual bodily harm. He was sentenced to life imprisonment for the attempted rape and four years' imprisonment for the assault. His appeal against sentence was rejected by the Court of Appeal in July 1997.

Introductory letter lodged	June 1996
Application registered	August 1996
Commission gave notice to UK government	February 1997
Government's observations lodged	May 1997
Applicant's observations in reply	July 1997

The Government argued that section 25 of the 1994 Act was intended to avoid the unacceptable risk of an error of judgment by the courts, with the possible serious consequences for the alleged victims that would entail. It was also argued that Article 5(3) did not prevent a state from deciding that in particular circumstances it would be an unacceptable risk to release such a person, provided that the person was tried within a reasonable period of time. In the Government's submission, the magistrates' court complied with Article 5(3) as being the 'judge or other officer authorised by law to exercise judicial power'. This requirement was still met by the remaining powers of the magistrates' court, such as the power at committal hearings to dismiss a case if there was insufficient evidence to continue the proceedings, the power to consider whether the defendant had been properly charged and treated, and to dismiss the case for abuse of process, and the power to ensure that the trial takes place speedily. According to the Government, section 25 of the 1994 Act was a carefully considered and rational scheme which was not arbitrary.

Admissibility

In December 1997 the Commission declared admissible the applicant's complaints under Articles 5(3), 5(5), 13 and 14. Given that the period of the applicant's pre-trial detention had been deducted from his sentence under section 67 of the Criminal Justice Act 1967, the first question for the Commission was whether the applicant could still claim to be a 'victim' of a violation of the Convention. However, in spite of the deduction, there had been no acknowledgement by the authorities that there had been a Convention violation and therefore the Commission found that C could still claim to be the victim of a Convention violation. The arguments under Articles 6(2) and 7 were declared inadmissible as being incompatible *ratione materiae* with the Convention: the points raised under those heads were to be considered under Article 5.

Commission merits

In June 1998 the European Commission adopted its report on the merits of the case (the Article 31 Report). The Commission found violations of Article 5(3) and 5(5), but no violations of Articles 13 or 14. Article 5(3) required that a judge must 'examine all the facts arguing for and against the existence of a genuine requirement of public interest justifying, with due regard to the presumption of innocence, a departure from the rule of respect for the accused's liberty'. Article 5(3) had been breached because any possibility of releasing C had been excluded in advance by Parliament. Article 5(5) was found to have been violated as it was undisputed that there had been no domestic remedy for detention violating Article 5(3). The submission under Article 13 was considered to amount to a complaint about the lack of a remedy to challenge a statutory provision, which was not guaranteed by that Article. Finally, the Commission found it unnecessary to consider the arguments under Article 14, given the decision in relation to Article 5(3). Notably, a significant minority of twelve members of the Commission voted against the nineteen-strong majority's decision of a violation of Article 5(3).

Legislative changes by the UK Parliament

In anticipation of the decision in Strasbourg, prior to the publication of the Commission's decision on the merits in 1998, the UK Government published the Crime and Disorder Bill which included a proposed amendment to section 25 of the Criminal Justice and Public Order Act 1994. In moving the amendment to the Bill in March 1998, Lord Falconer of Thoroton said:

> This amendment will restore to the police and to the courts their rightful discretion in relation to the granting of bail ... to remove the ability of the police and the courts to make that decision is not in the interests of justice. It cannot be right to fetter the judicial discretion of the court in this way.[2]

Section 56 of the Crime and Disorder Act 1998 came into force on 30 September 1998, amending section 25 of the 1994 Act, so that, in the particular circumstances, defendants 'shall be granted bail in those proceedings only if the court, or, as the case may be, the constable considering the grant of bail is satisfied that there are exceptional circumstances which justify it'.

European Court proceedings

In November 1998, in accordance with the changes brought about by Protocol 11, the case passed to the new Court. A date for a hearing was set for June 1999. However, in May 1999 the Government's Agent wrote to the Court to concede that there had been violations of Article 5(3) and 5(5). In view of those concessions, the Court decided that it was not necessary to hold a hearing to reach its judgment. The applicant's Memorial to the Court was lodged in May 1999. The applicant withdrew the complaint under Article 13, but maintained his submissions under Articles 5(3), 5(5) and 14.

The Court's judgment was published in February 2000. The Grand Chamber of the Court[3] unanimously accepted the Government's concession of a violation of Article 5(3) and 5(5), but found it unnecessary to consider whether there had been violations of Articles 13 or 14. The applicant was awarded the sum of £1,000 for non-pecuniary damage, plus a proportion of his legal costs, as 'just satisfaction' under Article 41.

It was a departure from the Court's previous practice not formally to find a violation of the Convention, but to accept the Government's concession of a violation. This was an unfortunate development (in the author's view) as the Court did not give any reasons for the violations, but merely accepted the Government's concession. This had the effect of depriving the applicant of

---

[2] *Hansard*, HL, vol. 558, col. 239, 31.3.98.
[3] The Grand Chamber included Sir Robert Carnwath as ad hoc judge, because the UK judge, Sir Nicolas Bratza, had previously been involved in the case as a member of the European Commission.

reasons and left the issue itself unsatisfactorily resolved, with only the Commission having provided reasons for its decision, and being split by 19 to 12. There was no explanation from the Court as to the circumstances when it will formally accept a Government's concession of a violation, rather than find a violation itself. Some may argue that this formula, particularly in the absence of reasons, risks letting respondent Governments off the hook.

Law Commission report

In November 1999 the Law Commission published its consultation paper on Bail and the Human Rights Act 1998.[4] The report questions whether even the revised wording of section 25 of the 1994 Act complies with Article 5 of the European Convention. The Law Commission provisionally concludes that the section can be applied in a way which would not violate the Convention, but that it is liable to be misunderstood and applied in a way which would violate the Convention.[5]

---

[4] Law Commission Consultation Paper No. 157.
[5] See paras 9.1–9.30.

Chapter Twelve

Sources of Information on the European Convention on Human Rights

12.1 LAW REPORTS

Since 1996 the official European Convention law reports are the Reports of Judgments and Decisions (RJD) published in English and French (Carl Heymanns Verlag KG).

> e.g., *John Murray* v *the United Kingdom*, Reports of Judgments and Decisions 1996-I.

Prior to 1996 the official law reports were the Series A reports (Carl Heymanns Verlag KG). The Series B reports include the pleadings and other documents.

> e.g., *McCann and others* v *the United Kingdom* (1995) Series A, No. 324.

From 1974, selected European Commission decisions were reproduced in the Decisions and Reports series.

> e.g., *D* v *France* (1983) 23 DR 199.

The European Human Rights Reports (EHRR) series includes selected judgments of the Court, plus some Commission decisions (Sweet & Maxwell). The first two volumes (1979 and 1980) cover the entire European Court case law from inception.

> e.g., *Smith and Grady* v *United Kingdom* (2000) 29 EHRR 493.

The usual convention in citing cases from the first two volumes is not to include the year of the volume (e.g., *Ireland* v *UK* 2 EHRR 25). The European Human Rights Reports also include summaries, extracts and admissibility decisions. Since 1993 there has been a separate section of Commission Decisions (CD).

> e.g., *Vollert v Germany* (1996) 22 EHRR CD 129.

Other reports have been published in the Collections of Decisions (CD) 1955–1974, the Yearbook of the European Convention on Human Rights (YB) and the Digest of Strasbourg case law (Digest).

Butterworths Human Rights Cases include selected judgments of the European Court.

> e.g., *Sürek v Turkey* (2000) 7 BHRC 339.

12.2   WEBSITES AND ONLINE SOURCES

Council of Europe website: http://www.coe.int

This site includes the texts of treaties, tables of signatures and ratification, information on the history and activities of the Council of Europe, publications and press releases. There is also a Council of Europe Treaties site: http://conventions.coe.int

European Court website: http://www.echr.coe.int

European Court judgments are posted on the Court's website on the day they are handed down (http://www.echr.coe.int/eng/Judgments.htm). The Court regularly produces press releases providing details of forthcoming hearings and judgments, summaries of judgments, developments in significant cases and statistics.

Admissibility decisions are also posted on the website, but there is often a delay between the date of adoption of the decision and its appearance on the website.

The Court website incorporates the HUDOC search system (http://www.echr.coe.int/hudoc) which includes Court judgments, admissibility decisions and European Commission Article 31 reports. It is a reasonably sophisticated system which allows searches, for example, by respondent state, title, date and text.

The text of the European Convention and the Court rules are at http://www.echr.coe.int/eng/basictexts.htm

The European Court site includes information on the composition of the Court, case law information notes, surveys of activities and brief notes on procedure (in twenty-one languages). There are also notes on the effects of judgments at http://www.echr.coe.int/eng/effects.html

Committee of Ministers website: http://www.coe.fr/cm

This site has Committee of Ministers' documents (including recommendations, resolutions, treaties and declarations) at http://coe.fr/cm/indexes/doc.0.html

Butterworths Human Rights Direct (via http://www.butterworths.com)

Online information service, including Butterworths Human Rights Cases, European Court of Human Rights case materials, commentary and current awareness services.

Westlaw UK Human Rights (Sweet & Maxwell) (via http://www.westlaw.co.uk)

Online information service, including European Human Rights Reports, Human Rights Law Reports and European Human Rights Law Review, cases and commentary.

12.3   COUNCIL OF EUROPE PUBLICATIONS

The following are published on a regular basis by the Council of Europe:

Survey of Activities — information and statistics.
Case Law Information Notes (monthly) — case statistics and summaries.
Information Bulletins (three editions per year) — update on human rights activities within the Council of Europe, including cases.

12.4   JOURNALS

Some suggested journals:

European Human Rights Law Review (EHRLR) (Sweet & Maxwell — six editions per year) includes articles, case summaries and commentaries.
Human Rights Alerter (Sweet & Maxwell — ten editions per year) includes brief summaries of European Court decisions (and domestic UK court decisions).
Legal Action (Legal Action Group) — article on recent European Convention cases in January and July editions.

12.5   SELECT BIBLIOGRAPHY

Some suggested texts on the European Convention and/or the Human Rights Act 1998:

Baker, C. (ed), *Human Rights Act 1998: A Practitioner's Guide*, Sweet & Maxwell, 1998

Beddard, R., *Human Rights and Europe*, 3rd edn, Cambridge University Press, 1994

Clayton, R. and Tomlinson, H., *The Law of Human Rights*, Oxford University Press, 2000

Clements, L., Mole, N. and Simmons, A., *European Human Rights: Taking a Case under the Convention*, 2nd edn, Sweet & Maxwell, 1999

Dickson, B. (ed), *Human Rights and the European Convention*, Sweet & Maxwell, 1997

Dijk, P. van and Hoof, G. van, *Theory and Practice of the European Convention on Human Rights*, 3rd edn, Kluwer, 1998

Emmerson, B. and Ashworth, A., *Criminal Law and the European Convention on Human Rights*, Sweet & Maxwell, 2000

Emmerson, B. and Simor, J., *Human Rights Practice*, Sweet & Maxwell, 2000

Farran, S., *The UK before the European Court of Human Rights*, Blackstone Press, 1996

Gearty, C.A. (ed), *European Civil Liberties and the European Convention on Human Rights*, Kluwer, 1997

Grosz, S., Beatson, J. and Duffy, P., *Human Rights: The 1998 Act and the European Convention*, Sweet & Maxwell, 1999

Harris, D.J., O'Boyle, M. and Warbrick, C., *Law of the European Convention on Human Rights*, Butterworths, 1995

Hunt, M. and Singh, R. (eds), *A Practitioner's Guide to the Impact of the Human Rights Act 1998*, Hart Publishing (forthcoming in 2001)

Jacobs, F. and White, R., *The European Convention on Human Rights*, 2nd edn, Clarendon Press, 1996

Janis, M., Kay, R. and Bradley, A., *European Human Rights Law — Text and Materials*, Clarendon Press, 1995

Kempees, P., *A Systematic Guide to the Case-Law of the European Court of Human Rights*, vols I and II, 1996, vol III, 1998, Martinus Nijhoff

Law Commission/Scottish Law Commission Report, Damages under the Human Rights Act 1998, Cm 4853, October 2000.

Lester, Lord and Pannick, D. (eds), *Human Rights Law and Practice*, Butterworths, 1999

Loucaides, L.G., *Essays on the Developing Law of Human Rights*, Martinus Nijhoff, 1995

Morgan, R., and Evans, M. (eds), *Protecting Prisoners — The Standards of the European Committee for the Prevention of Torture*, Oxford University Press, 1999.

Reid, K., *A Practitioner's Guide to the European Convention on Human Rights*, Sweet & Maxwell, 1998

Robertson, A.H. and Merrills, J.G., *Human Rights in Europe*, 3rd edn, Manchester University Press, 1993

Rodley, N., *The Treatment of Prisoners in International Law*, 2nd edn, Oxford University Press, 1999.

Shelton, D., *Remedies in International Human Rights Law*, Oxford University Press, 1999.

Starmer, K., *European Human Rights Law*, Legal Action Group, 1999

Uglow, S., Cheney, D., Dickson, L. and Fitzpatrick, J., *Criminal Justice and the Human Rights Act 1998*, Jordans, 1999

Wadham, J. and Mountfield, H., *Blackstone's Guide to the Human Rights Act 1998*, 2nd edn, Blackstone Press, 2000

Yourow, H.C., *The Margin of Appreciation Doctrine in the Dynamics of European Human Rights Jurisprudence*, Martinus Nijhoff, 1996

Zwart, *The Admissibility of Human Rights Petitions*, Martinus Nijhoff, 1994

Some suggested 'overview' articles

Bratza, N. and O'Boyle, M., 'The Legacy of the Commission to the New Court under the Eleventh Protocol' [1997] 3 EHRLR 211

Jones, T.H., 'The Devolution of Human Rights under the European Convention' [1995] Public Law 430

Lavender, N., 'The Problem of the Margin of Appreciation' [1997] EHRLR 380

Ryssdal, R., 'The Coming of Age of the Convention' [1996] EHRLR 18

Appendix One

Convention for the Protection of Human Rights and Fundamental Freedoms as amended by Protocol No. 11
(Date of entry into force 1 November 1998)

The governments signatory hereto, being members of the Council of Europe,

Considering the Universal Declaration of Human Rights proclaimed by the General Assembly of the United Nations on 10th December 1948;

Considering that this Declaration aims at securing the universal and effective recognition and observance of the Rights therein declared;

Considering that the aim of the Council of Europe is the achievement of greater unity between its members and that one of the methods by which that aim is to be pursued is the maintenance and further realisation of human rights and fundamental freedoms;

Reaffirming their profound belief in those fundamental freedoms which are the foundation of justice and peace in the world and are best maintained on the one hand by an effective political democracy and on the other by a common understanding and observance of the human rights upon which they depend;

Being resolved, as the governments of European countries which are like-minded and have a common heritage of political traditions, ideals, freedom and the rule of law, to take the first steps for the collective enforcement of certain of the rights stated in the Universal Declaration,

Have agreed as follows:

Article 1
Obligation to respect human rights

The High Contracting Parties shall secure to everyone within their jurisdiction the rights and freedoms defined in Section I of this Convention.

Section I — Rights and freedoms

Article 2
Right to life

1   Everyone's right to life shall be protected by law. No one shall be deprived of his life intentionally save in the execution of a sentence of a court following his conviction of a crime for which this penalty is provided by law.

2   Deprivation of life shall not be regarded as inflicted in contravention of this article when it results from the use of force which is no more than absolutely necessary:

a   in defence of any person from unlawful violence;

b   in order to effect a lawful arrest or to prevent the escape of a person lawfully detained;

c   in action lawfully taken for the purpose of quelling a riot or insurrection.

Article 3
Prohibition of torture

No one shall be subjected to torture or to inhuman or degrading treatment or punishment.

Article 4
Prohibition of slavery and forced labour

1   No one shall be held in slavery or servitude.

2   No one shall be required to perform forced or compulsory labour.

3   For the purpose of this article the term 'forced or compulsory labour' shall not include:

a   any work required to be done in the ordinary course of detention imposed according to the provisions of Article 5 of this Convention or during conditional release from such detention;

b   any service of a military character or, in case of conscientious objectors in countries where they are recognised, service exacted instead of compulsory military service;

c   any service exacted in case of an emergency or calamity threatening the life or well-being of the community;

d   any work or service which forms part of normal civic obligations.

Article 5
Right to liberty and security

1   Everyone has the right to liberty and security of person. No one shall be deprived of his liberty save in the following cases and in accordance with a procedure prescribed by law:

    a   the lawful detention of a person after conviction by a competent court;

    b   the lawful arrest or detention of a person for non-compliance with the lawful order of a court or in order to secure the fulfilment of any obligation prescribed by law;

    c   the lawful arrest or detention of a person effected for the purpose of bringing him before the competent legal authority on reasonable suspicion of having committed an offence or when it is reasonably considered necessary to prevent his committing an offence or fleeing after having done so;

    d   the detention of a minor by lawful order for the purpose of educational supervision or his lawful detention for the purpose of bringing him before the competent legal authority;

    e   the lawful detention of persons for the prevention of the spreading of infectious diseases, of persons of unsound mind, alcoholics or drug addicts or vagrants;

    f   the lawful arrest or detention of a person to prevent his effecting an unauthorised entry into the country or of a person against whom action is being taken with a view to deportation or extradition.

2   Everyone who is arrested shall be informed promptly, in a language which he understands, of the reasons for his arrest and of any charge against him.

3   Everyone arrested or detained in accordance with the provisions of paragraph 1.c of this article shall be brought promptly before a judge or other officer authorised by law to exercise judicial power and shall be entitled to trial within a reasonable time or to release pending trial. Release may be conditioned by guarantees to appear for trial.

4   Everyone who is deprived of his liberty by arrest or detention shall be entitled to take proceedings by which the lawfulness of his detention shall be decided speedily by a court and his release ordered if the detention is not lawful.

5   Everyone who has been the victim of arrest or detention in contravention of the provisions of this article shall have an enforceable right to compensation.

Article 6
Right to a fair trial

1   In the determination of his civil rights and obligations or of any criminal charge against him, everyone is entitled to a fair and public hearing within a reasonable time by an independent and impartial tribunal established by law. Judgment shall be pronounced publicly but the press and public may be excluded

from all or part of the trial in the interests of morals, public order or national security in a democratic society, where the interests of juveniles or the protection of the private life of the parties so require, or to the extent strictly necessary in the opinion of the court in special circumstances where publicity would prejudice the interests of justice.

2 Everyone charged with a criminal offence shall be presumed innocent until proved guilty according to law.

3 Everyone charged with a criminal offence has the following minimum rights:

a to be informed promptly, in a language which he understands and in detail, of the nature and cause of the accusation against him;

b to have adequate time and facilities for the preparation of his defence;

c to defend himself in person or through legal assistance of his own choosing or, if he has not sufficient means to pay for legal assistance, to be given it free when the interests of justice so require;

d to examine or have examined witnesses against him and to obtain the attendance and examination of witnesses on his behalf under the same conditions as witnesses against him;

e to have the free assistance of an interpreter if he cannot understand or speak the language used in court.

Article 7
No punishment without law

1 No one shall be held guilty of any criminal offence on account of any act or omission which did not constitute a criminal offence under national or international law at the time when it was committed. Nor shall a heavier penalty be imposed than the one that was applicable at the time the criminal offence was committed.

2 This article shall not prejudice the trial and punishment of any person for any act or omission which, at the time when it was committed, was criminal according to the general principles of law recognised by civilised nations.

Article 8
Right to respect for private and family life

1 Everyone has the right to respect for his private and family life, his home and his correspondence.

2 There shall be no interference by a public authority with the exercise of this right except such as is in accordance with the law and is necessary in a democratic society in the interests of national security, public safety or the economic well-being of the country, for the prevention of disorder or crime, for the protection of health or morals, or for the protection of the rights and freedoms of others.

Article 9
Freedom of thought, conscience and religion

1   Everyone has the right to freedom of thought, conscience and religion; this right includes freedom to change his religion or belief and freedom, either alone or in community with others and in public or private, to manifest his religion or belief, in worship, teaching, practice and observance.

2   Freedom to manifest one's religion or beliefs shall be subject only to such limitations as are prescribed by law and are necessary in a democratic society in the interests of public safety, for the protection of public order, health or morals, or for the protection of the rights and freedoms of others.

Article 10
Freedom of expression

1   Everyone has the right to freedom of expression. This right shall include freedom to hold opinions and to receive and impart information and ideas without interference by public authority and regardless of frontiers. This article shall not prevent States from requiring the licensing of broadcasting, television or cinema enterprises.

2   The exercise of these freedoms, since it carries with it dudes and responsibilities, may be subject to such formalities, conditions, restrictions or penalties as are prescribed by law and are necessary in a democratic society, in the interests of national security, territorial integrity or public safety, for the prevention of disorder or crime, for the protection of health or morals, for the protection of the reputation or rights of others, for preventing the disclosure of information received in confidence, or for maintaining the authority and impartiality of the judiciary.

Article 11
Freedom of assembly and association

1   Everyone has the right to freedom of peaceful assembly and to freedom of association with others, including the right to form and to join trade unions for the protection of his interests.

2   No restrictions shall be placed on the exercise of these rights other than such as are prescribed by law and are necessary in a democratic society in the interests of national security or public safety, for the prevention of disorder or crime, for the protection of health or morals or for the protection of the rights and freedoms of others. This article shall not prevent the imposition of lawful restrictions on the exercise of these rights by members of the armed forces, of the police or of the administration of the State.

Article 12
Right to marry

Men and women of marriageable age have the right to marry and to found a family, according to the national laws governing the exercise of this right.

Article 13
Right to an effective remedy

Everyone whose rights and freedoms as set forth in this Convention are violated shall have an effective remedy before a national authority notwithstanding that the violation has been committed by persons acting in an official capacity.

Article 14
Prohibition of discrimination

The enjoyment of the rights and freedoms set forth in this Convention shall be secured without discrimination on any ground such as sex, race, colour, language, religion, political or other opinion, national or social origin, association with a national minority, property, birth or other status.

Article 15
Derogation in time of emergency

1   In time of war or other public emergency threatening the life of the nation any High Contracting Party may take measures derogating from its obligations under this Convention to the extent strictly required by the exigencies of the situation, provided that such measures are not inconsistent with its other obligations under international law.

2   No derogation from Article 2, except in respect of deaths resulting from lawful acts of war, or from Articles 3, 4 (paragraph 1) and 7 shall be made under this provision.

3   Any High Contracting Party availing itself of this right of derogation shall keep the Secretary General of the Council of Europe fully informed of the measures which it has taken and the reasons therefor. It shall also inform the Secretary General of the Council of Europe when such measures have ceased to operate and the provisions of the Convention are again being fully executed.

Article 16
Restrictions on political activity of aliens

Nothing in Articles 10, 11 and 14 shall be regarded as preventing the High Contracting Parties from imposing restrictions on the political activity of aliens.

Article 17
Prohibition of abuse of rights

Nothing in this Convention may be interpreted as implying for any State, group or person any right to engage in any activity or perform any act aimed at the destruction of any of the rights and freedoms set forth herein or at their limitation to a greater extent than is provided for in the Convention.

Article 18
Limitation on use of restrictions on rights

The restrictions permitted under this Convention to the said rights and freedoms shall not be applied for any purpose other than those for which they have been prescribed.

Section II — European Court of Human Rights

Article 19
Establishment of the Court

To ensure the observance of the engagements undertaken by the High Contracting Parties in the Convention and the Protocols thereto, there shall be set up a European Court of Human Rights, hereinafter referred to as 'the Court'. It shall function on a permanent basis.

Article 20
Number of judges

The Court shall consist of a number of judges equal to that of the High Contracting Parties.

Article 21
Criteria for office

1   The judges shall be of high moral character and must either possess the qualifications required for appointment to high judicial office or be jurisconsults of recognised competence.

2   The judges shall sit on the Court in their individual capacity.

3   During their term of office the judges shall not engage in any activity which is incompatible with their independence, impartiality or with the demands of a full-time office; all questions arising from the application of this paragraph shall be decided by the Court.

Article 22
Election of judges

1   The judges shall be elected by the Parliamentary Assembly with respect to each High Contracting Party by a majority of votes cast from a list of three candidates nominated by the High Contracting Party.

2   The same procedure shall be followed to complete the Court in the event of the accession of new High Contracting Parties and in filling casual vacancies.

Article 23
Terms of office

1   The judges shall be elected for a period of six years. They may be re-elected. However, the terms of office of one-half of the judges elected at the first election shall expire at the end of three years.

2   The judges whose terms of office are to expire at the end of the initial period of three years shall be chosen by lot by the Secretary General of the Council of Europe immediately after their election.

3   In order to ensure that, as far as possible, the terms of office of one-half of the judges are renewed every three years, the Parliamentary Assembly may decide, before proceeding to any subsequent election, that the term or terms of office of one or more judges to be elected shall be for a period other than six years but not more than nine and not less than three years.

4   In cases where more than one term of office is involved and where the Parliamentary Assembly applies the preceding paragraph, the allocation of the terms of office shall be effected by a drawing of lots by the Secretary General of the Council of Europe immediately after the election.

5   A judge elected to replace a judge whose term of office has not expired shall hold office for the remainder of his predecessor's term.

6   The terms of office of judges shall expire when they reach the age of 70.

7   The judges shall hold office until replaced. They shall, however, continue to deal with such cases as they already have under consideration.

Article 24
Dismissal

No judge may be dismissed from his office unless the other judges decide by a majority of two-thirds that he has ceased to fulfil the required conditions.

Article 25
Registry and legal secretaries

The Court shall have a registry, the functions and organisation of which shall be laid down in the rules of the Court. The Court shall be assisted by legal secretaries.

Article 26
Plenary Court

The plenary Court shall

  a   elect its President and one or two Vice-Presidents for a period of three years; they may be re-elected;

  b   set up Chambers, constituted for a fixed period of time;

c   elect the Presidents of the Chambers of the Court; they may be re-elected;
d   adopt the rules of the Court, and
e   elect the Registrar and one or more Deputy Registrars.

Article 27
Committees, Chambers and Grand Chamber

1   To consider cases brought before it, the Court shall sit in committees of three judges, in Chambers of seven judges and in a Grand Chamber of seventeen judges. The Court's Chambers shall set up committees for a fixed period of time.

2   There shall sit as an *ex officio* member of the Chamber and the Grand Chamber the judge elected in respect of the State Party concerned or, if there is none or if he is unable to sit, a person of its choice who shall sit in the capacity of judge.

3   The Grand Chamber shall also include the President of the Court, the Vice-Presidents, the Presidents of the Chambers and other judges chosen in accordance with the rules of the Court. When a case is referred to the Grand Chamber under Article 43, no judge from the Chamber which rendered the judgment shall sit in the Grand Chamber, with the exception of the President of the Chamber and the judge who sat in respect of the State Party concerned.

Article 28
Declarations of inadmissibility by committees

A committee may, by a unanimous vote, declare inadmissible or strike out of its list of cases an application submitted under Article 34 where such a decision can be taken without further examination. The decision shall be final.

Article 29
Decisions by Chambers on admissibility and merits

1   If no decision is taken under Article 28, a Chamber shall decide on the admissibility and merits of individual applications submitted under Article 34.

2   A Chamber shall decide on the admissibility and merits of inter-State applications submitted under Article 33.

3   The decision on admissibility shall be taken separately unless the Court, in exceptional cases, decides otherwise.

Article 30
Relinquishment of jurisdiction to the Grand Chamber

Where a case pending before a Chamber raises a serious question affecting the interpretation of the Convention or the protocols thereto, or where the resolution of a question before the Chamber might have a result inconsistent with a judgment previously delivered by the Court, the Chamber may, at any time before it has rendered its judgment, relinquish jurisdiction in favour of the Grand Chamber, unless one of the parties to the case objects.

Article 31
Powers of the Grand Chamber

The Grand Chamber shall

    a   determine applications submitted either under Article 33 or Article 34 when a Chamber has relinquished jurisdiction under Article 30 or when the case has been referred to it under Article 43; and

    b   consider requests for advisory opinions submitted under Article 47.

Article 32
Jurisdiction of the Court

1   The jurisdiction of the Court shall extend to all matters concerning the interpretation and application of the Convention and the protocols thereto which are referred to it as provided in Articles 33, 34 and 47.

2   In the event of dispute as to whether the Court has jurisdiction, the Court shall decide.

Article 33
Inter-State cases

Any High Contracting Party may refer to the Court any alleged breach of the provisions of the Convention and the protocols thereto by another High Contracting Party

Article 34
Individual applications

The Court may receive applications from any person, non-governmental organisation or group of individuals claiming to be the victim of a violation by one of the High Contracting Parties of the rights set forth in the Convention or the protocols thereto. The High Contracting Parties undertake not to hinder in any way the effective exercise of this right.

Article 35
Admissibility criteria

1   The Court may only deal with the matter after all domestic remedies have been exhausted, according to the generally recognised rules of international law, and within a period of six months from the date on which the final decision was taken.

2   The Court shall not deal with any application submitted under Article 34 that

    a   is anonymous; or

    b   is substantially the same as a matter that has already been examined by the Court or has already been submitted to another procedure of international investigation or settlement and contains no relevant new information.

3   The Court shall declare inadmissible any individual application submitted under Article 34 which it considers incompatible with the provisions of the Convention or the protocols thereto, manifestly ill-founded, or an abuse of the right of application.

4   The Court shall reject any application which it considers inadmissible under this Article. It may do so at any stage of the proceedings.

Article 36
Third party intervention

1   In all cases before a Chamber of the Grand Chamber, a High Contracting Party one of whose nationals is an applicant shall have the right to submit written comments and to take part in hearings.

2   The President of the Court may, in the interest of the proper administration of justice, invite any High Contracting Party which is not a party to the proceedings or any person concerned who is not the applicant to submit written comments or take part in hearings.

Article 37
Striking out applications

1   The Court may at any stage of the proceedings decide to strike an application out of its list of cases where the circumstances lead to the conclusion that

    a   the applicant does not intend to pursue his application; or

    b   the matter has been resolved; or

    c   for any other reason established by the Court, it is no longer justified to continue the examination of the application.

However, the Court shall continue the examination of the application if respect for human rights as defined in the Convention and the protocols thereto so requires.

2   The Court may decide to restore an application to its list of cases if it considers that the circumstances justify such a course.

Article 38
Examination of the case and friendly settlement proceedings

1   If the Court declares the application admissible, it shall

    a   pursue the examination of the case, together with the representatives of the parties, and if need be, undertake an investigation, for the effective conduct of which the States concerned shall furnish all necessary facilities;

    b   place itself at the disposal of the parties concerned with a view to securing a friendly settlement of the matter on the basis of respect for human rights as defined in the Convention and the protocols thereto.

2   Proceedings conducted under paragraph 1.b shall be confidential.

Article 39
Finding of a friendly settlement

If a friendly settlement is effected, the Court shall strike the case out of its list by means of a decision which shall be confined to a brief statement of the facts and of the solution reached.

Article 40
Public hearings and access to documents

1   Hearings shall be in public unless the Court in exceptional circumstances decides otherwise.

2   Documents deposited with the Registrar shall be accessible to the public unless the President of the Court decides otherwise.

Article 41
Just satisfaction

If the Court finds that there has been a violation of the Convention or the protocols thereto, and if the internal law of the High Contracting Party concerned allows only partial reparation to be made, the Court shall, if necessary afford just satisfaction to the injured party.

Article 42
Judgments of Chambers

Judgments of Chambers shall become final in accordance with the provisions of Article 44, paragraph 2.

Article 43
Referral to the Grand Chamber

1   Within a period of three months from the date of the judgment of the Chamber, any party to the case may, in exceptional cases, request that the case be referred to the Grand Chamber.

2   A panel of five judges of the Grand Chamber shall accept the request if the case raises a serious question affecting the interpretation or application of the Convention or the protocols thereto, or a serious issue of general importance.

3   If the panel accepts the request, the Grand Chamber shall decide the case by means of a judgment.

Article 44
Final judgments

1   The judgment of the Grand Chamber shall be final.

2   The judgment of a Chamber shall become final

a   when the parties declare that they will not request that the case be referred to the Grand Chamber; or

b   three months after the date of the judgment, if reference of the case to the Grand Chamber has not been requested; or

c   when the panel of the Grand Chamber rejects the request to refer under Article 43.

3   The final judgment shall be published.

Article 45
Reasons for judgments and decisions

1   Reasons shall be given for judgments as well as for decisions declaring applications admissible or inadmissible.

2   If a judgment does not represent, in whole or in part, the unanimous opinion of the judges, any judge shall be entitled to deliver a separate opinion.

Article 46
Binding force and execution of judgments

1   The High Contracting Parties undertake to abide by the final judgment of the Court in any case to which they are parties.

2   The final judgment of the Court shall be transmitted to the Committee of Ministers, which shall supervise its execution.

Article 47
Advisory opinions

1   The Court may, at the request of the Committee of Ministers, give advisory opinions on legal questions concerning the interpretation of the Convention and the protocols thereto.

2   Such opinions shall not deal with any question relating to the content or scope of the rights or freedoms defined in Section I of the Convention and the protocols thereto, or with any other question which the Court or the Committee of Ministers might have to consider in consequence of any such proceedings as could be instituted in accordance with the Convention.

3   Decisions of the Committee of Ministers to request an advisory opinion of the Court shall require a majority vote of the representatives entitled to sit on the Committee.

Article 48
Advisory jurisdiction of the Court

The Court shall decide whether a request for an advisory opinion submitted by the Committee of Ministers is within its competence as defined in Article 47.

Article 49
Reasons for advisory opinions

1 Reasons shall be given for advisory opinions of the Court.

2 If the advisory opinion does not represent, in whole or in part, the unanimous opinion of the judges, any judge shall be entitled to deliver a separate opinion.

3 Advisory opinions of the Court shall be communicated to the Committee of Ministers.

Article 50
Expenditure on the Court

The expenditure on the Court shall be borne by the Council of Europe.

Article 51
Privileges and immunities of judges

The judges shall be entitled, during the exercise of their functions, to the privileges and immunities provided for in Article 40 of the Statute of the Council of Europe and in the agreements made thereunder.

Section III — Miscellaneous provisions

Article 52
Inquiries by the Secretary General

On receipt of a request from the Secretary General of the Council of Europe any High Contracting Party shall furnish an explanation of the manner in which its internal law ensures the effective implementation of any of the provisions of the Convention.

Article 53
Safeguard for existing human rights

Nothing in this Convention shall be construed as limiting or derogating from any of the human rights and fundamental freedoms which may be ensured under the laws of any High Contracting Party or under any other agreement to which it is a Party.

Article 54
Powers of the Committee of Ministers

Nothing in this Convention shall prejudice the powers conferred on the Committee of Ministers by the Statute of the Council of Europe.

Article 55
Exclusion of other means of dispute settlement

The High Contracting Parties agree that, except by special agreement, they will not avail themselves of treaties, conventions or declarations in force between them for the purpose of submitting, by way of petition, a dispute arising out of the interpretation or application of this Convention to a means of settlement other than those provided for in this Convention.

Article 56
Territorial application

1   Any State may at the time of its ratification or at any time thereafter declare by notification addressed to the Secretary General of the Council of Europe that the present Convention shall, subject to paragraph 4 of this Article, extend to all or any of the territories for whose international relations it is responsible.

2   The Convention shall extend to the territory or territories named in the notification as from the thirtieth day after the receipt of this notification by the Secretary General of the Council of Europe.

3   The provisions of this Convention shall be applied in such territories with due regard, however, to local requirements.

4   Any State which has made a declaration in accordance with paragraph 1 of this article may at any time thereafter declare on behalf of one or more of the territories to which the declaration relates that it accepts the competence of the Court to receive applications from individuals, non-governmental organisations or groups of individuals as provided by Article 34 of the Convention.

Article 57
Reservations

1   Any State may, when signing this Convention or when depositing its instrument of ratification, make a reservation in respect of any particular provision of the Convention to the extent that any law then in force in its territory is not in conformity with the provision. Reservations of a general character shall not be permitted under this article.

2   Any reservation made under this article shall contain a brief statement of the law concerned.

Article 58
Denunciation

1   A High Contracting Party may denounce the present Convention only after the expiry of five years from the date on which it became a party to it and after six months' notice contained in a notification addressed to the Secretary General of the Council of Europe, who shall inform the other High Contracting Parties.

2   Such a denunciation shall not have the effect of releasing the High Contracting Party concerned from its obligations under this Convention in respect of any act which, being capable of constituting a violation of such obligations, may have been performed by it before the date at which the denunciation became effective.

3   Any High Contracting Party which shall cease to be a member of the Council of Europe shall cease to be a Party to this Convention under the same conditions.

4   The Convention may be denounced in accordance with the provisions of the preceding paragraphs in respect of any territory to which it has been declared to extend under the terms of Article 56.

Article 59
Signature and ratification

1   This Convention shall be open to the signature of the members of the Council of Europe. It shall be ratified. Ratifications shall be deposited with the Secretary General of the Council of Europe.

2   The present Convention shall come into force after the deposit of ten instruments of ratification.

3   As regards any signatory ratifying subsequently, the Convention shall come into force at the date of the deposit of its instrument of ratification.

4   The Secretary General of the Council of Europe shall notify all the members of the Council of Europe of the entry into force of the Convention, the names of the High Contracting Parties who have ratified it, and the deposit of all instruments of ratification which may be effected subsequently.

Done at Rome this 4th day of November 1950, in English and French, both texts being equally authentic, in a single copy which shall remain deposited in the archives of the Council of Europe.

The Secretary General shall transmit certified copies to each of the signatories.

PROTOCOL [NO. 1] TO THE CONVENTION FOR THE PROTECTION OF HUMAN RIGHTS AND FUNDAMENTAL FREEDOMS, AS AMENDED BY PROTOCOL NO. 11

The governments signatory hereto, being members of the Council of Europe,

Being resolved to take steps to ensure the collective enforcement of certain rights and freedoms other than those already included in Section I of the Convention for the Protection of Human Rights and Fundamental Freedoms signed at Rome on 4 November 1950 (hereinafter referred to as 'the Convention'),

Have agreed as follows:

Article 1
Protection of property

Every natural or legal person is entitled to the peaceful enjoyment of his possessions. No one shall be deprived of his possessions except in the public interest and subject to the conditions provided for by law and by the general principles of international law.

The preceding provisions shall not, however, in any way impair the right of a State to enforce such laws as it deems necessary to control the use of property in accordance with the general interest or to secure the payment of taxes or other contributions or penalties.

Article 2
Right to education

No person shall be denied the right to education. In the exercise of any functions which it assumes in relation to education and to teaching, the State shall respect the right of parents to ensure such education and teaching in conformity with their own religious and philosophical convictions.

Article 3
Right to free elections

The High Contracting Parties undertake to hold free elections at reasonable intervals by secret ballot, under conditions which will ensure the free expression of the opinion of the people in the choice of the legislature.

Article 4
Territorial application

Any High Contracting Party may at the time of signature or ratification or at any time thereafter communicate to the Secretary General of the Council of Europe a declaration stating the extent to which it undertakes that the provisions of the present Protocol shall apply to such of the territories for the international relations of which it is responsible as are named therein.

Any High Contracting Party which has communicated a declaration in virtue of the preceding paragraph may from time to time communicate a further declaration modifying the terms of any former declaration or terminating the application of the provisions of this Protocol in respect of any territory.

A declaration made in accordance with this article shall be deemed to have been made in accordance with paragraph 1 of Article 56 of the Convention.

Article 5
Relationship to the Convention

As between the High Contracting Parties the provisions of Articles 1, 2, 3 and 4 of this Protocol shall be regarded as additional articles to the Convention and all the provisions of the Convention shall apply accordingly.

Article 6
Signature and ratification

This Protocol shall be open for signature by the members of the Council of Europe, who are the signatories of the Convention; it shall be ratified at the same time as or after the ratification of the Convention. It shall enter into force after the deposit of ten instruments of ratification. As regards any signatory ratifying subsequently, the Protocol shall enter into force at the date of the deposit of its instrument of ratification.

The instruments of ratification shall be deposited with the Secretary General of the Council of Europe, who will notify all members of the names of those who have ratified.

Done at Paris on the 20th day of March 1952, in English and French, both texts being equally authentic, in a single copy which shall remain deposited in the archives of the Council of Europe. The Secretary General shall transmit certified copies to each of the signatory governments.

PROTOCOL NO. 4 TO THE CONVENTION FOR THE PROTECTION OF HUMAN RIGHTS AND FUNDAMENTAL FREEDOMS, SECURING CERTAIN RIGHTS AND FREEDOMS OTHER THAN THOSE ALREADY INCLUDED IN THE CONVENTION AND IN THE FIRST PROTOCOL THERETO, AS AMENDED BY PROTOCOL NO. 11

The governments signatory hereto, being members of the Council of Europe,

Being resolved to take steps to ensure the collective enforcement of certain rights and freedoms other than those already included in Section 1 of the Convention for the Protection of Human Rights and Fundamental Freedoms signed at Rome on 4th November 1950 (hereinafter referred to as the 'Convention') and in Articles 1 to 3 of the First Protocol to the Convention, signed at Paris on 20th March 1952,

Have agreed as follows:

Article 1
Prohibition of imprisonment for debt

No one shall be deprived of his liberty merely on the ground of inability to fulfil a contractual obligation.

Article 2
Freedom of movement

1   Everyone lawfully within the territory of a State shall, within that territory, have the right to liberty of movement and freedom to choose his residence.

2   Everyone shall be free to leave any country, including his own.

3   No restrictions shall be placed on the exercise of these rights other than such as are in accordance with law and are necessary in a democratic society in the interests of national security or public safety, for the maintenance of *ordre public*, for the prevention of crime, for the protection of health or morals, or for the protection of the rights and freedoms of others.

4   The rights set forth in paragraph 1 may also be subject, in particular areas, to restrictions imposed in accordance with law and justified by the public interest in a democratic society.

Article 3
Prohibition of expulsion of nationals

1   No one shall be expelled, by means either of an individual or of a collective measure, from the territory of the State of which he is a national.

2   No one shall be deprived of the right to enter the territory of the state of which he is a national.

Article 4
Prohibition of collective expulsion of aliens

Collective expulsion of aliens is prohibited.

Article 5
Territorial application

1   Any High Contracting Party may, at the time of signature or ratification of this Protocol, or at any time thereafter, communicate to the Secretary General of the Council of Europe a declaration stating the extent to which it undertakes that the provisions of this Protocol shall apply to such of the territories for the international relations of which it is responsible as are named therein.

2   Any High Contracting Party which has communicated a declaration in virtue of the preceding paragraph may, from time to time, communicate a further declaration modifying the terms of any former declaration or terminating the application of the provisions of this Protocol in respect of any territory.

3   A declaration made in accordance with this article shall be deemed to have been made in accordance with paragraph 1 of Article 56 of the Convention.

4   The territory of any State to which this Protocol applies by virtue of ratification or acceptance by that State, and each territory to which this Protocol is applied by virtue of a declaration by that State under this article, shall be treated as separate territories for the purpose of the references in Articles 2 and 3 to the territory of a State.

5   Any State which has made a declaration in accordance with paragraph 1 or 2 of this Article may at any time thereafter declare on behalf of one or more of the territories to which the declaration relates that it accepts the competence of the

Court to receive applications from individuals, non-governmental organisations or groups of individuals as provided in Article 34 of the Convention in respect of all or any of Articles 1 to 4 of this Protocol.

Article 6
Relationship to the Convention

As between the High Contracting Parties the provisions of Articles 1 to 5 of this Protocol shall be regarded as additional Articles to the Convention, and all the provisions of the Convention shall apply accordingly.

Article 7
Signature and ratification

1   This Protocol shall be open for signature by the members of the Council of Europe who are the signatories of the Convention; it shall be ratified at the same time as or after the ratification of the Convention. It shall enter into force after the deposit of five instruments of ratification. As regards any signatory ratifying subsequently, the Protocol shall enter into force at the date of the deposit of its instrument of ratification.

2   The instruments of ratification shall be deposited with the Secretary General of the Council of Europe, who will notify all members of the names of those who have ratified.

In witness whereof the undersigned, being duly authorised thereto, have signed this Protocol.

Done at Strasbourg, this 16th day of September 1963, in English and in French, both texts being equally authoritative, in a single copy which shall remain deposited in the archives of the Council of Europe. The Secretary General shall transmit certified copies to each of the signatory states.

PROTOCOL NO. 6 TO THE CONVENTION FOR THE PROTECTION OF HUMAN RIGHTS AND FUNDAMENTAL FREEDOMS CONCERNING THE ABOLITION OF THE DEATH PENALTY, AS AMENDED BY PROTOCOL NO. 11

The member States of the Council of Europe, signatory to this Protocol to the Convention for the Protection of Human Rights and Fundamental Freedoms, signed at Rome on 4 November 1950 (hereinafter referred to as 'the Convention'),

Considering that the evolution that has occurred in several member States of the Council of Europe expresses a general tendency in favour of abolition of the death penalty;

Have agreed as follows:

Article 1
Abolition of the death penalty

The death penalty shall be abolished. No-one shall be condemned to such penalty or executed.

Article 2
Death penalty in time of war

A State may make provision in its law for the death penalty in respect of acts committed in time of war or of imminent threat of war; such penalty shall be applied only in the instances laid down in the law and in accordance with its provisions. The State shall communicate to the Secretary General of the Council of Europe the relevant provisions of that law.

Article 3
Prohibition of derogations

No derogation from the provisions of this Protocol shall be made under Article 15 of the Convention.

Article 4
Prohibition of reservations

No reservation may be made under Article 57 of the Convention in respect of the provisions of this Protocol.

Article 5
Territorial application

1   Any State may at the time of signature or when depositing its instrument of ratification, acceptance or approval, specify the territory or territories to which this Protocol shall apply.

2   Any State may at any later date, by a declaration addressed to the Secretary General of the Council of Europe, extend the application of this Protocol to any other territory specified in the declaration. In respect of such territory the Protocol shall enter into force on the first day of the month following the date of receipt of such declaration by the Secretary General.

3   Any declaration made under the two preceding paragraphs may, in respect of any territory specified in such declaration, be withdrawn by a notification addressed to the Secretary General. The withdrawal shall become effective on the first day of the month following the date of receipt of such notification by the Secretary General.

Article 6
Relationship to the Convention

As between the States Parties the provisions of Articles 1 to 5 of this Protocol shall be regarded as additional articles to the Convention and all the provisions of the Convention shall apply accordingly.

Article 7
Signature and ratification

The Protocol shall be open for signature by the member States of the Council of Europe, signatories to the Convention. It shall be subject to ratification, acceptance or approval. A member State of the Council of Europe may not ratify, accept or approve this Protocol unless it has, simultaneously or previously, ratified the Convention. Instruments of ratification, acceptance or approval shall be deposited with the Secretary General of the Council of Europe.

Article 8
Entry into force

1   This Protocol shall enter into force on the first day of the month following the date on which five member States of the Council of Europe have expressed their consent to be bound by the Protocol in accordance with the provisions of Article 7.

2   In respect of any member State which subsequently expresses its consent to be bound by it, the Protocol shall enter into force on the first day of the month following the date of the deposit of the instrument of ratification, acceptance or approval.

Article 9
Depositary functions

The Secretary General of the Council of Europe shall notify the member States of the Council of:

a   any signature;

b   the deposit of any instrument of ratification, acceptance or approval;

c   any date of entry into force of this Protocol in accordance with Articles 5 and 8;

d   any other act, notification or communication relating to this Protocol.

In witness whereof the undersigned, being duly authorised thereto, have signed this Protocol.

Done at Strasbourg, this 28th day of April 1983, in English and in French, both texts being equally authentic, in a single copy which shall be deposited in the archives of the Council of Europe. The Secretary General of the Council of

Europe shall transmit certified copies to each member State of the Council of Europe.

PROTOCOL NO. 7 TO THE CONVENTION FOR THE PROTECTION OF HUMAN RIGHTS AND FUNDAMENTAL FREEDOMS, AS AMENDED BY PROTOCOL NO. 11

The member States of the Council of Europe signatory hereto,

Being resolved to take further steps to ensure the collective enforcement of certain rights and freedoms by means of the Convention for the Protection of Human Rights and Fundamental Freedoms signed at Rome on 4 November 1950 (hereinafter referred to as 'the Convention'),

Have agreed as follows

Article 1
Procedural safeguards relating to expulsion of aliens

1   An alien lawfully resident in the territory of a State shall not be expelled therefrom except in pursuance of a decision reached in accordance with law and shall be allowed:

a   to submit reasons against his expulsion,

b   to have his case reviewed, and

c   to be represented for these purposes before the competent authority or a person or persons designated by that authority.

2   An alien may be expelled before the exercise of his rights under paragraph 1.a, b and c of this Article, when such expulsion is necessary in the interests of public order or is grounded on reasons of national security.

Article 2
Right of appeal in criminal matters

1   Everyone convicted of a criminal offence by a tribunal shall have the right to have his conviction or sentence reviewed by a higher tribunal. The exercise of this right, including the grounds on which it may be exercised, shall be governed by law.

2   This right may be subject to exceptions in regard to offences of a minor character, as prescribed by law, or in cases in which the person concerned was tried in the first instance by the highest tribunal or was convicted following an appeal against acquittal.

Article 3
Compensation for wrongful conviction

When a person has by a final decision been convicted of a criminal offence and when subsequently his conviction has been reversed, or he has been pardoned, on the ground that a new or newly discovered fact shows conclusively that there has been a miscarriage of justice, the person who has suffered punishment as a result of such conviction shall be compensated according to the law or the practice of the State concerned, unless it is proved that the non-disclosure of the unknown fact in time is wholly or partly attributable to him.

Article 4
Right not to be tried or punished twice

1   No one shall be liable to be tried or punished again in criminal proceedings under the jurisdiction of the same State for an offence for which he has already been finally acquitted or convicted in accordance with the law and penal procedure of that State.

2   The provisions of the preceding paragraph shall not prevent the reopening of the case in accordance with the law and penal procedure of the State concerned, if there is evidence of new or newly discovered facts, or if there has been a fundamental defect in the previous proceedings, which could affect the outcome of the case.

3   No derogation from this Article shall be made under Article 15 of the Convention.

Article 5
Equality between spouses

Spouses shall enjoy equality of rights and responsibilities of a private law character between them, and in their relations with their children, as to marriage, during marriage and in the event of its dissolution. This Article shall not prevent States from taking such measures as are necessary in the interests of the children.

Article 6
Territorial application

1   Any State may at the time of signature or when depositing its instrument of ratification, acceptance or approval, specify the territory or territories to which the Protocol shall apply and state the extent to which it undertakes that the provisions of this Protocol shall apply to such territory or territories.

2   Any State may at any later date, by a declaration addressed to the Secretary General of the Council of Europe, extend the application of this Protocol to any other territory specified in the declaration. In respect of such territory the Protocol shall enter into force on the first day of the month following the expiration of a period of two months after the date of receipt by the Secretary General of such declaration.

3   Any declaration made under the two preceding paragraphs may, in respect of any territory specified in such declaration, be withdrawn or modified by a notification addressed to the Secretary General. The withdrawal or modification

shall become effective on the first day of the month following the expiration of a period of two months after the date of receipt of such notification by the Secretary General.

4   A declaration made in accordance with this Article shall be deemed to have been made in accordance with paragraph 1 of Article 56 of the Convention.

5   The territory of any State to which this Protocol applies by virtue of ratification, acceptance or approval by that State, and each territory to which this Protocol is applied by virtue of a declaration by that State under this Article, may be treated as separate territories for the purpose of the reference in Article 1 to the territory of a State.

6   Any State which has made a declaration in accordance with paragraph 1 or 2 of this Article may at any time thereafter declare on behalf of one or more of the territories to which the declaration relates that it accepts the competence of the Court to receive applications from individuals, non-governmental organisations or groups of individuals as provided in Article 34 of the Convention in respect of Articles 1 to 5 of this Protocol.

Article 7
Relationship to the Convention

As between the States Parties, the provisions of Article 1 to 6 of this Protocol shall be regarded as additional Articles to the Convention, and all the provisions of the Convention shall apply accordingly.

Article 8
Signature and ratification

This Protocol shall be open for signature by member States of the Council of Europe which have signed the Convention. It is subject to ratification, acceptance or approval. A member State of the Council of Europe may not ratify, accept or approve this Protocol without previously or simultaneously ratifying the Convention. Instruments of ratification, acceptance or approval shall be deposited with the Secretary General of the Council of Europe.

Article 9
Entry into force

1   This Protocol shall enter into force on the first day of the month following the expiration of a period of two months after the date on which seven member States of the Council of Europe have expressed their consent to be bound by the Protocol in accordance with the provisions of Article 8.

2   In respect of any member State which subsequently expresses its consent to be bound by it, the Protocol shall enter into force on the first day of the month following the expiration of a period of two months after the date of the deposit of the instrument of ratification, acceptance or approval.

Article 10
Depositary functions

The Secretary General of the Council of Europe shall notify all the member States of the Council of Europe of:

a any signature;

b the deposit of any instrument of ratification, acceptance or approval;

c any date of entry into force of this Protocol in accordance with Articles 6 and 9;

d any other act, notification or declaration relating to this Protocol.

In witness whereof the undersigned, being duly authorised thereto, have signed this Protocol.

Done at Strasbourg, this 22nd day of November 1984, in English and French, both texts being equally authentic, in a single copy which shall be deposited in the archives of the Council of Europe. The Secretary General of the Council of Europe shall transmit certified copies to each member State of the Council of Europe.

Appendix Two

Rules of Procedure of the European Court of Human Rights

RULES OF COURT
(4 November 1998)

REGISTRY OF THE COURT
STRASBOURG

CONTENTS

Chapter II — Institution of Proceedings

Rule 45 Signatures
Rule 46 Contents of an inter-State application
Rule 47 Contents of an individual application

Chapter III — Judge Rapporteurs

Rule 48 Inter-State applications
Rule 49 Individual applications
Rule 50 Grand Chamber proceedings

Chapter IV — Proceedings on Admissibility

Inter-State applications

Rule 51

Individual applications

Rule 52 Assignment of applications to the Sections
Rule 53 Procedure before a Committee
Rule 54 Procedure before a Chamber

Inter-State and individual applications

Rule 55 Pleas of inadmissibility
Rule 56 Decision of a Chamber
Rule 57 Language of the decision

Chapter V — Proceedings after the Admission of an Application

Rule 58 Inter-State applications
Rule 59 Individual applications
Rule 60 Claims for just satisfaction
Rule 61 Third-party intervention
Rule 62 Friendly settlement

Chapter VI — Hearings

Rule 63 Conduct of hearings
Rule 64 Failure to appear — at a hearing
Rule 65 Convocation of witnesses, experts and other persons; costs of their appearance
Rule 66 Oath or solemn declaration by witnesses and experts
Rule 67 Objection to a witness or expert; hearing of a person for information purposes
Rule 68 Questions put during hearings
Rule 69 Failure to appear, refusal to give evidence or false evidence
Rule 70 Verbatim record of hearings

Chapter VII — Proceedings before the Grand Chamber

Rule 71 Applicability of procedural provisions
Rule 72 Relinquishment of jurisdiction by a Chamber in favour of the Grand Chamber
Rule 73 Request by a party for referral to the Grand Chamber

Chapter VIII — Judgments

Rule 74 Contents of the judgment
Rule 75 Ruling on just satisfaction
Rule 76 Language of the judgment
Rule 77 Signature, delivery and notification of the judgment
Rule 78 Publication of judgments and other documents
Rule 79 Request for interpretation of a judgment
Rule 80 Request for revision of a judgment
Rule 81 Rectification of errors in decisions and judgments

Chapter IX — Advisory Opinions

Rule 82
Rule 83
Rule 84
Rule 85
Rule 86
Rule 87
Rule 88
Rule 89
Rule 90

Chapter X — Legal Aid

Rule 91
Rule 92
Rule 93
Rule 94
Rule 95
Rule 96

TITLE III — Transitional Rules

Rule 97 Judges' terms of office
Rule 98 Presidency of the Sections
Rule 99 Relations between the Court and the Commission
Rule 100 Chamber and Grand Chamber proceedings
Rule 101 Grant of legal aid
Rule 102 Request for interpretation or revision of a judgment

TITLE IV — Final Clauses

Rule 103 Amendment or suspension of a Rule
Rule 104 Entry into force of the Rules

The European Court of Human Rights,
Having regard to the Convention for the Protection of Human Rights and
Fundamental Freedoms and the Protocols thereto,
Makes the present Rules:

Rule 1
(Definitions)

For the purposes of these Rules unless the context otherwise requires:

(a)   the term 'Convention' means the Convention for the Protection of
Human Rights and Fundamental Freedoms and the Protocols thereto;

(b)   the expression 'plenary Court' means the European Court of Human
Rights sitting in plenary session;

(c)   the term 'Grand Chamber' means the Grand Chamber of seventeen
judges constituted in pursuance of Article 27 § 1 of the Convention;

(d)   the term 'Section' means a Chamber set up by the plenary Court for a
fixed period in pursuance of Article 26(b) of the Convention and the expression
'President of the Section' means the judge elected by the plenary Court in
pursuance of Article 26(c) of the Convention as President of such a Section;

(e)   the term 'Chamber' means any Chamber of seven judges constituted in
pursuance of Article 27 § 1 of the Convention and the expression 'President of the
Chamber' means the judge presiding over such a 'Chamber';

(f)   the term 'Committee' means a Committee of three judges set up in
pursuance of Article 27 § 1 of the Convention;

(g)   the term 'Court' means either the plenary Court, the Grand Chamber, a
Section, a Chamber, a Committee or the panel of five judges referred to in Article
43 § 2 of the Convention;

(h)   the expression '*ad hoc* judge' means any person, other than an elected
judge, chosen by a Contracting Party in pursuance of Article 27 § 2 of the
Convention to sit as a member of the Grand Chamber or as a member of a
Chamber;

(i)   the terms 'judge' and 'judges' mean the judges elected by the
Parliamentary Assembly of the Council of Europe or *ad hoc* judges;

(j)   the term 'Judge Rapporteur' means a judge appointed to carry out the
tasks provided for in Rules 48 and 49;

(k)   the term 'Registrar' denotes the Registrar of the Court or the Registrar
of a Section according to the context;

(l)   the terms 'party' and 'parties' mean
    — the applicant or respondent Contracting Parties;

— the applicant (the person, non-governmental organisation or group of individuals) that lodged a complaint under Article 34 of the Convention;

(m) the expression 'third party' means any Contracting State or any person concerned who, as provided for in Article 36 §§ 1 and 2 of the Convention, has exercised its right or been invited to submit written comments or take part in a hearing;

(n) the expression 'Committee of Ministers' means the Committee of Ministers of the Council of Europe;

(o) the terms 'former Court' and 'Commission' mean respectively the European Court and European Commission of Human Rights set up under former Article 19 of the Convention.

TITLE I
ORGANISATION AND WORKING OF THE COURT

Chapter I
Judges

Rule 2
(Calculation of term of office)

1.   The duration of the term of office of an elected judge shall be calculated as from the date of election. However, when a judge is re-elected on the expiry of the term of office or is elected to replace a judge whose term of office has expired or is about to expire, the duration of the term of office shall, in either case, be calculated as from the date of such expiry.

2.   In accordance with Article 23 § 5 of the Convention, a judge elected to replace a judge whose term of office has not expired shall hold office for the remainder of the predecessor's term.

3.   In accordance with Article 23 § 7 of the Convention, an elected judge shall hold office until a successor has taken the oath or made the declaration provided for in Rule 3.

Rule 3
(Oath or solemn declaration)

1.   Before taking up office, each elected judge shall, at the first sitting of the plenary Court at which the judge is present or, in case of need, before the President of the Court, take the following oath or make the following solemn declaration:

'I swear' — or 'I solemnly declare' — 'that I will exercise my functions as a judge honourably, independently and impartially and that I will keep secret all deliberations.'

2.   This act shall be recorded in minutes.

Rule 4
(Incompatible activities)

In accordance with Article 21 § 3 of the Convention, the judges shall not during their term of office engage in any political or administrative activity or any professional activity which is incompatible with their independence or impartiality or with the demands of a full-time office. Each judge shall declare to the President of the Court any additional activity. In the event of a disagreement between the President and the judge concerned, any question arising shall be decided by the plenary Court.

Rule 5
(Precedence)

1.   Elected judges shall take precedence after the President and Vice-Presidents of the Court and the Presidents of the Sections, according to the date of their election; in the event of re-election, even if it is not an immediate re-election, the length of time during which the judge concerned previously held office as a judge shall be taken into account.

2.   Vice-Presidents of the Court elected to office on the same date shall take precedence according to the length of time they have served as judges. If the length of time they have served as judges is the same, they shall take precedence according to age. The same Rule shall apply to Presidents of Sections.

3.   Judges who have served the same length of time as judges shall take precedence according to age.

4.   *Ad hoc* judges shall take precedence after the elected judges according to age.

Rule 6
(Resignation)

Resignation of a judge shall be notified to the President of the Court, who shall transmit it to the Secretary General of the Council of Europe. Subject to the provisions of Rules 24 § 3 *in fine* and 26 § 2, resignation shall constitute vacation of office.

Rule 7
(Dismissal from office)

No judge may be dismissed from his or her office unless the other judges, meeting in plenary session, decide by a majority of two-thirds of the elected judges in office that he or she has ceased to fulfil the required conditions. He or she must first be heard by the plenary Court. Any judge may set in motion the procedure for dismissal from office.

Chapter II
Presidency of the Court

Rule 8
(Election of the President and Vice-Presidents of the Court and the Presidents and Vice-Presidents of the Sections)

1.   The plenary Court shall elect its President, two Vice-Presidents and the Presidents of the Sections for a period of three years, provided that such period shall not exceed the duration of their terms of office as judges. They may be re-elected.

2.   Each Section shall likewise elect for a renewable period of three years a Vice-President, who shall replace the President of the Section if the latter is unable to carry out his or her duties.

3.   The Presidents and Vice-Presidents shall continue to hold office until the election of their successors.

4.   If a President or a Vice-President ceases to be a member of the Court or resigns from office before its normal expiry, the plenary Court or the relevant Section, as the case may be, shall elect a successor for the remainder of the term of that office.

5.   The elections referred to in this Rule shall be by secret ballot; only the elected judges who are present shall take part. If no judge receives an absolute majority of the elected judges present, a ballot shall take place between the two judges who have received most votes. In the event of a tie, preference shall be given to the judge having precedence in accordance with Rule 5.

Rule 9
(Functions of the President of the Court)

1.   The President of the Court shall direct the work and administration of the Court. The President shall represent the Court and, in particular, be responsible for its relations with the authorities of the Council of Europe.

2.   The President shall preside at plenary meetings of the Court, meetings of the Grand Chamber and meetings of the panel of five judges.

3.   The President shall not take part in the consideration of cases being heard by Chambers except where he or she is the judge elected in respect of a Contracting Party concerned.

Rule 10
(Functions of the Vice-Presidents of the Court)

The Vice-Presidents of the Court shall assist the President of the Court. They shall take the place of the President if the latter is unable to carry out his or her duties or the office of President is vacant, or at the request of the President. They shall also act as Presidents of Sections.

Rule 11
(Replacement of the President and the Vice-Presidents)

If the President and the Vice-Presidents of the Court are at the same time unable to carry out their duties or if their offices are at the same time vacant, the office of President of the Court shall be assumed by a President of a Section or, if none is available, by another elected judge, in accordance with the order of precedence provided for in Rule 5.

Rule 12
(Presidency of Sections and Chambers)

The Presidents of the Sections shall preside at the sittings of the Section and Chambers of which they are members. The Vice-Presidents of the Sections shall take their place if they are unable to carry out their duties or if the office of President of the Section concerned is vacant, or at the request of the President of the Section. Failing that, the judges of the Section and the Chambers shall take their place, in the order of precedence provided for in Rule 5.

Rule 13
(Inability to preside)

Judges of the Court may not preside in cases in which the Contracting Party of which they are nationals or in respect of which they were elected is a party.

Rule 14
(Balanced representation of the sexes)

In relation to the making of appointments governed by this and the following chapter of the present Rules, the Court shall pursue a policy aimed at securing a balanced representation of the sexes.

Chapter III
The Registry

Rule 15
(Election of the Registrar)

1.   The plenary Court shall elect its Registrar. The candidates shall be of high moral character and must possess the legal, managerial and linguistic knowledge and experience necessary to carry out the functions attaching to the post.

2.   The Registrar shall be elected for a term of five years and may be re-elected. The Registrar may not be dismissed from office, unless the judges, meeting in plenary session, decide by a majority of two-thirds of the elected judges in office that the person concerned has ceased to fulfil the required conditions. He or she must first be heard by the plenary Court. Any judge may set in motion the procedure for dismissal from office.

3.   The elections referred to in this Rule shall be by secret ballot; only the elected judges who are present shall take part. If no candidate receives an absolute majority of the elected judges present, a ballot shall take place between the two candidates who have received most votes. In the event of a tie, preference shall be given, firstly, to the female candidate, if any, and, secondly, to the older candidate.

4.   Before taking up office, the Registrar shall take the following oath or make the following solemn declaration before the plenary Court or, if need be, before the President of the Court:

'I swear' — or 'I solemnly declare' — 'that I will exercise loyally, discreetly and conscientiously the functions conferred upon me as Registrar of the European Court of Human Rights.'

This act shall be recorded in minutes.

Rule 16
(Election of the Deputy Registrars)

1.   The plenary Court shall also elect two Deputy Registrars on the conditions and in the manner and for the term prescribed in the preceding Rule. The procedure for dismissal from office provided for in respect of the Registrar shall likewise apply. The Court shall first consult the Registrar in both these matters.

2.   Before taking up office, a Deputy Registrar shall take an oath or make a solemn declaration before the plenary Court or, if need be, before the President of the Court, in terms similar to those prescribed in respect of the Registrar. This act shall be recorded in minutes.

Rule 17
(Functions of the Registrar)

1.   The Registrar shall assist the Court in the performance of its functions and shall be responsible for the organisation and activities of the Registry under the authority of the President of the Court.

2.   The Registrar shall have the custody of the archives of the Court and shall be the channel for all communications and notifications made by, or addressed to, the Court in connection with the cases brought or to be brought before it.

3.   The Registrar shall, subject to the duty of discretion attaching to this office, reply to requests for information concerning the work of the Court, in particular to enquiries from the press.

4.   General instructions drawn up by the Registrar, and approved by the President of the Court, shall regulate the working of the Registry.

Rule 18
(Organisation of the Registry)

1.   The Registry shall consist of Section Registries equal to the number of Sections set up by the Court and of the departments necessary to provide the legal and administrative services required by the Court.

2.   The Section Registrar shall assist the Section in the performance of its functions and may be assisted by a Deputy Section Registrar.

3.   The officials of the Registry, including the legal secretaries but not the Registrar and the Deputy Registrars, shall be appointed by the Secretary General of the Council of Europe with the agreement of the President of the Court or of the Registrar acting on the President's instructions.

Chapter IV
The Working of the Court

Rule 19
(Seat of the Court)

1.   The seat of the Court shall be at the seat of the Council of Europe at Strasbourg. The Court may, however, if it considers it expedient, perform its functions elsewhere in the territories of the member States of the Council of Europe.

2.   The Court may decide, at any stage of the examination of an application, that it is necessary that an investigation or any other function be carried out elsewhere by it or one or more of its members.

Rule 20
(Sessions of the plenary Court)

1.   The plenary sessions of the Court shall be convened by the President of the Court whenever the performance of its functions under the Convention and under these Rules so requires. The President of the Court shall convene a plenary session if at least one-third of the members of the Court so request, and in any event once a year to consider administrative matters.

2.   The quorum of the plenary Court shall be two-thirds of the elected judges in office.

3.   If there is no quorum, the President shall adjourn the sitting.

Rule 21
(Other sessions of the Court)

1.   The Grand Chamber, the Chambers and the Committees shall sit full time. On a proposal by the President, however, the Court shall fix session periods each year.

2.   Outside those periods the Grand Chamber and the Chambers shall be convened by their Presidents in cases of urgency.

Rule 22
(Deliberations)

1.   The Court shall deliberate in private. Its deliberations shall remain secret.

2.   Only the judges shall take part in the deliberations. The Registrar or the designated substitute, as well as such other officials of the Registry and interpreters whose assistance is deemed necessary, shall be present. No other person may be admitted except by special decision of the Court.

3.   Before a vote is taken on any matter in the Court, the President may request the judges to state their opinions on it.

Rule 23

(Votes)

1.   The decisions of the Court shall be taken by a majority of the judges present. In the event of a tie, a fresh vote shall be taken and, if there is still a tie, the President shall have a casting vote. This paragraph shall apply unless otherwise provided for in these Rules.

2.   The decisions and judgments of the Grand Chamber and the Chambers shall be adopted by a majority of the sitting judges. Abstentions shall not be allowed in final votes on the admissibility and merits of cases.

3.   As a general rule, votes shall be taken by a show of hands. The President may take a roll-call vote, in reverse order of precedence.

4.   Any matter that is to be voted upon shall be formulated in precise terms.

Chapter V

The Chambers

Rule 24

(Composition of the Grand Chamber)

1.   The Grand Chamber shall be composed of seventeen judges and three substitute judges.

2.   The Grand Chamber shall be constituted for three years with effect from the election of the presidential office-holders referred to in Rule 8.

3.   The Grand Chamber shall include the President and Vice-Presidents of the Court and the Presidents of the Sections. In order to complete the Grand Chamber, the plenary Court shall, on a proposal by its President, divide all the other judges into two groups which shall alternate every nine months and whose membership shall be geographically as balanced as possible and reflect the different legal systems among the Contracting Parties. The judges and substitute judges who are to hear each case referred to the Grand Chamber during each nine-month period shall be designated in rotation within each group; they shall remain members of the Grand Chamber until the proceedings have been completed, even after their terms of office as judges have expired.

4.   If he or she does not sit as a member of the Grand Chamber by virtue of paragraph 3 of the present Rule, the judge elected in respect of any Contracting Party concerned shall sit as an *ex officio* member of the Grand Chamber in accordance with Article 27 §§ 2 and 3 of the Convention.

5. (a)   Where any President of a Section is unable to sit as a member of the Grand Chamber, he or she shall be replaced by the Vice-President of the Section.

(b)   If other judges are prevented from sitting, they shall be replaced by the substitute judges in the order in which the latter were selected under paragraph 3 of the present Rule.

(c)   If there are not enough substitute judges in the group concerned to complete the Grand Chamber, the substitute judges lacking shall be designated by a drawing of lots amongst the members of the other group.

6. (a)   The panel of five judges of the Grand Chamber called upon to consider requests submitted under Article 43 of the Convention shall be composed of

— the President of the Court,

— the Presidents or, if they are prevented from sitting, the Vice-Presidents of the Sections other than the Section from which was constituted the Chamber that dealt with the case whose referral to the Grand Chamber is being sought,

— one further judge designated in rotation from among the judges other than those who dealt with the case in the Chamber.

(b)   No judge elected in respect of, or who is a national of, a Contracting Party concerned may be a member of the panel.

(c)   Any member of the panel unable to sit shall be replaced by another judge who did not deal with the case in the Chamber, who shall be designated in rotation.

Rule 25
(Setting up of Sections)

1.   The Chambers provided for in Article 26(b) of the Convention (referred to in these Rules as 'Sections') shall be set up by the plenary Court, on a proposal by its President, for a period of three years with effect from the election of the presidential office-holders of the Court under Rule 8. There shall be at least four Sections.

2.   Each judge shall be a member of a Section. The composition of the Sections shall be geographically and gender balanced and shall reflect the different legal systems among the Contracting Parties.

3.   Where a judge ceases to be a member of the Court before the expiry of the period for which the Section has been constituted, the judge's place in the Section shall be taken by his or her successor as a member of the Court.

4.   The President of the Court may exceptionally make modifications to the composition of the Sections if circumstances so require.

5.   On a proposal by the President, the plenary Court may constitute an additional Section.

Rule 26
(Constitution of Chambers)

1.   The Chambers of seven judges provided for in Article 27 § 1 of the Convention for the consideration of cases brought before the Court shall be constituted from the Sections as follows.

(a)   The Chamber shall in each case include the President of the Section and the judge elected in respect of any Contracting Party concerned. If the latter judge is not a member of the Section to which the application has been assigned under Rule 51 or 52, he or she shall sit as an *ex officio* member of the Chamber in accordance with Article 27 § 2 of the Convention. Rule 29 shall apply if that judge is unable to sit or withdraws.

(b)   The other members of the Chamber shall be designated by the President of the Section in rotation from among the members of the relevant Section.

(c)   The members of the Section who are not so designated shall sit in the case as substitute judges.

2.   Even after the end of their terms of office judges shall continue to deal with cases in which they have participated in the consideration of the merits.

Rule 27
(Committees)

1.   Committees composed of three judges belonging to the same Section shall be set up under Article 27 § 1 of the Convention. After consulting the Presidents of the Sections, the President of the Court shall decide on the number of Committees to be set up.

2.   The Committees shall be constituted for a period of twelve months by rotation among the members of each Section, excepting the President of the Section.

3.   The judges of the Section who are not members of a Committee may be called upon to take the place of members who are unable to sit.

4.   Each Committee shall be chaired by the member having precedence in the Section.

Rule 28
(Inability to sit, withdrawal or exemption)

1.   Any judge who is prevented from taking part in sittings shall, as soon as possible, give notice to the President of the Chamber.

2.   A judge may not take part in the consideration of any case in which he or she has a personal interest or has previously acted either as the Agent, advocate or adviser of a party or of a person having an interest in the case, or as a member of a tribunal or commission of inquiry, or in any other capacity.

3.   If a judge withdraws for one of the said reasons, or for some special reason, he or she shall inform the President of the Chamber, who shall exempt the judge from sitting.

4.   If the President of the Chamber considers that a reason exists for a judge to withdraw, he or she shall consult with the judge concerned; in the event of disagreement, the Chamber shall decide.

Rule 29
(Ad hoc judges)

1.   If the judge elected in respect of a Contracting Party concerned is unable to sit in the Chamber or withdraws, the President of the Chamber shall invite that Party to indicate within thirty days whether it wishes to appoint to sit as judge either another elected judge or, as an *ad hoc* judge, any other person possessing the qualifications required by Article 21 § 1 of the Convention and, if so, to state at the same time the name of the person appointed. The same rule shall apply if the person so appointed is unable to sit or withdraws.

2.   The Contracting Party concerned shall be presumed to have waived its right of appointment if it does not reply within thirty days.

3.   An *ad hoc* judge shall, at the opening of the first sitting fixed for the consideration of the case after the judge has been appointed, take the oath or make the solemn declaration provided for in Rule 3. This act shall be recorded in minutes.

Rule 30
(Common interest)

1.   If several applicant or respondent Contracting Parties have a common interest, the President of the Court may invite them to agree to appoint a single elected judge or *ad hoc* judge in accordance with Article 27 § 2 of the Convention. If the Parties are unable to agree, the President shall choose by lot, from among the persons proposed as judges by these Parties, the judge called upon to sit *ex officio.*

2.   In the event of a dispute as to the existence of a common interest, the plenary Court shall decide.

TITLE II
PROCEDURE

Chapter 1
General Rules

Rule 31
(Possibility of particular derogations)

The provisions of this Title shall not prevent the Court from derogating from them for the consideration of a particular case after having consulted the parties where appropriate.

Rule 32
(Practice directions)

The President of the Court may issue practice directions, notably in relation to such matters as appearance at hearings and the filing of pleadings and other documents.

Rule 33
(Public character of proceedings)

1. Hearings shall be public unless, in accordance with paragraph 2 of this Rule, the Chamber in exceptional circumstances decides otherwise, either of its own motion or at the request of a party or any other person concerned.

2. The press and the public may be excluded from all or part of a hearing in the interest of morals, public order or national security in a democratic society, where the interests of juveniles or the protection of the private life of the parties so require, or to the extent strictly necessary in the opinion of the Chamber in special circumstances where publicity would prejudice the interests of justice.

3. Following registration of an application, all documents deposited with the Registry, with the exception of those deposited within the framework of friendly-settlement negotiations as provided for in Rule 62, shall be accessible to the public unless the President of the Chamber, for the reasons set out in paragraph 2 of this Rule, decides otherwise, either of his or her own motion or at the request of a party or any other person concerned.

4. Any request for confidentiality made under paragraphs 1 or 3 above must give reasons and specify whether the hearing or the documents, as the case may be, should be inaccessible to the public in whole or in part.

Rule 34
(Use of languages)

1. The official languages of the Court shall be English and French.

2. Before the decision on the admissibility of an application is taken, all communications with and pleadings by applicants under Article 34 of the Convention or their representatives, if not in one of the Court's official languages, shall be in one of the official languages of the Contracting Parties.

3. (a) All communications with and pleadings by such applicants or their representatives in respect of a hearing, or after a case has been declared admissible, shall be in one of the Court's official languages, unless the President of the Chamber authorises the continued use of the official language of a Contracting Party.

(b) If such leave is granted, the Registrar shall make the necessary arrangements for the oral or written translation of the applicant's observations or statements.

4.   (a)   All communications with and pleadings by Contracting Parties or third parties shall be in one of the Court's official languages. The President of the Chamber may authorise the use of a non-official language.

(b)   If such leave is granted, it shall be the responsibility of the requesting party to provide for and bear the costs of interpreting or translation into English or French of the oral arguments or written statements made.

5.   The President of the Chamber may invite the respondent Contracting Party to provide a translation of its written submissions in the or an official language of that Party in order to facilitate the applicant's understanding of those submissions.

6.   Any witness, expert or other person appearing before the Court may use his or her own language if he or she does not have sufficient knowledge of either of the two official languages. In that event the Registrar shall make the necessary arrangements for interpreting or translation.

Rule 35
(Representation of Contracting Parties)

The Contracting Parties shall be represented by Agents, who may have the assistance of advocates or advisers.

Rule 36
(Representation of applicants)

1.   Persons, non-governmental organisations or groups of individuals may initially present applications under Article 34 of the Convention themselves or through a representative appointed under paragraph 4 of this Rule.

2.   Following notification of the application to the respondent Contracting Party under Rule 54 § 3 (b), the President of the Chamber may direct that the applicant should be represented in accordance with paragraph 4 of this Rule.

3.   The applicant must be so represented at any hearing decided on by the Chamber or for the purposes of the proceedings following a decision to declare the application admissible, unless the President of the Chamber decides otherwise.

4.   (a)   The representative of the applicant shall be an advocate authorised to practise in any of the Contracting Parties and resident in the territory of one of them, or any other person approved by the President of the Chamber.

(b)   The President of the Chamber may, where representation would otherwise be obligatory, grant leave to the applicant to present his or her own case, subject, if necessary, to being assisted by an advocate or other approved representative.

(c)   In exceptional circumstances and at any stage of the procedure, the President of the Chamber may, where he or she considers that the circumstances or the conduct of the advocate or other person appointed under the preceding sub-paragraphs so warrant, direct that the latter may no longer represent or assist the applicant and that the applicant should seek alternative representation.

5.   The advocate or other approved representative, or the applicant in person if he or she seeks leave to present his or her own case, must have an adequate knowledge of one of the Court's official languages. However, leave to use a non-official language may be given by the President of the Chamber under Rule 34 § 3.

Rule 37
(Communications, notifications and summonses)

1.   Communications or notifications addressed to the Agents or advocates of the parties shall be deemed to have been addressed to the parties.

2.   If, for any communication, notification or summons addressed to persons other than the Agents or advocates of the parties, the Court considers it necessary to have the assistance of the Government of the State on whose territory such communication, notification or summons is to have effect, the President of the Court shall apply directly to that Government in order to obtain the necessary facilities.

3.   The same rule shall apply when the Court desires to make or arrange for the making of an investigation on the spot in order to establish the facts or to procure evidence or when it orders the appearance of a person who is resident in, or will have to cross, that territory.

Rule 38
(Written pleadings)

1.   No written observations or other documents may be filed after the time-limit set by the President of the Chamber or the Judge Rapporteur, as the case may be, in accordance with these Rules. No written observations or other documents filed outside that time-limit or contrary to any practice direction issued under Rule 32 shall be included in the case file unless the President of the Chamber decides otherwise.

2.   For the purposes of observing the time-limit referred to in paragraph 1, the material date is the certified date of dispatch of the document or, if there is none, the actual date of receipt at the Registry.

Rule 39
(Interim measures)

1.   The Chamber or, where appropriate, its President may, at the request of a party or of any other person concerned, or of its own motion, indicate to the parties any interim measure which it considers should be adopted in the interests of the parties or of the proper conduct of the proceedings before it.

2.   Notice of these measures shall be given to the Committee of Ministers.

3.   The Chamber may request information from the parties on any matter connected with the implementation of any interim measure it has indicated.

Rule 40
(Urgent notification of an application)

In any case of urgency the Registrar, with the authorisation of the President of the Chamber, may, without prejudice to the taking of any other procedural steps and by any available means, inform a Contracting Party concerned in an application of the introduction of the application and of a summary of its objects.

Rule 41
(Case priority)

The Chamber shall deal with applications in the order in which they become ready for examination. It may, however, decide to give priority to a particular application.

Rule 42
(Measures for taking evidence)

1.   The Chamber may, at the request of a party or a third party, or of its own motion, obtain any evidence which it considers capable of providing clarification of the facts of the case. The Chamber may, *inter alia*, request the parties to produce documentary evidence and decide to hear as a witness or expert or in any other capacity any person whose evidence or statements seem likely to assist it in the carrying out of its tasks.

2.   The Chamber may, at any time during the proceedings, depute one or more of its members or of the other judges of the Court to conduct an inquiry, carry out an investigation on the spot or take evidence in some other manner. It may appoint independent external experts to assist such a delegation.

3.   The Chamber may ask any person or institution of its choice to obtain information, express an opinion or make a report on any specific point.

4.   The parties shall assist the Chamber, or its delegation, in implementing any measures for taking evidence.

5.   Where a report has been drawn up or some other measure taken in accordance with the preceding paragraphs at the request of an applicant or respondent Contracting Party, the costs entailed shall be borne by that Party unless the Chamber decides otherwise. In other cases the Chamber shall decide whether such costs are to be borne by the Council of Europe or awarded against the applicant or third party at whose request the report was drawn up or the other measure was taken. In all cases the costs shall be taxed by the President of the Chamber.

Rule 43
(Joinder and simultaneous examination of applications)

1.   The Chamber may, either at the request of the parties or of its own motion, order the joinder of two or more applications.

2.   The President of the Chamber may, after consulting the parties, order that the proceedings in applications assigned to the same Chamber be conducted simultaneously, without prejudice to the decision of the Chamber on the joinder of the applications.

Rule 44
(Striking out and restoration to the list)

1.   When an applicant Contracting Party notifies the Registrar of its intention not to proceed with the case, the Chamber may strike the application out of the Court's list under Article 37 of the Convention if the other Contracting Party or Parties concerned in the case agree to such discontinuance.

2.   The decision to strike out an application which has been declared admissible shall be given in the form of a judgment. The President of the Chamber shall forward that judgment, once it has become final, to the Committee of Ministers in order to allow the latter to supervise, in accordance with Article 46 § 2 of the Convention, the execution of any undertakings which may have been attached to the discontinuance, friendly settlement or solution of the matter.

3.   When an application has been struck out, the costs shall be at the discretion of the Court. If an award of costs is made in a decision striking out an application which has not been declared admissible, the President of the Chamber shall forward the decision to the Committee of Ministers.

4.   The Court may restore an application to its list if it concludes that exceptional circumstances justify such a course.

Chapter II
Institution of Proceedings

Rule 45
(Signatures)

1.   Any application made under Articles 33 or 34 of the Convention shall be submitted in writing and shall be signed by the applicant or by the applicant's representative.

2.   Where an application is made by a non-governmental organisation or by a group of individuals, it shall be signed by those persons competent to represent that organisation or group. The Chamber or Committee concerned shall determine any question as to whether the persons who have signed an application are competent to do so.

3.   Where applicants are represented in accordance with Rule 36, a power. of attorney or written authority to act shall be supplied by their representative or representatives.

Rule 46
(Contents of an inter-State application)

Any Contracting Party or Parties intending to bring a case before the Court under Article 33 of the Convention shall file with the registry an application setting out

(a)   the name of the Contracting Party against which the application is made;

(b)   a statement of the facts;

(c)   a statement of the alleged violation(s) of the Convention and the relevant arguments;

(d)   a statement on compliance with the admissibility criteria (exhaustion of domestic remedies and the six-month rule) laid down in Article 35 § 1 of the Convention;

(e)   the object of the application and a general indication of any claims for just satisfaction made under Article 41 of the Convention on behalf of the alleged injured party or parties; and

(f)   the name and address of the person(s) appointed as Agent; and accompanied by

(g)   copies of any relevant documents and in particular the decisions, whether judicial or not relating to the object of the application.

Rule 47
(Contents of an individual application)

1.   Any application under Article 34 of the Convention shall be made on the application form provided by the registry, unless the President of the Section concerned decides otherwise. It shall set out

(a)   the name, date of birth, nationality, sex, occupation and address of the applicant;

(b)   the name, occupation and address of the representative, if any;

(c)   the name of the Contracting Party or Parties against which the application is made;

(d)   a succinct statement of the facts;

(e)   a succinct statement of the alleged violation(s) of the Convention and the relevant arguments;

(f)   a succinct statement on the applicant's compliance with the admissibility criteria (exhaustion of domestic remedies and the six-month rule) laid down in Article 35 § 1 of the Convention; and

(g)   the object of the application as well as a general indication of any claims for just satisfaction which the applicant may wish to make under Article 41 of the Convention; and be accompanied by

(h)   copies of any relevant documents and in particular the decisions, whether judicial or not, relating to the object of the application.

2.   Applicants shall furthermore

(a)   provide information, notably the documents and decisions referred to in paragraph 1(h) above, enabling it to be shown that the admissibility criteria (exhaustion of domestic remedies and the six-month rule) laid down in Article 35 § 1 of the Convention have been satisfied; and

(b)   indicate whether they have submitted their complaints to any other procedure of international investigation or settlement.

3.   Applicants who do not wish their identity to be disclosed to the public shall so indicate and shall submit a statement of the reasons justifying such a departure from the normal rule of public access to information in proceedings before the Court. The President of the Chamber may authorise anonymity in exceptional and duly justified cases.

4.   Failure to comply with the requirements set out in paragraphs 1 and 2 above may result in the application not being registered and examined by the Court.

5.   The date of introduction of the application shall as a general rule be considered to be the date of the first communication from the applicant setting out, even summarily, the object of the application. The Court may for good cause nevertheless decide that a different date shall be considered to be the date of introduction.

6.   Applicants shall keep the Court informed of any change of address and of all circumstances relevant to the application.

Chapter III
Judge Rapporteurs

Rule 48
(Inter-State applications)

1.   Where an application is made under Article 33 of the Convention, the Chamber constituted to consider the case shall designate one or more of its judges as Judge Rapporteur(s), who shall submit a report on admissibility when the written observations of the Contracting Parties concerned have been received. Rule 49 § 4 shall, in so far as appropriate, be applicable to this report.

2.   After an application made under Article 33 of the Convention has been declared admissible, the Judge Rapporteur(s) shall submit such reports, drafts and other documents as may assist the Chamber in the carrying out of its functions.

Rule 49
(Individual applications)

1.   Where an application is made under Article 34 of the Convention, the President of the Section to which the case has been assigned shall designate a judge as Judge Rapporteur, who shall examine the application.

2.   In their examination of applications Judge Rapporteurs

(a)   may request the parties to submit, within a specified time, any factual information, documents or other material which they consider to be relevant;

(b)   shall, subject to the President of the Section directing that the case be considered by a Chamber, decide whether the application is to be considered by a Committee or by a Chamber.

3.   Where a case is considered by a Committee in accordance with Article 28 of the Convention, the report of the Judge Rapporteur shall contain

(a)   a brief statement of the relevant facts;

(b)   a brief statement of the reasons underlying the proposal to declare the application inadmissible or to strike it out of the list.

4.   Where a case is considered by a Chamber pursuant to Article 29 § 1 of the Convention, the report of the Judge Rapporteur shall contain

(a)   a statement of the relevant facts, including any information obtained under paragraph 2 of this Rule;

(b)   an indication of the issues arising under the Convention in the application;

(c)   a proposal on admissibility and on any other action to be taken, together, if need be, with a provisional opinion on the merits.

5.   After an application made under Article 34 of the Convention has been declared admissible, the Judge Rapporteur shall submit such reports, drafts and other documents as may assist the Chamber in the carrying out of its functions.

Rule 50
(Grand Chamber proceedings)

Where a case has been submitted to the Grand Chamber either under Article 30 or under Article 43 of the Convention, the President of the Grand Chamber shall designate as Judge Rapporteur(s) one or, in the case of an inter-State application, one or more of its members.

Chapter IV
Proceedings on Admissibility

Inter-State applications

Rule 51

1.   When an application is made under Article 33 of the Convention, the President of the Court shall immediately give notice of the application to the respondent Contracting Party and shall assign the application to one of the Sections.

2.   In accordance with Rule 26 § 1 (a), the judges elected in respect of the applicant and respondent Contracting Parties shall sit as *ex officio* members of the Chamber constituted to consider the case. Rule 30 shall apply if the application has been brought by several Contracting Parties or if applications with the same

object brought by several Contracting Parties are being examined jointly under Rule 43 § 2.

3.   On assignment of the case to a Section, the President of the Section shall constitute the Chamber in accordance with Rule 26 § 1 and shall invite the respondent Contracting Party to submit its observations in, writing on the admissibility of the application. The observations so obtained shall be communicated by the Registrar to the applicant Contracting Party, which may submit written observations in reply.

4.   Before ruling on the admissibility of the application, the Chamber may decide to invite the parties to submit further observations in writing.

5.   A hearing on the admissibility shall be held if one or more of the Contracting Parties concerned so requests or if the Chamber so decides of its own motion.

6.   After consulting the Parties, the President of the Chamber shall fix the written and, where appropriate, oral procedure and for that purpose shall lay down the time-limit within which any written observations are to be filed.

7.   In its deliberations the Chamber shall take into consideration the report submitted by the Judge Rapporteur(s) under Rule 48 § 1.

Individual applications

Rule 52
(Assignment of applications to the Sections)

1.   Any application made under Article 34 of the Convention shall be assigned to a Section by the President of the Court, who in so doing shall endeavour to ensure a fair distribution of cases between the Sections.

2.   The Chamber of seven judges provided for in Article 27 § 1 of the Convention shall be constituted by the President of the Section concerned in accordance with Rule 26 § 1 once it has been decided that the application is to be considered by a Chamber.

3.   Pending the constitution of a Chamber in accordance with the preceding paragraph, the President of the Section shall exercise any powers conferred on the President of the Chamber by these Rules.

Rule 53
(Procedure before a Committee)

1.   In its deliberations the Committee shall take into consideration the report submitted by the Judge Rapporteur under Rule 49 § 3.

2.   The Judge Rapporteur, if he or she is not a member of the Committee, may be invited to attend the deliberations of the Committee.

3.   In accordance with Article 28 of the Convention, the Committee may, by a unanimous vote, declare inadmissible or strike out of the Court's list of cases an

application where such a decision can be taken without further examination. This decision shall be final.

4.   If no decision pursuant to paragraph 3 of the present Rule is taken, the application shall be forwarded to the Chamber constituted under Rule 52 § 2 to examine the case.

Rule 54
(Procedure before a Chamber)

1.   In its deliberations the Chamber shall take into consideration the report submitted by the Judge Rapporteur under Rule 49 § 4.

2.   The Chamber may at once declare the application inadmissible or strike it out of the Court's list of cases.

3.   Alternatively, the Chamber may decide to

  (a)   request the parties to submit any factual information, documents or other material which it considers to be relevant;

  (b)   give notice of the application to the respondent Contracting Party and invite that Party to submit written observations on the application;

  (c)   invite the parties to submit further observations in writing.

4.   Before taking its decision on admissibility, the Chamber may decide, either at the request of the parties or of its own motion, to hold a hearing. In that event, unless the Chamber shall exceptionally decide otherwise, the parties shall be invited also to address the issues arising in relation to the merits of the application.

5.   The President of the Chamber shall fix the procedure, including time-limits, in relation to any decisions taken by the Chamber under paragraphs 3 and 4 of this Rule.

Inter-State and individual applications

Rule 55
(Pleas of inadmissibility)

Any plea of inadmissibility must, in so far as its character and the circumstances permit, be raised by the respondent Contracting Party in its written or oral observations on the admissibility of the application submitted as provided in Rule 51 or 54, as the case may be.

Rule 56
(Decision of a Chamber)

1.   The decision of the Chamber shall state whether it was taken unanimously or by a majority and shall be accompanied or followed by reasons.

2.   The decision of the Chamber shall be communicated by the Registrar to the applicant and to the Contracting Party or Parties concerned.

Rule 57
(Language of the decision)

1.   Unless the Court decides that a decision shall be given in both official languages, all decisions shall be given either in English or in French. Decisions given shall be accessible to the public.

2.   Publication of such decisions in the official reports of the Court, as provided for in Rule 78, shall be in both official languages of the Court.

Chapter V
Proceedings after the Admission of an Application

Rule 58
(Inter-State applications)

1.   Once the Chamber has decided to admit an application made under Article 33 of the Convention, the President of the Chamber shall, after consulting the Contracting Parties concerned, lay down the time-limits for the filing of written observations on the merits and for the production of any further evidence. The President may however, with the agreement of the Contracting Parties concerned, direct that a written procedure is to be dispensed with.

2.   A hearing on the merits shall be held if one or more of the Contracting Parties concerned so requests or if the Chamber so decides of its own motion. The President of the Chamber shall fix the oral procedure.

3.   In its deliberations the Chamber shall take into consideration any reports, drafts and other documents submitted by the Judge Rapporteur(s) under Rule 48 § 2.

Rule 59
(Individual applications)

1.   Once the Chamber has decided to admit an application made under Article 34 of the Convention, it may invite the parties to submit further evidence and written observations.

2.   A hearing on the merits shall be held if the Chamber so decides of its own motion or, provided that no hearing also addressing the merits has been held at the admissibility stage under Rule 54 § 4, if one of the parties so requests. However, the Chamber may exceptionally decide that the discharging of its functions under Article 38 § 1 (a) of the Convention does not require a hearing to be held.

3.   The President of the Chamber shall, where appropriate, fix the written and oral procedure.

4.   In its deliberations the Chamber shall take into consideration any reports, drafts and other documents submitted by the Judge Rapporteur under Rule 49 § 5.

Rule 60
(Claims for just satisfaction)

1.   Any claim which the applicant Contracting Party or the applicant may wish to make for just satisfaction under Article 41 of the Convention shall, unless the President of the Chamber directs otherwise, be set out in the written observations on the merits or, if no such written observations are filed, in a special document filed no later than two months after the decision declaring the application admissible.

2.   Itemised particulars of all claims made, together with the relevant supporting documents or vouchers, shall be submitted, failing which the Chamber may reject the claim in whole or in part.

3.   The Chamber may, at any time during the proceedings, invite any party to submit comments on the claim for just satisfaction.

Rule 61
(Third-party intervention)

1.   The decision declaring an application admissible shall be notified by the Registrar to any Contracting Party one of whose nationals is an applicant in the case, as well as to the respondent Contracting Party under Rule 56 § 2.

2.   Where a Contracting Party seeks to exercise its right to submit written comments or to take part in an oral hearing, pursuant to Article 36 § 1 of the Convention, the President of the Chamber shall fix the procedure to be followed.

3. In accordance with Article 36 § 2 of the Convention, the President of the Chamber may, in the interests of the proper administration of justice, invite or grant leave to any Contracting State which is not a party to the proceedings, or any person concerned who is not the applicant, to submit written comments or, in exceptional cases, to take part in an oral hearing. Requests for leave for this purpose must be duly reasoned and submitted in one of the official languages, within a reasonable time after the fixing of the written procedure.

4.   Any invitation or grant of leave referred to in paragraph 3 of this Rule shall be subject to any conditions, including time-limits, set by the President of the Chamber. Where such conditions are not complied with, the President may decide not to include the comments in the case file.

5.   Written comments submitted in accordance with this Rule shall be submitted in one of the official languages, save where leave to use another language has been granted under Rule 34 § 4. They shall be transmitted by the Registrar to the parties to the case, who shall be entitled, subject to any conditions, including time-limits, set by the President of the Chamber, to file written observations in reply.

Rule 62
(Friendly settlement)

1.   Once an application has been declared admissible, the Registrar, acting on the instructions of the Chamber or its President, shall enter into contact with the parties with a view to securing a friendly settlement of the matter in accordance with Article 38 § 1 (b) of the Convention. The Chamber shall take any steps that appear appropriate to facilitate such a settlement.

2.   In accordance with Article 38 § 2 of the Convention, the friendly settlement negotiations shall be confidential and without prejudice to the parties' arguments in the contentious proceedings. No written or oral communication and no offer or concession made in the framework of the attempt to secure a friendly settlement may be referred to or relied on in the contentious proceedings.

3.   If the Chamber is informed by the Registrar that the parties have agreed to a friendly settlement, it shall, after verifying that the settlement has been reached on the basis of respect for human rights as defined in the Convention and the protocols thereto, strike the case out of the Court's list in accordance with Rule 44 § 2.

Chapter VI
Hearings

Rule 63
(Conduct of hearings)

1.   The President of the Chamber shall direct hearings and shall prescribe the order in which Agents and advocates or advisers of the parties shall be called upon to speak.

2.   Where a fact-finding hearing is being carried out by a delegation of the Chamber under Rule 42, the head of the delegation shall conduct the hearing and the delegation shall exercise any relevant power conferred on the Chamber by the Convention or these Rules.

Rule 64
(Failure to appear at a hearing)

Where, without showing sufficient cause, a party fails to appear, the Chamber may, provided that it is satisfied that such a course is consistent with the proper administration of justice, nonetheless proceed with the hearing.

Rule 65
(Convocation of witnesses, experts and other persons; costs of their appearance)

1.   Witnesses, experts and other persons whom the Chamber or the President of the Chamber decides to hear shall be summoned by the Registrar.

2.   The summons shall indicate

(a) the case in connection with which it has been issued;

(b) the object of the inquiry, expert opinion or other measure ordered by the Chamber or the President of the Chamber;

(c) any provisions for the payment of the sum due to the person summoned.

3. If the persons concerned appear at the request or on behalf of an applicant or respondent Contracting Party, the costs of their appearance shall be borne by that Party unless the Chamber decides otherwise. In other cases, the Chamber shall decide whether such costs are to be borne by the Council of Europe or awarded against the applicant or third party at whose request the person summoned appeared. In all cases the costs shall be taxed by the President of the Chamber.

Rule 66
(Oath or solemn declaration by witnesses and experts)

1. After the establishment of the identity of the witness and before testifying, every witness shall take the following oath or make the following solemn declaration:

'I swear' — or 'I solemnly declare upon my honour and conscience' — 'that I shall speak the truth, the whole truth and nothing but the truth.'

This act shall be recorded in minutes.

2. After the establishment of the identity of the expert and before carrying out his or her task, every expert shall take the following oath or make the following solemn declaration:

'I swear' — or 'I solemnly declare' — 'that I will discharge my duty as an expert honourably and conscientiously.'

This act shall be recorded in minutes.

3. This oath may be taken or this declaration made before the President of the Chamber, or before a judge or any public authority nominated by the President.

Rule 67
(Objection to a witness or expert; hearing of a person for information purposes)

The Chamber shall decide in the event of any dispute arising from an objection to a witness or expert. It may hear for information purposes a person who cannot be heard as a witness.

Rule 68
(Questions put during hearings)

1. Any judge may put questions to the Agents, advocates or advisers of the parties, to the applicant, witnesses and experts, and to any other persons appearing before the Chamber.

2. The witnesses, experts and other persons referred to in Rule 42 § 1 may, subject to the control of the President of the Chamber, be examined by the Agents

and advocates or advisers of the parties. In the event of an objection as to the relevance of a question put, the President of the Chamber shall decide.

Rule 69
(Failure to appear, refusal to give evidence or false evidence)

If, without good reason, a witness or any other person who has been duly summoned fails to appear or refuses to give evidence, the Registrar shall, on being so required by the President of the Chamber, inform the Contracting Party to whose jurisdiction the witness or other person is subject. The same provisions shall apply if a witness or expert has, in the opinion of the Chamber, violated the oath or solemn declaration provided for in Rule 66.

Rule 70
(Verbatim record of hearings)

1.   The Registrar shall, if the Chamber so directs, be responsible for the making of a verbatim record of a hearing. The verbatim record shall include

(a)   the composition of the Chamber at the hearing;

(b)   a list of those appearing before the Court, that is to say Agents, advocates and advisers of the parties and any third party taking part;

(c)   the surnames, forenames, description and address of each witness, expert or other person heard;

(d)   the text of statements made, questions put and replies given;

(e)   the text of any decision delivered during the hearing by the Chamber or the President of the Chamber.

2.   If all or part of the verbatim record is in a non-official language, the Registrar shall, if the Chamber so directs, arrange for its translation into one of the official languages.

3.   The representatives of the parties shall receive a copy of the verbatim record in order that they may, subject to the control of the Registrar or the President of the Chamber, make corrections, but in no case may such corrections affect the sense and bearing of what was said. The Registrar shall lay down, in accordance with the instructions of the President of the Chamber, the time-limits granted for this purpose.

4.   The verbatim record, once so corrected, shall be signed by the President and the Registrar and shall then constitute certified matters of record.

Chapter VII
Proceedings before the Grand Chamber

Rule 71
(Applicability of procedural provisions)

Any provisions governing proceedings before the Chambers shall apply, *mutatis mutandis*, to proceedings before the Grand Chamber.

Rule 72
(Relinquishment of jurisdiction by a Chamber in favour of the Grand Chamber)

1.   In accordance with Article 30 of the Convention, where a case pending before a Chamber raises a serious question affecting the interpretation of the Convention or the protocols thereto or where the resolution of a question before it might have a result inconsistent with a judgment previously delivered by the Court, the Chamber may, at any time before it has rendered its judgment, relinquish jurisdiction in favour of the Grand Chamber, unless one of the parties to the case has objected in accordance with paragraph 2 of this Rule. Reasons need not be given for the decision to relinquish.

2.   The Registrar shall notify the parties of the Chamber's intention to relinquish jurisdiction. The parties shall have one month from the date of that notification within which to file at the Registry a duly reasoned objection. An objection which does not fulfil these conditions shall be considered invalid by the Chamber.

Rule 73
(Request by a party for referral of a case to the Grand Chamber)

1.   In accordance with Article 43 of the Convention, any party to a case may exceptionally, within a period of three months from the date of delivery of the judgment of a Chamber, file in writing at the Registry a request that the case be referred to the Grand Chamber. The party shall specify in its request the serious question affecting the interpretation or application of the Convention or the protocols thereto, or the serious issue of general importance, which in its view warrants consideration by the Grand Chamber.

2.   A panel of five judges of the Grand Chamber constituted in accordance with Rule 24 § 6 shall examine the request solely on the basis of the existing case file. It shall accept the request only if it considers that the case does raise such a question or issue. Reasons need not be given for a refusal of the request.

3.   If the panel accepts the request, the Grand Chamber shall decide the case by means of a judgment.

Chapter VIII
Judgments

Rule 74
(Contents of the judgment)

1.   A judgment as referred to in Articles 42 and 44 of the Convention shall contain
  (a)   the names of the President and the other judges constituting the Chamber concerned, and the name of the Registrar or the Deputy Registrar;
  (b)   the dates on which it was adopted and delivered;

   (c)   a description of the parties;

   (d)   the names of the Agents, advocates or advisers of the parties;

   (e)   an account of the procedure followed;

   (f)   the facts of the case;

   (g)   a summary of the submissions of the parties;

   (h)   the reasons in point of law;

   (i)   the operative provisions;

   (j)   the decision, if any, in respect of costs;

   (k)   the number of judges constituting the majority;

   (l)   where appropriate, a statement as to which text is authentic.

2.   Any judge who has taken part in the consideration of the case shall be entitled to annex to the judgment either a separate opinion, concurring with or dissenting from that judgment, or a bare statement of dissent.

Rule 75
(Ruling on just satisfaction)

1.   Where the Chamber finds that there has been a violation of the Convention, it shall give in the same judgment a ruling on the application of Article 41 of the Convention if that question, after being raised in accordance with Rule 60, is ready for decision; if the question is not ready for decision, the Chamber shall reserve it in whole or in part and shall fix the further procedure.

2.   For the purposes of ruling on the application of Article 41 of the Convention, the Chamber shall, as far as possible, be composed of those judges who sat to consider the merits of the case. Where it is not possible to constitute the original Chamber, the President of the Court shall complete or compose the Chamber by drawing lots.

3.   The Chamber may, when affording just satisfaction under Article 41 of the Convention, direct that if settlement is not made within a specified time, interest is to be payable on any sums awarded.

4.   If the Court is informed that an agreement has been reached between the injured party and the Contracting Party liable, it shall verify the equitable nature of the agreement and, where it finds the agreement to be equitable, strike the case out of the list in accordance with Rule 44 § 2.

Rule 76
(Language of the judgment)

1.   Unless the Court decides that a judgment shall be given in both official languages, all judgments shall be given either in English or in French. Judgments given shall be accessible to the public.

2.   Publication of such judgments in the official reports of the Court, as provided for in Rule 78, shall be in both official languages of the Court.

Rule 77
(Signature, delivery and notification of the judgment)

1.   Judgments shall be signed by the President of the Chamber and the Registrar.

2.   The judgment may be read out at a public hearing by the President of the Chamber or by another judge delegated by him or her. The Agents and representatives of the parties shall be informed in due time of the date of the hearing. Otherwise the notification provided for in paragraph 3 of this Rule shall constitute delivery of the judgment.

3.   The judgment shall be transmitted to the Committee of Ministers. The Registrar shall send certified copies to the parties, to the Secretary General of the Council of Europe, to any third party and to any other person directly concerned. The original copy, duly signed and sealed, shall be placed in the archives of the Court.

Rule 78
(Publication of judgments and other documents)

In accordance with Article 44 § 3 of the Convention, final judgments of the Court shall be published, under the responsibility of the Registrar, in an appropriate form. The Registrar shall in addition be responsible for the publication of official reports of selected judgments and decisions and of any document which the President of the Court considers it useful to publish.

Rule 79
(Request for interpretation of a judgment)

1.   A party may request the interpretation of a judgment within a period of one year following the delivery of that judgment.

2.   The request shall be filed with the Registry. It shall state precisely the point or points in the operative provisions of the judgment on which interpretation is required.

3.   The original Chamber may decide of its own motion to refuse the request on the ground that there is no reason to warrant considering it. Where it is not possible to constitute the original Chamber, the President of the Court shall complete or compose the Chamber by drawing lots.

4.   If the Chamber does not refuse the request, the Registrar shall communicate it to the other party or parties and shall invite them to submit any written comments within a time-limit laid down by the President of the Chamber. The President of the Chamber shall also fix the date of the hearing should the Chamber decide to hold one. The Chamber shall decide by means of a judgment.

Rule 80
(Request for revision of a judgment)

1.   A party may, in the event of the discovery of a fact which might by its nature have a decisive influence and which, when a judgment was delivered, was unknown to the Court and could not reasonably have been known to that party, request the Court, within a period of six months after that party acquired knowledge of the fact, to revise that judgment.

2.   The request shall mention the judgment of which revision is requested and shall contain the information necessary to show that the conditions laid down in paragraph 1 have been complied with. It shall be accompanied by a copy of all supporting documents. The request and supporting documents shall be filed with the Registry.

3.   The original Chamber may decide of its own motion to refuse the request on the ground that there is no reason to warrant considering it. Where it is not possible to constitute the original Chamber, the President of the Court shall complete or compose the Chamber by drawing lots.

4.   If the Chamber does not refuse the request, the Registrar shall communicate it to the other party or parties and shall invite them to submit any written comments within a time-limit laid down by the President of the Chamber. The President of the Chamber shall also fix the date of the hearing should the Chamber decide to hold one. The Chamber shall decide by means of a judgment.

Rule 81
(Rectification of errors in decisions and judgments)

Without prejudice to the provisions on revision of judgments and on restoration to the list of applications, the Court may, of its own motion or at the request of a party made within one month of the delivery of a decision or a judgment, rectify clerical errors, errors in calculation or obvious mistakes.

Chapter IX
Advisory Opinions

Rule 82

In proceedings relating to advisory opinions the Court shall apply, in addition to the provisions of Articles 47, 48 and 49 of the Convention, the provisions which follow. It shall also apply the other provisions of these Rules to the extent to which it considers this to be appropriate.

Rule 83

The request for an advisory opinion shall be filed with the Registry. It shall state fully and precisely the question on which the opinion of the Court is sought, and also

(a)   the date on which the Committee of Ministers adopted the decision referred to in Article 47 § 3 of the Convention;

(b)   the names and addresses of the person or persons appointed by the Committee of Ministers to give the Court any explanations which it may require.

The request shall be accompanied by all documents likely to elucidate the question.

Rule 84

1.   On receipt of a request, the Registrar shall transmit a copy of it to all members of the Court.

2.   The Registrar shall inform the Contracting Parties that the Court is prepared to receive their written comments.

Rule 85

1.   The President of the Court shall lay down the time-limits for filing written comments or other documents.

2.   Written comments or other documents shall be filed with the Registry. The Registrar shall transmit copies of them to all the members of the Court, to the Committee of Ministers and to each of the Contracting Parties.

Rule 86

After the close of the written procedure, the President of the Court shall decide whether the Contracting Parties which have submitted written comments are to be given an opportunity to develop them at an oral hearing held for the purpose.

Rule 87

If the Court considers that the request for an advisory opinion is not within its consultative competence as defined in Article 47 of the Convention, it shall so declare in a reasoned decision.

Rule 88

1.   Advisory opinions shall be given by a majority vote of the Grand Chamber. They shall mention the number of judges constituting the majority.

2.   Any judge may, if he or she so desires, attach to the opinion of the Court either a separate opinion, concurring with or dissenting from the advisory opinion, or a bare statement of dissent.

Rule 89

The advisory opinion shall be read out in one of the two official languages by the President of the Court, or by another judge delegated by the President, at a public hearing, prior notice having been given to the Committee of Ministers and to each of the Contracting Parties.

Rule 90

The opinion, or any decision given under Rule 87, shall be signed by the President of the Court and by the Registrar. The original copy, duly signed and sealed, shall be placed in the archives of the Court. The Registrar shall send certified copies to the Committee of Ministers, to the Contracting Parties and to the Secretary General of the Council of Europe.

Chapter X
Legal Aid

Rule 91

1.   The President of the Chamber may, either at the request of an applicant lodging an application under Article 34 of the Convention or of his or her own motion, grant free legal aid to the applicant in connection with the presentation of the case from the moment when observations in writing on the admissibility of that application are received from the respondent Contracting Party in accordance with Rule 54 § 3 (b), or where the time-limit for their submission has expired.

2.   Subject to Rule 96, where the applicant has been granted legal aid in connection with the .presentation of his or her case before the Chamber, that grant shall continue in force for purposes of his or her representation before the Grand Chamber.

Rule 92

Legal aid shall be granted only where the President of the Chamber is satisfied

(a)   that it is necessary for the proper conduct of the case before the Chamber;

(b)   that the applicant has insufficient means to meet all or part of the costs entailed.

Rule 93

1.   In order to determine whether or not applicants have sufficient means to meet all or part of the costs entailed, they shall be required to complete a form of declaration stating their income, capital assets and any financial commitments in respect of dependants, or any other financial obligations. The declaration shall be certified by the appropriate domestic authority or authorities.

2.   The Contracting Party concerned shall be requested to submit its comments in writing.

3.   After receiving the information mentioned in paragraphs 1 and 2 above, the President of the Chamber shall decide whether or not to grant legal aid. The Registrar shall inform the parties accordingly.

Rule 94

1.   Fees shall be payable to the advocates or other persons appointed in accordance with Rule 36 § 4. Fees may, where appropriate, be paid to more than one such representative.

2.   Legal aid may be granted to cover not only representatives' fees but also travelling and subsistence expenses and other necessary expenses incurred by the applicant or appointed representative.

Rule 95

On a decision to grant legal aid, the Registrar shall

     (a)   fix the rate of fees to be paid in accordance with the legal-aid scales in force;

     (b)   the level of expenses to be paid.

Rule 96

The President of the Chamber may, if satisfied that the conditions stated in Rule 92 are no longer fulfilled, revoke or vary a grant of legal aid at any time.

TITLE III
TRANSITIONAL RULES

Rule 97
(Judges' terms of office)

The duration of the terms of office of the judges who were members of the Court at the date of the entry into force of Protocol No. 11 to the Convention shall be calculated as from that date.

Rule 98
(Presidency of the Sections)

For a period of three years from the entry into force of Protocol No. 11 to the Convention,

     (a)   the two Presidents of Sections who are not simultaneously Vice-Presidents of the Court and, the Vice-Presidents of the Sections shall be elected for a term of office of eighteen months;

     (b)   the Vice-Presidents of the Sections may not be immediately re-elected.

Rule 99
(Relations between the Court and the Commission)

1.   In cases brought before the Court under Article 5 §§ 4 and 5 of Protocol No. 11 to the Convention the Court may invite the Commission to delegate one or more of its members to take part in the consideration of the case before the Court.

2.   In cases referred to in the preceding paragraph the Court shall take into consideration the report of the Commission adopted pursuant to former Article 31 of the Convention.

3.   Unless the President of the Chamber decides otherwise, the said report shall be made available to the public through the Registrar as soon as possible after the case has been brought before the Court.

4.   The remainder of the case file of the Commission, including all pleadings, in cases brought before the Court under Article 5 §§ 2 to 5 of Protocol No. 11 shall remain confidential unless the President of the Chamber decides otherwise.

5.   In cases where the Commission has taken evidence but has been unable to adopt a report in accordance with former Article 31 of the Convention, the Court shall take into consideration the verbatim records, documentation and opinion of the Commission's delegations arising from such investigations.

Rule 100
(Chamber and Grand Chamber proceedings)

1.   In cases referred to the Court under Article 5 § 4 of Protocol No. 11 to the Convention, a panel of the Grand Chamber constituted in accordance with Rule 24 § 6 shall determine, solely on the basis of the existing case file, whether a Chamber or the Grand Chamber is to decide the case.

2.   If the case is decided by a Chamber, the judgment of the Chamber shall, in accordance with Article 5 § 4 of Protocol No. 11, be final and Rule 73 shall be inapplicable.

3.   Cases transmitted to the Court under Article 5 § 5 of Protocol No. 11 shall be forwarded by the President of the Court to the Grand Chamber.

4.   For each case transmitted to the Grand Chamber under Article 5 § 5 of the Protocol No 11, the Grand Chamber shall be completed by judges designated by rotation within one of the groups mentioned in Rule 24 § 3, the cases being allocated to the groups on an alternate basis.

Rule 101
(Grant of legal aid)

Subject to Rule 96, in cases brought before the Court under Article 5 §§ 2 to 5 of Protocol No. 11 to the Convention, a grant of legal aid made to an applicant in the proceedings before the Commission or the former Court shall continue in force for the purposes of his or her representation before the Court.

Rule 102
(Request for interpretation or revision of a judgment)

1.   Where a party requests interpretation or revision of a judgment delivered by the former Court, the President of the Court shall assign the request to one of

the Sections in accordance with the conditions laid down in Rule 51 or 52, as the case may be.

2. The President of the relevant Section shall, notwithstanding Rules 79 § 3 and 80 § 3, constitute a new Chamber to consider the request.

3. The Chamber to be constituted shall include as *ex officio* members

(a) the President of the Section; and, whether or not they are members of the relevant Section,

(b) the judge elected in respect of any Contracting Party concerned or, if he or she is unable to sit, any judge appointed under Rule 29;

(c) any judge of the Court who was a member of the original Chamber that delivered the judgment in the former Court.

4. (a) The other members of the Chamber shall be designated by the President of the Section by means of a drawing of lots from among the members of the relevant Section.

(b) The members of the Section who are not so designated shall sit in the case as substitute judges.

TITLE IV
FINAL CLAUSES

Rule 103
(Amendment or suspension of a Rule)

1. Any Rule may be amended upon a motion made after notice where such a motion is carried at the next session of the plenary Court by a majority of all the members of the Court. Notice of such a motion shall be delivered in writing to the Registrar at least one month before the session at which it is to be discussed. On receipt of such a notice of motion, the Registrar shall inform all members of the Court at the earliest possible moment.

2. A Rule relating to the internal working of the Court may be suspended upon a motion made without notice, provided that this decision is taken unanimously by the Chamber concerned. The suspension of a Rule shall in this case be limited in its operation to the particular purpose for which it was sought.

Rule 104
(Entry into force of the Rules)

The present Rules shall enter into force on 1 November 1998.

Appendix Three

Application Form

Voir note explicative
See Explanatory Note

COUR EUROPÉENNE DES DROITS DE L'HOMME
EUROPEAN COURT OF HUMAN RIGHTS

Conseil de l'Europe — *Council of Europe*
Strasbourg, France

REQUÊTE

APPLICATION

présentée en application de l'article 34 de la Convention européenne des Droits de l'Homme, ainsi que des articles 45 et 47 du Reglement de la Cour

under Article 34 of the European Convention on Human Rights and Rules 45 and 47 of the Rules of Court

IMPORTANT: La presente requête est un document juridique et peut affecter vos droits et obligations.
This application is a formal legal document and may affect your rights and obligations.

I— LES PARTIES
THE PARTIES

A. LE REQUERANT/LA REQUERANTE
THE APPLICANT

(Renseignements a fournir concernant le requérant(e) et son/sa représentant(e) eventuel(le))
(Fill in the following details of the applicant and the representative, if any)

1 Nom de famille   2. Prénom(s)
   Surname...............   *First name(s)*...............

   Sexe: masculin/féminin
   Sex: male/female

3. Nationalité   4. Profession
    Nationality...............   *Occupation*...............

5. Date et lieu de naissance
    Date and place of birth...

6. Domicile
    Permanent address...

7. Tel No....................

8. Adresse actuelle (si différente de 6.)
    Present address (if different from 6)...

9. Nom et prénom du/de la représentant(e)*
    *Name of representative**...

10. Profession du/de la représentant(e)
    Occupation of representative..

11. Adresse du/de la représentant(e)
    Address of representative...

12. Tel. No...............   Fax No...............

B. LA HAUTE PARTIE CONTRACTANTE
THE HIGH CONTRACTING PARTY

(Indiquer ci-après le nom de l'Etat/des Etats contre le(s)quel(s) la requête est dirigée)
(Fill in the name of the State(s) against which the application is directed)

13.   ....

---

*Si le/la requerant(e) est represente(e), joindre une procuration signée par le/la requérant(e) en faveur du/de la représentant(e)
A form of authority signed by the applicant should be submitted if a representative is appointed

II— EXPOSÉ DES FAITS
STATEMENT OF THE FACTS

(Voir chapitre II de la note explicative)
(see Part II of the Explanatory Note)

14.

Si necessaire, continuer sur une feuille séparée
Continue on a separate sheet if necessary

III— EXPOSÉ DE LA OU DES VIOLATION(S) DE LA CONVENTION ET/OU DES
PROTOCOLES ALLÉGUÉE(S), AINSI QUE DES ARGUMENTS À L'APPUI
*STATEMENT OF ALLEGED VIOLATION(S) OF THE CONVENTION AND/OR
PROTOCOLS AND OF RELEVANT ARGUMENTS*

(Voir chapitre 111 de la note explicative)
(see Part III of the Explanatory Note)

15.

IV— EXPOSÉ RELATIF AUX PRESCRIPTIONS DE L'ARTICLE 35(1) DE LA CONVENTION
STATEMENT RELATIVE TO ARTICLE 35(1) OF THE CONVENTION

(Voir chapitre IV de la note explicative. Donner pour chaque grief, et au besoin sur une feuille séparée, les renseignements demandés sous les points 16 à 18 ci-apres)
(See Part IV of the Explanatory Note. If, necessary, give the details mentioned below under points 16 to 18 on a separate sheet for each separate complaint)

16. Décision interne définitive (date et nature de la décision, organe — judiciare ou autre — l'ayant rendue)
Final decision (date, court or authority and nature of decision).

17. Autres décisions (énumérées dans l'ordre chronologique en indiquant, pour chaque décision, sa date, sa nature et l'organe — judiciare ou autre — l'ayant rendue)
Other decisions (list in order, giving date, court or authority and nature of decision for each of them)

18. Dispos(i)ez-vous d'un recours que vous n'avez pas exercé? Si oui, lequel et pour quel motif n'a-t-il pas été exercé?
Is there or was there any other appeal or other remedy available which you have not used? If so, explain why you have not used it.

Si necessaire, continuer sur une feuille séparée
Continue on a separate sheet if necessary

V— EXPOSÉ DE L'OBJET DE LA REQUÊTE ET PRÉTENTIONS PROVISOIRES
POUR UNE SATISFACTION EQUITABLE
*STATEMENT OF THE OBJECT OF THE APPLICATION AND PROVISIONAL
CLAIMS FOR JUST SATISFACTION*

(Voir chapitre V de la note explicative)
(See Part V of the Explanatory Note)

19.

VI— AUTRES INSTANCES INTERNATIONALES TRAITANT OU AYANT
TRAITÉ L'AFFAIRE
STATEMENT CONCERNING OTHER INTERNATIONAL PROCEEDINGS

(Voir chapitre VI de la note explicative)
(See Part VI of the Explantory Note)

20.   Avez-vous soumis à une autre instance internationale d'enquête ou de règlement
les griefs énoncés dans la présente requête? Si oui, fournir des indications
détaillées à ce sujet.
*Have you submitted the above complaints to any other procedure of international
investigation or settlement? If so, give full details*

VII— PIÈCES ANNEXÉES
     LIST OF DOCUMENTS

**(PAS D'ORIGINAUX,
UNIQUEMENT DES COPIES)**
*(NO ORIGINAL DOCUMENTS,
ONLY PHOTOCOPIES)*

(Voir chapitre VII de la note explicative. Joindre copie de toutes les décisions mentionnées sous ch. IV et VI ci-dessus. Se procurer, au besoin, les copies nécessaires et, en cas impossibilité, expliquer pourquoi celles-ci ne peuvent pas être obtenues. Ces documents ne vous seront pas retournés)
(See Part VII of the Explanatory Note. Include copies of all decisions referred to in Parts IV and VI above. If you do not have copies, you should obtain them. If you cannot obtain them, explain why not. No documents will be returned to you)

21.   a)..

       b)..

       c)..

VIII— DÉCLARATION ET SIGNATURE
DECLARATION AND SIGNATURE

(Voir chapitre IX de la note explicative)
(See Part IX of the Explanatory Note)

22.   Je déclare en toute conscience et loyauté que les renseignments qui figurent sur la présente formule de requête sont exacts.
I hereby declare that, to the best of my knowledge and belief, the information I have given in the present application form is correct.

Lieu/Place . . . .
Date/Date . . . .

(Signature du/de la requérant(e) ou du/de la représentant(e))
(Signature of the applicant or of the representative)

Appendix Four

Form of Authority

EUROPEAN COURT OF HUMAN RIGHTS

A U T H O R I T Y

I, ...

....

(name and address of applicant)

hereby authorise...

....

....

(name and address of representative)

to represent me in the proceedings before the European Court of Human Rights,

and in any subsequent proceedings under the European Convention on Human

Rights, concerning my application introduced under Article 34 of the Convention

against

....

(respondent State)

on ....
(date of letter of introduction)

....
(place and date)

....
(signature)

Appendix Five

Conditional Fee Agreement

CONDITIONAL FEE AGREEMENT

(European Convention on Human Rights: pay as you go)

The agreement is a legally binding contract between you and your legal representative. The Law Society Conditions are part of the agreement. Before you sign, please read everything carefully. Please also read 'Conditional Fees Explained', a Law Society leaflet we have given you.

For an explanation of words like 'our disbursements', 'win', and 'lose', see condition 3 of the Law Society Conditions.

Agreement date

. . . .

We, the legal representative

You, the client

What is covered by the agreement

- Your claim for violation of your rights under the European Convention on Human Rights ('the Convention') before the European Court of Human Rights ('the Court')

Paying us

If you win the case, you are liable to pay our costs and disbursements (to the extent that we have not recovered them from any Council of Europe legal aid payments). You may be able to recover some of these from your opponent. For full details, see condition 4.

If you lose the case, you pay our disbursements (to the extent that we have not recovered them from any Council of Europe legal aid payments). For full details see condition 5.

If you end the agreement before the case is won or lost, you pay our disbursements. If you go on to win this case, you pay our costs. For full details, see condition 7.

Costs

These are for work done from now until the review date, [   ].
Our hourly rates are:

- Partner   £
- Assistant Solicitor   £
- Trainee Solicitor   £

We add VAT at the rate that applies when the work is done (now 17.5%). The hourly rates are the same as would be charged if the work was done under a non-conditional fee agreement.

Success fee

- 2 % of the basic costs plus
- 4 % of the basic costs if an extra success fee is payable under condition 6.

The total of the success fee and any barrister's uplift fee (see condition 6) will not be more than 25% of the damages or settlement you win

Immediately before you sign the agreement, we explained the following points to you. They are also explained in the Law Society Conditions.

Legal Aid

- Whether you can get legal aid for this case.
- Under what conditions you can get legal aid.
- How those conditions apply to this case.

Costs and Disbursements

- In what circumstances you may have to pay our disbursements and costs.
- In what circumstances (if any) you can have our bills checked by a court (known as taxation), and how to do so.

Our disbursements

Pay-as-you-go option

You agree to pay our disbursements now and as the case goes on.

Signatures

. . . .

Signed for the legal
Representative

. . . .

Signed by the Client

LAW SOCIETY CONDITIONS

1. Our responsibilities
We must:
- always act in your best interests in pursuing your claim for compensation and obtaining for you the best possible result, subject to our duty to the court;
- explain to you the risks and benefits of taking legal action;
- give you our best advice about whether to accept any offer of settlement;
- at the outset, give you the best information possible about the likely costs of your case;
- every six months, inform you of the approximate amount of the basic costs.

2. Your responsibilities
You must:
- give us instructions that allow us to do our work properly;
- not ask us to work in an improper or unreasonable way;
- not deliberately mislead us;
- co-operate with us when asked;
- go to any court hearing when asked;
- pay for disbursements as the case goes on.

3. Explanation of words used
(a) *Advocacy*
Appearing for you at court hearings.

(b) *Basic costs*
Our costs for legal work. You pay them — and a success fee — if you win. Basic costs are worked out in line with the agreement. But we will review the rates in the agreement on the review date and on each anniversary of the review date. We will not increase the rates by more than the rise in the Retail Price Index.

(c) *Case*
Your claim for breach of your rights under the Convention.

(d) *Compensation*
Money that a court says you or your opponent must pay (or money that you or your opponent agree to pay) in settlement of the case.

(e) *Our disbursements*
Payments we make on your behalf to others involved in the case.
Fees for advocacy may also be counted as our disbursements (see condition 6).

You have to pay all our disbursements, whether you win or lose. if you win, we may recover on your behalf the money for our disbursements from your opponent.

(f) *Lien*

Our right to keep all papers, documents, money or other property held on your behalf until all money due to us is paid. A lien may be applied after the agreement ends.

(g) *Lose*

The Commission or the Court has dismissed your proccedings or you have stopped them on our advice.

(h) *Opponent*

The United Kingdom Government.

Success fee

The percentage of basic costs that we add to your bill if you win the case. It cannot be more than 100% of the basic costs. It is paid out of your damages.

The percentage reflects:

- our opinion of the level of risk we are taking — if you lose, we will not earn anything;
- the fact that we are not receiving our basic costs in advance.

It may be that your opponent makes a payment into court which you reject and, on our advice, the case goes ahead to trial where you recover damages that are less than the payment-in. If so, we will not add our success fee to the basic costs for the work done after you rejected the payment-in.

The total of our success fee and any barrister's uplift fee (see condition 6) is capped — it will not be more than 25% of damages recovered. This calculation excludes any money your opponent pays to the DSS in repayment of any benefits you receive.

(i) *Win*

The Court finds that your right under the Convention has been violated, or there is a 'friendly settlement' of the application, or the Court decides that the application has been resolved and accordingly is to be struck out of the list of cases, or any other resolution which you consider satisfactory.

4. What happens, if you win?

If you win, you are liable to pay our disbursements our basic costs and the success fee promptly, and in any event not later than 3 months from the date on which the matter was successfully concluded. Normally, however, you will be able to recover part or all of our disbursements and basic costs from your opponent. The Court will decide how much you can recover if you and your opponent cannot agree the amount. If the amount agreed or allowed by the court does not cover all our work, you pay the difference.

You agree that we may receive the damages and costs your opponent has to pay. If your opponent refuses to accept our receipt, you will pay the cheque you receive from your opponent into a joint bank account in your name and ours. Out of the money, you agree to let us take the balance of the costs, disbursements and VAT. You take the rest.

We are allowed to keep any interest your opponent pays on the costs.

Payment for advocacy is explained in condition 6.

5. What happens if you lose?

If you lose, you do not have to pay any of the costs. You do have to pay us for any disbursements which are not met by the Council of Europe's legal aid scheme.

Payment for advocacy is dealt with in condition 6.

If your opponent pays you the costs of any hearing, they belong to us.

6. Payment for advocacy

Costs of advocacy undertaken by us or by any solicitor agent on our behalf form part of our basic costs and are not a disbursement.

Barristers who have a conditional fee agreement with us

If you win, their fee is a disbursement which can be recovered from your opponent. You must pay the barrister's uplift fee shown in a separate conditional fee agreement we make with the barrister. We will discuss the barrister's uplift fee with you before we instruct him or her. If you lose, you pay nothing.

Barristers who do not have a conditional fee agreement with us

We are responsible for paying the barrister's fees, whether you win or lose. Because of this, we will normally only instruct a barrister who has a conditional fee agreement with us. If you want to instruct another barrister, you will have to agree to be responsible for his or her fees, whether you win or lose the case.

Other points concerning barristers

If you choose a barrister we do not recommend, we may decide not to seek a conditional fee agreement with him or her. The points in the previous paragraph will then apply.

If we ask a barrister to provide advice or to draft documents, the fees will be treated as set out in this section.

If you reject our advice to use a barrister, you may not compel us to provide advocacy ourselves. Following our refusal to provide advocacy, we can end the agreement if you still reject our advice to use a barrister.

7.   What happens when the agreement ends before the case itself ends?

Paying us if you end the agreement
You can end the agreement at any time. We then have the right to decide whether you must:

- pay the basic costs and disbursements when we ask for them; or
- pay the basic costs, disbursements and success fee if you go on to win the case.

Paying us if we end the agreement
We can end the agreement if you do not keep to your responsibilities in condition 2. We then have the right to decide whether you must:

- pay the basic costs and disbursements when we ask for them; or
- pay the basic costs, disbursements and success fee if you go on to win the case.

We can end the agreement if we believe you are unlikely to win but you disagree with us. If this happens, you will only have to pay disbursements.

We can end the agreement if you reject our opinion about making a settlement with your opponent. You must then

- pay the basic costs immediately.
- pay the success fee if you go on to win the case (unless your damages or settlement are at least 20% more than the offer we advised you to accept);
- pay disbursements.

If you ask us to get a second opinion from a specialist legal representative outside our firm, we will do so. You pay the cost of a second opinion.

8.   What happens after the agreement ends

After the agreement ends, we will apply to have our name removed from the record of any court proceedings in which we are acting.

We have the right to preserve our lien unless another solicitor working for you undertakes to pay us what we are owed.

Appendix Six

Court Acknowledgement Letter and Explanatory Note

COUR EUROPEENNE
DES
DROITS DE L'HOMME

CONSEIL DE L'EUROPE
STRASBOURG

EUROPEAN COURT
OF
HUMAN RIGHTS

COUNCIL OF EUROPE
STRASBOURG

[ADDRESSEE]

Our Ref.
[Name of Case]

Dear Sir/Madam,

I acknowledge receipt of your letter of [date]

I now enclose a form on which you should set out your clients' application to the Court. You should complete and return this, together with a photocopy of all relevant documents which you wish to submit, as soon as possible (normally within six weeks). I should draw your attention to the fact that these documents will not be returned to you. Consequently, it is in your interests only to send photocopies, not original documents.

An explanatory note to assist you in completing the form is annexed to it. As you will see from the explanatory note, the Court will examine the case on the basis of the completed form. You should therefore take care to complete it fully and accurately, but you may refer to submissions already made in previous correspondence or pleadings. Failure to return promptly the application form duly completed and signed might affect the date of introduction of your application and thus the six months' time-limit under Article 35 § 1 of the Convention.

You are also requested to return the attached letter of authority, duly completed and signed by the applicants.

Yours faithfully,
For the Registrar

[name]
Legal Secretary

Encs. Application form and explanatory note
　　　Letter of authority

EXPLANATORY NOTE

for persons completing the Application Form
under Article 34 of the Convention

INTRODUCTION

These notes are intended to assist you in drawing up your application to the Court. **Please read them carefully before completing the form**, and then refer to them as you complete each section of the form.

The completed form will be your application to the Court under Article 34 of the Convention. It will be the basis for the Court's examination of your case. It is therefore important that you **complete it fully and accurately even if this means repeating information you have already given the Registry in previous correspondence**.

You will see that there are eight sections to the form. You should complete all of these so that your application contains all the information required under the Court's Rules of Procedure. Below you will find an explanatory note relating to each section of the form. You will also find at the end of these notes the text of Rules 45 and 47 of the Court's Rules of Procedure.

NOTES RELATING TO THE APPLICATION FORM

I. THE PARTIES — Rule 47 § 1(a), (b) and (c)

If there is more than one applicant, you should give the required information for each one, on a separate sheet if necessary.

An applicant may appoint a person to represent him. Such representative shall be an advocate authorised to practise in any of the Contracting Parties and resident in the territory of one of them, or any other person approved by the Court. When an applicant is represented, relevant details should be given in this part of the application form, and the Registry will correspond only with the representative.

II. STATEMENT OF THE FACTS — Rule 47 § 1(d)

You should give clear and concise details of the facts you are complaining about. Try to describe the events in the order in which they occured. Give exact dates. If your complaints relate to a number of different matters (for instance different sets of court proceedings) you should deal with each matter separately.

III. STATEMENT OF ALLEGED VIOLATION(S) OF THE CONVENTION AND/OR PROTOCOLS AND OF RELEVANT ARGUMENTS — Rule 47 § 1(e)

In this section of the form should explain as precisely as you can what your complaint **under the Convention** is. Say which provisions of the Convention you rely on and explain why you consider that the facts you have set out in Part II of the form involve a violation of these provisions.

You will see that some of the articles of the Convention permit interferences with the rights they guarantee in certain circumstances — (see for instance sub-paras (a) to (f) of Article 5 § 1 and 2 of Articles 8 to 11). If you are relying on such an article, try to explain why you consider the interference about which you are complaining is not justified.

IV. STATEMENT RELATIVE TO ARTICLE 35 § 1 OF THE CONVENTION — Rule 47 § 2 (a)

In this section you should set out details of the remedies you have pursued before the national authorities. You should fill in each of the three parts of this section and give the same information separately for each separate complaint. In part 18 you should say whether or not any other appeal or remedy is available which could redress your complaints and which you have not used. If such a remedy is available, you should say what it is (e.g., name the court or authority to which an appeal would lie) and explain why you have not used it.

V. STATEMENT OF THE OBJECT OF THE APPLICATION — Rule 47 § 1(a)

Here you should state briefly what you want to achieve through your application to the Court. You should give a general indication of any claims for just satisfaction which you may wish to make under Article 41 of the Convention.

VI. STATEMENT CONCERNING OTHER INTERNATIONAL PROCEEDINGS — Rule 47 § 2(b)

Here you should say whether or not you have ever submitted the complaints in your application to any other procedure of international investigation or settlement. If you have, you should give full details, including the name of the body to which you submitted your complaints, dates and details of any proceedings which took place and details of decisions taken. You should also submit copies of relevant decisions and other documents.

VII. LIST OF DOCUMENTS — Rule 47 § 1(h)
(NO ORIGINAL DOCUMENTS, ONLY PHOTOCOPIES)

Do not forget to enclose with your application and to mention on the list all judgments and decisions referred to in Sections IV and VI, as well as any other documents you wish the Court to take into consideration as evidence (transcripts, statements of witnesses, etc.). Include any documents giving the reasons for a court or other decision as well as the decision itself. Only submit documents which are relevant to the complaints you are making to the Court.

VIII.   DECLARATION AND SIGNATURE — Rule 45 § 3

If the application is signed by the representative of the applicant, it should be accompanied by a form of authority signed by the applicant (unless this has already been submitted).

Appendix Seven

Rule 36 Form of Appointment of Representative

**APPOINTMENT OF THE APPLICANT'S (TS') REPRESENTATIVE
IN THE PROCEEDINGS BEFORE
THE EUROPEAN COURT OF HUMAN RIGHTS**
(Rule 36 of the Rules of Court)

Application no.

TO BE SIGNED BY THE APPLICANT

I/We the undersigned

Family name   *First name(s)*

Address

Telephone number

Telefax number

hereby appoint as my/our representative in the proceedings before the Court:

Family name *First name(s)*

Address

Telephone number

Telefax number

. . . .
(place, date, signature(s) of applicant(s))

TO BE SIGNED BY THE PERSON APPOINTED AS REPRESENTATIVE

I the undersigned

Family name *First name(s)*

Address for correspondence

Telephone number

Telefax number

Information concerning the bank (send bank identity slip, if available)[1]

Name of bank:

Bank Agency number:

Address of the Agency:

Account number:

certify:
— that I am an advocate authorised to practise in a Contracting State and resident in a Contracting State;[2]
— that I accept the above appointment, subject, if need be, to the approval of the President of the Court.[2]

I wish to correspond in English/French (Rule 34 § 3).

. . . .
(place, date, signature of the person appointed)

---

[1] For any funds that may be payable to the applicant(s).
[2] Please delete as appropriate.

Appendix Eight

Declaration of applicant's means

DECLARATION OF APPLICANT'S MEANS

1. Name of applicant and case number:

   _____

   _____

   _____

2. Are you married, divorced or single?

   _____

3. Nature of your employment, name of employer:
   (if not at present employed, give details of your last employment)

   _____

   _____

   _____

   _____

4. Details of net salary and other net income (e.g., interest from loans and investments, allowances, pensions, insurance benefits, etc.) after deduction of tax:

   _____

   _____

   _____

   _____

5. List and value of capital assets owned by you:
   (a) Immovable property (e.g., land, house, business premises)
   (b) Moveable property and nature thereof (e.g., bank balance, savings account, motor-car valuables)

   _____

   _____

   _____

   _____

   _____

6. List your financial commitments:
   (a) Rent, mortgage and other charges

   _____

   _____

   (b) Loans and interst payable thereon

   _____

   _____

   (c) Maintenance of dependants

   _____

   _____

   (d) Any other financial obligations

   _____

   _____

7. What contribution can you make towards your legal representation before the Court of Human Rights?

   _____

   _____

8. The name of the person whom you propose to assist you:
   (see Rule 94 of the Rules of Court)

   _____

I certify that the above information is correct.

Signed   Dated:

Appendix Nine

Legal Services Commission Certificate of Indigence

LEGAL SERVICES COMMISSION

London Region
29–37 Red Lion Street, London.
WC1R 4PP DX: 170
Tel: 0207.759.1500 Fax: 0207.759.1953

ADDRESS

Our ref:
Your ref:
Please ask for: Means Assessment Team

Date:
Dear Sirs,

EUROPEAN COURT OF HUMAN RIGHTS:
CERTIFICATE OF INDIGENCE FOR [APPLICANT'S NAME]

The financial circumstances of the above applicant have been assessed as requested. Had they applied for legal aid for court proceedings in England or Wales, and had their means been assessed under the Civil Legal Aid (Assessment of Resources) Regulations 1989 then the result of the financial assessment would have been as follows:

The disposable income and disposable capital are such that they would have been within the financial limits for civil legal aid, and they would not have been required to make a contribution towards the legal costs.

Yours faithfully

LEGAL SERVICES COMMISSION
MEANS ASSESSMENT SECTION

LEGAL SERVICES COMMISSION

London Region
29–37 Red Lion Street, London.
WC1R 4PP DX: 170
Tel: 0207.759.1500 Fax: 0207.759.1953

ADDRESS

Our ref:
Your ref:
Please ask for: Means Assessment Team

Date:
Dear Sirs,

EUROPEAN COURT OF HUMAN RIGHTS: CERTIFICATE OF INDIGENCE FOR [APPLICANT'S NAME]

The financial circumstances of the above applicant have been assessed as requested. Had they applied for legal aid for court proceedings in England or Wales, and had their means been assessed under the Civil Legal Aid (Assessment of Resources) Regulations 1989 then the result of the financial assessment would have been as follows:

The disposable income and disposable capital are such that they would have been within the financial limits for civil legal aid, but they would have been required to make a contribution of £XXXXX per month from income and £XXXXX from capital towards the legal costs.

I enclose a breakdown of the assessment in this case.

Yours faithfully

LEGAL SERVICES COMMISSION
MEANS ASSESSMENT SECTION

LEGAL SERVICES COMMISSION

London Region
29–37 Red Lion Street, London.
WC1R 4PP DX: 170
Tel: 0207.759.1500 Fax: 0207.759.1953

ADDRESS

Our ref:
Your ref:
Please ask for: Means Assessment Team

Date:
Dear Sirs,

EUROPEAN COURT OF HUMAN RIGHTS:
CERTIFICATE OF INDIGENCE FOR [APPLICANT'S NAME]

The financial circumstances of the above applicant have been assessed as requested. Had they applied for legal aid for court proceedings in England or Wales, and had their means been assessed under the Civil Legal Aid (Assessment of Resources) Regulations 1989 then the result of the financial assessment would have been as follows.

The disposable income and disposable capital are such that they would have been above the financial limits for civil legal aid, and their application would have been refused on that basis.

I enclose a breakdown of the assessment in this case.

Yours faithfully

LEGAL SERVICES COMMISSION
MEANS ASSESSMENT SECTION

Appendix Ten

European Court Legal Aid Rates

Legal aid rates[1]
applicable as from 1 July 2000

		[Euros]	
A. **FEES**		Average	Maximum
1.	Preparation of the case	305 €	460 €
2.	Filing written pleadings (on the admissibility or merits of the case)	275 €	305 €
3.	Filing supplementary written pleadings at the request of the Court (on the admissibility or merits of the case)	155 €	185 €
	(observations on just satisfaction or friendly settlement)	95 €	140 €
4.	Appearance at hearing (including preparation)	275 €	305 €
5.	Assisting in friendly settlement negotiations	155 €	185 €

B. **EXPENSES**

1 Normal secretarial expenses (telephone, postage, photocopies etc) lump sum per case   50 €

2. Special items (translations, procurement of documents that the applicant has to pay for) will be reimbursed only exceptionally upon receipts following prior authorisation by the Registrar in charge (with indication of a maximum amount).

---

[1] The average fee is most likely to be offered in most cases, the maximum being in exceptional cases.

3. Travelling costs incurred in connection with appearance at a hearing (lawyer and applicant(s)) or with friendly settlement negotiations (lawyer only) according to receipts (shortest route between lawyer's office/applicant's residence and Strasbourg plus return, by air (economy class and airport taxes) or rail (second class). If a private car is used the reimbursement will be effected on the basis of the price of the second class rail ticket).

4. Subsistence allowance in connection with appearance at a hearing (lawyer and applicant(s)) or with friendly settlement negotiations (lawyer only), including local transport at place of office or residence and in Strasbourg):
   per diem (maximum 3 days)   152 € per person

Appendix Eleven

Admissibility Decision by a Committee

<table>
<tr><td>CONSEIL
DE L'EUROPE</td><td>COUNCIL
OF EUROPE</td></tr>
</table>

COUR EUROPÉENNE DES DROITS DE L'HOMME
EUROPEAN COURT OF HUMAN RIGHTS

FOURTH SECTION

DECISION

AS TO THE ADMISSIBILITY OF

Application no. 56125/00
by THAI TRADING
against the United Kingdom

The European Court of Human Rights (Fourth Section) sitting as a Committee composed of

Mr J. HEDIGAN, *President*,
Mr M. PELLONPÄÄ,
Mrs S. BOTOUCHAROVA, *Judges*,
and Mr V. BERGER, *Section Registrar*,

Delivered the following unanimous decision on 11 May 2000:

The Court has examined the applicant's complaints as they have been submitted and has noted that the applicant has been informed of the possible obstacles to the admissibility of the application. In the light of all the material in its possession, and in so far as the matters complained of are within its competence, the Court finds that they do not disclose any appearance of a violation of the rights and freedoms set out in the Convention or its Protocols. It follows that the application must be rejected, in accordance with Article 35 § 4 of the Convention.

Accordingly, the Court

Declares the application inadmissible.

Vincent BERGER   John HEDIGAN
Registrar   President

Appendix Twelve

Notes for Guidance of Persons Appearing at Hearings before the European Court of Human Rights

NOTES FOR THE GUIDANCE OF PERSONS APPEARING AT HEARINGS BEFORE THE EUROPEAN COURT OF HUMAN RIGHTS

These notes are intended to provide general guidance on some aspects of the Court's normal practice in relation to oral hearings and on certain practical points. Arrangements may of course differ from case to case.

Location

1. Hearings are held in the Court's hearing room in the new Human Rights Building in Strasbourg.

Publicity and information

2. The proceedings before the Court are public. A press release containing some information about the case is normally issued by the Registrar of the Court in advance of a hearing and further details are given in a second release issued on the day of the hearing. The texts of the Court's decisions and judgments are available to the public.

Persons present

3. The parties' representatives and advisers and any individual applicant or witness should be present. The parties are required to submit **at least 2 weeks in**

advance of the hearing a list of those who will be present on their behalf. The Court may limit the number of persons who may appear.

Times, duration and hearing briefs

4.   Hearings normally take place from **9.00 to 11.00 am or 2.30 to 4.30 pm** with a break of about 15 minutes. The parties' initial submissions shall not exceed 30 minutes each and their further submissions shall be limited to 15 minutes.

5.   The President meets the parties' representatives before the hearing at **8.45 am or 2.15 pm.**

Order of proceedings

6.   The order of proceedings is fixed for each case individually and depends partly on the stage the proceedings have reached. Commonly in a hearing on admissibility and merits the Government will open and the applicant will reply. At a hearing on the merits this order is reversed. There will then be questions from judges and a short second round of pleadings.

7.   The parties' representatives are not required to wear robes but may do so if they so wish. They stand in order to address the Court.

Language and interpreting

8.   The official languages of the Court are English and French and simultaneous interpreting between those two languages is provided in all cases. The parties should immediately indicate to the Registrar in which official language their submissions will be delivered. The parties should bear in mind that many of those present will be listening to the proceedings in a language which is not their own.

9.   On request, a party may be given leave to use another official language of a High Contracting Party (see Rule 34 of the Rules of Court).

10.   To assist accurate interpreting of their argument into the other language(s) used, pleaders are advised:

— to speak clearly and at moderate speed;

— if speaking from a prepared text, to make a copy available before the hearing for the exclusive use of the interpreters (even an outline or notes can be helpful; there is no need to adhere rigidly to the text provided).

Recording of proceedings

11.   The proceedings are recorded on tape, but are not transcribed into a verbatim record unless the Chamber so decides. In the latter case, the parties will

be provided with a copy of the draft verbatim record for the purpose of making corrections in the statements made on their behalf.

<u>Miscellaneous</u>

12.   There is a self-service cafeteria in the Human Rights Building, on the ground floor.

13.   It is the parties' responsibility to make their own hotel bookings etc. There is sometimes pressure on accommodation in Strasbourg, particularly during sessions of the European Parliament.

14.   Mobile telephones must be switched off during the hearing.

Appendix Thirteen

Rules of the Committee of Ministers

Rules adopted by the Committee of Ministers concerning the application of Article 54 of the European Convention on Human Rights

Text approved by the Committee of Ministers at the 254th Meeting of the Ministers' Deputies in February 1976.

Rule 1

When a judgment of the Court is transmitted to the Committee of Ministers in accordance with Article 54 of the Convention, the case shall be inscribed on the agenda of the Committee without delay.

Rule 2

a. When, in the judgment transmitted to the Committee of Ministers in accordance with Article 54 of the Convention, the Court decides that there has been a violation of the Convention and/or affords just satisfaction to the injured party under Article 50 of the Convention, the Committee shall invite the state concerned to inform it of the measures which it has taken in consequence of the judgment, having regard to its obligation under Article 53 of the Convention to abide by the judgment.[1]

---

[1] At the 215th meeting of the Ministers' Deputies (November 1972), it was agreed that the Committee of Ministers is entitled to consider a communication from an individual who claims that he has not received damages in accordance with a decision of the Court under Article 50 of the Convention affording him just satisfaction as an injured party, as well as any further information furnished to it concerning the execution of such a judgment of the Court, and that, consequently, any such communication should be distributed to the Committee of Ministers.

b.   If the state concerned informs the Committee of Ministers that it is not yet in a position to inform it of the measures taken, the case shall be automatically inscribed on the agenda of a meeting of the Committee taking place not more than six months later, unless the Committee of Ministers decides otherwise; the same Rule will be applied on expiration of this and any subsequent period.

Rule 3

The Committee of Ministers shall not regard its functions under Article 54 of the Convention as having been exercised until it has taken note of the information supplied in accordance with Rule 2 and, when just satisfaction has been afforded, until it has satisfied itself that the state concerned has awarded this just satisfaction to the injured party.

Rule 4

The decision in which the Committee of Ministers declares that its functions under Article 54 of the Convention have been exercised shall take the form of a resolution.

Appendix Fourteen

Tables of Ratifications of the Convention and its Protocols

DATES OF RATIFICATION

28.11.2000

STATE	CONVENTION	PROTOCOL No. 1	PROTOCOL No. 4	PROTOCOL No. 6	PROTOCOL No. 7
Albania	02.10.1996	02.10.1996	02.10.1996	21.09.2000	02.10.1996
Andorra	22.01.1996	—	—	22.01.1996	—
Austria	03.09.1958	03.09.1958	18.09.1969	05.01.1984	14.05.1986
Belgium	14.06.1955	04.06.1955	21.09.1970	10.12.1998	—
Bulgaria	07.09.1992	07.09.1992	04.11.2000	29.09.1999	04.11.2000
Croatia	05.11.1997	05.11.1997	05.11.1997	05.11.1997	05.11.1997
Cyprus	06.10.1962	06.10.1962	03.10.1989	19.01.2000	—
Czech Republic	08.03.1992	08.03.1992	18.03.1992	18.03.1992	18.03.1992
Denmark	13.04.1953	03.04.1953	30.09.1964	01.12.1983	18.08.1988
Estonia	16.04.1996	16.04.1996	16.04.1996	17.04.1998	16.04.1996
Finland	10.05.1990	10.05.1990	10.05.1990	10.05.1990	10.05.1990
France	03.05.1974	03.05.1974	03.05.1974	17.02.1986	17.02.1986
Georgia	20.05.1999	—	13.04.2000	13.04.2000	13.04.2000
Germany	05.12.1952	13.02.1957	01.06.1968	05.07.1989	—
Greece	28.11.1974	28.11.1974	—	08.09.1998	29.10.1987
Hungary	05.11.1992	05.11.1992	05.11.1992	05.11.1992	05.11.1992
Iceland	29.06.1953	29.06.1953	16.11.1967	22.05.1987	22.05.1987
Ireland	25.02.1953	25.02.1953	29.10.1968	24.06.1994	—
Italy	26.10.1955	26.10.1955	27.05.1982	29.12.1988	07.11.1991
Latvia	27.06.1997	27.06.1997	27.06.1997	07.05.1999	27.06.1997

STATE	CONVENTION	PROTOCOL No. 1	PROTOCOL No. 4	PROTOCOL No. 6	PROTOCOL No. 7
Liechtenstein	08.09.1982	4.11.1995	—	15.11.1990	—
Lithuania	20.06.1995	24.05.1996	20.06.1995	08.07.1999	20.06.1995
Luxembourg	03.09.1953	03.09.1953	02.05.1968	19.02.1985	19.04.1989
Malta	23.01.1967	23.01.1967	—	26.03.1991	—
Moldova	12.09.1997	12.09.1997	12.09.1997	12.09.1997	12.09.1997
Netherlands	31.08.1954	31.08.1954	23.06.1982	25.04.1986	—
Norway	15.01.1952	18.12.1952	12.06.1964	25.10.1988	25.10.1988
Poland	19.01.1993	10.10.1994	10.10.1994	31.10.2000	—
Portugal	09.11.1978	09.11.1978	09.11.1978	02.10.1986	—
Roumania	20.06.1994	20.06.1994	20.06.1994	20.06.1994	20.06.1994
Russia	05.05.1998	05.05.1998	05.05.1998	—	05.05.1998
San Marino	22.03.1989	22.03.1989	22.03.1989	22.03.1989	22.03.1989
Slovak Republic	18.03.1992	18.03.1992	18.03.1992	18.03.1992	18.03.1992
Slovenia	28.06.1994	28.06.1994	28.06.1994	28.06.1994	28.06.1994
Spain	04.10.1979	27.11.1990	—	14.01.1985	—
Sweden	04.02.1952	22.06.1953	13.06.1964	09.02.1984	08.11.1985
Switzerland	28.11.1974	—	—	13.10.1987	24.02.1988
TFYR. Macedonia	10.04.1997	10.04.1997	10.04.1997	10.04.1997	10.04.1997
Turkey	18.05.1954	8.05.1954	—	—	—
Ukraine	11.09.1997	1.09.1997	11.09.1997	04.04.2000	11.09.1997
United Kingdom	08.03.1951	03.11.1952	—	20.05.1999	—

Appendix Fifteen

List of Judges (Sections and Grand Chamber)

17 January 2001

M. Luzius WILDHABER, President (Swiss)
Mme Elisabeth PALM, Vice-President (Swedish)
M. Christos ROZAKIS, Vice-President (Greek)
M. Georg RESS, Section President (German)
M. Jean-Paul COSTA, Section President (French)
M. Antonio PASTOR RIDRUEJO (Spanish)
M. Luigi FERRARI BRAVO (Italian)*
M. Gaukur JÖRUNDSSON (Icelandic)
M. Giovanni BONELLO (Maltese)
M. Lucius CAFLISCH (Swiss)**
M. Loukis LOUCAIDES (Cypriot)
M. Jerzy MAKARCZYK (Polish)
M. Pranas KURIS (Lithuanian)
M. Ireneu CABRAL BARRETO (Portuguese)
M. Riza TÜRMEN (Turkish)
Mme Françoise TULKENS (Belgian)
Mme Viera STRÁZNICKÁ (Slovakian)
M. Corneliu BÎRSAN (Romanian)
M. Peer LORENZEN (Danish)

M. Willi FUHRMANN (Austrian)
M. Karel JUNGWIERT (Czech)
Sir Nicolas BRATZA (British)
M. Marc FISCHBACH (Luxemburger)
M. Volodymyr BUTKEVYCH (Ukrainian)
M. Josep CASADEVALL (Andorran)
M. Bostjan ZUPANCIC (Slovenian)
Mme Nina VAJIC (Croatian)
M. John HEDIGAN (Irish)
Mme Wilhelmina THOMASSEN (Dutch)
M. Matti PELLONPÄÄ (Finnish)
Mme Margarita TSATSA-NIKOLOVSKA (citizen of 'the Former Yugoslav
Republic of Macedonia')
M. Tudor PANTIRU (Moldovian)
Mme Hanne Sophie GREVE (Norwegian)
M. András BAKA (Hungarian)
M. Rait MARUSTE (Estonian)
M. Egils LEVITS (Latvian)
M. Kristaq TRAJA (Albanian)
Mme Snejana BOTOUCHAROVA (Bulgarian)
M. Mindia UGREKHELIDZE (Georgian)
M. Anatoly KOVLER (Russian)
M. Michele de SALVIA, Registrar (Italian)
M. Paul MAHONEY, Deputy Registrar (British)
Mme Maud DE BOER-BUQUICCHIO, Deputy Registrar (Dutch)

 * Elected as the judge in respect of San Marino. The seat of the judge in respect
   of Italy is currently vacant.
**Elected as the judge in respect of Liechtenstein.

COMPOSITION OF SECTIONS

	SECTION I	SECTION II	SECTION III	SECTION IV
President	Mme E. Palm	M. C. Rozakis	M. J.-P. Costa	M. G. Ress
Vice-President	Mme W. Thomassen	M. A. Baka	M. W. Fuhrmann	M. A. Pastor Ridruejo
	M. L. Ferrari Bravo	M. L. Wildhaber	M. L. Loucaides	M. L. Caflisch
	M. Gaukur Jörundsson	M. B. Conforti	M. P. Kuris	M. J. Makarczyk
	M. R. Türmen	M. G. Bonello	Mme F. Tulkens	M. I. Cabral Barreto
	M. C. Bîrsan	Mme V. Stráznická	M. K. Jungwiert	M. V. Butkevych
	M. J. Casadevall	M. P. Lorenzen	Sir Nicolas Bratza	Mme N. Vajic
	M. B. Zupancic	M. M. Fischbach	Mme H. S. Greve	M. J. Hedigan
	M. T. Pantiru	Mme M. Tsatsa-Nikolovska	M. K. Traja	M. M. Pellonpää
	M. R. Maruste	M. E. Levits	M. M. Ugrekhelidze	Mme S. Botoucharova
		M. A. Kovler		
Section Registrar	M. M. O'Boyle	M. E. Fribergh	Mme S. Dollé	M. V. Berger

COMPOSITION OF GRAND CHAMBERS

Grand Chamber 1	Grand Chamber 2
M. L. Wildhaber, *President*	M. L. Wildhaber, *President*
Mme E. Palm, *Vice-President, President of Section I*	Mme E. Palm, *Vice-President, President of Section I*
M. C. Rozakis, *Vice-President, President of Section II*	M. C. Rozakis, *Vice-President, President of Section II*
M. J.-P. Costa *President of Section III*	M J.-P. Costa, *President of Section III*
M. G. Ress *President of Section IV*	M G. Ress *President of Section IV*
M. B. Conforti	(M A. Pastor Ridruejo *Vice-President of Section IV*)
M. A. Pastor Ridruejo *Vice-President of Section IV*	M. L. Ferrari Bravo
M. G. Bonello	M. Gaukur Jörundsson
M. J. Makarezyk	M. L. Caflisch
M. P. Kuris	M. L. Loucaides
Mr R. Türmen	M. I. Cabral Barreto
Mme F. Tulkens	M. W. Fuhrmann *Vice-President of Section III*
Mme V. Stráznická	M. K. Jungwiert
M. C. Bîrsan	Sir Nicolas Bratza
M. P. Lorenzen	M. B. Zupancic
(M. W. Fuhrmann *Vice-President of Section III*)	Mme N. Vajic
M. M. Fischbach	M. J. Hedigan
M. V. Butkevych	Mme W. Thomassen *Vice-President of Section I*
M. J. Casadevall	M. Pellonpää
(Mme W. Thomassen *Vice-President of Section I*)	Mme M. Tsatsa-Nikolovska
Mme H. S. Greve	M. T. Pantiru
M. A. Baka *Vice-President of Section II*	(M . A. Baka *Vice-President of Section II*)
M. R. Maruste	E. Levits
Mme S. Botoucharova	K. Traja
M. M. Ugrekhelidze	A. Kovler

Appendix Sixteen

UK Declarations Concerning Territorial Application (Article 56; former Article 63)

ARTICLE 63 DECLARATIONS

Declaration contained in a letter from the Permanent Representative, dated November 8, 1983, registered at the Secretariat General on November 9, 1983

I have the honour to refer to Article 63 of the Convention for the Protection of Human Rights and Fundamental Freedoms, under which the Convention was extended to the Leeward Islands (including St. Kitts-Nevis) in 1953.

On instructions from Her Majesty's Principal Secretary of State for Foreign and Commonwealth Affairs, I now have the honour to inform you that since the independence of St. Kitts-Nevis from September 19, 1983, the Government of the United Kingdom is no longer responsible for this territory.

Declaration contained in a letter from the Permanent Representative, dated April 3, 1984, registered at the Secretariat General on April 3, 1984

I have the honour to refer to Article 63 of the Convention for the Protection of Human Rights and Fundamental Freedoms, under which the Convention was extended to Brunei on September 12, 1967.

On instructions from Her Majesty's Principal Secretary of State for Foreign and Commonwealth Affairs, I now have the honour to inform you that since Brunei Darussalam resumed full international responsibility as a sovereign and independent State on December 13, 1983, the Government of the United Kingdom is no longer responsible for her external affairs.

List of territories for whose international relations Her Majesty's Government in the United Kingdom are responsible and to which the European Convention on Human Rights has been extended:

Anguilla	Guernsey
Bermuda	Isle of Man
British Virgin Islands	Jersey
Cayman Islands	Montserrat
Falkland Islands	St. Helena
Gibraltar	Turks and Caicos Islands

April 1984

Appendix Seventeen

UK Reservation (1952) and Derogations (1988 & 1989)

RESERVATION

At the time of signing the present (First) Protocol, I declare that, in view of certain provisions of the Education Acts in the United Kingdom, the principle affirmed in the second sentence of Article 2 is accepted by the United Kingdom only so far as it is compatible with the provision of efficient instruction and training, and the avoidance of unreasonable public expenditure.

Dated 20 March 1952

Made by the United Kingdom Permanent Representative to the Council of Europe.

DEROGATION

The 1988 notification

The United Kingdom Permanent Representative to the Council of Europe presents his compliments to the Secretary General of the Council, and has the honour to convey the following information in order to ensure compliance with the obligations of Her Majesty's Government in the United Kingdom under Article 15(3) of the Convention for the Protection of Human Rights and Fundamental Freedoms signed at Rome on 4 November 1950.

There have been in the United Kingdom in recent years campaigns of organised terrorism connected with the affairs of Northern Ireland which have manifested themselves in activities which have included repeated murder, attempted murder, maiming, intimidation and violent civil disturbance and in bombing and fire raising which have resulted in death, injury and widespread destruction of property. As a result, a public emergency within the meaning of Article 15(1) of the Convention exists in the United Kingdom.

The Government found it necessary in 1974 to introduce and since then, in cases concerning persons reasonably suspected of involvement in terrorism connected with the affairs of Northern Ireland, or of certain offences under the legislation, who have been detained for 48 hours, to exercise powers enabling further detention without charge, for periods of up to five days, on the authority of the Secretary of State. These powers are at present to be found in Section 12 of the Prevention of Terrorism (Temporary Provisions) Act 1984, Article 9 of the Prevention of Terrorism (Supplemental Temporary Provisions) Order 1984 and Article 10 of the Prevention of Terrorism (Supplemental Temporary Provisions) (Northern Ireland) Order 1984.

Section 12 of the Prevention of Terrorism (Temporary Provisions) Act 1984 provides for a person whom a constable has arrested on reasonable grounds of suspecting him to be guilty of an offence under Section 1, 9 or 10 of the Act, or to be or to have been involved in terrorism connected with the affairs of Northern Ireland, to be detained in right of the arrest for up to 48 hours and thereafter, where the Secretary of State extends the detention period, for up to a further five days. Section 12 substantially reenacted Section 12 of the Prevention of Terrorism (Temporary Provisions) Act 1976 which, in turn, substantially re-enacted Section 7 of the Prevention of Terrorism (Temporary Provisions) Act 1974.

Article 10 of the Prevention of Terrorism (Supplemental Temporary Provisions) (Northern Ireland) Order 1984 (SI 1984/417) and Article 9 of the Prevention of Terrorism (Supplemental Temporary Provisions) Order 1984 (SI 1984/418) were both made under Sections 13 and 14 of and Schedule 3 to the 1984 Act and substantially re-enacted powers of detention in Orders made under the 1974 and 1976 Acts. A person who is being examined under Article 4 of either Order on his arrival in, or on seeking to leave, Northern Ireland or Great Britain for the purpose of determining whether he is or has been involved in terrorism connected with the affairs of Northern Ireland, or whether there are grounds for suspecting that he has committed an offence under Section 9 of the 1984 Act, may be detained under Article 9 or 10, as appropriate, pending the conclusion of his examination. The period of this examination may exceed 12 hours if an examining officer has reasonable grounds for suspecting him to be or to have been involved in acts of terrorism connected with the affairs of Northern Ireland.

Where such a person is detained under the said Article 9 or 10 he may be detained for up to 48 hours on the authority of an examining officer and thereafter, where the Secretary of State extends the detention period, for up to a further five days.

In its judgment of 29 November 1988 in the Case of *Brogan and Others*, the European Court of Human Rights held that there had been a violation of Article

5(3) in respect of each of the applicants, all of whom had been detained under Section 12 of the 1984 Act. The Court held that even the shortest of the four periods of detention concerned, namely four days and six hours, fell outside the constraints as to time permitted by the first part of Article 5(3). In addition, the Court held that there had been a violation of Article 5(5) in the case of each applicant.

Following this judgment, the Secretary of State for the Home Department informed Parliament on 6 December 1988 that, against the background of the terrorist campaign, and the overriding need to bring terrorists to justice, the Government did not believe that the maximum period of detention should be reduced. He informed Parliament that the Government were examining the matter with a view to responding to the judgment. On 22 December 1988, the Secretary of State further informed Parliament that it remained the Government's wish, if it could be achieved, to find a judicial process under which extended detention might be reviewed and where appropriate authorised by a judge or other judicial officer. But a further period of reflection and consultation was necessary before the Government could bring forward a firm and final view.

Since the judgment of 29 November 1988 as well as previously, the Government have found it necessary to continue to exercise, in relation to terrorism connected with the affairs of Northern Ireland, the powers described above enabling further detention without charge for periods of up to 5 days, on the authority of the Secretary of State, to the extent strictly required by the exigencies of the situation to enable necessary enquiries and investigations properly to be completed in order to decide whether criminal proceedings should be instituted. To the extent that the exercise of these powers may be inconsistent with the obligations imposed by the Convention the Government has availed itself of the right of derogation conferred by Article 15(1) of the Convention and will continue to do so until further notice.

Dated 23 December 1988.

The 1989 notification

The United Kingdom Permanent Representative to the Council of Europe presents his compliments to the Secretary General of the Council, and has the honour to convey the following information.

In his communication to the Secretary General of 23 December 1988, reference was made to the introduction and exercise of certain powers under section 12 of the Prevention of Terrorism (Temporary Provisions) Act 1984, Article 9 of the Prevention of Terrorism (Supplemental Temporary Provisions) Order 1984 and Article 10 of the Prevention of Terrorism (Supplemental Temporary Provisions) (Northern Ireland) Order 1984.

These provisions have been replaced by section 14 of and paragraph 6 of Schedule 5 to the Prevention of Terrorism (Temporary Provisions) Act 1989, which make comparable provision. They came into force on 22 March 1989. A copy of these provisions is enclosed.

The United Kingdom Permanent Representative avails himself of this opportunity to renew to the Secretary General the assurance of his highest consideration.

23 March 1989.

Appendix Eighteen

European Agreement Relating to Persons Participating in Proceedings of the European Court of Human Rights (1996)

COUNCIL OF EUROPE	CONSEIL DE
European Treaties	L'EUROPE
	Traités Européens
ETS No. 161	STE N° 161

EUROPEAN AGREEMENT RELATING TO PERSONS PARTICIPATING
IN PROCEEDINGS OF THE EUROPEAN COURT OF HUMAN RIGHTS

Strasbourg, 5.III.1996

The member States of the Council of Europe, signatories hereto,

Having regard to the Convention for the Protection of Human Rights and Fundamental Freedoms, signed at Rome on 4 November 1950 (hereinafter referred to as 'the Convention');

Recalling the European Agreement relating to Persons Participating in the Proceedings of the European Commission and Court of Human Rights, signed at London on 6 May 1969;

Having regard to Protocol No. 11 to the Convention, restructuring the control machinery established thereby, signed at Strasbourg on 11 May 1994 (hereinafter referred to as 'Protocol No. 11 to the Convention'), which establishes a permanent

European Court of Human Rights (hereinafter referred to as 'the Court') to replace the European Commission and Court of Human Rights;

Considering, in the light of this development, that it is advisable for the better fulfilment of the purposes of the Convention that persons taking part in proceedings before the Court be accorded certain immunities and facilities by a new Agreement, the European Agreement relating to Persons Participating in Proceedings of the European Court of Human Rights (hereinafter referred to as 'this Agreement'),

Have agreed as follows:

Article 1

1.   The persons to whom this Agreement applies are:

(a)   any persons taking part in proceedings instituted before the Court as parties, their representatives and advisers;

(b)   witnesses and experts called upon by the Court and other persons invited by the President of the Court to take part in proceedings.

2.   For the purposes of this Agreement, the term 'Court' shall include committees, chambers, a panel of the Grand Chamber, the Grand Chamber and the judges. The term 'taking part in proceedings' shall include making communications with a view to a complaint against a State Party to the Convention.

3.   If in the course of the exercise by the Committee of Ministers of its functions under Article 46, paragraph 2, of the Convention, any person mentioned in paragraph 1 above is called upon to appear before, or to submit written statements to the Committee of Ministers, the provisions of this Agreement shall apply in relation to him.

Article 2

1.   The persons referred to in paragraph 1 of Article 1 of this Agreement shall have immunity from legal process in respect of oral or written statements made, or documents or other evidence submitted by them before or to the Court.

2.   This immunity does not apply to communication outside the Court of any such statements, documents or evidence submitted to the Court.

Article 3

1.   The Contracting Parties shall respect the right of the persons referred to in paragraph 1 of Article 1 of this Agreement to correspond freely with the Court.

2.   As regards persons under detention, the exercise of this right shall in particular imply that:

(a)   their correspondence shall be despatched and delivered without undue delay and without alteration;

(b)   such persons shall not be subject to disciplinary measures in any form on account of any communication sent through the proper channels to the Court;

(c)   such persons shall have the right to correspond, and consult out of hearing of other persons, with a lawyer qualified to appear before the courts of the country where they are detained in regard to an application to the Court, or any proceedings resulting therefrom.

3. In application of the preceding paragraphs, there shall be no interference by a public authority except such as is in accordance with the law and is necessary in a democratic society in the interests of national security, for the detection or prosecution of a criminal offence or for the protection of health.

Article 4

1. (a) The Contracting Parties undertake not to hinder the free movement and travel, for the purpose of attending and returning from proceedings before the Court, of persons referred to in paragraph 1 of Article 1 of this Agreement.

(b) No restrictions shall be placed on their movement and travel other than such as are in accordance with the law and necessary in a democratic society in the interests of national security or public safety, for the maintenance of *ordre public*, for the prevention of crime, for the protection of health or morals, or for the protection of the rights and freedoms of others.

2. (a) Such persons shall not, in countries of transit and in the country where the proceedings take place, be prosecuted or detained or be subjected to any other restriction of their personal liberty in respect of acts or convictions prior to the commencement of the journey.

(b) Any Contracting Party may, at the time of signature, ratification, acceptance or approval of this Agreement, declare that the provisions of this paragraph will not apply to its own nationals. Such a declaration may be withdrawn at any time by means of a notification addressed to the Secretary General of the Council of Europe.

3. The Contracting Parties undertake to re-admit on his return to their territory any such person who commenced his journey in the said territory.

4. The provisions of paragraphs 1 and 2 of this Article shall cease to apply when the person concerned has had, for a period of fifteen consecutive days from the date when his presence is no longer required by the Court, the opportunity of returning to the country from which his journey commenced.

5. Where there is any conflict between the obligations of a Contracting Party resulting from paragraph 2 of this Article and those resulting from a Council of Europe convention or from an extradition treaty or other treaty concerning mutual assistance in criminal matters with other Contracting Parties, the provisions of paragraph 2 of this Article shall prevail.

Article 5

1. Immunities and facilities are accorded to the persons referred to in paragraph 1 of Article 1 of this Agreement solely in order to ensure for them the freedom of speech and the independence necessary for the discharge of their functions, tasks or duties, or the exercise of their rights in relation to the Court.

2.   (a)   The Court shall alone be competent to waive, in whole or in part, the immunity provided for in paragraph 1 of Article 2 of this Agreement; it has not only the right but the duty to waive immunity in any case where, in its opinion, such immunity would impede the course of justice and waiver in whole or in part would not prejudice the purpose defined in paragraph 1 of this Article.

(b)   The immunity may be waived by the Court, either *ex officio* or at the request of any Contracting Party or of any person concerned.

(c)   Decisions waiving immunity or refusing the waiver shall be accompanied by a statement of reasons.

3.   If a Contracting Party certifies that waiver of the immunity provided for in paragraph 1 of Article 2 of this Agreement is necessary for the purpose of proceedings in respect of an offence against national security, the Court shall waive immunity to the extent specified in the certificate.

4.   In the event of the discovery of a fact which might, by its nature, have a decisive influence and which at the time of the decision refusing waiver of immunity was unknown to the author of the request, the latter may make a new request to the Court.

Article 6

Nothing in this Agreement shall be construed as limiting or derogating from any of the obligations assumed by the Contracting Parties under the Convention or its protocols.

Article 7

1.   This Agreement shall be open for signature by the member States of the Council of Europe, which may express their consent to be bound by:

(a)   signature without reservation as to ratification, acceptance or approval; or

(b)   signature, subject to ratification, acceptance or approval, followed by ratification, acceptance or approval.

2.   Instruments of ratification, acceptance or approval shall be deposited with the Secretary General of the Council of Europe.

Article 8

1.   This Agreement shall enter into force on the first day of the month following the expiration of a period of one month after the date on which ten member States of the Council of Europe have expressed their consent to be bound by the Agreement in accordance with the provisions of Article 7 or on the date of entry into force of Protocol No. 11 to the Convention, whichever is the later.

2.   In respect of any member State which subsequently expresses its consent to be bound by it, this Agreement shall enter into force on the first day of the month following the expiration of a period of one month after the date of such signature or of the deposit of the instrument of ratification, acceptance or approval.

Article 9

1.   Any Contracting State may, when depositing its instrument of ratification, acceptance or approval or at any later date, by declaration addressed to the Secretary General of the Council of Europe, extend this Agreement to any territory or territories specified in the declaration and for whose international relations it is responsible or on whose behalf it is authorised to give undertakings.

2.   This Agreement shall enter into force for any territory or territories specified in a declaration made pursuant to paragraph 1 on the first day of the month following the expiration of one month after the date of receipt of the declaration by the Secretary General.

3.   Any declaration made pursuant to paragraph 1 may, in respect of any territory mentioned in such declaration, be withdrawn according to the procedure laid down for denunciation in Article 10 of this Agreement.

Article 10

1.   This Agreement shall remain in force indefinitely.

2.   Any Contracting Party may, insofar as it is concerned, denounce this Agreement by means of a notification addressed to the Secretary General of the Council of Europe.

3.   Such denunciation shall take effect six months after the date of receipt by the Secretary General of such notification. Such denunciation shall not have the effect of releasing the Contracting Parties concerned from any obligation which may have arisen under this Agreement in relation to any person referred to in paragraph 1 of Article 1.

Article 11

The Secretary General of the Council of Europe shall notify the member States of the Council of:

(a)   any signature;

(b)   the deposit of any instrument of ratification, acceptance or approval;

(c)   any date of entry into force of this Agreement in accordance with Articles 8 and 9 thereof,

(d)   any other act, notification or communication relating to this Agreement.

In witness whereof the undersigned, being duly authorised thereto, have signed this Agreement.

Done at Strasbourg, this 5th day of March 1996, in English and French, both texts being equally authentic, in a single copy which shall be deposited in the archives of the Council of Europe. The Secretary General of the Council of Europe shall transmit certified copies to each member State of the Council of Europe.

Appendix Nineteen

Vienna Convention (Articles 31–33)

VIENNA CONVENTION ON THE LAW OF TREATIES

Section 3   Interpretation on Treaties

Article 31   General rule of interpretation

1.   A treaty shall be interpreted in good faith in accordance with the ordinary meaning to be given to the terms of the treaty in their context and in the light of its object and purpose.

2.   The context for the purpose of the interpretation of a treaty shall comprise, in addition to the text, including its preamble and annexes:

(a)   any agreement relating to the treaty which was made between all the parties in connexion with the conclusion of the treaty;

(b)   any instrument which was made by one or more parties in connection with the conclusion of the treaty and accepted by the other parties as an instrument related to the treaty.

3.   There shall be taken into account, together with the context:

(a)   any subsequent agreement between the parties regarding the interpretation of the treaty or the application of its provisions;

(b)   any subsequent practice in the application of the treaty which establishes the agreement of the parties regarding its interpretation;

(c)   any relevant rules of international law applicable in the relations between the parties.

4.   A special meaning shall be given to a term if it is established that the parties so intended.

Article 32   Supplementary means of interpretation

Recourse may be had to supplementary means of interpretation, including the preparatory work of the treaty and the circumstances of its conclusion, in order to confirm the meaning resulting from the application of article 31, or to determine the meaning when the interpretation according to article 31:

(a)   leaves the meaning ambiguous or obscure; or

(b)   leads to a result which is manifestly absurd or unreasonable.

Article 33   Interpretation of treaties authenticated in two or more languages

1.   When a treaty has been authenticated in two or more languages, the text is equally authoritative in each language, unless the treaty provides or the parties agree that, in case of divergence, a particular text shall prevail.

2.   A version of the treaty in a language other than one of those in which the text was authenticated shall be considered an authentic text only if the treaty so provides or the parties so agree.

3.   The terms of the treaty are presumed to have the same meaning in each authentic text.

4.   Except where a particular text prevails in accordance with paragraph 1, when a comparison of the authentic texts discloses a difference of meaning which the application of articles 31 and 32 does not remove, the meaning which best reconciles the texts, having regard to the object and purpose of the treaty, shall be adopted.

Appendix Twenty

Protocol 12 to the European Convention and Explanatory Report

PROTOCOL No. 12 TO THE CONVENTION FOR THE PROTECTION OF HUMAN RIGHTS AND FUNDAMENTAL FREEDOMS

The member states of the Council of Europe signatory hereto,

Having regard to the fundamental principle according to which all persons are equal before the law and are entitled to the equal protection of the law;

Being resolved to take further steps to promote the equality of all persons through the collective enforcement of a general prohibition of discrimination by means of the Convention for the Protection of Human Rights and Fundamental Freedoms signed at Rome on 4 November 1950 (hereinafter referred to as 'the Convention');

Reaffirming that the principle of non-discrimination does not prevent States Parties from taking measures in order to promote full and effective equality, provided that there is an objective and reasonable justification for those measures,

Have agreed as follows:

Article 1   General prohibition of discrimination

1.   The enjoyment of any right set forth by law shall be secured without discrimination on any ground such as sex, race, colour, language, religion, political or other opinion, national or social origin, association with a national minority, property, birth or other status.

2.   No one shall be discriminated against by any public authority on any ground such as those mentioned in paragraph 1.

Article 2   Territorial application

1.   Any state may, at the time of signature or when depositing its instrument of ratification, acceptance or approval, specify the territory or territories to which this Protocol shall apply.

2.   Any state may at any later date, by a declaration addressed to the Secretary General of the Council of Europe, extend the application of this Protocol to any other territory specified in the declaration. In respect of such territory the Protocol shall enter into force on the first day of the month following the expiration of a period of three months after the date of receipt by the Secretary General of such declaration.

3.   Any declaration made under the two preceding paragraphs may, in respect of any territory specified in such declaration, be withdrawn or modified by a notification addressed to the Secretary General. The withdrawal or modification shall become effective on the first day of the month following the expiration of a period of three months after the date of receipt of such notification by the Secretary General.

4.   A declaration made in accordance with this article shall be deemed to have been made in accordance with paragraph 1 of Article 56 of the Convention.

5.   Any state which has made a declaration in accordance with paragraph 1 or 2 of this article may at any time thereafter declare on behalf of one or more of the territories to which the declaration relates that it accepts the competence of the Court to receive applications from individuals, non-governmental organisations or groups of individuals as provided by Article 34 of the Convention in respect of Article 1 of this Protocol.

Article 3   Relationship to the Convention

As between the States Parties, the provisions of Articles 1 and 2 of this Protocol shall be regarded as additional articles to the Convention, and all the provisions of the Convention shall apply accordingly.

Article 4   Signature and ratification

This Protocol shall be open for signature by member states of the Council of Europe which have signed the Convention. It is subject to ratification, acceptance or approval. A member state of the Council of Europe may not ratify, accept or approve this Protocol without previously or simultaneously ratifying the Convention. Instruments of ratification, acceptance or approval shall be deposited with the Secretary General of the Council of Europe.

Article 5   Entry into force

1.   This Protocol shall enter into force on the first day of the month following the expiration of a period of three months after the date on which ten member states of the Council of Europe have expressed their consent to be bound by the Protocol in accordance with the provisions of Article 4.

2. In respect of any member state which subsequently expresses its consent to be bound by it, the Protocol shall enter into force on the first day of the month following the expiration of a period of three months after the date of the deposit of the instrument of ratification, acceptance or approval.

Article 6 Depositary functions

The Secretary General of the Council of Europe shall notify all the member states of the Council of Europe of.

(a)   any signature;

(b)   the deposit of any instrument of ratification, acceptance or approval;

(c)   any date of entry into force of this Protocol in accordance with Articles 2 and 5;

(d)   any other act, notification or communication relating to this Protocol.

In witness whereof the undersigned, being duly authorised thereto, have signed this Protocol.

Done at .... this ... day of .... 2000, in English and French, both texts being equally authentic, in a single copy which shall be deposited in the archives of the Council of Europe. The Secretary General of the Council of Europe shall transmit certified copies to each member state of the Council of Europe.

EXPLANATORY REPORT

Introduction

1.   Article 1 of the Universal Declaration of Human Rights proclaims: 'All human beings are born free and equal in dignity and rights'. The general principle of equality and non-discrimination is a fundamental element of international human rights law. It has been recognised as such in Article 7 of the Universal Declaration of Human Rights, Article 26 of the International Covenant on Civil and Political Rights and in similar provisions in other international human rights instruments. The relevant provision in the European Convention on Human Rights (ECHR) in this respect is Article 14. However, the protection provided by Article 14 of the Convention with regard to equality and non-discrimination is limited in comparison with those provisions of other international instruments. The principal reason for this is the fact that Article 14, unlike those provisions in other instruments, does not contain an independent prohibition of discrimination, that is, it prohibits discrimination only with regard to the 'enjoyment of the rights and freedoms' set forth in the Convention. Since 1950, certain specific further guarantees concerning only equality between spouses have been laid down in Article 5 of Protocol No. 7 to the ECHR.

2.   Various ways of providing further guarantees in the field of equality and non-discrimination through a protocol to the Convention have been proposed or studied from the 1960s onwards by both the Parliamentary Assembly and the competent intergovernmental committees of experts of the Council of Europe.

An important fresh impetus was given by work carried out in recent years in the field of equality between women and men and that of combating racism and intolerance. The European Commission against Racism and Intolerance (ECRI), the Steering Committee for Equality between Women and Men (CDEG) and the Steering Committee for Human Rights (CDDH), have actively considered a possible reinforcement of ECHR guarantees in these two areas.

3.   Participants at the 7th International Colloquy on the European Convention on Human Rights (Copenhagen, Oslo and Lund, from 30 May to 2 June 1990) affirmed that the principles of equality and non-discrimination are fundamental elements of international human rights law. With regard to the possibility of broadening, through the development of the Strasbourg case-law, the protection offered by Article 14 of the Convention beyond the above-mentioned limit (see paragraph 1 above), participants recognised that there was little scope for further expansion of the case-law on this score since the prohibition in Article 14 is clearly accessory to the other, substantive guarantees in the Convention.

4.   Since 1990, the examination of a possible strengthening of the Convention's guarantees with regard to equality and non-discrimination was initially pursued separately, and from specific standpoints, by the Steering Committee for Equality between Women and Men and the European Commission against Racism and Intolerance.

5.   In the course of its work, the CDEG underlined the fact that there is no legal protection for equality between women and men as an independent fundamental right in the context of the binding instruments of the Council of Europe. Considering, that a legal norm to that is one of the prerequisites for achieving de jure and de facto equality, the CDEG focused the major part of its activities on the inclusion in the European Convention on Human Rights of a fundamental right of women and men to equality. The work of the CDEG resulted in a reasoned proposal to include such a right in a protocol to the ECHR. In 1994, the Committee of Ministers instructed the Steering Committee for Human Rights to consider the necessity for and the feasibility of such a measure, taking into consideration, inter alia, the report submitted by the CDEG. On the basis of the work of its Committee of Experts for the Development of Human Rights (DH-DEV), the CDDH agreed in October 1996 that there was a need for standard-setting work by the Council of Europe in the field of equality between women and men but expressed reservations, from the point of view of the principle of universality of human rights, about a draft protocol based on a sectoral approach. Further to a request made by the CDDH, the Committee of Ministers subsequently (in December 1996) instructed the CDDH to examine, and submit proposals for, standard-setting solutions regarding equality between women and men other than a specific draft protocol to the ECHR.

6.   In the meantime, work in the Council of Europe on the problem of racism and intolerance had intensified as a direct result of the 1st Summit of Heads of

State and Government of its member States, held in Vienna on 8 and 9 October 1993. The Declaration and Plan of Action on combating racism, xenophobia, anti-Semitism and intolerance adopted at this meeting expressed alarm over the resurgence of these phenomena as well as the development of a climate of intolerance. As part of a global approach for tackling these problems set out in the Plan of Action, the heads of state and government agreed to establish the European Commission against Racism and Intolerance and gave it, among other things, the task of working on the strengthening of the guarantees against all forms of discrimination and, in that context, studying the applicable international legal instruments with a view to their reinforcement where appropriate.

7.   Having studied all existing, international human rights instruments which deal with discrimination issues, ECRI submitted its findings to the Committee of Ministers. ECRI considered that the protection offered by the ECHR from racial discrimination should be strengthened by means of an additional protocol containing a general clause against discrimination on the grounds of race, colour, language, religion or national or ethnic origin. In proposing, a new protocol, ECRI recognised that the law alone cannot eliminate racism in its many forms vis-à-vis various groups, but it stressed also that efforts to promote racial justice cannot succeed without the law. ECRI was convinced that the establishment of a right to protection from racial discrimination as a fundamental human right would be a significant step towards combating the manifest violations of human rights which result from racism and xenophobia. It emphasised that discriminatory attitudes and racist violence are currently spreading in many European countries and observed that the resurgence of racist ideologies and religious intolerance is adding, to daily tension in our societies an attempt to legitimise discrimination.

8.   In the light of ECRI's proposal, the Committee of Ministers decided in April 1996 to instruct the Steering Committee for Human Rights to examine the advisability and feasibility of a legal instrument against racism and intolerance taking account of ECRI's reasoned report on the reinforcement of the non-discrimination clause of the ECHR.

9.   On the basis of preparatory work done by the DH-DEV, which included the identification of arguments for and against possible standard-setting solutions (namely, an additional protocol based on ECRI's proposal; an additional protocol broadening, in a general fashion, the field of application of Article 14; a framework convention or other convention; or a recommendation of the Committee of Ministers), the CDDH adopted, in October 1997, a report for the attention of the Committee of Ministers concerning both the question of equality between women and men and that of racism and intolerance. The CDDH was of the opinion that an additional protocol to the ECHR was advisable and feasible, both as a standard-setting solution regarding equality between women and men and as a legal instrument against racism and intolerance.

10. It was on the basis of this report that, at the 622nd meeting of the Ministers' Deputies (10–11 March 1998), the Committee of Ministers gave the CDDH terms of reference to draft an additional protocol to the European Convention on Human Rights broadening in a general fashion the field of application of Article 14, and containing a non-exhaustive list of discrimination grounds.

11. The CDDH and its committee of experts, the DH-DEV, elaborated the draft protocol and an explanatory report in 1998 and 1999. As had been the case during previous stages of this activity, the CDEG and ECRI were associated with this work through their representatives. During this period, further support for the rapid conclusion of the elaboration of the draft protocol was expressed by the participants at the European regional colloquy 'In Our Hands — The Effectiveness of Human Rights Protection 50 Years after the Universal Declaration' (Strasbourg, 2–4 September 1998), organised by the Council of Europe as a contribution to the commemoration of the 50th anniversary of the Universal Declaration of Human Rights, and in the political declaration adopted by the Committee of Ministers on 10 December 1998 on the occasion of the same anniversary.

12. The CDDH, after having *consulted* the European Court of Human Rights and the Parliamentary Assembly, finalised the text of the draft protocol at an extraordinary meeting held on 9 and 10 March 2000 and decided to transmit it, together with the draft explanatory report, to the Committee of Ministers.

13. The Committee of Ministers adopted the text of the Protocol on 26 June 2000 at the 715th meeting of the Ministers' Deputies and opened it for signature by member states of the Council of Europe on . . . 2000.

Commentary on the provisions of the Protocol

Preamble

14. The brief Preamble refers, in the first recital, to the principle of equality before the law and equal protection of the law. This is a fundamental and well-established general principle, and an essential element of the protection of human rights, which has been recognised in constitutions of member states and in international human rights law (see also paragraph 1 above).

15. While the equality principle does not appear explicitly in the text of either Article 14 of the Convention or Article 1 of this Protocol, it should be noted that the non-discrimination and equality principles are closely intertwined. For example, the principle of equality requires that equal situations are treated equally and unequal situations differently. Failure to do so will amount to discrimination unless an objective and reasonable justification exists (see paragraph 18 below). The Court, in its case-law under Article 14, has already made reference to the 'principle of equality of treatment' (see, for example, the Court's judgment of 23 July 1968 in the 'Belgian Linguistic' case, Series A, No. 6, paragraph 10) or to

'equality of the sexes' (see, for example, the judgment of 28 May 1985 in the case of *Abdulaziz. Cabales and Balkandali* v *the United Kingdom*, Series A, No. 94, paragraph 78).

16.   The third recital of the preamble refers to measures taken in order to promote full and effective equality and reaffirms that such measures shall not be prohibited by the principle of non-discrimination, provided that there is an objective and reasonable justification for them (this principle already appears in certain existing international provisions: see, for example, Article 1, paragraph 4, of the International Convention on the Elimination of All Forms of Racial Discrimination. Article 4, paragraph 1, of the Convention on the Elimination of All Forms of Discrimination against Women and, at the regional level, Article 4, paragraph 3, of the Framework Convention for the Protection of National Minorities). The fact that there are certain groups or categories of persons who are disadvantaged, or the existence of de facto inequalities, may constitute justifications for adopting, measures providing for specific advantages in order to promote equality, provided that the proportionality principle is respected. Indeed, there are several international instruments obliging or encouraging states to adopt positive measures (see, for example, Article 2, paragraph 2, of the International Convention on the Elimination of All Forms of Racial Discrimination, Article 4, paragraph 2, of the Framework Convention for the Protection of National Minorities and Recommendation No. R (85) 2 of the Committee of Ministers to member states on legal protection against sex discrimination). However, the present Protocol does not impose any obligation to adopt such measures. Such a programmatic obligation would sit ill with the whole nature of the Convention and its control system which are based on the collective guarantee of individual rights which are formulated in terms sufficiently specific to be justiciable.

Article 1   General prohibition of discrimination

17.   This article contains the main substantive provisions of the Protocol. Its wording is based on the following general considerations.

18.   The notion of discrimination has been interpreted consistently by the European Court of Human Rights in its case-law concerning Article 14 of the Convention. In particular, this case-law has made clear that not every distinction or difference of treatment amounts to discrimination. As the Court has stated, for example, in the judgment in the case of *Abdulaziz, Cabales and Balkandali* v *the United Kingdom*: 'a difference of treatment is discriminatory if 'has no objective and reasonable justification', that is, if it does not pursue a 'legitimate aim' or if there is not a 'reasonable relationship of proportionality between the means employed and the aim sought to be realised' (judgment of 28 May 1985, Series A, No. 94, paragraph 72). The meaning of the term 'discrimination' in Article 1 is intended to be identical to that in Article 14 of the Convention. The wording of the French text of Article 1 ('sans discrimination aucune') differs slightly from

that of Article 14 ('sans distinction aucune'). No difference of meaning is intended; on the contrary, this is a terminological adaptation intended to reflect better the concept of discrimination within the meaning of Article 14 by bringing the French text into line with the English (see, on this precise point, the Court's judgment of 23 July 1968 in the 'Belgian Linguistic' case, Series A, No. 6, paragraph 10).

20. Since not every distinction or difference of treatment amounts to discrimination, and because of the general character of the principle of non-discrimination, it was not considered necessary or appropriate to include a restriction clause in the present Protocol. For example, the law of most if not all member states of the Council of Europe provides for certain distinctions based on nationality concerning certain rights or entitlements to benefits. The situations where such distinctions are acceptable are sufficiently safeguarded by the very meaning of the notion 'discrimination' as described in paragraph 18 above, since distinctions for which an objective and reasonable justification exists do not constitute discrimination. In addition, it should be recalled that under the case-law of the European Court of Human Rights a certain margin of appreciation is allowed to national authorities in assessing whether and to what extent differences in otherwise similar situations justify a different treatment in law. The scope of the margin of appreciation will vary according to the circumstances, the subject-matter and its background (see, for example, the judgment of 28 November 1984 in the case of *Rasmussen* v *Denmark*, Series A, No. 87, paragraph 40). For example, the Court has allowed a wide margin of appreciation as regards the framing and implementation of policies in the area of taxation (see, for example, the judgment of 3 October 1997 in the case of *National and Provincial Building Society and Others* v *the United Kingdom*, Reports of Judgments and Decisions 1997-VII, paragraph 80).

20. The list of non-discrimination grounds in Article 1 is identical to that in Article 14 of the Convention. This solution was considered preferable over others, such as expressly including certain additional non-discrimination grounds (for example, physical or mental disability, sexual orientation or age), not because of a lack of awareness that such grounds have become particularly important in today's societies as compared with the time of drafting of Article 14 of the Convention, but because such an inclusion was considered unnecessary from a legal point of view since the list of non-discrimination grounds is not exhaustive, and because inclusion of any particular additional ground might give rise to unwarranted a contrario interpretations as regards discrimination based on grounds not so included. It is recalled that the European Court of Human Rights has already applied Article 14 in relation to discrimination grounds not explicitly mentioned in that provision (see, for example, as concerns the ground of sexual orientation, the judgment of 21 December 1999 in the case of *Salgueiro da Silva Mouta* v *Portugal*).

21. Article 1 provides a general non-discrimination clause and thereby affords a scope of protection which extends beyond the 'enjoyment of the rights and freedoms set forth in [the] Convention'.

22. In particular, the additional scope of protection under Article 1 concerns cases where a person is discriminated against:

(i)   in the enjoyment of any right specifically granted to an individual under national law;

(ii)   in the enjoyment of a right which may be inferred from a clear obligation of a public authority under national law, that is, where a public authority is under an obligation under national law to behave in a particular manner;

(iii)   by a public authority in the exercise of discretionary power (for example, granting certain subsidies);

(iv)   by any other act or omission by a public authority (for example, the behaviour of law enforcement officers when controlling a riot).

23. In this respect, it was considered unnecessary to specify which of these four elements are covered by the first paragraph of Article 1 and which by the second. The two paragraphs are complementary and their combined effect is that all four elements are covered by Article 1. It should also be borne in mind that the distinctions between the respective categories (i)–(iv) are not clear-cut and that domestic legal systems may have different approaches as to which case comes under which category.

24. The wording of Article 1 reflects a balanced approach to possible positive obligations of the Parties under this provision. This concerns the question to what extent Article 1 obliges the Parties to take measures to prevent discrimination, even where discrimination occurs in relations between private persons (so-called 'indirect horizontal effects'). The same question arises as regards measures to remedy instances of discrimination. While such positive obligations cannot be excluded altogether, the prime objective of Article 1 is to embody a negative obligation for the Parties: the obligation not to discriminate against individuals.

25. On the one hand, Article 1 protects against discrimination by public authorities. The Article is not intended to impose a general positive obligation on the Parties to take measures to prevent or remedy all instances of discrimination in relations between private persons. An additional protocol to the Convention, which typically contains justiciable individual rights formulated in concise provisions, would not be a suitable instrument for defining, the various elements of such a wide-ranging obligation of a programmatic character. Detailed and tailor-made rules have already been laid down in separate conventions exclusively devoted to the elimination of discrimination on the specific grounds covered by them (see, for example, the Convention on Elimination of All Forms of Racial Discrimination and the Convention on the Elimination of All Forms of Discrimination against Women, which were both elaborated within the United

Nations). It is clear that the present Protocol may not be construed as limiting or derogating from domestic or treaty provisions which provide further protection from discrimination (see the comment on Article 3 in paragraph 32 below).

26.   On the other hand, it cannot be totally excluded that the duty to 'secure' under the first paragraph of Article 1 might entail positive obligations. For example, this question could arise if there is a clear lacuna in domestic law protection from discrimination. Regarding more specifically relations between private persons, a failure to provide protection from discrimination in such relations might be so clear-cut and grave that it might engage clearly the responsibility of the State and then Article 1 of the Protocol could come into play (see, mutatis mutandis, the judgment of the Court of 26 March 1985 in the case of *X and Y* v *the Netherlands*, Series A, No 91, paragraphs 23–24, 27 and 30).

27.   Nonetheless, the extent of any positive obligations flowing, from Article 1 is likely to be limited. It should be borne in mind that the first paragraph is circumscribed by the reference to the 'enjoyment of any right set forth by law' and that the second paragraph prohibits discrimination 'by any public authority'. It should be noted that, in addition, Article 1 of the Convention sets a general limit on state responsibility which is particularly relevant in cases of discrimination between private persons.

28.   These considerations indicate that any positive obligation in the area of relations between private persons would concern, at the most, relations in the public sphere normally regulated by law, for which the state has a certain responsibility (for example, arbitrary denial of access to work, access to restaurants, or to services which private persons may make available to the public such as medical care or utilities such as water and electricity, etc). The precise form of the response which the state should take will vary according to the circumstances. It is understood that purely private matters would not be affected. Regulation of such matters would also be likely to interfere with the individual's right to respect for his private and family life, his home and his correspondence, as guaranteed by Article 8 of the Convention.

29.   The first paragraph of Article 1 refers to 'any right set forth by law'. This expression seeks to define the scope of the guarantee provided for in this paragraph and to limit its possible indirect horizontal effects (see paragraph 27 above). Since there may be some doubt as to whether this sentence on its own covers all four elements which constitute the basic additional scope of the Protocol (the question could arise in particular with respect to elements (iii) and (iv) — see paragraph 22 above), it should be recalled that the first and second paragraphs of Article 1 are complementary. The result is that those four elements are at all events covered by Article 1 as a whole (see paragraph 23 above). The word 'law' may also cover international law, but this does not mean that this provision entails jurisdiction for the European Court of Human Rights to examine compliance with rules of law in other international instruments.

30.   The term 'public authority' in paragraph 2 has been borrowed from Article 8, paragraph 2, and Article 10, paragraph 1, of the Convention and is intended to have the same meaning as in those provisions. It covers not only administrative authorities but also the courts and legislative bodies (see paragraph 23 above).

Article 2   Territorial application

31.   This is the territorial application clause contained in the Model Final Clauses adopted by the Committee of Ministers in February 1980. Paragraph 5 follows closely Article 56, paragraph 4 of the Convention.

Article 3   Relationship to the Convention

32.   The purpose of this article is to clarify, the relationship of this Protocol to the Convention by indicating that all the provisions of the latter shall apply in respect of Articles 1 and 2 of the Protocol. Among those provisions, attention is drawn in particular to Article 53, under the terms of which 'Nothing in this Convention shall be construed as limiting or derogating from any of the human rights and fundamental freedoms which may be ensured under the laws of any High Contracting Party or under any other agreement to which it is a Party'. It is clear that this article will apply in the relations between the present Protocol and the Convention itself. It was decided not to include a reference to Article 16 of the Convention in this Protocol.

33.   As has already been mentioned in paragraph 21 above. Article 1 of the Protocol encompasses, but is wider in scope than the protection offered by Article 14 of the Convention. As an additional Protocol, it does not amend or abrogate Article 14 of the Convention, which will therefore continue to apply, also in respect of States Parties to the Protocol. There is thus an overlap between the two provisions. In accordance with Article 32 of the Convention, any further questions of interpretation concerning the precise relationship between these provisions fall within the jurisdiction of the Court.

Article 4   Signature and ratification

Article 5   Entry into force

Article 6   Depositary functions

34.   The provisions of Articles 4 to 6 correspond to the wording of the Model Final Clauses adopted by the Committee of Ministers of the Council of Europe.

Appendix Twenty-One

Application in *Caballero* v *United Kingdom*

IN THE EUROPEAN COMMISSION OF HUMAN RIGHTS

B E T W E E N:

CLIVE CABALLERO   Applicant

and

THE UNITED KINGDOM   Respondent

GROUNDS OF ALLEGED VIOLATION OF THE CONVENTION

A. SUMMARY

1.   The Applicant has been charged with attempted rape and remanded in custody pending trial. His primary complaint is that his rights under Article 5(3) of the Convention have been violated in that, although his pre-trial detention cannot be justified under the Convention, no court in England or Wales has power to order his release. The Applicant further complains that as a result his rights under Article 6(2), Article 7, Article 5(5), Article 13 and Article 14 of the Convention have been breached.

B. FACTUAL FRAMEWORK

2.   The facts of this case are relatively straight-forward. The Applicant is an old aged pensioner (aged 69), who lives at [address] with his son. On 2nd January 1996, he was arrested for an alleged offence of attempted rape. The complainant is [name]

3.   The full facts are clear from the Affidavit of Mr Skinner (attached to this application), the solicitor with conduct of the Applicant's case in the domestic criminal courts. In summary, the complainant visited the Applicant in the afternoon of 2nd January 1996 for a New Year drink. She says that the Applicant gave her whisky and that, after about half an hour, she blacked out for a period of about four hours. She has no recollection of the alleged rape itself — the next thing she remembers is finding herself in the Applicant's bed with her clothing in a state of disarray and various scratching and bruising to her body.

4.   For his part, the Applicant maintains that after the complainant became drunk, a consensual sexual act took place at her instigation. He denies causing any of the injuries to her and suggests that they may have been caused by her boyfriend when she later returned to her own flat. On that basis, he vehemently denies the charges brought against him.

5.   When he was arrested, the Applicant was taken to Battersea Police Station and held overnight. He was interviewed on 3rd January 1996 in the presence of his solicitor and then taken before the South Western Magistrates' Court on 4th January 1996. The Applicant instructed his solicitors to apply for bail on his behalf, indicating that he was prepared to abide by any conditions the court wished to impose on him (see, more fully, the Affidavit of Mr Skinner).

6.   Until 10th April 1995, anyone in the Applicant's position would have been entitled to release from custody pending trial unless the prosecution could show that there were 'substantial grounds for believing' that he or she would fail to surrender to custody, commit an offence whilst on bail or interfere with witnesses or otherwise obstruct the course of justice (see 'Relevant Domestic Law' below).

7.   On 10th April 1995, section 25 of the Criminal Justice and Public Order Act 1994 came into force (see copy attached). In a nutshell, this section prohibits any court from granting bail to anyone charged with an offence of murder, attempted murder, manslaughter, rape or attempted rape, who has previously been convicted of any such offence (again, see below under 'Relevant Domestic Law'). There are no exceptions.

8.   The Applicant is an old man with only two previous convictions — one for criminal damage in 1973 when he was fined £10, and one in 1987 when he pleaded guilty to an offence of manslaughter, which was wholly unrelated either to the earlier conviction or to the present charge, and for which he received a four year term of imprisonment (note: in 1983 he was also bound over to keep the peace, which is not a criminal conviction). Since the Applicant is now charged with attempted rape, section 25 of the Criminal Justice and Public Order Act 1994

prevents any court from releasing him from custody pending trial *whatever the circumstances.* The South Western Magistrates' Court (rightly) refused to even consider any application for bail on the Applicant's behalf — it simply remanded him in custody until trial.

9. Initially, the Applicant was held at Wandsworth Prison. He was then moved to Brixton Prison on 9th May 1996. The prison regime has been very harsh for the Applicant, particularly in view of his age and failing health. For the first eight days at Wandsworth Prison, the Applicant was subjected to cellular confinement for about 23 hours a day. Then, after about two weeks, he agreed to a suggestion from the prison authorities that, as a person charged with attempted rape, he be segregated from other prisoners for his own protection under rule 43 of the Prison Rules 1964. The Applicant has remained segregated ever since.

10. The Applicant's health has also deteriorated in prison. He has long suffered from chronic bronchitis, which has become much worse in prison. In addition, he now suffers from high blood pressure. Furthermore, the Applicant's state pension of £67.04 per week has been stopped whilst he is in prison and, although it now seems safe, for many months the Applicant worried about losing his flat because he was not living in it. The combination of old age, failing health and worry has made the imposition of imprisonment upon the Applicant particularly severe.

C. RELEVANT DOMESTIC LAW

11. The full effect of section 25 of the Criminal Justice and Public Order Act 1994 on domestic law is dramatic. It can only been fully understood by a short analysis of the Bail Act 1976, which would have applied to the Applicant before section 25 came into force, and which continues to govern all cases not covered by section 25.

The Bail Act 1976

12. The Bail Act 1976 was passed by Parliament following the publication of a Home Office working party report, 'Bail Procedures in Magistrates' Courts' (HMSO 1974). The aim of the legislation was to balance the rights of the individual, the needs of society and the practical considerations which flow from people being remanded to prison custody. At the heart of the Act is the entrenchment of the old common law right to bail, which can be traced to Magna Carta. Section 4(1) provides that:

A person to whom this section applies *shall* be granted *bail* except as provided by Schedule 1 to this Act (emphasis added).

By section 4(2), this section applies to anyone accused of an offence when he or she appears or is brought before a magistrates' court or the Crown Court.

13.   Defined exceptions to this general right to bail are laid down in Schedule 1 of the Bail Act 1976 according to the status of the offence and the stage in the proceedings. If an exception does apply, the court then has a *discretion* to grant or refuse bail. For imprisonable offences, such as attempted rape, bail can be refused if the court is satisfied that there are *substantial ground for believing* that the accused, if released on bail, would:

    (a)   fail to surrender to custody;

    (b)   commit an offence while on bail;

    (c)   interfere with witnesses or otherwise obstruct the course of justice.

14.   Thus, before 10th April 1995, a person in the exactly the same position as the Applicant would have had a right to bail unless one of the exceptions was made out *and* the court, in the exercise of its discretion, considered that bail ought to be refused. If necessary, and as an alternative to pre-trial detention, conditions could be imposed on the accused person to ensure that he or she surrendered to custody, did not commit an offence whilst on bail, did not interfere with witnesses or otherwise obstruct the course of justice or made himself or herself available for the purpose of inquiries or a report.

15.   The likely outcome of an application for bail by this Applicant — had the law not changed — is obviously a matter of some speculation. However, Mr Skinner, the solicitor with conduct of the Applicant's case, sets out the approach he would have adopted in paragraphs 8 to 21 of his Affidavit and his conclusion, based on ten years professional experience of making bail applications in all criminal courts, is that the Applicant would have had a *realistic chance* of being granted bail after a few weeks (see paragraph 20 of his Affidavit).

The Criminal Justice and Public Order Act 1994

16.   On 10th April 1995, section 25 of the Criminal Justice and Public Order Act 1994 came into force, fundamentally changing the law on pre-trial detention for small group of people, including the Applicant.

17.   Section 25(1) provides that:

    (1)   A person who in any proceedings has been charged with or convicted of an offence to which this section applies in circumstances to which it applies *shall not be granted bail in those proceedings'*. (emphasis added)

    (2)   This section applies, subject to subsection (3) below, to the following offences, that is to say—

    (a)   murder;

    (b)   attempted murder;

    (c)   manslaughter;

    (d)   rape; or

    (e)   attempted rape.

(3)   This section applies to a person charged with or convicted of any such offence only if he has been previously convicted by or before a court in any part of the United Kingdom of any such offence or of culpable homicide and, in the case of a previous conviction of manslaughter or of culpable homicide, if he was then sentenced to imprisonment or if he was then a child or young person, to long-term detention under any of the relevant enactments.

. . .

In other words, anyone charged with one of the five specified offences who has a previous conviction for the same offence or any of the other four offences, shall be detained pending trial with no exceptions.

18.   The effect of section 25 is to deprive the courts of any jurisdiction to inquire into the question of whether a person falling within its terms should be detained pending trial or released on bail. The courts now have no option but to order that he or she be detained pending trial. And, it follows, there is no basis for a 'hearing' to consider and determine the question of bail.

D.   ALLEGED VIOLATION OF ARTICLE 5(3) OF THE CONVENTION GENERAL PRINCIPLES

19.   Article 5(3) is specifically concerned with the rights of those who are arrested or detained in accordance with Article 5(1)(c), that is with those arrested or detained for the purpose of being brought before a competent legal authority on reasonable suspicion of having committed an offence, or when it is reasonably considered necessary to prevent their committing an offence, or fleeing after having done so. It provides that in such cases the individual has two distinct rights. First, he or she must be 'brought promptly before a judge or other officer authorised by law to exercise judicial power'; secondly, he or she is 'entitled to trial within a reasonable time or release pending trial'.

The right to be brought before a judge or other officer authorised by law to exercise judicial power

20.   The wording 'judge or other judicial officer authorised by law' in Article 5(3) has the same meaning as 'competent legal authority' in Article 5(1)(c) (*Schiesser* v *Switzerland* 1979 Series A, No. 34). Bringing an accused person before a magistrates' court would be sufficient, so long as that court exercised the *function* required under Article 5(3).

21.   According to the Court in *Schiesser v Switzerland* (above), the function of the 'judge or other judicial officer authorised by law' before whom an accused person must be brought under Article 5(3) is three-fold:

(a)   First, the judge or other judicial officer has the task of 'reviewing the circumstances militating for and against detention' (para. 31).

(b)   Second, he or she must decide 'by reference to legal criteria, whether there are reasons to justify detention' (para. 31).

(c)   Finally, he or she should order release of the accused person if no such reasons exist (para. 31).

Any person or body unable to order the immediate release of the detained person will lack the judicial qualities necessary for compliance with Article 5(3) (*De Jong, Baliet and Van den Brink* v *Netherlands* (1984) Series A, No. 77).

22.   In order to carry out the function required by Article 5(3), the 'judge or other judicial officer authorised by law' is under an 'obligation of himself hearing the individual brought before him' (*Schiesser* v *Switzerland* (above).

The right to release pending trial

23.   The right under Article 5(3) of the Convention to release pending trial is not absolute and both the Court and Commission have recognised that pre-trial detention is justified in some circumstances. However, the Court has long recognised that the mere fact that a reasonable suspicion that the accused person has committed an offence persists is not enough since it would justify pre-trial detention in every case failing under Article 5(1)(c) (*Wemhoff* v *Germany* (1968) Series A, No. 7; *Neumeister* v *Austria* (1968) Series A, No. 8; *Stögmüller* v *Germany* (1969) Series A, No. 9; *Matznetter* v *Austria* (1969) Series A, No. 10; *Ringeisen* v *Austria* (1969) Series A, No. 13; and *Letellier* v *France* (1991) Series A, No. 207).

24.   According to the Court in *Letellier* v *France* (above):

The persistence of reasonable suspicion that the person arrested has committed an offence is a condition *sina qua non* for the validity of the continued detention, but, after a certain lapse of time, it no longer suffices; the court must then establish whether the other grounds cited by the judicial authorities continue to justify the deprivation of liberty. Where such grounds are 'relevant' and 'sufficient', the court must also ascertain whether the competent national authorities displayed 'special diligence' in the conduct of the proceedings. (para. 35).

In other words, the persistence of a reasonable suspicion that the person arrested has committed an offence remains a condition of the accused's continued detention under Article 5(1)(c). But, once Article 5(3) comes into play, the national authorities must also show that there are also 'relevant and sufficient' public interest reasons to justify further interference with the 'right to liberty' of a person presumed to be innocent.

25.   In their case-law, the Court and Commission have identified four grounds upon which pre-trial detention may be justified: fear of absconding, interference with the course of justice, the prevention of crime and the preservation of public order. In each case, a general statement that the accused will abscond or engage

in the prohibited activity is not enough; supporting evidence must be provided (*Clooth* v *Belgium* (1991) Series A, No. 225). So, for example, when assessing the refusal of bail on the ground that the accused might abscond, the Court has stated:

> There must be a whole set out circumstances ... which give reason to suppose that the consequences and hazards of flight will seem to him to be a lesser evil than continued imprisonment. (*Stögmüller* v *Germany* above para. 44).

Moreover, the danger of flight cannot be gauged solely on the basis of the severity of the sentenced risked, which does not constitute a separate ground for refusing bail and cannot by itself warrant detention on remand (*Letellier* v *France* above para. 43).

APPLICATION OF GENERAL PRINCIPLES TO FACTS

26. The Applicant submits that his continued detention breaches each of the rights guaranteed under Article 5(3) of the Convention in that:

(a) Although he was brought before a magistrates' court on 4th January 1996 (and on several occasions subsequently), by virtue of section 25 of the Criminal Justice and Public Order Act 1994, no court in England or Wales has jurisdiction to carry out the function required by Article 5(3).

(b) Further, the only grounds for his pre-trial detention are that he is charged with attempted rape and that he has an unrelated previous conviction for manslaughter. Neither is 'relevant' or 'sufficient' to justify continued interference with his 'right to liberty' under Article 5.

Each of these points will be developed in turn.

The right to be brought before a judge or other officer authorised by law to exercise judicial power

27. The Applicant submits that where a court in England or Wales is faced with an accused person charged with an offence of murder, attempted murder, manslaughter, rape or attempted rape, who has previously been convicted of any such offence, it no longer has jurisdiction to carry out the function required by Article 5(3) of the Convention. In particular, it cannot perform the tasks identified by the Court as necessary in *Schiesser* v *Switzerland* (above) — it cannot review 'the circumstances militating for and against detention', decide 'by reference to legal criteria, whether there are reasons to justify detention' or 'order release of the accused person if no such reasons exist'. It has no option but to order pre-trial detention.

28. In other words, every court in England and Wales has been stripped of the very attributes considered by the Commission and the Court to be the vital properties of a 'judge or other officer authorised by law to exercise judicial power' under Article 5(3).

29.   Hence, no court has ever 'considered' whether the Applicant should be detained pending his trial or released on bail in the sense that it has heard evidence and submissions, considered the merits and exercised its discretion: since the Applicant is charged with attempted rape and has an unrelated previous conviction for manslaughter, no court in England or Wales can grant him bail whatever the circumstances. So, for example, when the South Western Magistrates' Court ordered that the Applicant be detained pending trial, it did not even consider questions such as whether there was any evidence that the Applicant might fail to surrender to custody in the future, whether he might commit offences whilst on bail, whether he might interfere with witnesses or otherwise obstruct justice etc. (see exhibit 'JS/1' to the affidavit of John Skinner). It simply justified its decision by reference to section 25 of the Criminal Justice and Public Order Act 1994.

30.   In the circumstances, the Applicant submits that he has never been brought before a 'judge or other officer authorised by law to exercise judicial power' as required by Article 5(3) of the Convention and that the essential purpose of Article 5(3) — the protection of individuals from arbitrary interference with their liberty by bringing them under the protection of the judiciary — has been thwarted by the enactment of section 25 of the Criminal Justice and Public Order Act 1994.

The right to release pending trial

31.   The sole basis for the Applicant's continued pre-trial detention is section 25 of the Criminal Justice and Public Order Act 1994. The section applies to the Applicant because he is charged with attempted rape and has a previous conviction for manslaughter. Neither is 'relevant' or 'sufficient' to justify continued interference with his 'right to liberty' under Article 5.

32.   The Applicant submits that the fact that he has been charged with attempted rape means no more than that the prosecuting authorities have a reasonable suspicion that he has committed the offence of attempted rape. The persistence of such a reasonable suspicion remains a condition of the Applicant's continued detention under Article 5(1)(c), but alone cannot satisfy Article 5(3) (see *Letellier* v *France* above). Nor can the severity of the sentenced risked by virtue of such a charge — which does not constitute a separate ground for refusing bail — justify the Applicant's pre-trial detention (*Letellier* v *France* above). Article 5(3) requires the Respondent to establish that there are 'relevant and sufficient' public interest reasons to justify further interference with the Applicant's 'right to liberty' *other* than the fact that he has been charged with attempted rape.

33.   Since the Applicant has never been given the opportunity to advance any evidence or arguments on the question of whether there is any likelihood that he might fail to surrender to custody in the future, commit offences whilst on bail, interfere with witnesses or otherwise obstruct justice, and since no court has

jurisdiction to determine any such question, the Applicant submits that it is not open to the Respondent to seek to advance any further justification for his pre-trial detention other than the fact that he has an unrelated previous conviction for manslaughter.

34. Yet the mere existence of an unrelated previous conviction for manslaughter cannot amount to a 'relevant and sufficient' public interest reason to justify further interference with the Applicant's 'right to liberty'. On its own it discloses nothing about the likelihood of the Applicant absconding, interfering with witnesses, otherwise obstructing justice or committing offences whilst on bail. And no exceptions are permitted — so, for example, even if there was *overwhelming evidence* that the Applicant would not abscond or engage in any such activity, a court would have no power to release him.

35. In any event, before the introduction of section 25 of the Criminal Justice and Public Order Act 1994, the courts had to consider cases such as the Applicant's on countless occasions. If a court considered that the previous conviction of an accused person was relevant, it could be taken it into proper account when deciding whether to grant bail or not under the Bail Act 1976. And the grounds on which a court could have refused bail under that Act — i.e. that 'substantial grounds' existed for believing that the accused person, if released on bail, would fail to surrender to custody, commit an offence while on bail, interfere with witnesses or otherwise obstruct the course of justice — squarely corresponded with those approved by the Commission and Court interpreting Article 5(3) the Convention. Moreover, when the Criminal Justice and Public Order Act 1994 was being debated in Parliament, the Government was unable to justify the need for section 25. During the debate in the House of Lord, Lord Ackner, a distinguished Law Lord, pressed the Government to give examples of the judiciary failing to exercise their powers under the Bail Act 1976 properly. And when none were forthcoming, he made the following comments:

The risk has been in existence for years and years and years. Yet he [the minister] can give no example of the risk being wrongly taken. He fails in that regard, while seeking to justify interference with judicial discretion.' (HL Deb, 17th May 1994, c. 182).

And again:

Where the Executive seeks to interfere with the established discretion of the judiciary, it has a very heavy burden to discharge and the government have not got within miles of doing so on this occasion. (HL Deb, 15th July 1994 c. 1234).

36. In the circumstances, the Applicant submits that there are strong reasons for the Commission to call on the Respondent to explain its reasons for enacting

section 25 of the Criminal Justice and Public Order Act 1994 and to demonstrate how its operation in the Applicant's case complies with Article 5(3) of the Convention.

E.   ALLEGED VIOLATION OF ARTICLES 6(2) AND 7 OF THE CONVENTION

37.   The Applicant submits that by requiring the courts to order his pre-trial detention without any reference whatsoever to the facts of his case, his personal circumstances and without hearing any evidence on the likelihood that he might fail to surrender to custody in the future, commit offences whilst on bail, interfere with witnesses or otherwise obstruct justice, section 25 of the Criminal Justice and Public Order Act 1994 violates his rights under Article 6(2) and Article 7 of the Convention.

38.   Article 6(2) provides that a person 'charged with a criminal offence shall be presumed innocent until proved guilty according to law'. The Applicant accepts that there are circumstances in which an accused person can be detained pending trial without any violation of Article 6(2), but submits that such cases only arise where the national authorities can show that there are 'relevant and sufficient' reasons, *specific to the individual concerned*, to justify such pre-trial detention. To withdraw the Applicant's right to bail simply because he has been charged with attempted rape is to suggest that there is deep significance in the charge itself. Had the Applicant been charged with another serious offence — for example, armed robbery — he would retain his 'right to bail' despite his previous conviction for manslaughter.

39.   Equally to seek to advance the Applicant's unrelated previous conviction as justification for the *automatic* withdrawal of his 'right to bail' is to impose a heavier penalty on him than the one that was applicable at the time the offence of manslaughter was committed, contrary to Article 7 of the Convention. In other words, the effect of section 25 of the Criminal Justice and Public Order Act 1994 is to increase the Applicant's sentence for manslaughter by adding the further penalty that if he ever finds himself charged with murder, attempted murder, manslaughter, rape or attempted rape after release from his sentence for manslaughter, he will be *automatically* detained pending trial without regard to the facts of his case, his personal circumstances and without hearing any evidence on the likelihood that he might fail to surrender to custody in the future, commit offences whilst on bail, interfere with witnesses or otherwise obstruct justice.

F.   ALLEGED VIOLATION OF ARTICLE 5(5), ARTICLE 13 AND ARTICLE 14 OF THE CONVENTION

Article 5(5)

40.   Article 5(5) of the Convention requires that '[E]veryone who has been the victim of arrest or detention in contravention of the provisions of this Article shall

have an enforceable right to compensation'. Yet, as the Court recognised in *Brogan* v *United Kingdom* (1988) Series A, No. 145B, '[A]s Article 5 is not considered part of the domestic law of the United Kingdom, no claim for compensation lies for breach of any provision of Article 5 which does not at the same time constitute a breach of United Kingdom law' (para. 66).

41.   The Applicant's pre-trial detention clearly does not breach United Kingdom law since it is authorised by section 25 of the Criminal Justice and Public Order Act 1994. Therefore, even if the Applicant succeeds in showing that his rights under Article 5(3) have been violated by his pre-trial detention, he will not have any enforceable right to compensation in the United Kingdom. In the circumstances, the Applicant submits that his complaint that his rights under Article 5(5) of the Convention have been violated must be upheld if the Commission finds that his rights under Article 5(3) have been breached.

Article 13

42.   The Applicant submits that the complaints he raises in this Application under Article 5(3), Article 6(2), Article 7, Article 5(5) and Article 14 are clearly 'arguable' within the meaning given to that term in *Boyle and Rice* v *United Kingdom* (1988) Series A, No. 131. It follows that under Article 13, the Respondent is under a duty to provide a domestic process for adjudicating upon the Applicant's complaints. Since no such process exists, the Applicant submits that his rights under Article 13 of the Convention have also been violated.

Article 14

43.   If the Applicant did not have a previous conviction for manslaughter, he would have a 'right to bail' under the Bail Act 1976 (see above). Since he does have such a conviction his pre-trial detention is *automatic*. The Applicant submits that it is therefore clear that he is being discriminated against in the enjoyment of his rights and freedoms under the Convention — in particular his Article 5(3) rights — solely on the basis of his status as a man with a previous conviction for manslaughter. The Applicant accepts that the fact that an accused person has a previous conviction for manslaughter might, in some circumstances, lead a court to order pre-trial detention rather than bail, but submits that since section 25 of the Criminal Justice and Public Order Act 1994 deprives the courts in England and Wales of any jurisdiction to consider the individual circumstances of his case, his rights under Article 14 of the Convention have been violated.

G.   OTHER INTERNATIONAL HUMAN RIGHTS STANDARDS ON PRE-TRIAL DETENTION

44.   The Applicant submits in its determination of the issues raised in this Application, it is legitimate for the Commission to refer to other international human rights treaties and other agreements to ensure that, so far as the text of the Convention allows, its interpretation of Article 5(3) is in harmony with them.

Furthermore, the Applicant notes that under Article 60, nothing in the Convention is to be construed as limiting or derogating from any of the human rights and fundamental freedoms which have been ensured under any other agreement to which the Respondent is a party.

45. In particular, the Applicant urges the Commission to have regard to the terms of Article 9(3) of the International Covenant on Civil and Political Rights, which is framed in almost identical terms to Article 5(3) of the European Convention on Human Rights — 'Anyone arrested or detained on a criminal charge shall be brought promptly before a judge or other officer authorised by law to exercise judicial power and shall be entitled to trial within a reasonable period or to release . . .' — but goes on to state specifically that, '*[I]t shall not be the general rule that persons awaiting trial shall be detained in custody . . .*' (emphasis added).

46. The United Nations Human Rights Committee has interpreted this provision to mean that detention before trial should be used only where it is lawful, reasonable and necessary. The 'necessity' requirement should be interpreted narrowly. According to the Human Rights Committee, detention may be necessary 'to prevent flight, interference with evidence or the recurrence of crime' (*Hugo van Alphen* v *The Netherlands*, Application No. 305 of 1988) or 'where the person concerned constitutes a clear and serious threat to society which cannot be contained in any other manner' (*David Alberto Campora Schweizer* v *Uruguay*, Application No. 66 of 1980). The seriousness of a crime or the need for continued investigation, considered alone, do not justify prolonged pre-trial detention (*Floresmilo Bolanos* v *Ecuador*, Application No. 238 of 1987).

47. The Applicant draws the Commission's attention specifically to the statements of members of the Human Rights Committee in *Floresmilo Bolanos* v *Ecuador* (above). In particular, their finding that, in relation to the right to release pending trial, a national system whose only alternative to confinement before trial was supervised release, which was granted only in certain circumstances, and which had no provision for bail did not conform to the requirements of Article 9(3) of the International Covenant on Civil and Political Rights.

48. The Applicant further submits that the principles adopted by the Eighth United Nations Congress on the Prevention of Crime and the Treatment of Offenders (27th August–7th September 1990) should also be taken into account by the Commission in its interpretation of Article 5(3) of the Convention. Whilst not binding in the same way as the European Convention or the International Covenant, these principles are authoritative and persuasive since they reflect the current trend in international human rights standards on pre-trial detention which forms part of the United Nations programme on crime prevention and criminal justice. Paragraph 2 of the principles reads as follows:

   (a) Persons suspected of having committed offences and deprived of their liberty should be brought promptly before a judge or other officer authorised by law to exercise judicial functions who should hear them and take a decision concerning pre-trial detention without delay.

(b) Pre-trial detention may be ordered only if there are reasonable grounds to believe that the persons concerned have been involved in the commission of the alleged offences and there is a danger of their absconding or committing further serious offences or a danger that the course of justice will be seriously interfered with if they are left free.

(c) In considering whether pre-trial detention should be ordered, account should be taken of the circumstances of the individual case, in particular the nature and seriousness of the alleged offence, the strength of the evidence, the penalty likely to be incurred, and the conduct and personal and social circumstances of the person concerned, including his or her community ties.

49. Finally, the Applicant draws the Commission's attention to the United Nations Standard Minimum Rules for Non-Custodial Measures (Tokyo Rules: adopted by the General Assembly on 14th December 1990), which state that, '[P]re-trial detention shall be used as a means of last resort in criminal proceedings, with due regard to the investigation of the alleged offence and for the protection of society and the victim' (rule 6.1). And further, that, '[T]he offender shall have the right to appeal to a judicial or other competent independent authority in cases where pre-trial detention is employed' (rule 6.3).

H. CONCLUSION

50. The Applicant submits that facts and matters set out above give rise to a very grave breach of his rights under the Convention — particularly bearing in mind his age, failing health and the harsh prison regime which he has been subjected to unnecessarily. The Applicant therefore urges the Commission to find that this Application raises serious issues under Article 5(3), Article 6(2), Article 7, Article 5(5), Article 13 and Article 14 of the Convention, which are well-founded on the facts.

Appendix Twenty-Two

Correspondence Relating to the Third Party Intervention in *Khan* v *UK*

The Registrar of the Third Section
The European Court of Human Rights
BY FAX 00 333 8841 2730

30 June 1999

Dear Sir

Sultan Khan v UK: Hearing 26 October

I am writing to ask for permission pursuant to Article 36(2) of the Convention to make representations in the above case.

Liberty (the National Council for Civil Liberties) was formed in 1934 and is an independent and non-party-political organisation which seeks to defend and extend human rights and civil liberties. It has some six thousand individual members and several hundred affiliated organisations established by a constitution.

As you may know Liberty has been given permission in the past to intervene in a number of cases. Most recently: *Sheffield and Horsham* v *UK*; *Ahmed* v *UK*; *McGinley & Egan* v *UK; Halford* v *UK*; *Chahal* v *UK*; *Saunders* v *UK*. In Chahal for instance the Court commented that it particularly welcomed our work on international comparisons.

In the case of Khan itself we intervened in the House of Lords appeal and again our contribution was welcomed by their Lordships. In fact this was the first time an NGO had been given permission to intervene in a House of Lords appeal.

In line with previous practice we will of course keep our written submission short (to below 15 pages) and deliver this to you well in advance of the hearing itself (by 17 September).

We would particularly like to assist the Court by outlining the importance to the right to a fair trial of decisions about the admissibility of evidence within the UK tradition. We would also like to consider how other common law countries like New Zealand, the USA and Canada have dealt with this issue. Finally we would like to set out the way in which this issue will impact on the Human Rights Act 1998 which incorporates the European Convention on Human Rights in domestic English law.

The Court now has a power to allow third parties to make representations at the hearing itself and we would also like to assist the Court by instructing a leading expert to set out our findings at the hearing itself. We would of course wish to limit any presentation by us strictly to a maximum of 20 minutes. We are particularly concerned to assist the Court in this way because of the crucial importance this case may have in protecting and promoting the Convention once the Convention is part of our law.

We understand that JUSTICE, another NGO based in the UK, will also be seeking to assist the Court. We would be very happy to co-operate with them on any intervention.

I hope that you will allow us to assist the Court in its consideration of this important case.

Yours faithfully

[Name]
Liberty Legal Department

COUR EUROPEENNE	EUROPEAN COURT
DES	OF
DROITS DE L'HOMME	HUMAN RIGHTS

CONSEIL DE L'EUROPE	COUNCIL OF EUROPE
STRASBOURG	STRASBOURG

[Address]

THIRD SECTION

ECHR-   8 July 1999
JSP/dp

Application no. 35394/97
Sultan KHAN v *the United Kingdom*

Dear Sir,

I acknowledge receipt of your letter of 30 June 1999 and inform you that on 7 July 1999 the President granted leave to Liberty and JUSTICE to submit *joint* written comments in connection with the above case, pursuant to Article 36 § 2 of the Convention and Rule 61 § 3 of the Rules of Court.

These joint comments should be limited to *ten* pages, should not take the form of pleadings in the case, and should be limited to comparative law material about the admissibility of unlawfully obtained evidence. The comments should be submitted by **17 September 1999**.

I enclose a copy of the letter sent today to JUSTICE for information.

Yours faithfully,

[name]
Section Registrar

Appendix Twenty-Three

Third Party Intervention of JUSTICE in *T and V* v *United Kingdom* (1999)

APPLICATION No. 24888/94

V   against the UNITED KINGDOM
T   against the UNITED KINGDOM

WRITTEN COMMENTS OF JUSTICE

1.   The purpose of this intervention is to provide the Court with a brief survey of how international Conventions apply to juveniles in serious criminal cases; and to consider how the principles in those Conventions are applied in practice in particular countries. We attach copies of the JUSTICE report, *Children and homicide*, published to coincide with the Court's judgment in *Hussain and Singh* v *UK* (21 February 1996), and copies of JUSTICE's intervention in the present case when it was before the House of Lords.

International law principles

2.   Certain principles in regard to the age and extent of criminal responsibility, the appropriate mode of trial, and the sentencing or juveniles can be drawn from international law, as it has developed.

Criminal responsibility

3.   The Convention on the Rights of the Child points to the importance of the establishment of a minimum age below which children shall be presumed not to

have the capacity to infringe the penal law.[1] Rule 4 of the Beijing Rules urges that 'the beginning of that age shall not be fixed at too low an age level, bearing in mind the facts of emotional, mental, and intellectual maturity'. The Commentary to the Rules makes it clear that 'In general, there is a close relationship between the notion of responsibility for delinquent or criminal behaviour and other social rights and responsibilities (such as marital status, civil majority etc.) Efforts should therefore be made to agree on a reasonable lowest age limit that is applicable internationally'.

4.   The Committee on the Rights of the Child has commented that 'even cases where the child was aware that its action was wrong might well reflect the fact that it was not in full control of its situation. Very young child offenders should be seen more as victims than as culprits, since statistics showed that almost all came from difficult family backgrounds ... the overwhelming majority of countries had set the age of criminal responsibility much higher [than 10], and even 14 was considered too low ...'[2]

Mode of trial

5.   Mode of trial is closely connected with these concerns. Article 12(2) of the Convention on the Rights of the Child states that the child shall be provided with the opportunity to be heard in judicial and administrative hearings. This implies that the trial environment must be conducive to understanding and participation, and that it should not be too overawing. The Convention on the Rights of the Child, the Beijing Rules, and the International Convention on Civil and Political Rights insist on the child's right to privacy at all stages of the proceedings. The Commentary to the Rules stresses that young people are particularly susceptible to stigmatisation, and refer to the detrimental effects of labelling as 'delinquent' and 'criminal', and of publicity.

Sentencing

6.   The relevant principles on the sentencing of juveniles were first set out in detail in the UN's Beijing Rules. The Commentary notes that the conflicts between rehabilitation and just deserts, assistance and punishment, and general deterrence and individual loss of liberty, are more pronounced in a child criminal justice context. It acknowledges that the Rules do not attempt to prescribe the preferred approach, beyond setting out basis principles, such as proportionality and the fact that there should be limited use of deprivation of liberty. However, this apparent conflict has now been resolved by the later UN Convention on the Rights of the Child. This establishes as the aim of juvenile justice the entitlement of children to be treated in a manner consistent with 'the child's age and the desirability of promoting the child's reintegration and the child's assuming a

---

[1] Article 40(3)(a).
[2] Initial report of UK dependent territory: Hong Kong, SR. 329, para. 79.

constructive role in society'.[3] This approach is strengthened further by Article 3, which also governs criminal justice, and declares that the best interests of the child shall be a primary consideration.

7.   International law takes a holistic approach to child criminal justice: in other words, it does not lay down one set of principles for less serious offences and another for offences such as murder. This is also evidenced by the legal principles governing the most heinous offences under the Statute of the International Criminal Court, which remove from its jurisdiction those under the age of 18.

8.   International law does not ignore the needs of society, but considers that they are satisfied if the child is shown how to reintegrate and assume a constructive role in society. The Convention on the Rights of the Child emphasises the 'promotion of a child's sense of dignity and worth', and this cannot be undertaken where a State Party adopts a policy which is characterised as being of general deterrence and punitive.

9.   The twin principles of proportionality and a State's duty to take into consideration the child's well-being underline much of the detail found in international law concerning the aims, restrictions and prohibitions on the sentencing of children. A further fundamental principle is that deprivation of liberty, if used at all, should be a measure of last resort, and should be for the shortest appropriate period of time.[4] Consequently, international law regulating the sentencing of children is characterised by an emphasis on the constructive purpose of the disposition, rather than its punitive side.

10.   Deprivation of liberty is thus the least favoured alternative. International law recognises the findings of criminological research, demonstrating the many adverse effects of institutionalisation. These are not always remedied by treatment. According to the research, children are particularly vulnerable to negative influences, because the combined effect of loss of liberty and separation from their accustomed daily social life may have acutely deleterious consequences. By aiming for the reintegration of children, international law seeks to assist them in beginning to believe that they are valued members of the community: whereas institutionalisation risks alienating them.[5] Indeed, Article 40 of the Convention on the Rights of the Child (see above) indicates that the child needs to be reintegrated as a child, not as an adult: this cannot happen in the context of excessive sentences.

11.   International law prohibits specific forms of punishment from being imposed on children. The Convention on the Rights of the Child states that life imprisonment without the possibility of release is a form of prohibited punishment in the case of those who have committed offences below the age of 18. This

---

[3] Article 40.
[4] Article 37(b) Convention on the Rights of the Child; Rule 17(6) Beijing Rules.
[5] Commentary to Beijing Rules

is included in the same Article (Article 36) as the prohibition on torture, cruel, inhuman and degrading treatment, and the prohibition on the death penalty.

12.   Although under 18 year olds can be sentenced to detention for an indeterminate period, the sentence must be proportionate to the offence and offender, and there must be an effective mechanism for reviewing the sentence. The undoubted trend in international law is for sentences of imprisonment on children to be imposed for the shortest appropriate period. This points to a sparing use of indeterminate sentences, and for the period of detention within such sentences to be as short as possible.

13.   The key principles of international law are therefore:

- a child-centred approach, recognising a child's needs and developmental stage
- proportionality and flexibility in sentencing
- the use of detention only as a last resort and for the shortest appropriate period
- the child's right to privacy.

Principles in practice

14.   We go on to examine the way that these principles find effect in two other Council of Europe states, Germany and Spain, and in the common law jurisdiction of Canada.

Germany

15.   The German approach to criminal responsibility may be instructive, and contrasts with England and Wales, where children are now fully criminally responsible from the age of 10. Germany recognises three separate levels of responsibility, based upon age. Those under 14 are not criminally responsible. Article 1 of the Juvenile Justice Act (Jugendgerichtsgesetz, JGG) then distinguishes between juveniles (14–18 year olds) and young adults (18–21 year olds). Juveniles are regarded as criminally responsible if they are morally and intellectually mature enough to understand the unlawfulness of the offence (Article 3). Those suffering from grave mental, psychological or developmental disorders will not be regarded as responsible (Article 20), and in less serious offences where responsibility is diminished, sentence will be mitigated (Article 21). Young adults may be dealt with either as juveniles or as adults, depending upon an assessment of their circumstances (Article 105).

16.   In continuation of this approach, 14–21 year olds are dealt with in specialised juvenile courts. More serious offences, including murder, will be tried in the juvenile chambers of the regional courts, staffed by three professional and two lay judges. All the judges, as well as the prosecutors, are specially trained, and the proceedings are in private.

17.   German law also defines the purpose and sets limits to the duration of youth custody. Article 91 defines the purpose of youth custody as to educate the convicted to lead a law-abiding and responsible life. Juveniles (including young

adults assessed as juveniles) cannot be sentenced to life imprisonment — the mandatory sentence for adults convicted of certain types of murder — but only to the upper limit of youth custody, which is 10 years (Article 105). Young adults assessed as being mature may be sentenced to 10–15 years (Article 106) and can also be sentenced to life, but this is rare.

18.   In cases of murder where there is no criminal responsibility, the juvenile court acts as a guardianship court, and may transfer the young person to a residential home. This can only be until the age of 18. Alternatively, there can be transfer to a psychiatric hospital for an indeterminate time, but with annual judicial review. Under 14 year olds are dealt with by guardianship courts under civil law provisions, and in cases of murder would be sent to a residential home for rehabilitative purposes.

19.   Youth custody is entirely separate from adult prisons, and transfer to an adult establishment must take place if the sentence is not due to expire until after the young person is 24 years old. Otherwise, it may be done at any appropriate stage from the age of 18, as the juvenile judge decides (Article 92). Article 88 provides for judicial re-examination of sentences, and their possible suspension. Thus, if the juvenile judge is satisfied that the juvenile will lead a law-abiding life, after a percentage of the sentence has been served, conditional release may be authorised.

Spain

20.   In Spain also, there are clear distinctions in the Penal Code between the sentences available for children (those under 16), juveniles (16–18 year olds), and young adults (those over 18).

21.   Under 16 year olds are not criminally responsible (Article 8.2). If convicted of murder they can be confined only for a maximum of two years, on an educational programme. If they commit an act punishable by law, they will be dealt with by the Juzgados de Menores (juvenile courts), introduced in 1992 (Ley 4/92 reguladora de los Juzgados de Menores). The judges in these courts are specialists in law relating to young people, and are assisted by psychologists and teachers. The State has no role in the proceedings, which are conducted in private.

22.   No punishments or penalties may be imposed, but the child may be required to undertake a rehabilitative or educational programme (medida). The purpose is education rather than punishment. In order to decide the length and nature of the educational programme, the court takes into account both the nature of the offence and the character of the young offender. The most severe measure possible is closed confinement for a maximum of two years. Confinement will be imposed for serious offences only.

23.   Juveniles (16–18 year olds) who are convicted of murder may be given a determinate sentence of between 6 and 12 years. 16–18 year olds are criminally responsible for their actions, but their youth has the effect of mitigating sentence

(Article 9.3) from reclusion mayor (which an adult would receive for murder) to prision mayor (from 6 to 12 years with three intermediate lengths). An assessment is made of the dangerousness of the offender, resulting in a classification into one of three categories which affects the conditions attaching to the sentence. Punishment is a relevant consideration at this stage; and there are special young people's prisons for 16–21 year olds.

24.   Movement to an open prison may occur after one-quarter of the sentence has been served. Parole is also available: for example, for those serving the middle length (8 years and a day to 10 years), 38 days' parole per annum are allowed. Prision mayor is determinate and is not reviewable; but in practice the whole sentence will not be served, as sentences are reduced by one day for each two days of prison work (Article 100).

Canada

25.   The Canadian youth justice system offers an interesting example, because it has been the subject of recent reform (by amendments to the 1984 Young Offenders Act in 1992 and 1995) and considerable public debate. There is now a mode of trial recognising the special needs of children; a trial and sentencing regime graduated according to age; and provisions for regular review. The Declaration of Principle in the 1984 Act requires that the limited maturity and dependency of youth be taken into account, and that decisions about young people should reflect their 'special needs'. Both the protection of society and the rehabilitation of the offender are seen as best achieved by addressing the relevant needs and circumstances of young people.

26.   The age of criminal responsibility is 12, and any child under that age is dealt with under child protection legislation. 12–14 year olds charged with first or second degree murder must be tried in the youth court. This consists of trial in private by a specialised judge. The youth court may also try 14–18 year olds, subject to procedures which vary according to age. Broadly, for 14–16 year olds the presumption will be in favour of trial in youth courts. For 16–17 year olds the presumption is that proceedings will be in ordinary courts in accordance with the law applying to adults. Applications for transfer to and from youth courts can be made by either party, and the point at issue will be whether the interests of society, which includes the protection of the public and the rehabilitation of the young person, can properly be served if the case remains within the youth court's jurisdiction. One murder case involving a girl of almost 18[6] resulted in a trial in the youth court because of the absence of criminal record, no tendency to violence, the advantages of the youth correctional system, and the belief that an adult sentence was not required.

27.   There are no mandatory or indeterminate sentences in the youth court. There is a maximum of 10 years for first degree murder: 6 years' maximum

---

[6] Nathalie, B., N.B. (1985) 21c.c.c. (3d) 374 (Que.C.A.).

detention, followed by 4 years maximum conditional supervision. For those 14–16 year olds convicted in the adult courts the judge sets a tariff of between 5 and 7 years. 16–18 year olds convicted in adult courts are subject to the mandatory life sentence: but their parole eligibility occurs after 10 years for first degree murder, and after 7 years for second degree murder.

28.   All custodial sentences are subject to automatic annual review by the youth court. This allows for arrangements to be modified, and if necessary amended, to reflect the young person's development and change. Reviews require the submission of progress reports. The period of sentence to be spent in detention may be shortened, or indeed lengthened until the end of the maximum period, if circumstances justify it. Additional reviews may be held with the leave of the youth court judge if there is sufficient progress or other circumstances have changed.

29.   Following review, the youth court may confirm the disposition, order transfer to open custody, place the young person under conditional supervision, or order continuation of custody until the end of the maximum period.

30.   In deciding between open and secure custody, the youth court must take into account the principle that the level of custody should involve the least degree of containment and restraint, having regard to the seriousness of the offence and the circumstances in which it was committed. It must also consider the needs and circumstances of the young person, including proximity to family, school, employment and support services. Applications may be made to alter the level of custody. Young people may remain in youth custody until they are 20, if that is appropriate. Even after transfer to adult prison the Young Offenders Act will continue to apply.

Conclusion

31.   The above jurisdictions are all instructive in terms of their application of the key principles identified. They offer examples of how to recognise the particular needs of children in relation to the age of criminal responsibility, mode of trial, and sentence. They meet the requirements of fairness and international law; and assist in the process of examining current procedures in England and Wales.

32.   Finally, we draw to the Court's attention the research in *Children and homicide*, which showed that, with the possible exception of Ireland, there was no other European country where the executive, rather than the courts, determined the length of detention or the appropriate time for release.

JUSTICE
July 1999

Index

BLACKSTONE'S HUMAN RIGHTS SERIES

TITLES IN THE SERIES